WOMEN AND THE
WAR STORY

WOMEN AND THE WAR STORY

MIRIAM COOKE

UNIVERSITY OF CALIFORNIA PRESS
BERKELEY   LOS ANGELES   LONDON

For my grandmothers,
Meta and Harriet

University of California Press
Berkeley and Los Angeles, California

University of California Press, Ltd.
London, England

© 1996 by
The Regents of the University of California

Library of Congress Cataloging-in-Publication Data

Cooke, Miriam.
    Women and the war story / Miriam Cooke.
      p.   cm.
    Includes bibliographical references and index.
    ISBN 0-520-20612-6.—ISBN 0-520-20613-4 (pbk.)
    1. War stories—Women authors, Arab—History and
criticism.   2. War in literature.   3. Women and war.   4. Arabic
fiction—20th century—History and criticism.   5. Arabic fiction—
Women authors—History and criticism.   I. Title.
    PN23448.W3C66   1996
    892'.73609358—dc20   96-11601

The paper used in this publication meets the minimum re-
quirements of American National Standard for Information
Sciences—Permanence of Paper for Printed Library Materials,
ANSI Z39.48-1984.

Excerpt from "Dulce et Decorum Est" by Wilfred Owen is
reprinted from *Collected Poems of Wilfred Owen*, ed. C. Day
Lewis, © 1963 Chatto and Windus, Ltd. Reprinted by permission
of New Directions Publishing Corp.
    "Guerrilla War" is reprinted from *To Those Who Have Gone
Home Tired* by W. D. Ehrhart (New York: Thunder's Mouth
Press, 1984) by permission of the author.

An earlier version of chapter 6 appeared in the *South Atlantic
Quarterly* 94:4 (Fall 1995).

Contents

List of Illustrations   vii

Acknowledgments   ix

Introduction   1

1. Subvert the Dominant Paradigm   13

2. Culture Degree Zero   68

3. Silence Is the Real Crime   118

4. Talking Democracy   167

5. Flames of Fire in Qadisiya   220

6. Reimagining Lebanon   267

    Conclusion   291

    Notes   301

    Cited Works   323

    Index   349

Illustrations

(following p. 43)

Captions are taken from the book *Harb Lubnan* (Lebanon's War)

1. Front cover
2. Back cover
3. The 'Ayn al-Rummana bus incident
4. A bulldozer removes the barricade of buses
5. Al-Rada'—peace by force
6. They arrived, and the cannons were silent
7. A smile . . . a cannon
8. He lies on the bed of death
9. UNESCO parade on 1 May 1977
10. President Elias Sarkis conducted consultations
11. A meeting at the Mathaf traffic circle
12. [Uncaptioned photograph]
13. A human corpse under the rubble
14. The children's hunger is stronger than the war
15. The father led his family to the parliament
16. And the police stopped him
17. But the policeman's and the deputies' hearts are hard
18. They left everything behind them
19. "He's lost . . . where's my husband?"
20. They weep for everything
21. Childhood survives to carry the future
22. He carried him in the first stage

23. And his mother carried him in the difficult stage
24. [Uncaptioned full-page image]
25. [Uncaptioned full-page image]
26. The Holiday Inn sniper
27. Photographers and journalists
28. They grabbed hold of his arms
29. The bulldozers of the dialogue committee
30. A witness to the massacre in Burj Square
31. In Bab Idris, streets of elegance and beauty
32. One of the Irtibat armed elements in Shiyah

Acknowledgments

At Duke University, to the Women's Studies Faculty Seminar and
the faculty of Asian and African Languages and Literature and
the students in my war and gender classes;

to all the fellows of the 1990 Gender and War Institute, Dartmouth
College

to the Rockefeller Institute at Bellagio, Italy;

to institutions that have invited me to speak on aspects of the book:
Bryn Mawr College, University of California at Riverside, University of California at Santa Cruz, University of Chicago, Cor-
nell University (especially Davydd Greenwood); Croatian Academy of Science and Art (Zagreb, Croatia), Dayton University,
Emory University, College of the Holy Cross, University of Illinois at Champaign-Urbana, Kuwaiti Writers Union (Kuwait),
University of Michigan, Muhammad V University (Rabat, Morocco), University of Nijemegen (Holland), University of Sabah
(Malaysia), Stanford University, Syracuse University, Tel Aviv
University (Israel), Vanderbilt University, University of Vermont
at Burlington.

To individuals:

Evelyne Accad for friendship, intense conversations, and the sharing of inaccessible texts;

Francine d'Amico for introducing me to the IR and the IPE crowd at the ISA;

Daisy al-Amir for making chapter five possible;

Elizabet Boyi and Valentin Mudimbe for believing in the project when it was only half-baked;

Dale Eickelmann for entertaining conversations about war and music;

Alex Roland for enlightening me about military historians;

Roshni Rustomji-Kerns for reminding me how rooted I am in Western cultural paradigms, and how hard I must struggle to see the strange so as not to reinscribe what I challenge;

Ghada al-Samman for her unfailing interest and thoughtfulness in sending me books that she thought, correctly, might help me in this project;

Faiza Shereen for warm hospitality and great talks in Dayton and Rabat;

Judith Stiehm for making me understand the relation between the argument of my book and the transformations in the gender arrangements of the U.S. military;

Kristine Stiles for pushing me toward the visual;

Klaus Theweleit for urging me to work on propaganda and to look for its fantasy;

Susan Thorn for a sobering contextualizing of wars I was describing;

Layla al-'Uthman for inviting me to meet with writers in Kuwait;

Candice Ward for meticulous editing of chapter six, which first appeared in *South Atlantic Quarterly* (fall 1995).

Above all, I owe the deepest debt of gratitude and heaps of love to Arthur Cooke, my brother, for insights into arms technology and great Gulf War talks about how Martin-Marietta was making weapons for the media; to Hedley Cooke, my father, for persistent challenges to my enthusiasm about postmodern wars, and for his quietly shining inspiration to work for peace; and to Bruce Lawrence, my soul-mate, for infinite moral and intellectual support and stimulation, for his nurturing care of my horror-filled nights, and, of course, for the title!

Introduction

I was born in 1948, the year of the war between the Palestinian Arabs and the Jews that culminated in the establishment of the state of Israel. My brother was born in 1956, the year of the war in Suez. In 1967, a few months after the Six-Day War, I went to Edinburgh University to study Arabic. Two years later I spent the summer and fall in a Lebanon still shaken by its first serious military encounter with its southern neighbor. In 1980 I returned to Lebanon as a stringer for the London-based *Middle East* magazine. I chose to interview women, particularly those who had written on their five-year-old war. The interviews led to a book-length project, and I went back two years later to collect more material. During my stay the Israelis invaded and dropped bombs all around the area in which I was staying. I went back the next year to collect the books that I had had to leave in my hurry. Then, when I had finished writing *War's Other Voices* and was ready to move on, I realized that I could not, that the project had become so much part of me that I could not just turn my back on it. I wanted to know how what I had done fitted into the larger scheme. And so I started to read novels and poetry about the wars in Algeria, Vietnam, Iraq, and the Israeli-occupied territories.

A life in a paragraph organized by violence: I arrange the dots that draw me around the spaces of Middle Eastern wars. Why do I not include in this dot outline the first man on the moon? The first flight of Concorde? Then I remember Wilfred Owen. It is 1960, a dank afternoon in May when I, a twelve-year-old in the Tunbridge Wells County Grammar School for Girls, am asked to read out a poem. At first, haltingly because I have not had time to scan the text and then breathlessly as I tumble through the lines that from that day become part of my life . . .

> Men marched asleep. Many had lost their boots,
> But limped on blood-shod. . . .
>   . . . deaf even to the hoots
> Of gas-shells dropping softly behind. . . .
> If in some smothering dreams, you too could pace
> Behind the wagon that we flung him in,
> And watch the white eyes writhing in his face,
> His hanging face, like a devil's full of sin;
> If you could hear, at every jolt, the blood
> Come gargling from the froth-corrupted lungs . . .
> My friend, you would not tell with such high zest
> To children ardent for some desperate glory,
> The old Lie: Dulce et decorum est
> Pro patria mori.

This poem tied me to a man twice my age whose agony seared my innocence. Today I look back fondly on that surprised child and an anguished young man, now half my age, and I marvel at the power of his words that have made him my friend. The pacifist physicist Freeman Dyson was surely right when he wrote that if "we are searching for meaning in a world of shifting standards, literature is one place where we can find it. All of us have periods in our lives when meaning is lost, and other periods when it is found again. It is an inescapable part of the human condition to be borrowing meaning from one another" (Dyson 1985, 299–300). The tragedy of the poem is the story it tells but also the fate of the poet whose death for his country was neither sweet nor appropriate. Forty years after his death, Wilfred handed me his poem, and now thirty years later I am trying to borrow meaning from this fragment that survives, trying to understand how his opposition from within the war sheds light on what, throughout my life, women halfway across the world have been writing on war. Does their participation give them a special right to speak?

More than most human activities, war has been considered the literary purview of those few who have experienced combat. Those who had not been at the front had no authority to speak of the dead and dying. Women, therefore, clearly had no right to speak. Yet what of Helen Zenna Smith, who wrote *Not So Quiet . . .* in 1930, or Stephen Crane, who wrote *Red Badge of Courage* in 1895? Neither writer had even approached a war zone, and both works have been hailed as stunning exemplars of war fiction that vividly evoke the experiences of combatants and their caretakers. These two novels suggest that experience does not necessarily bestow authority. I take my cue.

And yet, in this world increasingly split between North and South, between a homogenizing global culture and myriad resistance movements, how can an American woman write about Arab women without privileging herself as norm? In 1980, when I began to work on Arab women's writings on the Lebanese civil war, my colleagues' only objection was the value of the enterprise: did I really want to waste my time on these *dames de salon?* Now, however, things have changed. As Arab women's writings are increasingly translated into all the major, and even not so major, languages of the world and some Arab women are receiving a recognition that few of their male colleagues have enjoyed, all feminist criticism on Arabic literature is coming under investigation. Western feminists have been criticized for viewing women from the South as victims bound by a shared oppression at the hands of an undifferentiated patriarchy. Their interventions in the affairs of Asian and African women, their outrages at the inflicting of what they consider to be harmful cultural practices, such as veiling, clitoridectomy and foot binding have been linked to Euro-American cultural imperialism. Is there a way to work together without suspicion and silencing?

My answer has been to focus on literature because it allows for the articulation of individual women's different experiences, beliefs, choices, and aspirations. Clearly I am implicated in what Chandra Mohanty calls the "global hegemony of western scholarship—i.e., the production, publication, distribution, and consumption of information and ideas" (Mohanty 1991, 55). I acknowledge that I am interested in those moments of women's empowerment, though they seem to be invisible. Above all, I believe in the power of women's oppositional discourses wherever they happen. My work is premised on the hope that women's contestatory narratives can create alternative spaces and that in these new spaces conflicts may be resolved without automatic resort to organized and lethal violence.

Women and the War Story is about wars and gender in the contemporary literature of the Arab world. It attempts to situate Arab wars and primarily women's writings about them in a cross-cultural context. It is clearly a sequel to *War's Other Voices,* but it is also a departure from it in that it interrogates more deeply the conditions that enable the production of particular kinds of war texts. In the earlier work I spoke about women who wrote unconventionally about the Lebanese war. They told a story of chaos, not of revolution, of daily surviving, not of relentless hatred and fighting. Their stories opened up for me a new way of reading about other wars in the Arab world in the second half of the twentieth century: the Algerian war of independence from the French 1954–62; the Palestinian-Israeli wars of 1948 and 1967 and the Intifada (1987–93); and the Iraq-Iran War 1980–88. This literature inscribes the changes in the experience and expression of war from the colonial to the postcolonial period.

Women and the War Story suggests that there is no one history, no one story about war, that has greater claim to truth but that history is made up of multiple stories, many of them herstories, which emanate from and then reconstruct events. Each story told by someone who experienced a war, or by someone who saw someone who experienced a war, or by someone who read about someone who saw someone who experienced a war, becomes part of a mosaic the many colors and shapes of which make up the totality of that war. Yet however exhaustive my research and reach, I cannot encompass this totality: I can always only tell an individual story.

I am interested in the choices that Arab women make as they pick up their pens to write about their experiences in wars others declare they have lived as noncombatants. How do they begin to imagine narratives that do not fit the mold of the War Story? How does the way they position themselves affect the knowledge they produce and their right to express it? How do they challenge the archetypes of the Mater Dolorosa, the Patriotic Mother, the Spartan Mother, or the Amazon? How can such iconoclasts then fashion a new persona: the woman who has lived war not as a victim but as a survivor, who may not have borne arms but who has played all the other roles a war culture prescribes? Should she submit her experiences to others' labeling? How can she force others to acknowledge the variety of roles she has taken in what is supposed to be a men-only domain? How can she guarantee that this time she will not find herself written out of the War Story and civic belonging? It is not merely whim that drives women everywhere to claim their war experiences as combat. It is the growing understanding of the ways in which patriarchy seizes and then articulates women's experiences so that they will be seem to be marginal and apolitical that now drives women as creative artists and as critics to re-member their pasts and then to write them.

I am looking in postcolonial Arab war literature for alternatives to the master narrative of war. I have spent the past thirteen years studying the emergence of an imagined community of oppositional writers. With Benedict Anderson and Chandra Mohanty I use the term "imagined community" to point out how people forge alliances that are neither biological nor cultural but political, to form what Mohanty calls a "common context of struggle . . . [for r]esistance is encoded in the practices of remembering and of writing." As Algerian, Lebanese, Palestinian, and Iraqi women re-member their experiences in war and then write of its dailiness, they figure their agency (Mohanty 1991, 7, 38). As I interpret these writings I inscribe them further into a global movement of women's empowerment. Women who have had experiences that have changed their conceptions of who they are must write to inscribe their transformed consciousness. Women must fight to retain the authority to write about an experience that they are supposed not to have had.

In chapter one, "Subvert the Dominant Paradigm," I discuss the persistence of the War Story, a narrative frame that has for millennia shaped the articulation of the war experience. I try to account for its influence on the waging of war as well as on the gender composition of the military. I have been struck by the parallels between women writing about war and women entering into the military. In each case, women who have traditionally been associated with peace are intervening in wars and revealing that the ways in which war stories have been told were deeply flawed. These women who fight with weapons or with their determination to survive or with their pens draw attention to what they are doing and how they are changing the norms. I compare the perceived role of enlisted women with that of mother warriors. These are women—not necessarily actual mothers—who have used the role of mother to enter public space whence they demand justice. These women, who are not substituting for male fighters but who have evolved their own way of fighting, are demanding that the meanings attached to war experience be reviewed and revised. Finally, I connect the military women and the self-styled women combatants with women writers who have scripted multiple stories about the wars in which they have participated. I ask whether acknowledgement of women's presence in what was considered to be no-woman's land (Higonnet 1993) will make a difference to the ways in which wars are narrated and consequently fought in the future.

In chapter two, "Culture Degree Zero," I describe ways in which the conduct, constitution, and above all the representation of war have changed in the nuclear age. The role of film and the media has been critical to altering the historical debates about the meanings, causes, and cures of war. Such is the case because until recently the reality of war was said to precede and thus to be separate from its representation. This is no longer possible. I analyze aspects of the representation of the war in Vietnam to make connections between other oppositions crucial to the War Story, for example, combatant and civilian; beginnings and endings. The very category of war is destabilized as it is shown to be integral to what was thought to be its opposite, namely, peace. Wars today are called civil, revolutionary, drug, gang, feudal, ideological, but they are linked by the fact that they refuse the easy oppositions that had marked, in fact constituted, the War Story. There are risks attendant on the dismantling of the War Story. Why go to war if victory and defeat are not clear-cut, mutually exclusive concepts? Low-intensity conflict may spill into a non-militarized zone, but people still need to believe in the separation of space into dangerous front—men's space—and danger-free home—women's space. And then who would venture into battle if there were doubt about the goodness and loyalty of troops and allies and the total evil of the enemy? People's beliefs, hopes, and needs notwithstanding, the reality, or better the realities, of nuclear age wars fly in the face of such distortions. Those who continue to function in terms of black and white categorizations are neither mad nor stupid, they are nostalgic. They long for a world that I suspect never existed; it allocated special terrain for fighting and designated safe space. Certainties of space imparted other assurances about identity in terms of gender, class, and nationalism. So critical have these identities been to sane survival in an insane world that ambiguity and ambivalence in experience were obstinately recast as certainties.

Chapter three, "Silence Is the Real Crime," compares men's and women's writings on the Algerian war of independence. This war was widely acclaimed for mobilizing women into the revolutionary forces. How did contemporary writers assess women's participation as it was happening? Although women writers gradually came to write about the war, at the time they were more concerned with issues like gender inequality. The war would have seemed to open up opportunities to escape or even to change such a fate. It did not. The women did not know how to profit from their war experiences—nor indeed that they might do so. In the absence of a concerted attempt on the women's part to change their conditions, the men quickly established a neotraditional system that deprived the women of any voice. Literary evidence supports a recent contention that Algerian women were not so much forced back into oppression as they were blocked from pursuing opportunities they did not at the time recognize. Even feminist writers like Djamila Débèche and Assia Djebar did not describe the war as liberating. Why? Algerian women did not have a feminist context within which to situate their struggle. The revolution came too soon in the history of modern Arab women's activism to be recognized as a catalyst for the inscription of feminist issues into the nationalist agenda. War was declared an opportunity that women had failed to exploit. Ironically the men, among them Mohamed Dib and Malek Haddad, wrote with anxiety about women's growing roles and strength during the war. A comparison of women's and men's writings suggests why women were disempowered in the aftermath. The women did not realize and certainly did not write about their potential social transformation. The men did write and they acted on their writing. It was only in the 1980s, when the fundamentalist Front Islamique de Salut and their armed counterparts began to mount lethal attacks in their war against their secular government and nonobservant civilians, that Algerian women began to learn the lessons of those—like the Iranian and Palestinian women—who had learned the Algerian Lesson: silence is the real crime.

Chapter four, "Talking Democracy," considers the writings of Palestinian women during two periods immediately following Israeli occupations, the first in 1948 and the next in 1967 leading to the Intifada. These writings exemplify within one literature how women shifted from acting and writing like men to adopt a woman-centered behavior and discourse. Unlike other colonized peoples, Palestinians experienced renewed colonialism in a period said to be beyond it. When the British left in the late 1940s, European refugees replaced them. Some Palestinians remained, and for them the relationship with the occupiers was complex. Were they new neighbors or enemies? Palestinian men and women writers of this period reflect great ambivalence about the Israelis as well as about their own status and future. The major concerns are survival with dignity and the establishment of a just if patriarchal society. The literary reaction to the defeat of 1967 was quite different. Five years after the end of the Algerian revolution, Palestinians were invoking its lessons: the importance of the use of violence in the struggle for independence; the indispensability of women to national liberation. Palestinian women writers took the latter a step further to claim that not only were women as actors indispensable to the nationalist revolution but so was feminism as an ideology of radical social change. The poetry, autobiographies, novels, and short stories of Fadwa Tuqan, Sahar Khalifa, and Halima Jauhar early draw the contours of the Intifada. This popular uprising derived its name from the term the women had been using for twenty years to describe their women-specific ways of resisting the occupation in Gaza and the West Bank. The women writers demonstrate how the conventional binary structures thought to be proper to war no longer pertained despite valiant attempts to hold on to them. Men's writings, mirroring women's literary assessments of men's political actions and attitudes, seem oblivious to the new strategies and realities.

In chapter five, "Flames of Fire in Qadisiya," I consider the writings of one of the major global conflicts of the 1980s, the Iraq-Iran War. Most of this literature, like most of the art produced under the Baathist regime of Saddam Hussein, was state-commissioned often before the events they were supposed to celebrate and commemorate had actually taken place. Conferences were held to give a platform to this new literature. So insular and preoccupied were Iraqi writers with their project that they debated the term "war literature" as though they were the first to invent it. Some artists collaborated with the government: victory monuments were constructed before any victory was in sight, martyr monuments were conceived before the war. Were they producing art or propaganda? Can they claim innocence of collaboration with an evil regime? What are we to make of the writer's responsibility to society? Can patronized but also terrorized writers question the validity of a patriotic war? How do we read such texts? Many men did not hold back as they touted the glories of the war. The women, however, were not so easily co-opted. Daisy al-Amir, Suhayla Salman, Lutfiya al-Dulaymi, and 'Aliya Talib ventured cautious recognitions of the hollowness of victory and of martyrdom. They even interrogated the ways in which propaganda was made and used against Iraqi citizens. These women were able to overcome atomization and retain the sense of responsibility that some claimed all Iraqi writers enlisted into state service had lost.

Chapter six, "Reimagining Lebanon," turns to the civil war in the aftermath of the Israeli invasion of 1982. Women like Huda Barakat and Nur Salman, who had not written about the war until that point, join others like Emily Nasrallah, who wrote throughout, to urge the national importance of remaining on the soil of Lebanon. In their texts they have begun to fashion a new form of nationalism—what I call humanist nationalism—that does not predicate itself on the existence of a state. They are deliberately writing against the grain of the War Story. I have chosen to conclude *Women and the War Story* with a return to my earlier interest but at a later period so as to frame the question of war in the postcolonial period. To use the Lebanese war as a prism is to acknowledge its difference from these other wars but also its centrality to their interpretation.

Two of these wars were considered by their women participants to be "just," the other two were not. The Algerians had to rise up as a people against the French if they were to gain independence; the Palestinians, particularly in the post-1967 period, realized that they had to unite against the Israelis if they were to regain some form of homeland. In contrast, the Iraqi people found themselves in a war they could not understand against a people they were not sure they hated. The same was true for many Lebanese who recognized that their internecine chaos served no one but the war profiteers. In each conflict women became involved and wanted their role to be acknowledged. When they supported the nationalist cause, they assumed that their unprecedented contribution would reap its own automatic rewards. When it did not, these women later struggled for recognition. In Iraq and Lebanon the women writers described the wars in which their countries were embroiled as being unjustifiably destructive. They resisted the violence, working against a system they understood to be responsible for perpetuating the war. They drew attention to the falseness of the rhetoric used to mobilize the population as well as to the fact that this system was mostly managed by men. They tried to change what was happening by resisting as women and by showing how effective were their different forms of resistance. Their stories describe the reality underlying and contradicting the nationalist rhetoric.

Study of the literature of these four wars reveals that the date of their occurrence is very important. The situation of women in the anticolonial war is different from that of women in postcolonial wars. In the 1950s and early 1960s Algerian and Palestinian women in Israel considered themselves to be *exceptionally* part of a political movement. They fought as the men did, and their goal was to liberate the country, not to change society. The situation of Iraqi and Lebanese women, and Palestinian women in the Occupied Territories of the West Bank and the Gaza Strip in the late 1970s and 1980s, provides a stark contrast. These women all write of fighting for their country but they do not give priority to the political. For them, the social takes precedence. They have seen that victory in the political sphere has no necessary connection with societal change; political victory brings few if any advantages to the lives of the people. Yet political mobilization provides opportunities for change because it is there that ad hoc social accommodations must begin to create the climate for political success. Women in the 1970s, 1980s, and 1990s recognize the social possibilities inherent in political resistance and bring to their war participation the awareness that if political victory is to have any meaning at all, it must entail social transformation. Armed with this awareness, these women improvise ways of participating that are unlike those of their male counterparts, ways that do not negate their identities as women. Their resistance becomes self-consciously feminine. They insist on this difference in activism while emphasizing the commonality of the goal. These women write out of their own experiences, transforming the meanings others have traditionally attached to what they have done and to who they are, demanding recognition at the time of participation. They write to express their own needs and link these with the needs of their country, which is both a political entity and a community of precious individuals.

In these postcolonial wars, women generally criticize men's ways of fighting regardless of their personal attitudes to the war in question. They object to the ways in which men have generally overlooked their involvement, whether active or passive. Their writings show how women wage peace, in other words how women fight for justice without necessarily engaging in destruction. They may see aggression to be necessary, but they propose new ways, strategies, and targets. Sometimes they try to reveal ways in which some form of resolution can be reached without resort to lethal violence. Their stories allow us to ask new questions. For example, would the Palestinian-Israeli peace process—however volatile its current incarnation—have been conceivable without the Intifada, and would the Intifada have been possible had the women for years not invented new ways of resisting without arms?

In this world of shifting standards I borrow meaning from these women. I build my story on foundations they have laid. My hope for myself and for all embarked on this venture, this cultural crossing, is that a recognition of our own strangeness will not serve to silence but will rather allow for the proliferation of multiple stories each of which will contribute to the flourishing of shared understandings based on mutual respect.

Chapter One

Subvert the Dominant Paradigm

War has become a constant presence in our everyday lives, whether through telecasting of ethnic cleansings in Cambodia or Bosnia or Rwanda, or through experience of militarization. We may seem further away from nuclear night than we were as recently as 1989, but smaller-scale widespread explosions of violence force us to ask just why it is that communities that were living together in "peace" suddenly turn to killing each other. The causes of war must be explored; surely war is not inevitable; it is only made to seem that way.

Two Paradigms

A bumper sticker on the car in front of me reads Subvert the Dominant Paradigm. My mind wanders from the "Morning Edition" broadcast story about Serbian aggressions in Gorazde to the two dominant paradigms I study: war and gender.

War is conventionally defined as organized armed conflict among states, that is, among political entities having or aspiring to have a monopoly on armed force within their territory. The goal of war is definitive resolution—victory. Even when such a resolution is not reached, and it rarely is, it is often *said* to be reached. Victory is declared; fighting ceases. The war is over. Therefore, the new state must be one of peace. During peace, society no longer needs to be divided between spaces where certain tasks are performed by men and other tasks are performed by women. Previously, this sex segregation was so accepted that few questioned what the philosopher J. Glenn Gray calls the "artificial separation of the sexes or, at best, a maldistribution" (Gray 1970, 62).

Unlike convents and monasteries, as well as boys' and girls' schools, the front and home front have not usually been analyzed as gendered spaces. Until recently these emergency, gender-specific spaces have not been so different from peacetime, patriarchal arrangements. Women occupied spaces that had little if any direct access to the spaces of power that the men in general occupied. In the Arab world this absence was marked by such words as "veil" and "harem." In the West the absence had to be uncovered. As David Harvey writes, space allocation constructs power and privilege, because "the assignment of place within a sociospatial structure indicates distinctive roles, capacities for action, and access to power within the social order."[1] The inequities built into military space are grounded in the fact that where women are not, is the space of privilege.

Like war and peace, gender is thought of in binary terms that are said to be natural. But gender, far from being natural, is a cultural code that describes, prescribes, and thus shapes social expectations for sexed bodies: men and women grow up differently and most act in ways consonant with their culture's prevalent images and values. The literary critic Eve Sedgwick defines gender as the "dichotomized social production and reproduction of male and female identities and behaviors . . . in a culture for which 'male/female' functions as a primary and perhaps model binarism affecting the structure and meaning of many, many other binarisms . . . the meaning of gender is seen as culturally mutable and variable, highly relational . . . and inextricable from a history of power differentials between genders" (Sedgwick 1990, 27–28). Gender is constructed in a discourse that the psychologist Carol Cohn describes as being "not only about words or language but about a system of meanings, of ways of thinking, images and words that first shape how we experience, understand, and represent ourselves as men and women, but that also do more than that; they shape many other aspects of our lives and culture. In this symbolic system, human characteristics are dichotomized" (Cohn 1993, 228–29). Thus, our images come to polarize both war and gender. If war and gender so powerfully organize the world dyadically, their reconception and rearticulation may become the instrument for recreating that world.

I am interested in the blurring of binaries in contemporary wars. I am also concerned with the ways in which people who have lived through wars tell their stories, because stories influence how the next wars will be fought—and then told. Until quite recently, most wars were recounted within a narrative frame that the British military historian John Keegan argues has remained essentially unchanged since Thucydides. This frame I call the War Story with thanks to Tim O'Brien for drawing our attention to the problem of war story telling, and for his passionate plea to believe the "crazy stuff" and to resign ourselves to the fact that "in a true war story nothing is ever absolutely true" (O'Brien 1990, 79, 88).

The War Story gives order to wars that are generally experienced as confusion. It justifies not changing the rules, laws, and strategies of engagement, despite the fact that as a German commander once declared: "Every scheme, every pattern is wrong. No two situations are identical. That is why the study of military history can be extremely dangerous" (Dyson 1985, 153). Put otherwise, that is why writing the War Story can be extremely dangerous. Nevertheless, military historians force a grid on the anarchy; they arrange experience and actors into neat pairs: beginning and ending; foe and friend; aggression and defense; war and peace; front and home; combatant and civilian. Emphasizing that such splits occur, they explain women's need for protection as the reason men must fight. The War Story reinforces mythic wartime roles. It revives outworn essentialist clichés of men's aggressivity and women's pacifism. It divides the world between the *politikon,* where men play "political" roles, including the warrior as *homo furens,* whom Glenn Gray describes as being a subspecies of *H. sapiens* (Gray 1970, 27), and the *oikon,* where women are lovers or mothers, the latter category including the Mater Dolorosa (the weeping madonna), the Patriotic Mother (the ever-ready womb for war), the Spartan Mother (the jingoistic mother who prefers her sons dead to defeated). The War

Story proclaims that this sex segregation is justified for biological reasons: the men are strong, therefore they must protect the women who are weak.[2] It is written in their genes that men shall be active and women passive.

How to Tell the War Story

War is messy but until recently it was not told that way. Men have generally turned their messy war experiences into coherent stories, poems, memoirs, films, and photograph albums and even into official records. The dichotomies of the War Story organize the confusion so that aggression should not be confused with defense, victory with defeat, civilian with combatant, home with front, women's work with men's work.

Lebanon's ordeal between 1975 and 1992 offers a telling example of this ordering and dichotomization. I went to Lebanon in 1980 to interview women who were writing fiction on the civil war that had raged in the eastern Mediterranean for five years. I was surprised to find that literary activity was intense, that the war had inspired many to write and paint. Women and men were churning out novels, short stories, and poetry. The women's descriptions of the war seemed to preclude the possibility of arranging the chaos into a coherent narrative, whereas most men's war stories lined up oppositions. It was my comparative analysis of women's and men's differing senses of responsibility during the war that gave me a clue as to how the War Story grid remains even in the most intractable chaos.

By acknowledging chaos, the women presented the situation as out of control and urged each individual to assume responsibility for ending the war. Responsibility in the women's writings entailed *duties* toward others, duties that had to be fulfilled so that the war might stop. In the men's writings, responsibility adhered to a notion of *rights:* protagonists protected what was theirs against others. After disavowing chaos, the men transformed it into the clarity of friend and foe (Cooke 1988).

It was only years after the writing of *War's Other Voices,* my analysis of the war writings, that I was to realize that the most enlightening example of how to tell the Lebanese War Story might be through photographs. In 1980 and then again in 1982, I had noticed war albums with their full-page pictures of blood and guts in Beirut living rooms. I assumed that this phenomenon was peculiar to Lebanon, and beyond a cursory glance at the mostly gruesome contents I paid them little attention.

When I traveled to Croatia in the late summer of 1993 I began to suspect that this expensive packaging and marketing of war images might be more pervasive than I had thought. While in Zagreb, I bought Zoran Jovicic's *War Crimes Committed by the Yugoslav Army 1991–1992*. This oversized photo-illustrated book with its text in Croatian, English, and German was published in 1992 by the Croatian Information Centre. Although more sober than its Lebanese counterparts, this book too was a handsome production with many stunning photographs. Further, Jovicic or his publishers added a titillating detail: the last four pages were sealed with a piece of red tape. Like Madonna's presentation of her autobiography, this book was not accessible to the casual browser but had to be bought to be seen in whole.[3] I went straight to this section whose cover page carried the following message in three languages: "WARNING. The sealed pages contain some of many available photos depicting brutal murders and massacres committed by the YU-Army and Serbian irregular units against the civilian population in Croatia during the years of 1991 and 1992." To my relief, but also I must confess somewhat to my disappointment, the pictures were not as grim as I expected; I had seen worse in the uncensored Lebanese versions (among them, color photos).[4] Why did the publisher use the red tape trick here? Clearly, it made people buy the book and not just skim the pages in the store. Beyond the mercenary motive was a stated moral purpose: "This book has been outlined to identify the crimes committed by the YU-Army" (Jovicic 1992, 95). Jovicic and his team of twenty-two photographers assumed the role of detectives and lawyers for the prosecution. Jovicic sent me back to the Lebanese war albums. Maybe they, too, were not just examples of macabre commercialism.

The most popular of the Lebanese albums was *Harb Lubnan* (Lebanon's war), which came out in 1977 and was reprinted in

1980. Other than a two-page introduction and a war chronology, it had no written text—160 pages of photographs with as many as four per page. For the first time, I read the introduction. It was signed "The Publisher," but I could not tell whether this person was Layla Badi' 'Itani, who prepared the volume, or the photographer, 'Abd al-Razzaq al-Sayyid, or the editor, Sami Dhabyan, or someone else in the Dar al-Masira publishing house. Unlike the Croatian volume, *Harb Lubnan* did not set itself the task of identifying the enemy, although the format and nature of the subjects photographed suggested sympathies. Its avowed intent was to chronicle the war truthfully: "This is exactly what happened. Here it is between the two covers of a book. . . . Photo after photo out of which pour blood, stream rockets, burst shrapnel. A torn out eye, a cut off hand, a burned cadaver, a skinned body may slap you in the face. . . . Here is the nation, Lebanon, which *they* [this "they," I emphasize, indicating the enemy, whoever that might be] crucified for two years. We present it in pictures, events and documents. . . . We wanted to touch its wounds and then to bring them together in ink on paper because we do not want the tragedy to happen again. . . . We are less interested in whether this war was a victory or a defeat than we are in bringing it into your house, your office, into every corner of your house. . . . May it be a war on war itself and on you if you were one of its instigators, one of those who lit its fire or poured oil on it or failed to put it out. . . . This war might have been noble had the many revolutionaries and fighters not been joined by thieves and criminals, killers, drunks and ignoramuses. . . . [a paragraph later:] The war has ended." The writer urges the reader to look to the present and the future which must guarantee four aims: that Lebanon remain independent and united; that it be part of a pan-Arab ethos; that it no longer remain indifferent to Israel but confront its territorial ambitions in Lebanon; that it function in terms of its newly awakened consciousness.

What are we to make of such an introduction? It establishes the project as moral: this photojournal is supposed to make us experience the war and its horrors so as to assume responsibility for ending the war. But then, oddly, it announces that the war is over. Now it is time to build the future and this book plays a role in constructing this future. The very last sentence declares: "Our ambition is that you should read with us the *brilliant future* in the pictures, documents, and events" (my emphasis). Everything about the book says that it is time to rebuild, although from the perspective of 1994 we know that the seventeen-year war was in its second year only.[5] But what this album does is not *re*-build, but simply build. The author has used fragments of the Lebanese civil war to build the Lebanese War Story. The volume is a concrete example of how the confusion of war can be streamlined into the black and white certainties of a binary narrative.

Let us look at the way in which *Harb Lubnan* uses photographs and their captions to set up a binary structure. The pairs at issue are war and peace, and men's and women's spaces. The gendering of space points to another dichotomy, that of combatant versus civilian. We begin with war and peace. How does this volume frame the action? The covers are a good place to start. The front image represents the war front in medias res: burned-out buildings and bullet-pocked walls, sandbags, young men in khaki—two in helmets—alert with their Kalashnikov rifles at the ready, no women, in fact no sign of civilian life (Fig. 1; see the section of illustrations that follows p. 43). The back photograph is quite different (Fig. 2). It suggests that the war is over. We surmise this because the young men are sprawled over a tank, they are smiling and chatting, some have even returned to civvies. These masculine soldiers will protect us; they are in charge. We know this because although they are at ease, their tank's phallic gun thrusts out aggressively from the epicenter of the image; it fills the vision; it is pointed at us, between the eyes, so much so that it blocks out part of the image, including the head of one of the "soldiers." He sits on the shaft of the gun; opposite and facing him is a very relaxed man. The homoerotics of the scene are unmistakable. In this space of men and victory, men can with impunity love each other both emotionally and physically. On the right edge of the frame we see the peaceful background, absent from the rest of the volume, and we note unharmed residential buildings with hints of the cheerful orange awnings and a cedarlike tree. This tree serves two functions: it represents the return of life, but above all, the cedar is the tree of Lebanon. Its presence in this photograph suggests that the good guys have won. These cover images are the most important in the entire book because they are there on the coffee table, next to the afternoon teacup and the preprandial snacks. Family members and their guests can linger over two moments: the middle and the end of the war.

But what about the photographs inside? The images with their captions inside fill out the message of the covers: they move from being at war to beginning peace. They trace the progression of the war from its onset on 13 April 1975 when members of a fascist militia, called the Phalangists, shot up a bus of Palestinians in 'Ayn al-Rummana, a neighborhood in Beirut (Fig. 3), to its "end" on 1 May 1977. This ending is anticipated by some boiler-plate images and captions. First, "The al-Hoss government has dealt [note the past tense] with many problems that were a legacy of the war" (141)—so, the war is dead and the inheritance is being disposed of. Next, we see a bulldozer mopping up (Fig. 4). It is the beginning of a new day: "They [this 'they' is never specified, but at this late stage of the volume 'they' are always confident, relaxed young men in some military context] came with the dawn to make fast the peace of Rada' [prevention forces]—peace by force" (141; Fig. 5). "They" enter the city—I say "enter" because, presumably, we are in the city and they are approaching us; they are friendly and relaxed. Next, we recognize another take of the scene on the back cover. This image, however, is much less aggressive: the gun is smaller in the picture and off to the right, it is still pointed toward us but not at our eyes, there are more civilians hanging around—a man with a camera and some Roman ruins to balance the residence on the right—and in this case there is a caption: "They arrived—and the cannons were silent. A smile . . . a cannon" (141; Figs. 6 and 7). In other words, we are friendly, but don't mess with us! Clean-up operations in the devastated city are underway.

The absolute end is conclusively established with four photographs on unnumbered pages, as though they were outside the war that the book has been presenting. The first shows a leader—Kamal Jumblat—lying in state; the caption does not say who he is or that he was assassinated, only that "he lies on the bed of death between his two companions in life and death" (Fig. 8). The next shows the fortieth-day remembrance of Jumblat's death being observed, we are told, by 150,000 citizens and, as we can see, by "soldiers" lined up in organized rows; this picture seems to hark back to much earlier pictures of marching and victorious soldiers (15, 105), but these men look more disciplined (Fig. 9). The third photo assures us that things are moving in the right direction: a meeting of politicians in earnest and friendly conversation—the caption announces: "Before beginning to govern, President Elias Sarkis conducted consultations and initiated contacts," followed by names that include the Palestine Liberation Organization leader Yasser Arafat and the commander of the Syrian Air Force (Fig. 10). Thus, we get the impression that all the warring parties are represented here and that they are in agreement. Fourth, a group of civilians—marked by the fact that there are young women among them—meet at the Mathaf (museum) traffic circle (Fig. 11). After the Lebanese capital was divided in the mid-1970s, this Mathaf was one of the most dangerous crossing points from East to West Beirut. This last picture is the most reassuring: if it is safe enough for women to be at the Mathaf then the city will not continue to be divided for long. More than any other image, this one convinces us that peace is at hand.

The photographs create a sense that this was a war like many before it. It could even turn out to have been a good war. As we were told in the introduction, "This war might have been noble had the many revolutionaries and fighters not been joined by thieves and criminals, killers, drunks, and ignoramuses." We leaf through images of war made familiar by the plethora of World War II representations: crowds running, demonstrating, buying bread, setting up temporary shops in the streets, dragging the wounded out of sniper shot; refugees leaving town; bad guys gleefully celebrating with champagne (Fig. 12). We see gutted buildings, exploded cars, streets littered with military debris ("The Game of Death," 35) and the charred (120, a color photo), bloated, or crushed remains of "collateral damage" that are sometimes so mangled that a superposed arrow must point them out (48–49; Fig. 13). We see armored cars carrying "troops" (19) who are never referred to as the militiamen or thugs they actually were; we watch children playing on piles of sandbags. Interspersed among these images of violence are the calm takes of politicians huddled around conference tables. The captions are laconic, for example, "A meeting to find a solution" followed by the list of those in attendance (65). Clearly, these men are the ones who are waging war and deploying troops. They know what is going on. Others know that they know and that is why they still trust them [whoever they might be], even if "they" are not always willing to help. In a series of four photographs (Figs. 14–17), a father of five is pictured on his way to parliament to register a complaint about his children's hunger, but "the policeman's and the deputies' hearts are hard" (74–75). Had they not been hard, the images and the captions seem to say, they could have done something.

The images tell the story of a war that separated the men from the women and by extension the combatants from the civilians. Although early on we are allowed to see women soldiers (15), soon women disappear from photographs depicting anything that might be construed to be the front. A bizarre exception is the image of an image of a woman: after a shoot-out in the Basta market all we can see are scattered fruits and above them a billboard depicting a woman in a slip; the banner running behind her says: "When love collapses and marriage fails, what is the fate of the divorced, wronged woman?" (88; Fig. 18). This poster reminds the men that this is a time to reassess past behavior and to make sure that women are not wronged but defended. Early in the book, and therefore in the war as presented in this album, a woman has lost her husband and her desperate search announces that "the war entered every house" (24; Fig. 19). At rare intervals we see women weeping, in this case within the cramped space of a simple home (39; Fig. 20). Children—quintessential noncombatants—are pictured lost in the ruined streets-become-war front (Fig. 21). Their jarring presence reminds us of the inevitable transgression of segregation that they thereby serve to reinforce. The ironic caption reads: "Childhood survives to carry the future" (38). There are occasional images of women defending and preserving, an apparent role reversal that endangers the home/front binary. In two juxtaposed images (Figs.

22–23) a very young father and a mother are holding an infant. The first image suggests domesticity: the father stands quietly by a wall, looking toward what we assume to be his home. He seems contented as he holds the baby, its bottle, and its pillow; the caption reads: "War births: they are trying to escape to peace. He carried him in the first stage." When a father can hold his baby at home, all must be well abroad. The second image suggests present danger: the mother is rushing along a street, the baby tightly clasped to her bosom: "And his mother carried him in the difficult stage" (81). The caption announces that she is the one who really protects the weak. But another interpretation of this second image is that when there was danger in the streets, the men were out there protecting the women who were protecting the children. That is, the subtext reinforces the reassuring binaries of the War Story. In this self-contained narrative of a war that is told as finished, possibly won, Beirut appears to be clearly divided between home and front, between combatants and civilians, between men's action and women's reaction.

The cause of the war becomes clear: identity. With a cause to defend, combatants line up on opposing sides. Several images of corpses carry captions that explain the cause of death as being related to their identity but without elaboration: "Streets of corpses. Massacring identity" (31) and "Tragedy. They kidnapped them and killed them. Because of their identity" (93). The captions, and not the photographs alone, confirm that the war was about the politics of identity. Further, the pictures of desecrated sanctuaries (28; Fig. 24) and religious leaders remind the reader that yes, the identity in question is religious and the enemy is the religious other who kills our god in the name of his.

The book aims to persuade us that this chronicle of the war is true, total, and unbiased. Again, the introduction claims: "This is exactly what happened. Here it is between the two covers of a book" (4). Above all, we—unlike those who merely lived through the war but were not privileged to share this ubiquitous vision—are allowed the photographer's special access: we are made privy to the most inaccessible meetings; we get the impression that we have seen all parties to the conflict. We have even been up on the roof and in hideaways with the snipers (18, 77, 97; Fig. 25). Crucially, we have also seen one of them shot down, stripped of his threat, of his clothes, and of his gender, for had the caption not said that this was "The Holiday Inn sniper [masculine] who fell naked from the twenty-second floor" (107; Fig. 26), we would not know if this were a man or a woman. Indeed, the latter seems more likely because with the underwear yanked down and the beaten up body this image suggests a victim of rape.[6] Feminizing the sniper is consonant with the book's principal aim, which is to turn the chaos of the civil war into the militarized order of the War Story. For whereas the militiamen could be and indeed were represented as soldiers, the Lebanese sniper cannot be glorified. His job is to be alone, not to cohere with the group. The sniper is the quintessential symbol of anarchy, for his assignment is not to kill the enemy but rather to sow terror by hitting precisely those whom the military men are supposed to be protecting. The military men have to get rid of this loose cannon who detracts from the justness of the fight. Best of all, he should be shown to be different from them, should be humiliated, and what could be more humiliating than to look like a woman? (Jeffords 1989, 171–75). The photographer was there when this particular monster was killed, he witnessed the feminization, took the picture from close up, he was standing right above the body. He was participating in eliminating such undesirable elements. He is masculinized in this act of witnessing and feminizing, and so are we. It is this masculinization that is the sine qua non of victory, as we saw on the back cover.

We are given further assurance that we have been where few others dared to tread because we see those who are supposed to be managing the violence—journalists, through camera control, and politicians, who have otherwise been shown in consultation that promises resolution—out of control, running, ducking and "jumping" in fear for their lives (138, 139). The photographer, 'Abd al-Razzaq al-Sayyid, is in greater control of the violence than are the politicians; he was able to get a steady shot of the jumping deputies (Fig. 27)! He is braver than the other photographers who are cowering, feminized by their fear. The caption reads: "The photographers and journalists were there. . . . But!" The heavy sarcasm seems unwarranted when we think a bit about the angle of his camera; is he not lower than the woman whose frightened face he shoots? So maybe he was a little scared, but that is less important than the fact that our photographer is always there at the right moment (Fig. 28): a man is kidnapped on his return from shopping, and al-Sayyid catches the moment of shock that we later revisit (65). Two photos of planes: in one, it has just landed with its cargo of flour; in the next, the charred remains are recorded still smoking (119).

We are not restricted to painful emotions, we can also appreciate the moments of irony that wars produce. Sometimes we shake our heads in disbelief, as when a bulldozer is pictured trying to conquer a mountain of rubble (69; Fig. 29). At other times we are moved, as by the photograph of a corpse lying behind the wheels of an abandoned United Nations car (Fig. 30); the caption reads: "A witness to the massacre in Burj Square" (88). And then we smile in relief with the militiaman who is amusing himself by putting together the scattered limbs of a mannequin (Fig. 31): "In Bab Idris, streets of elegance and beauty. Will she walk through death?"

The sense of having had the experience that we are viewing in stills is enhanced by the inclusion of an unmarked section of fifteen full-page color glossies without captions. This section, entitled "The Crime: In Color," is introduced by a few lines explaining why color. It is "not a luxury, but rather another way of describing. Colors say what black and white cannot . . . they have ceased to serve as decoration and have become a *witness for the prosecution of a crime* and of those who committed the crime thinking that they were living a film on a wide screen . . . and in color" (my emphasis). This language is much closer to that used in the Croatian volume that emphasized the ethical aspect of the project. But there is a prurient quality to these brilliant images that, as Sontag writes in her comparison of color with black and white photographs, are more voyeuristic, sentimental even because they are so crudely lifelike (Sontag 1977, 114).

We are so much there with al-Sayyid that we witness a man's shooting and the ensuing suffering (Fig. 32): "One of the Irtibat armed elements in Shiyah was hit by a sniper's bullet. 3 June 1975."

This series compels us to share al-Sayyid's choices: to intervene or to record? To save a life or capture a death? Here the choice is dragged out over several images—three shots of a man asking for help (30). If al-Sayyid found three photos good enough for inclusion in this book, how many were there on the contact sheet from which he chose? Did it ever occur to al-Sayyid that he might choose between intervening and recording? Was he, and are we with him, inured to the victim's pain and terrible need so that we can over-look, literally, the fact that in the last two images this man is looking straight at him/us, screaming at him/us to do something for God's sake? Neither we nor al-Sayyid are going to do anything, unless it be to get closer for the perfect shot. As Susan Sontag notes, "Pho-tographing is essentially an act of non-intervention. . . . To take a picture is to . . . be in complicity with whatever makes a subject interesting, worth photographing—including, when that is the in-terest, another person's pain or misfortune" (Sontag 1977, 10, 11). The fact that the man was directly engaging the photographer and begging for his help meant that he was peculiarly photogenic.

For al-Sayyid what mattered was documentation. Here was just another event he was representing. But what of the other event, the one that involved him, the wounded man addressing him and us? More than most of the images in this book, this series alerts us to the role of the photographer in war. He is not a disinterested agent mediating reality, he is using fragments of his individual experience to construct another reality that he projects as objective.[7] These three frozen moments tell us that this book is the sum of an indi-vidual's choices. His camera has indeed proven to be what Sontag calls "a sublimation of the gun." He has gained double control over this man's life: the mere act of taking the image is "a sublimated murder—a soft murder" (Sontag 1977, 13); additionally, he has chosen to let him suffer, die if necessary. He has made other choices: of subject matter, of angle, of juxtaposition, and of captioning. Above all, he has chosen to assemble these images in a book that must be read in the order that he adopted. As Walter Benjamin states, such organization of photographs is comparable to what happens in film "where the meaning of each single picture appears to be prescribed by the sequence of all the preceding ones" (Benjamin 1969 [1936], 226). Once the sequence is broken, the meaning assigned by the context is lost or at least deferred until the advent of another organizer, and so on. That is the power and weakness of this democratic technology that allows anyone to subvert a dominant paradigm and then to pastiche together a convincing reality, at least until someone else comes along with a new idea or ideology. Each montage or collage authenticates itself by reference to these transparencies on to reality that in fact relays a fragment of someone else's experience. To paraphrase Sontag, 'Abd al-Razzaq al-Sayyid has explored the war, duplicated aspects of it, fragmented its continuities, and fed "the pieces into an interminable dossier, thereby providing possibilities of control that could not even be dreamed of under the earlier system of recording information: writing" (Sontag 1977, 95, 138). This control has created a visual version of the Lebanese War Story more powerful even than the novels and short stories that some men produced during the early years of the civil war.

Why question the photographer's story? Without the war photographer we would lose compelling evidence to prosecute criminals and also to remind ourselves and the world of what the war had been like. In 1964 Robert Capa reminded us of World War II: a few poignant, clear images, each with its own page of text. Although his project also tidies up the war into the War Story, it does so with less voyeuristic profusion. It does not allow the viewer the filmic sense of having been there. It is the profusion and its arrangement that allow al-Sayyid's fabrication to work so well that we accept that this is the way things happened in Lebanon even though this is not the story that many individuals, and particularly women, told while the war was raging. Photographs are particularly suitable building blocks in the construction of the War Story. Photography and later film allowed noncombatants to observe and witness war in a way that had never before been possible. The evidence provided by still and moving images of death and destruction from what was said to be the front gave the impression of being there. This "witness," you, may not have *actually* been there, but you feel that you know what it must have been like because you know what it *looked like*. For those of you who feel

guilty about surviving unharmed physically and also psychologically you can feel partially vindicated. You can appropriate this war
as your own, talk about it with the authority of experience, even
though what you experienced was a perception of a fragment of
what the photographer framed. "War and photography now seem
inseparable," writes Sontag. "The feeling of being exempt from
calamity stimulates interest in looking at painful pictures, and
looking at them suggests and strengthens the feeling that one is
exempt. . . . In the real world, something *is* happening and no one
knows what is *going* to happen. In the image world, it *has* happened, and it *will* forever happen in that way. . . . The powers of
photography have in effect de-Platonized our understanding of
reality, making it less and less plausible to reflect upon our experience according to the distinction between images and things,
between copies and originals" (Sontag 1977, 147–48, 158). We
have the illusion of having been present at the crucial moments and
in the turning-point places.[8] Since we were there, we have a stake
in confirming that this war was not fought for nothing. The war
may not have deprived us of a loved one, but it did rob us of our
innocence. We have interest in its being told as a good war.

   Photography throws into relief what happens when war experiences are codified into the War Story. The connection between
what actually happened and its documenting is never transparent.
Keegan graphically illustrates this point when he writes that the
General Staff historian's "mind is made up for him by *prevailing
staff doctrine about the proper conduct of war* and he will accord-
ingly *select* whatever facts endorse that view, while *manhandling*
those which offer resistance. . . . The rhetoric of [battle history] is
so strong, so inflexible and above all so time-hallowed that it exerts
virtual powers of dictatorship over the historian's mind" (Keegan
1978, 34–35). In other words, the accounts of war that have come
down to us are the products of careful screening by politicians,
military historians, creative writers even, all of whom have at least
some sense of what it is that they are doing. Although he understands how and why the War Story has remained unchanged for
millennia, Keegan is not so much critical as he is impressed by the
inspirational value of such stories (Keegan 1978, 20). The War

Story shapes reality as we would like it to be or as the government says it was. That is why the War Story has usually been written very soon after war at a time when, as Elaine Showalter writes, "canon formation has been particularly aggressive . . . when nationalist feeling runs high there is a strong wish to define a tradition" (Showalter 1985b, 11).

The resort to a familiar war narrative and attitude is not restricted to governments and militaries who demand that the war they have just fought be told in a particular way; it is almost a reflex. During the Spanish civil war there was much side-swapping, much confusion, and yet it is now narrated as the romance of right against wrong. As Frederick R. Benson writes, many idealized the war and explained their participation as "a humanitarian desire for a world in which poverty, injustice, and misery might be eliminated." Benson quotes Malraux as believing that the war could restore to the intellectual "his fertility, his fundamental sense of *belonging* to a definite time, a definite place, and a specific milieu, without which a meaningful life and true understanding of the self, cannot be achieved" (Benson 1967, 7). In *Homage to Catalonia* George Orwell writes that he was less frightened by the violence of the Spanish civil war than he was by the "immediate reappearance in left-wing circles of the mental atmosphere of the Great War" (Dyson 1985, 129). It made little difference that these two wars were utterly different, the one total and the other civil. To be at war entailed a remembering of what other wars had been so as to understand what was and would be happening and so as to know how to proceed.

Nuclear age wars, however, lend themselves ill to the streamlining of the War Story. The film director Francis Coppola is only one example, if one of the best, of the implementation of a new narrative frame. As he struggled to make sense of the experience of Vietnam, he lit upon the Polish-English Joseph Conrad and followed him—with his camera crew and a reluctant Marlon Brando—into the heart of darkness. It was there that he shot *Apocalypse Now*. Coppola did not know how otherwise to express the unspeakable that war always is. Wars today increasingly involve combatants and targets rarely officially acknowledged. The stories that today's warriors—many of them women—tell of the wars they have known stray further and further from the binarized structure of the War Story. Since women are no longer everywhere systematically excluded from the military and war, the War Story will eventually have to take account of them.

Derailing the Paradigms: Women in the Military

In the wake of the Cold War and the triumph in the Persian Gulf, an anti-militarist became president of the United States and commander-in-chief of the armed forces of a country whose military includes some 11 percent women, namely among the highest percentage of women personnel of all NATO countries (Stanley and Segal 1988, 559–85). The U.S. Congress voted to eliminate the clause excluding women from combat on ships. Dearly held beliefs about the appropriateness and feasibility of women fighting to defend the country, which they have often mythically represented, began to crumble. Proponents of equal access to all areas of national service, including military, began to argue that it constituted a central tenet of citizenship in a democracy.

What do American advocates for equal opportunity in the military, many of whom are women and feminists, really want? Few are uncompromising pacifists, most are concerned with justice. The historian Joyce Berkman argues that feminists' assessment of the "'justness' of their nation's military action would pretty much shape the position they would take on the war . . . short of countenancing a global war, most European and American women, with countless feminists among them, support a strong national military establishment" (Berkman 1990, 150, 157). A less jingoistic perspective is articulated by the political scientist Kathleen Jones. She encourages women to "demand access to the military only as a means to acquire the power base from which to redefine the range of responsibilities included in the concept of citizenship . . . and to enrich the meaning of citizenship" (Jones 1990, 133). Sheila Tobias is the most instrumental in her argument that women should be allowed to enlist without restriction. War experience, she writes, has been "a convenient stepping stone for politics" (Elshtain and Tobias 1990, 183). Judith Stiehm criticizes anti-militarists in North

America whose "interest too often stops when they are no longer threatened, and U.S. women feel threatened only by nuclear war. A serious and consistent critic [of the military] should analyze the wars fought by surrogates, the consequences of profiting from arms sales, the effects of 'winning' miniature wars" (Stiehm 1988, 105).

Some fear that increasing the number of women in the armed forces may strengthen the military and therefore—perhaps—make the country readier to go to war. They recall military historians like Carl von Clausewitz, Hans Delbrueck, and John Keegan who argue that this readiness for war constitutes a defining characteristic of the state and that citizenship is tied to the obligation to defend one's country. This argument would seem to doom us to wage war ad infinitum and to embrace it if we want to be citizens. What is to be done? Feminists are divided. Some advocate boycotting military service, arguing that war might become less likely if fewer people predicated their lives on its possibility, and if citizenship was not linked to war service. Others believe, however, that unilateral demilitarization is not an answer at a time when increasing numbers of new nations are expanding their militaries with easily procured arsenals of lethal arms. Also, feminist advocates of equal opportunity in the military want citizenship for all in a strong country whose military is rational and democratic, and has a humanitarian commitment to the promotion of freedom and the maintenance of a just peace.[9]

Objection in the United States as elsewhere to women combat soldiers has been vehement.[10] Opponents claim that opening up combat positions for women jeopardizes military effectiveness largely by disrupting men's cohesiveness. Yet combat duty is clearly not for everyone. Some, including men, are just not qualified, and many more may not want to participate. Further, a few women have long been "frontline combatants" without being publicly acknowledged as such. Women have stoked cannons and then stepped aside to make room for the men to fire (Enloe 1983, 123). In short, the War Story has long not been true, its dichotomies never absolute.

Wars today challenge more than ever the conventional binaries and their consequent exclusions that have organized war stories throughout history. In our Geneva Convention era, international military lawyers are entrusted with the task of establishing a war taxonomy, of determining who is a civilian, where a particular event happened, under what circumstances, and so on, in order to be able to judge the legality of behavior in a war situation. Yet some are beginning to acknowledge that they are not quite sure how to differentiate the space, activities, and actors of war. More and more lawyers are deployed with troops to the war theater. During the Gulf War the U.S. Army brought two hundred of them, and one of the lawyers' tasks was to establish clear categories according to the law of war and to draw up "a target list for the following day and pass it on to the commander." It was they who then had to work out the legalities of hitting a civilian shelter that had been disguised as a bunker.[11] We have at our disposal sophisticated surveillance technology, yet not even those who have been trained to observe and judge the conduct of wars can in the final analysis separate the combatant from the noncombatant, the warring from the peaceful village, and the one who pulls the trigger from the one who stokes the gun or receives the shock of the explosion. In spite of all this, the War Story continues to survive.

Cross-culturally and historically, combat has been reserved for male defenders as that arena in which they could test, prove, and be rewarded for their virility (Stiehm 1983). John Keegan writes of men who regret, even repudiate, machismo yet when the fight is on think it to be necessary. The inclusion in combat of women and also of men who are ambivalent about their sexuality may complicate a mobilization and a cohesion made attractive because of its promise to turn boys into men. How important is male bonding? Can the military's rhetoric about "cohesion, sense of mission, mood of self-sacrifice, local as well as national patriotism . . . self-confidence and credulity" (Keegan 1978, 277)—along with the hope for immortality that subsumes an individual's death to the group's survival (Gray 1970, 40–47)—motivate large numbers of women and gay men to kill or be killed?

Women's presence in the quintessentially male domain makes several important differences. Stiehm writes that "it alters the military if service is no longer a way to demonstrate manhood. It alters the assumptions of military incentive systems to have mother-soldiers." It challenges basic beliefs or myths that are "fundamental to the military enterprise: 1) War is manly; 2) Warriors protect; 3) Soldiers are substitutable." She suggests that women who do not understand their own role as protectee will not realize that they are "essential to legitimate violence. The protectee is its justification" (Stiehm 1989, 7, 224, 230). Moreover women's physical presence undermines the unmarked aspects of soldiers' lives. These soldiers are no longer "our boys" whom we are reluctantly but proudly prepared to sacrifice. Rather, they are women and men who are above all parents and spouses who saw in the military a chance for employment and even for social mobility. Several myths and realities of the military are having to give, although, as Stiehm writes, they give less easily in connection with women than they do with men: "accommodations are regularly made for fathers that are not compatible with the myth that every service person is always available for worldwide assignment" (Stiehm 1989, 119). Our "neo-mercenary military" has brought a new focus to the costs of patriotism. As coverage of the Gulf War demonstrated, the new questions raised by the new face of the military may be responsible for the brevity of the war. Just how long would we be willing to expose mother soldiers to danger when their babies were waiting at home with their perplexed fathers? And as we focus on mother soldiers, father soldiers also demand attention to their needs. At the "Just War–Gulf War" conference at Vanderbilt in January 1992, an officer in the audience challenged a panelist who had argued for the elimination of women from combat positions. After praising women's achievements in the Gulf War and describing his own and fellow father soldiers' pain at parting from their families, he urged us all to remember that the American military is no longer an institution attracting single young men only, it is now made up of families. Thus, these are simultaneously the families that the military is supposed to protect *and* the families who are supposed to do the protecting. The military is no longer so different from civilian society.

When the military analysts Mady Segal and David Segal were writing in 1983, they noted that public opinion tolerated women in military roles that had civilian counterparts but that it had "not gone the next step and defined as acceptable women serving in the traditionally male ground combat specialties that do not have counterparts in the civilian labor force. . . . [Yet i]f the military continues to expand women's participation, or even maintains it at present levels, it will in the process be serving as a critical agent for future social change" (Segal and Segal 1983, 255–256). In other words, the military might pioneer social reform, even if such reform originates in what Stiehm calls "coerced behavior changes" (Stiehm 1989, 107). D'Ann Campbell counters that the armed forces since World War II have been more progressive than civilian society. Women officers "were trained for leadership positions and were paid more than an average college-educated woman could earn in the private sector." These women who had done so well in the military were less successful outside: "Putting women in uniform was simply too radical a step for most Americans. A handful of years could not erase deeply ingrained norms and stereotypes" (Elshtain and Tobias 1990, 117, 118). They shared the experience of women fighters in revolutionary situations, like Algeria and Eritrea. For example, Amair Adhana, a former guerrilla fighter in the successful thirty-year struggle of the Eritrean People's Liberation Front against the Soviet-backed dictatorship, told an *Economist* reporter: "In the field, the men respected us—our brains, our strength. . . . They now respect make-up, nice hair, being a proper housewife." Whereas before 1991 the women fighters were "treated with awe," their attire and demeanor emulated, in 1994 many of the demobbed women were back in their kitchens.[12] And yet enlisted women are different both from the conscripted women and those in revolutions because they are not doing men's work in an emergency. They have chosen and have been chosen to do as a career what has been considered to be a man's job.

The thesis thus far rests on a paradox: feminists advocate the opening up of opportunities for killing to women in the hope that they will choose to exercise their right only when they see no other solution. Such a discourse elides the apparent chasm that divides those who speak about national security from those who speak about citizenship rights. It invests hope in the nightmare of the military effectiveness mavens: if a government must send women and families to war, it will be more reluctant to fight. It elaborates a link between military and civilian societies so that when the military eliminates discrimination, civilian society will follow suit, that when civilian society criminalizes the killing of civilians, the military will do the same. Having established the link, this discourse then seeks to destroy the link.

Feminist pacifists, like Mary Wollstonecroft, Sara Ruddick, and Klaus Theweleit, might well be skeptical about such a paradoxical discourse, questioning the acceptability of any collaboration with a militarized system. Although they would doubtless affirm the political importance of sexual equality, they would oppose swelling the military ranks with "natural" advocates of nonviolent resolutions to conflict.[13] If aggressivity is learned and women are as prone to violence as men, the ungendering of the makeup of the military may mean that aggressive behavior will spread throughout society. Such fears seem to be justified by blockbuster movies like *Aliens* whose androgynous female grunts are braver, brawnier, and more brutal than male peers in countering xenomorphs. In his Vietnam novel-memoir *The Things They Carried*, Tim O'Brien describes how the jungle transformed the proper, middle-class Mary Anne into "part of the land. She was wearing her culottes, her pink sweater, and a necklace of human tongues. She was dangerous. She was ready for the kill" (O'Brien 1990, 125). This might be a description of women in Peru's Shining Path (Sendero luminoso), or, to a lesser extent, of women settlers in the Israeli Occupied Territories. Throughout the period of the rule of the Imam Khomeini, Americans were regaled with media images of chador-swathed women toting Kalashnikovs. The war in Bosnia has provided images of Serb women blocking humanitarian aid to Muslims and Croats, of Croat women who make up 5 percent of their national army and who, like Sanja Arbanas, "feel best when I sleep with a hand grenade," and of Muslim women in the Bosnian army with "head scarves and Kalashnikovs."[14] These women, whom Jean Bethke Elshtain describes as the "Ferocious Few" (Elshtain 1987, 163–80), do not accord well with their traditional images as representatives of a culture and a land to be

protected. Their transformation dramatizes their group's determination to destroy whatever stands in its way. Stiehm believes that
the "pictures of women with guns appear when a country is under
siege. Their purpose is to mobilize civilians. Their purpose is to
demonstrate unified commitment. It is to tell an enemy that it will
have to occupy the country and pacify every citizen before it can
claim victory. But, perhaps most importantly, it is a way of mobilizing young men . . . few men are able to resist the call to service
when women are serving" (Stiehm 1988, 96). These women's pictures are flat embodiments of the desire of their nation. And feminist pacifists do not take such images lightly; they do not dismiss
their threat as part of rhetorical hype. They fear that women in
combat do not portend a kinder, gentler military but rather that
they prefigure the worst that is yet to come.

In response to such a list of fearsome Amazons I would propose
another: mother warriors who risk all for their children, real or
adopted.[15] Such women fighters have become popular idols of the
American screen. This is true of *Terminator 2* and the *Star Wars*
trilogy, and even of *Aliens* where the reluctant Sigourney Weaver
has to play the part of the ultimate marine, fearlessly diving down
deep into the bowels of the space colony to save the little girl she
had "adopted" from the monsters. The *madres* and *abuelas* for
years successfully opposed the military regimes of Chile and Argentina with nothing more than patience and placards. In 1984 the
"Mothers of Algiers [women divorced from Algerian men and
seeking access to or custody of their children, denied them for many
years] marched from Paris to Geneva to present their case to the
Commission of Human Rights of the United Nations" (Hélie-Lucas
1993, 56). The Palestinian mothers on the West Bank and in Gaza,
Zapatista mothers in Mexico, and the mothers of Soweto have
evolved with their children a form of resistance with sticks, stones,
and machetes that renders life for the resident oppressor as arduous
as possible. In the summer of 1994 Chechnya mothers were tele-
vised keeping the Russian army at bay. They scored few victories,
but they were a presence.

These activist mothers are committed to a cause but above all they
have adopted responsibility for another on behalf of whom they

improvise new forms of resistance and opposition that pay attention to the survival and preservation of the largest number of people possible. Writing of Edna St. Vincent Millay, Susan Schweik says that the "maternal metaphor allowed her to represent women in active political engagement, and to represent active political engagement as womanly—to claim women's right, power, and responsibility to speak of and to act knowingly and protectively in the war effort" (Schweik 1991, 78). These mother warriors have forced themselves on public awareness. They draw attention to themselves and to the roles that they have played in war and in the playing have transformed. Their activism in the "battlefield" contrasts with expectations that they should be passive, or, best of all, absent. They and their counterparts in the military as well as the growing battalions of women reporters in war zones sensitize the world to what happens to women in war. They do so especially in situations when governments sanction rape as a weapon. News from Bosnia of the Serb rape camps raised a furor. Demonstrations worldwide reminded a forgetful world that this is not the first time that women's bodies have been officially and systematically targeted. Even only in the past sixty years the list of mass rapes includes those during the 1930s by Japanese against Chinese women; during World War II by Nazis against Russian and Jewish women, by Soviets against German women, and by Japanese against Korean women (Brownmiller 1975); during the 1960s and 1970s by Americans against Vietnamese women; during the early 1970s by Pakistanis against Bengali women; during the late 1980s by Iraqis against Kurdish women and then Kuwaiti and Palestinian women during the Gulf War.[16] In 1992 alone, rapes by personnel in military organizations were reported from several widely separated locales, all happening simultaneously with the Serb military attacks on Muslim women in Bosnia. Human Rights Watch reported rapes by Peruvian soldiers against more than forty women, by Indian security and militant groups against women in Jammu and Kashmir, by Burmese government troops against Rohingya Muslim women. In each case, the rapes were officially sanctioned as part of a considered attempt to demoralize the people and even to drive them from their homes.[17] These are only the better known cases.

The ungendering of combat further undermines the "normality" of rape in war. Women in combat positions will not rape and they may report those who do. If the International Tribunal at the Hague indicts, tries, and condemns the Serb rapists and their leaders, officially organized and sanctioned rape will be punished as a crime against humanity on a par with Nazi genocide and Japanese war crimes. Will women civilians thus targeted be accorded the rights of combatants?

Many Little War Stories

Never before has the fictionality of the War Story been so obvious. In nuclear age wars the women and the children—whom the War Story had described as at home and safe because defended by their men at the front—are increasingly acknowledged to be attractive military targets. They are not being protected. Their men cannot protect them. This fact has never before been so openly and widely acknowledged as it is now, because war is no longer the province of military historians and national security analysts and advisers, all of them men, but has now become a magnet for humanists, many of them women and feminists.

Less rigidly bound by conventions that confine the understanding of war to extended battle, these cultural analysts of war are revealing connections that may allow for new ways of thinking. For example, the threat of war is in itself a kind of war. It is with hindsight that we can now look back on the Soviet-U.S. standoff and say, yes—I survived the forty-year Cold War! Soon, geologically speaking, the numbers of those who have had that experience, and who know that this war was lived as an uneasy peace, will dwindle. When added to the list of the world's long wars, our forty-year standoff may be remembered as devastating. I am not trying to minimize the very real fear that we all felt as we imagined and campaigned against the nuclear holocaust for which Hiroshima and Nagasaki seemed to be curtain-raisers, but I do want to record a fact that is as true for the Cold War as it is for the hot little wars exploding all over the globe: war behind the front lines, when such lines can be defined, often becomes another normality, a kind of charged "peace." Except in an idealized Kantian formulation of Perpetual Peace, peace is not the opposite of war but is rather a provisional tolerance of differences, of the conflicts they engender, and of the knowledge that absolute resolution may not be possible.[18] Peace thus construed is linked with war on a continuum of conflict negotiation spanning absolute nonviolence through mayhem. War is not always unspeakable horror. It can be, but it entails more commonly an intensity, a heightened awareness, a massive human displacement, and a preparedness to move from being at peace to being at war.

Can affairs of state function within such ambiguity? When split-second decisions have to be made can notions of continuity, uncertainty, and instability be tolerated? In general, governance and control have required clear-cut categories. Dyson writes that the "public voice of the military establishment cannot be critical of its own purposes. The military machine is designed to carry out the missions which it has established for itself, irrespective of the thoughts and feelings of individual commanders" (Dyson 1985, 8). Clarity is also essential for the public image of the military. Voters demand attention to their welfare and safety. The wise ruler must create the illusion of peace so that war shall always be utterly different.

Women's prominence as guerrilla fighters, as military targets of bombs and rapes, and as subjects of debate about the gendering of the military and of combat has complicated the telling of the War Story. These women are telling their own counternarratives, revealing that what we had thought to be self-evidently true is true only for some, for those for whom this particular truth is useful. This truth is of course the War Story, which is not just a story but a paradigm that lies at the heart of our inability to understand war and to construct a culture of peace, to paraphrase Alexandre Bloch, the director of International P.E.N.[19] Their stories help us see the ways in which war compels men and women to take over unfamiliar roles. For the duration, men and women fill in for one another—military men as medics and secretaries, women in munitions factories. A few male writers like Glenn Gray and Erich Maria Remarque even described men who nurtured and loved each other, whereas women like Helen Zenna Smith (*Not So Quiet . . .* 1989 [1930]) showed that the women who volunteered, like the ambulance drivers, became hard and fearless. Performance of new tasks and roles allowed for temporary transgressions of gender-prescribed behavior—women could act like men without losing their femininity, men could act like women without risking the knee-jerk label of "wimp."

Yet in the aftermath of war—and particularly its paradigmatic version, the War Story—this wavering, this gender instability and ambiguity, had to be sanitized. How can we retrieve the detritus? This is the task of the responsible intellectual: to make sure that the binary frame narrative does not predetermine the articulation of the experience. Instead of endlessly repeating tales of roles and experiences in which each war mirrors the experience of its predecessors, war stories should allow for the narration of war's dynamism and incomprehensibility, but also of other aspects usually excluded from the War Story. A vivid example can be found in O'Brien's Vietnam stories where he describes boredom. This less than heroic condition is portrayed as "dripping inside you like a leaky faucet, except it wasn't water, it was a sort of acid, and with each little droplet you'd feel the stuff eating away at important organs." For this man to write the story of his experience in Southeast Asia was not to replicate some outworn formula but rather to interrogate memory, to question what had seemed to be so self-evidently true: "Stories are for joining the past to the future. Stories are for those late hours in the night when you can't remember how you got from where you were to where you are. Stories are for eternity, when memory is erased, when there is nothing to remember except the story. . . . If a story seems moral, do not believe it. If at the end of a war story you feel uplifted, or if you feel that some small bit of rectitude has been salvaged from the larger waste, then you have been made the victim of a very old and terrible lie. . . . By telling stories, you objectify your own experience. You separate it from yourself. You pin down certain truths. You make up others" (O'Brien 1990, 37, 40, 76, 179). These stories are not for others only but mostly for an individual author, and yet in the process they create open areas of access for those others who have not had the experience that entitles them to tell the War Story. These stories do not silence, because as Tim O'Brien suggests provocatively, "a true war story is never about war" (O'Brien 1990, 91).

Such are the stories that Lebanese, Bosnian, Iraqi, Algerian, and Palestinian women are telling today. These stories offer some understanding and an alternative. They describe an experience of war that all can understand because it does not take place in a special privileged elsewhere but is rather the heightened awareness and management of lethal conflict that is different from ordinary life only in terms of its intensity. What women experience in war repeats in stereo the daily experience of violence that has become ordinary. This telling of the ordinariness of war bypasses the age-old prohibition on women writing about war. In these accounts women are not trespassing on men's space, threatening to deprive them of the glory of having been there where only heroes and martyrs tread. In these stories women assign their own meanings to what they have felt and done. What used to be labeled civilian experience—being bombed, raped, expropriated, and salvaging shreds of living in a refugee camp—some name combat experience. Everyone can have this experience and it is this acknowledgement of universality that is critical in re-imagining a world where conflict is a constant fact of life and survival depends on the ability to confront conflict without the automatic use of violence. We begin to understand women writers who have represented women in Lebanon, Bosnia, and Eritrea not as passive victims but as active survivors and even resisters. We can recognize the parallels between military women in combat and literary women authorizing themselves to name and inscribe women's experiences in war as "war experiences." If women with their different experiences of war write at the time that war is happening, and if they recognize that the collapsing of feeling and language undergirds the silencing and excluding discourse that finds its authentication in the "authority of experience," they may be able to intervene in how the War Story is finally told, and how future wars will be fought and then told. Their iconoclastic stories may make it hard indeed to continue to believe that *dulce et decorum est pro patria mori.*

Women's counternarratives of war and changes in the gender arrangements of the military allow us to frame new questions that reject either-or explanations. When does a war begin? Does the first shot to be fired launch a war, or do we have to take into account the buildup? When does it end? What are we to make of the negotiations of outcome? If war is not declared, if it is in fact Pure War, how can we "stop something that wasn't a war" (Virilio 1983, 26)? When does a civilian become a warrior? Does being targeted, as in total war, entail such a transformation? Or is there less at stake in defining who is a civilian when men and women can both be combatants?

I am increasingly persuaded that a binary epistemology facilitates the declaration of war and the consequent semiotic transformations; it sanctions what are otherwise considered crimes. To be militarily effective, people must be convinced that what they do in war bears no relation to actions and their meanings elsewhere. They can only be good soldiers if they believe and do not question the fact that war transforms the meaning of actions. For the duration, violence is normalized, even glorified as the experience of the sublime. The Martiniquais revolutionary psychiatrist Frantz Fanon refers to the violence that the Algerians employed in their struggle against the French colonizers as "sacred," and Gray writes of the horror of murder but of the pleasure and glory in heroic killing. Gray concedes that there is a growing problem, because "the warrior who slays an impersonal enemy has traditionally not been regarded as a criminal, a murderer. Yet in the era of total war the distinction becomes ever more blurred. And the dissociation in our lives between soldiering and civilian pursuits grows at the very period when distinguishing between combatants and noncombatants threatens to disappear altogether." Later he writes that this differentiation is essential lest killing be confused with murder. Murderers are criminals, but "killers [i.e., soldiers] come to feel like high priests" (Gray 1970, 33–36, xvi, 131–32, 154). Even a pacifist can say that killing may acquire the aura of sanctity if it happens in the right place. In 1984, the State Department announced that "it will no longer use the word 'killing,' much less 'murder,' in official reports on the status of human rights in allied countries. The new term is 'unlawful or arbitrary deprivation of life'" (Cohn 1990, 51). Language matters. In women's writings, there is no right place for killing or theft or rape. These women refuse the polarization of space that conceals the fact that the violence of war is not so different from the violence of peace. They reject black and white certainties and thus cast doubt on the validity of semiotic transformations occasioned because of the space and action with which they are attached.

Once we judge what happens in war by the same standards that we invoke to assess equivalent actions and events outside war, we may begin to understand the ways in which violence is so often not only justified but actively pursued. We can begin to think in these new ways because all around us the old structures are cracking. Women are in contemporary wars—whether by fiat of a governing body or because they find themselves in a place that has burst into violence. Women who have experienced this explosion of the normal and who have decided to talk and write about it draw attention to the reality of what women and those like them actually do and endure during war. It is by putting women into the war stories that we can begin to recognize the strangeness of the unchanging metanarrative that the War Story has always been. If we render transparent the process whereby the War Story not only legitimizes but also necessitates what in peacetime is considered criminal behavior, we may make it a little harder for governments and gangs to sally off to war.

Feminist praxis gives individuals the courage to be active witnesses whose words may serve to subvert dominant paradigms. These witnesses are elaborating survival strategies that include the forging of alternative visions and stories. They are voicing dissension from the status quo, they are making visible the linguistic strategies of patriotism and patriarchy, they are examining the role of consciousness and constructing a memory that is responsible to the future.

حرب لبنان

صُوَر • وثائق • أحداث

Figure 1. Front cover of the book *Harb Lubnan*—Lebanon's War—with title and subtitle.

Figure 2. Back cover of *Harb Lubnan*, also bearing the title.

Figure 3. *On Sunday afternoon 13 April 1975, the famous 'Ayn al-Rummana bus incident occurred. The beginning of the burning of Lebanon.*

Figure 4. *A workshop: a bulldozer removes the barricade of buses!*

Figure 5. *Al-Rada'—peace by force.*

Figure 6. *They arrived, and the cannons were silent.*

Figure 7. *A smile . . . a cannon.*

Figure 8. *He lies on the bed of death between his two companions in life and death.*

Figure 9. *The parade at UNESCO on 1 May 1977. The forty-day memorial for the martyr Kamal Jumblat, attended by more than 150,000 citizens.*

Figure 10. *Before beginning to govern, President Elias Sarkis conducted consultations and initiated contacts. . . . Here with Lieutenant Colonel Ahmad al-Hajj, commander of the Internal Security Forces; Colonel Muhammad al-Khuli; the assistant secretary-general to the Arab League, Hasan Sabri al-Khuli; Yasser Arafat, president of the Palestinian Liberation Organization; General Naji Jumayyil, commander of the Syrian Air Force; Henri Lahhud, governor of the Biqa'.*

Figure 11. *A meeting at the Mathaf traffic circle.*

Figure 12. Uncaptioned photograph—one of sixteen full-page colored photographs grouped at the end of the book and introduced with a short paragraph entitled "The Crime: In Color."

Figure 13. *A human corpse—under the rubble of the Arabi Hotel after it was destroyed and burned on 21 September 1975.*

Figure 14. *The children's hunger is stronger than the war.*

Figure 15. *The father could not feed his family because of the war . . . so he led them to the parliament (26 October 1975). Full of hope he climbed the stairs with them.*

Figure 16. *And the police stopped him—and he tried to convince them of the children's hunger.*

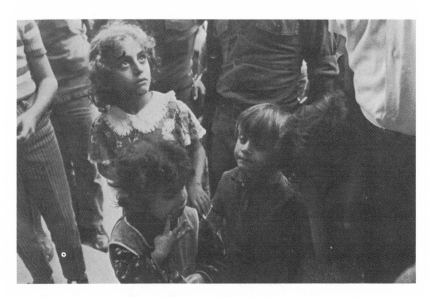

Figure 17. *But the policeman's and the deputies' hearts are hard. They were not touched by the children and they did not relieve their hunger or stop their tears.*

Figure 18. *They left everything behind them. . . . Basta* [a market in Beirut], *above and below. . . . Apples, beware of the bullets.*

Figure 19. *"He's lost . . . where's my husband?" That is how the war entered every house!*

Figure 20. *They weep for everything because they have nothing left.*

Figure 21. *Childhood survives to carry the future.*

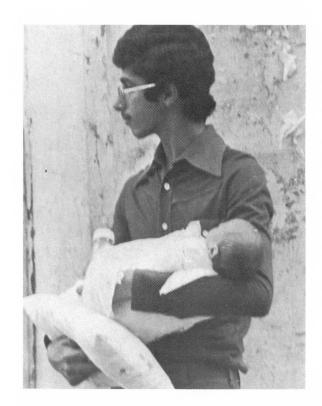

Figure 22. *War births: they are trying to escape to peace. He carried him in the first stage.*

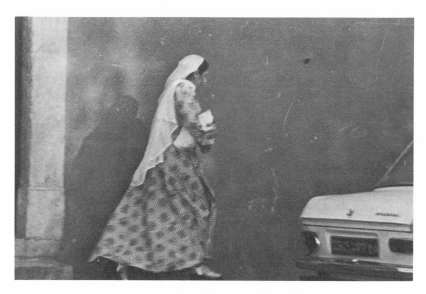

Figure 23. *And his mother carried him in the difficult stage.*

Figure 24. Uncaptioned full-page image.

Figure 25. Uncaptioned full-page image.

Figure 26. *The Holiday Inn sniper who fell naked from the twenty-second floor.*

Figure 27. *The photographers and journalists were there. . . . But!*

Figure 28. *They grabbed hold of his arms . . . then to the car . . . perhaps to the earth. The war continues in Beirut.*

Figure 29. *The bulldozers moved on 15 October 1975 to remove the rubble of the Arabi Hotel in Martyrs' Square in Beirut, and the dialogue committee bulldozer removes the barricades in Shiyah.*

Figure 30. *A witness to the massacre in Burj Square.*

في باب ادريس، شوارع الأناقة والجمال.. هل تمشي وسط الموت؟

Figure 31. *In Bab Idris, streets of elegance and beauty. Will she walk through death?*

Figure 32. *One of the Irtibat armed elements in Shiyah was hit by a sniper's bullet. 3 June 1975.*

Chapter Two

Culture Degree Zero

To the martial spirit every enemy is a Hitler and every ally is a freedom lover. This either-or mentality dooms us to live in dread of nations with whom we could well live in peace.
  Donald A. Wells (1967)

I kept thinking about all the kids who got wiped out by 17 years of war movies before coming to Vietnam to get wiped out for good. You don't know what a media freak is until you've seen the way a few of those grunts would run around during a fight when they knew that there was a television crew nearby; they were actually making war movies in their heads, doing little guts-and-glory Leath-erneck tap dances under fire, getting their pimples shot off for the networks. They were insane but the war hadn't done that to them.
  Michael Herr (1978)

During the nuclear age the experience of war has been changing, and this change is enmeshed in the new means and systems of representing wars. Postmodern wars resist the binaries believed to be necessary to the conduct and description of war and show the War Story to be less a transparent text than an event, not so much a lens on the war as a veil drawn over it. Readers who examine its text can only guess at what the veil hides. They need to learn how to read flat cloth. Some few, particularly creative artists like George Bernard Shaw in *Arms and the Man,* have been conscious witnesses to the process that reduces the multiple ambiguities of combat to the black and white distinctions of the War Story, and they have remembered how that happened. Such witnesses were in general too few, too unorthodox, too unsystematic to call the War Story into serious question.

68

In 1990s North America it is easier to conduct such an inquiry. The memory of the Gulf War, which was seen and talked about as though it were a Nintendo video game, lingers. Then there were the endless anomalies and vagaries that were discussed openly at the time and are now being forgotten or rearranged: the mother soldiers; the line-in-the-sand front; the seeing screen of the warhead; the networks filming the Cable News Network (CNN) as though it were the site of combat; foreplay maneuvers on both American and Iraqi televisions (Cooke 1991); the constantly changing causes for American intervention; even an uncertain enemy—so recently America's staunch ally against the inveterate Iranian foe; and of course, the living-room war-ness of it all. Just as important for understanding how the postmodern condition undermines the War Story is the fact that suspicion of dichotomous thinking has become part of our current culture. In the wake of the Stonewall rebellion, queer theory has shown how the fixing and naming of categories is in fact symptomatic of their actual instability.[1] Such categorization may also be instrumental in making visible and then breaking down other hitherto unquestioned dyads. For instance, the designation of one group as homosexual brings into existence its counterpart as heterosexual, and the assumption of their absolute natural separation is predicated on eliminating the private-public distinction (Sedgwick 1990).

What are the critical differences in today's wars? First, we have new weapons and image-making technology. Second, women are inventing new ways of participating in combat and then telling their actions as war stories.

Conquest of the Image

Over the past ten years library and bookstore shelves have sagged under the growing weight of books devoted to postmodernism. Scholars have waxed lyrical about irony, parody, permeable boundaries, pastiche, collage, collaboration, hybridization, hyperreality, empty shells, flat surfaces, simulacra, fragmentation and decentering, all against the backdrop of the technological revolution. Some argue that the way we know our world today is radically different from what it was even only fifty years ago. For example, the architect Christopher Jencks dates the "passage to the post-modern as 3:32 P.M. on 15 July 1972, when the Pruitt-Igoe housing development in St.Louis was dynamited" (in Harvey 1989, 39). Others counter that there is not so much a rupture between the modern and the postmodern as an intensification of conditions. For example, Jean François Lyotard describes postmodernism as "not modernism at its end but in the nascent state, and this state is constant" (Lyotard 1987, 79, 81).

My study of some late-twentieth-century wars has convinced me that conditions have changed sufficiently to warrant a label marking a break with the past. In each war the changes are different and specific to local conditions. In Lebanon, as in Vietnam, the involvement of civilians blurred the distinctions between combatant and noncombatant; the challenge to that hallowed binary had repercussions that rendered other battle-necessary conditions equally ambiguous. In Iraq, however, what changed was the manipulation of representation, particularly in monumental architecture. In the Israeli occupied territories, the role of the media was to be critical in changing the nature of the warfare. Rather than a uniform set of circumstances that makes a war postmodern, there is an awareness of the changed conditions of possibility that affect different wars to greater or lesser degrees. I date this break from modern to postmodern wars to the late twentieth century when colonized peoples wrested their freedom from European imperialisms. This does not mean that I equate postcolonialism with postmodernism, for I see the former to be a contestatory practice and the latter an analytical strategy. But I suggest a rough simultaneity. I accept the philosopher Kwame Anthony Appiah's distinction that describes the postcolonial as retaining the master narrative of resistance to the "Western *imperium* but also the nationalist project of the post-colonial national bourgeoisie," and postmodernism as "a retheo-rization of the proliferation of distinctions that reflects the under-lying dynamic of cultural modernity, the need to clear oneself a space" (Appiah 1991, 353, 346). The dissolution of colonial enterprises in places like Vietnam, Lebanon, Iraq, and Eastern Europe has produced conditions in which wars are waged, experienced, and expressed in radically new ways. These wars represent more than Derrida's "postmodernist excess of arms."[2] Rather, I detect a simultaneous change not only in the technology of war and its representation but also in the emerging symbiosis between them that has put into question many classical oppositions, most significantly the one between reality and appearance.[3]

Military leaders have always enlisted artists to record and glorify their wars. Assia Djebar writes of the retinue of artists that the invading French forces brought with them to record the takeover of Algeria in 1830 (Djebar 1985, 12); and in chapter five I talk about the armies of artists Saddam Hussein dispatched to battlefields. With time, these representations take on the aura of reality, and it is these representations, and not the wars themselves, that military scholars study and amplify. The philosopher Paul Virilio, who has written with such insight about the transformation of war technology and its consequences for the representation of wars, has declared that there "is no war, then, without representation. . . . Since the battlefield has always been a field of perception, the war machine appears to the military commander as an instrument of representation comparable to the painter's palette and brush" (Virilio 1989, 6, 20). Yet, however interdependent the war machine and its representation, the two were always thought of as radically different—there was the experience on the battlefield and then, later, there was the representation in a book or on a canvas. Certainly, the one approximated the other, but there was no suspicion that they might be so enmeshed that they might influence each other, even be parts of a single entity. A somber piece of evidence to support this argument may be found in the changing attitudes to war correspondents. On 25 February 1994 the *New York Times* published an editorial entitled "Slaughtering the Messengers." Reporters who brought back the message from the front used to be saluted for what they did; today, however, they are no longer tolerated or even accommodated by the military authorities. They can no longer act as though they were separate from the action they are representing. Today, the editor wrote, if somewhat hyperbolically so as to get his message across, these reporters are "not only exposed to fire but deliberately targeted, as in Bosnia, or taken hostage, as in Beirut."

In the twentieth century, the connection between wars and their representations reached a new level when their interdependence created a new technology: the cinema. Unlike photography that freezes moments that can be rearranged according to taste, desire, and need, filming captures process and movement and with time it became necessary for the waging of total war. The whole of the battlefield could no longer be taken in by the naked human eye: "only the lens-shutter could capture the film of events, the fleeting shape of the front line, the sequences of its gradual disintegration. Only serial photography was capable of registering changing troop positions or the impact of long-range artillery, and hence the capacity of new weapons for serial destruction" (Virilio, 1989, 70). In effect, World War I was the reason for Hollywood. Conversely, during World War II, American military propagandists sought help from Hollywood.[4] They did their job so well that World War II movies have become models for future warriors. In the *New York Times* of 27 May 1990, Thomas Bird wrote an article entitled "Man and Boy Confront the Images of War," which describes the overwhelming impact of these war movies. He explains: "It took me six months in Vietnam to wake up and turn all the World War II movies off in my mind."

World War II became the stage rehearsal for future wars that were to be marked by "transparency, ubiquitousness, instant information . . . comings and goings were less those of troops than of the output from detection and transmission equipment. Visual or audiovisual technology now began to reproduce not only the forced march or distant incursion—as it did in the 1914–18 war—but the actual movement of armies, with automatic feed-back and retransmission in real time." These wars were fought by "cine-commando units," units who had to look in two directions at once: at the enemy and through the camera lens at the audience back home. In other words, they were serving under a new kind of high command that was "at once absent and omnipresent" (Virilio 1989, 78–79).

It is not the fact of hyperrepresentation, then, that makes wars postmodern but its enmeshment in their construction, whether before, during, or after the event. James Der Derian writes that Saddam Hussein modeled the Iraq-Iran War on the "macro-strategic game which the consulting company BDM International sold to Iraq, just as the invasion of Kuwait, according to General Schwarzkopf, was rehearsed in the form of computer simulations provided by an American company" (quoted in Stam 1992, 111). Shots do not have to be fired for a war to be represented but simulation, alas, rarely occurs. Proleptic representation sets the stage for the "real" encounter. Michael Clark wrote about Vietnam that "monuments (and cultural myths) participate in the explicit and deliberate anti-referentiality of post-modernism" (Clark 1985b, 5). We see this principle at work in Iraq. Not only did Saddam Hussein model the Iraq-Iran War on a game, he arranged for it to be recorded and glorified in ink, stone, and paint by subsidizing armies of artists, journalists, and other writers to memorialize a victory that had not yet been won. In Baghdad building of the monument to celebrate the war began before the war was declared in September 1980 (al-Khalil 1991). The artists' paid vision was to substantiate the victory. It is such a "victory" that made the invasion into Kuwait and the takeover of the Arabian oilfields a self-evident next step. The War Story sorts out the confusion and draws the clear lines. The Iraq-Iran War began in September 1980 when Saddam Hussein declared war. Obviously.

Film revolutionized the waging and representing of war, but television both as camera and screen—as seer and seen—has had the most profound effect. In an era increasingly marked by the pressure of public opinion, television authorities are acquiring unprecedented authority. They focus on a war, or on one of its aspects, for as long as they or the government likes, while claiming to respond to the viewers' wishes and needs and to the dictates of responsibility: if the war is "important" it must be covered—but who judges what is important and what criteria are used?[5] The line between the sender and the receiver of the message becomes blurred within the message itself. When discussing American policy toward

Lebanon in the early 1980s, the media consultant David Gergen was quoted as saying: "I can tell you that television had an enormous impact on our policy in Lebanon. We withdrew those marines from Lebanon in part because of television. We asked the Israelis to stop bombing in part because of the television pictures that were coming back from Beirut" (quoted in Valeriani 1991). In her analysis of television coverage of the civil war in El Salvador, Denise Kervin writes that "television news came to define 'reality'" (Kervin 1985, 6). CNN did the same for the Gulf War. So much so that other television stations broadcast CNN as though it were itself the site of the war to be covered. The only news was often the news about the news. A brilliant example came two days after the air strikes began. The Iraqis hit Tel Aviv with a SCUD missile. An American Broadcasting Corporation reporter on site was in a panic. He could not tell Peter Jennings what was happening because CNN was showing nothing but file pictures of Jerusalem!

As early as the 1960s, Marshall McLuhan foretold that the media would turn the world into a village where everyone is potentially affected by everyone else. He was, of course, right. Wars that would otherwise escape international notice are beamed into every home; hijackings succeed because of world media attention. But what impact do the media have on war's destruction and its victims? Is the transfer of information in itself salutary? Writing out of besieged Bosnia, where she directed a surreal performance of *Waiting for Godot,* Susan Sontag reflects the unease of many who are confronted with the central role of media representation. She reports that "television, print, and radio journalism are an important part of this war. When in April I heard the French intellectual André Glucksmann . . . explain to the people of Sarajevo who had come to his press conference, that 'war is now a media event' and 'wars are won or lost on TV,' I thought to myself: try telling that to all the people who have lost their arms and legs. But there is a sense in which Glucksmann's indecent statement was on the mark. It's not that war has completely changed its nature, and is only or principally a media event, but that the media's coverage is a principal object of attention, and the very fact of media attention sometimes becomes the main story"

(Sontag 1993, 58). When the Serbs bombed a market in Sarajevo in the spring of 1994, international journalists covered the massacre meticulously. The ensuing calm was attributed by some to the positive role this coverage had played. Misha Glenny writes: "There is no better example to underscore the decisive impact television can have on policy makers. . . . The mortar attack has been transformed into a moment of history much more powerful than the explosion itself" (Glenny 1994, 6). There were some, however, who claimed that the media in fact served to endorse the Serb conquest of the city.

Enthusiasm about the positive role the media can play must be kept in check by a sober understanding of the ways in which the media can be manipulated for destructive ends. Nenad Pejic, a television director in Bosnia, explains how the media in former Yugoslavia created ethnic identity and rivalry. He writes that "the new television authorities, who were appointed by the governmental political parties, have started to produce programs 'in the name of ethnic interest'. . . . The public television stations in Zagreb and Belgrade . . . produce hatred between ethnic groups" (Pejic 1992, 36–37). Paul Parin, the ethnopsychoanalyst who worked as a doctor with Tito's Partisans during the liberation of Yugoslavia, calls television "*the* key element fanning the flames of the Serbo-Croatian war" (Parin 1994, 41). Catherine McKinnon adds that this use of television to create, record, broadcast, and commercialize atrocities, including mass rape, for the purposes of propaganda makes this war peculiarly postmodern (McKinnon 1994, 192).

But what is truly postmodern is the way in which the media have deliberately blurred the line between representation of actual events and the choreography of historical images in the service of propaganda. The role of media authorities has not gone unnoticed. In November 1994 I attended a meeting during which Richard Goldstone, the chief judge of the International Tribunal at the Hague, told a group of Duke law professors that in addition to prosecuting individuals in the military hierarchies for the commission of crimes against humanity, the Tribunal was going to indict individuals responsible for creating and broadcasting programs that could be shown to have a role in the genocidal policies of their governments.[6]

The war in Bosnia was mediated but also conducted and experienced according to filmic models. Mate Boban, a Croatian militia leader, explained to the reporter Robert Block: "I teach our soldiers ethics and moral lessons using American cowboy films."[7] Each event harked back to an image of another, earlier war. Stanko Cerovic, a Montenegran journalist working for Radio-France Internationale, compares the ruins of Sarajevo with those pictured in American films: "You have the impression of having lived this experience thousands of times before, cliché after cliché, the one more banal than the next. . . . The war is no more authentic than a television mini-series" (Cerovic 1993, 170, 171). This, of course, is not true. The war is authentic enough to have killed and maimed hundreds of thousands of civilians. But wars often occupy that edge of reality that slips seamlessly into its own representation. At times a filmic screen is useful; it can halt the slaughter for a while. During the Serbs' 1993 attempted naval blockade of Dubrovnic, the Croatian Admiral Torevic found himself cornered on this peninsula town with no armaments and the prospect of a certain defeat. In desperation he contacted the local television station and asked them to show ten seconds of "Top Gun" on the evening news. The ploy worked. Minutes later, the Serbian fleet had turned and withdrawn.[8] War as simulacrum—and then the killing resumes.

The reality of the moment blurs into the memory of a similar scene watched on a screen that projects into a future when this moment, preserved in representation, will be played out again. The re-play is usually for others, but not always. On 21 May 1995 the *New York Times* used the term "postmodern war" for the first time and on the front page. It was in connection with a report about the fighting in Sarajevo. A twenty-year-old Muslim man is lying in his hospital bed, paralyzed from the waist down, watching a video of himself being shot. He tells Roger Cohen, the reporter who is covering the story, what it feels like to watch this film: "I feel like it's somebody else. But I remember it so well." He remembers how the United Nations peacekeeping soldier just watched and did nothing. He remembers how the television cameraman who had been "waiting at a dangerous crossroads to see somebody killed or mutilated, films the shooting." But he also knows that had the cameraman not been there, the United Nations soldiers would not have brought him to the hospital (Cohen 1995, 1, 8). How similar is this story to that of the Lebanese photographer 'Abd al-Razzaq al-Sayyid and his shots of the "Irtibat armed element" that I discuss in chapter one. Whereas we do not know if the Lebanese militiaman survived, in this Bosnian story we have the chilling sequel of the wounded man viewing and re-viewing himself being shot as though he were not the victim. He is viewing and re-viewing the film that derealized his own injury but also made possible the treatment of that injury. The film may have saved his life. It certainly served to draw international attention to his injury as also to his war and to one of the reporters who covered the event—the next week National Public Radio carried an interview with Roger Cohen about his designation of the war as postmodern. Filming the shooting thus constituted a concrete intervention in the waging of the war in the former Yugoslavia.

International media today are continuing the practices of American journalists as they covered the war in Vietnam. Many blamed the media for the defeat. In an interview with Jonathan Mirsky, General William C. Westmoreland announced that "Vietnam was the first war in history lost on the front page of the *New York Times*." David James writes that with "American and world opinion necessary for the continuation of the war, the media became then as much the site of the war as the place where it was depicted or recorded . . . the contest of representation was inseparable not only from the contestation of the agencies of representation but also of the modes of representation" (James 1989, 45, 46). In a quirky turn of events, the media came to symbolize the horrors of war: whereas the Vietnamese would remove eyes from corpses and place them in the corpses' backs as a symbol of ubiquity, the Americans countered and used not real eyes but paper cutouts of the CBS motif fashioned in the shape of an eye.[9]

The media covered the war but in some ways also created it. A former Saigon bureau chief pointed out that it was "considered standard operating procedure for troops to fire their weapons for the benefit of the cameramen. If our cameramen had to wait until a fire fight with the Viet Cong broke out, we'd have less footage—

and perhaps cameramen."[10] This method of covering the war is demonstrated in the film *Apocalypse Now,* where Francis Coppola has a reporter stop the invading troops so that they might pose for him.

Like the war in Vietnam, the Intifada in the territories occupied by the Israelis was intimately linked to international media attention. The women and children fought nonviolently with sticks, stones, burning tires but also cameras.[11] The Palestinian-American cultural critic Edward Said cautions Palestinians against the dangerous seduction of media attention, lest the "glamorous search for recognition and negotiations" entail the loss of "the moral and cultural detail of our cause, which is a cause after all and not just a sordid game to control images" (Said 1989, 22). Some, like the Palestinian writer Ghassan al-Masri, retort that success may lie precisely in that sordid game to control images. Al-Masri says that the Intifada constituted the highest achievement of the preceding resistance because it "placed the heroic image of the Palestinian woman in front of all television lenses so that it might appear in every home all over the world" (Abu Samra 1989, 8). The child with the stone, David, disarms the soldier with the automatic assault weapon, Goliath. How? Beyond surprise and confusion, this act works into the politics of representation: in the global limelight Israeli soldiers must keep moral faith; their uniforms compel a particular kind of self-image and hence behavior. For the eyes of the world are on David and Goliath: every move made by the Israeli soldier is closely monitored, and army reactions to unarmed women and children are judged by an international tribunal.

In *Wild Thorns,* the 1976 novel by the West Bank writer Sahar Khalifa, soldiers search the house of a revolutionary who is under suspicion of murdering an Israeli officer. When the Israeli soldiers notice his mother looking unwell, they leave for fear that "word would spread all over town that Israeli soldiers had killed a poor woman in her seventies for no reason. . . . Israel's peace-loving image would be distorted and attacked" (Khalifa 1985a [1976], 169–70). Other characters in *Wild Thorns* are less sanguine about the role of the media, mocking those who believe that the "radio broadcasts will take care of everything" (75). They confirm Said's concerns as well as those of other activists. Jean Genet quotes Arafat as having said about the Intifada that "for some months now our revolution has been fashionable. We owe this to Israel. The papers, the photographers, the television companies, all the cameramen in the world came to see us and produce romantic stories and pictures. But suppose they overdo it? The Palestinian Revolution will cease to exist because it doesn't produce any more stories and pictures." Genet's friend Abu Omar comments that "the revolution's in danger of becoming unreal through rhetoric, images on screens, and metaphor and hyperbole in everyday speech. Our battles are in danger of turning into poses—they look heroic, but in fact they're performed. But what if our play were interrupted, forgotten, and . . . " (Genet 1992, 275). The moral is, use the media but beware the risks of manipulation.

The media have made possible the waging of a new kind of war. Such wars do not demand many dead, although many may and do die. When Reagan staged his 1980s television miniseries in Grenada and Lebanon and Bush his 1990–91 Gulf War, all they needed was for the media to cover the storming of some target described as strategic for the front-page story and for top items on the evening news. In February 1991 American citizens were there with the American military in the Persian Gulf. They entered the briefing room. They joined the journey of the bomb from its launch to the moment when the electronic eye warned that it was about to hit its target. And then its seeing screen and that of every American TV viewer went snowy. It was entirely unnecessary for the thousands of Iraqis stationed in the desert to be plowed into the sand. Robert Stam writes that "Gulf War media coverage endowed the spectator's eye with the symbolic function of a weapon . . . the spectator identifies both with the camera looking and with what it sees . . . war became familiar and strangely unifying for an ephemeral communitas of war-watchers . . . jointly bound in spectatorship, linked in a common tele-existence . . . [they were] protected witnesses. . . . With the Gulf War, the representation of war seemed to shift from classical realist representation to the brave new public-relations world of hyperreality evoked by Baudrillard" (Stam 1992, 102, 104, 106, 107, 110).[12] The eye of the spectator and that of the weapon have become one. Virilio writes that "nothing now distinguishes the functions of the weapon and the eye; the projectile's image and the image's projectile form a single composite" (Virilio 1989, 83). The lethal reality of this weapon of postmodern war is inseparable from its recording-representing function.

Vietnam: The Prototype

Breaking the reality-representation binary is only one example of the ways in which postmodern wars challenge dichotomous thinking and reveal connections whose former invisibility allowed for their survival. Yet is it possible to conceive of war except in binary terms? War, as conventionally defined and narrated, could be understood only relationally, namely in terms of what was considered to be its opposite: peace. War designated gender-specific tasks as well as arenas where these tasks might be executed. There was war and peace, front and home front, combatant and civilian, victory and defeat. Men made war and women kept the peace; men went to the front and women stayed at home; men fought and women were fought for; analogously speaking, men were masculinized if their side won, they were feminized if it lost. War valorizes another, subtler binary: between the ruler and the ruled. In many countries, to qualify for citizenship, the ruled must be prepared to die for their ruler who must not die. War sorts out potential citizens and excludes those who cannot aspire to citizenship because they do not fight and defend but who, as the signifiers of the nation under threat, are fought for and defended.

When I first began to explore the changing nature and representation of wars in the nuclear age it seemed to me that wars of independence in Asia and Africa were among the last wars to be described unequivocally as being separated from normal life; directed against an unambiguous enemy; and susceptible to definitive resolution. The colonized knew who the oppressor was, both when they launched resistance and when they drove the colonizer out. With earlier wars they shared the War Story that clarified confusion. However, I came to understand that the War Story is resilient enough to survive even the Gulf War. What is different today is that some analysts of war are highlighting, questioning, and showing the binaries to be constructed, artificial, even as military historians struggle to reinforce them.

References to postmodern wars usually serve to describe the American experience in Vietnam. Many observers hailed this war in Southeast Asia between the leader of the capitalist world and representatives of the communist world as the first of its kind. McLuhan and Fiore call it the "first television war [which] has meant the end of the dichotomy between civilian and military. The public is now participant in every phase of the war, and the main actions of the war are now being fought in the American home itself" (McLuhan and Fiore 1968, 134). Virilio labels the Vietnam War the "first electronic war in history . . . devised at Harvard and MIT" (Virilio 1989, 82); Jameson calls it the "first terrible postmodernist war" (Jameson 1991, 44).

Other scholars agree with Jameson's assessment of the war as postmodern. John Carlos Rowe writes that Marxists interpreted Vietnam as postmodern because its "contradictions turned apparently stable ground into the quagmire secretly at the base of capitalist theories and practices. . . . American ideology in the aftermath of the Vietnam War has managed to live up to Jean François Lyotard's definition of the postmodern: 'The presentation of the unpresentable' . . . the *unpresentable* is precisely what is made so by those presentations by which a certain artificial *unconscious* is produced" (Rowe 1988, 2, 12, 16–17). Philip Francis Kuberski describes Vietnam as postmodern because "its boundaries were hard to define. . . . A chaotic, visual, abrupt collage, it failed expectations generated by World War II. . . . If one adds this to the questioning of Man, the questioning of representation, and the collapse of the arche or beginning, one may well have made Vietnam into the Allegory . . . of a postmodern, poststructuralist world" (Kuberski 1985, 181, 187–88). Simon During, however, argues that the war in Vietnam was not so much unrepresentable as it was enmeshed in its representation. So linked to its mediation was the war that with time it was not clear which was which: "not only is war theatre, but film is war." When writing of *Apocalypse Now*, he describes Coppola hiring arms and equipment from the Filipino army and lending it back whenever the army needed matériel. During writes that the "film is enabled by acts of neo-imperialist war: it cannot disengage itself from what it represents. The collapse of distinction here between making films and making war is not primarily a cultural fact or a theme, but an outcome of specific material conditions. Its effects remain ideological however: this particular system induces theories of the loss of distinction between the image and the imaged. . . . The film itself becomes war within the frame of neo-imperialism. . . . The Vietnamese enemy are nowhere in Coppola's movie. The film achieves its sense of total irreality by wiping them out of the screen. If the discourse of postmodernity characterizes the postmodern as that which knows no Other, then in this film that Other is eliminated by fiat. If there were an enemy available for representation, perhaps then there would be narrative rather than just citation" (During 1987, 37, 39).

Vietnam was a precursor to a new kind of war that was honed in Lebanon and found its logical outcome in the Gulf War and most recently in the former Yugoslavia, South Africa, and in the American inner city.

The War-Peace Continuum

Religious wars, just wars, wars of succession, civil wars, total wars, and now postmodern wars. We name and categorize wars so as to give ourselves the illusion that we understand, and therefore that we can put order into the suspension of order. Above all, we name an event or series of events "war" so as to effect a separation from peace, from what we fondly like to think of as normality. If we were not told that there have been six Arab-Israeli wars over the past forty-eight years, would we not be excused for thinking that it was in fact just one long war of attrition with occasional flare-ups? After 1967 and for twenty years, Palestinian women and children resisted the Israeli occupation with sticks, stones, and burning tires. Then in December 1987 Palestinian men adopted this women-initiated nonlethal struggle. They named the dispersed women's actions *intifada*, or the Shaking Off. The women had invented the term and long used it to denote a kind of resistant domesticity: like dust from a rug, they were shaking off individual instances of the Occupation. But as soon as their decentered actions were collected under a single nomenclature, people assumed that a new revolution had been launched. So when did that war begin? Before the current interest in the violence perpetrated by Islamists in Algeria, it was assumed that the war of independence began in 1954 and ended in 1962. From the perspective of 1996 we must question those dates. The international terrorism specialist Ahmad Jalal 'Izz al-Din argues persuasively that the French suppression of Islam had already in 1930 led to the formation of Islamist groups all over Algeria, many of them with militarist agendas. When the war of independence brought little change in the religious situation they resumed their activities, which were now directed against the government and not the French as before. 'Izz al-Din warns of civil war if "the army does not take on the extremists soon." But is not what they have been doing since 1930 war? And does their activism not connect directly to the resistance that the Algerians had been putting up to the French since 1830? ('Izz al-Din 1995, 30–34). Had the Lebanese not carefully named the first two years of their civil war the "two-year war" and the rest of the war "the situation" or *les événements,* could the average observer or participant tell the difference between war and peace?

When did the Gulf War begin? Had George Bush not officially *declared* war on Iraq at 9 P.M. on 16 January 1991—on prime time television—it might have been hard for the uninitiated to recognize that it was only the carpet bombing that was war and that the mobilization that preceded it was not. If it was not on 16 January, was it on 2 August 1990 when Iraq invaded Kuwait? Or at an earlier stage in its media history? Let us pick at random. On 4 May 1990 I was leafing through the *New York Times,* when I came across an article that quoted Mohamed al-Mashat, the Iraqi ambassador to the United States, as saying that the "current speculation about Iraq's weapons program is strikingly similar to, if not even stronger than the propaganda campaign that preceded Israel's unprovoked attack on Iraq's nuclear research facility in 1981. This leads us to conclude that Israel once again is preparing to attack us. President Hussein wants Israeli political leaders and military planners to

know that Israel could not again attack Iraq with impunity. Thus
[Saddam Hussein's] warning to Israel was not a bluff or a bellicose
threat but an effort to maintain peace and avoid the suffering that
would result from such an exchange between Israel and Iraq." Iraq
claims that Israel claims that Iraq is about to launch an unprovoked
aggression. Iraq counters that this latter assumption is false and
that, moreover, Israel cannot play the media and then attack and
then hope that the world will buy its self-defense line because it,
Iraq, has preempted the next move in the media war. That was in
1990. But are we not here talking about an earlier stage? Did the
war start in 1981 when Israel bombed Iraq's nuclear reactor? What
led up to that bombing? Even Bush added to the confusion when
he annulled his own highly publicized declaration of the war. On
24 January he announced: "We did not begin the war seven days
ago. We are finishing a war begun on August 2." The military's
solution to all this vagary was to tell a War Story with three acts:
"a beginning (Desert Shield), a middle (Desert Sword), and an end
(Desert Storm) . . . the threefold articulation of the narrative recalls
the triple forms that Lévi-Strauss found characteristic of 'primitive'
myth" (Stam 1992, 122–23). After all, the War Story is the most
primitive of myths.

The indeterminacy of the beginnings of wars, even those that
have been officially declared, is not peculiarly postmodern. By and
large wars emerge out of war-like conditions, hence their beginnings are not easy to pinpoint. When wars are declared we have the
illusion of a beginning, even if the declaration was made ex post
facto. This analeptic marking of the beginning of a war is probably
not so different from what has always happened, but writers and
especially military historians have intervened with their penchant
for "making romantic landscapes in which they can deploy forces
like any Hollywood producers" (McLuhan and Fiore 1968, 38–
39). In the nuclear age, the artificiality of naming and defining
aspects of war dichotomously is becoming evident. As national
economies pour more and more resources into military spending,
these distinctions are blurring and reversing Clausewitz's description of war as the continuation of politics by other means.

In *Pure War,* his radical exposé of the human costs of global militarization, Virilio writes: "All of us are already civilian soldiers, without knowing it. . . . People don't recognize the militarized part of their identity, of their consciousness." For him, contemporary society knows only one state of being, and that is war, or what he calls "pure war." Pure war is the child of technology, it is perpetual war "which isn't acted out in representation, but in infinite preparation [which leads] toward a generalized non-development . . . of civilian societies." He extends his dystopia to describe these wartime economies, and their armies, as evolving not to defend but to target and colonize their own citizens "with, of course, a few skirmishes in the Third World" (Virilio 1983, 18, 54, 92–93, 94). These skirmishes sometimes target the citizens of the aggressor also. After the Gulf War, veterans complained of Gulf War Syndrome and were told they were suffering from PTSD (post-trauma stress disorder). Later they learned that while the U.S. military in the air was dropping depleted uranium on fleeing Iraqis, it was nuking its ground counterparts.

The boundaries believed to separate war and peace are crumbling and have been in a state of decay for some time. During the social upheavals of late 1960s Europe, Michel Foucault asked: "Isn't power simply a form of warlike domination? Shouldn't one therefore conceive all problems of power in terms of relations of war? Isn't power a sort of generalized war which assumes at particular moments the forms of peace and the State? Peace would then be a form of war, and the State a means of waging it" (Foucault 1980, 123). Is this collapsing of the war-peace binary too radical? Was the French poststructuralist philosopher a lone voice anticipating what would become more acceptable only two decades later? No, there were others, including Hannah Arendt who was writing at about the same time. She describes war as "the basic social system, within which other secondary modes of social organization conflict or conspire" (Arendt 1970, 9). More recently, Susan Jeffords notes that war discourse has become the "structuring frame that designates a time different from that which existed before 1952 . . . war spills over into life and seems not to be separated from it . . . war is not a specific but a general feature of these decades so that those who are not in the war must live by its rules or become exiles to its system" (Jeffords 1989, 185). Each of these three writers comes close to describing what Virilio names pure war, each sees this pure war to be part of daily life in a "non-war situation." If pure war is our current condition extending into every corner of human existence, how are we to function? Can we choose to become exiles to its system?

Certainly war-consciousness is pervasive, but war as organized, lethal engagement for the resolution of conflict is not. Elaine Scarry describes war as a "reciprocal activity of injuring to produce a non-reciprocal outcome" (Scarry 1985, 150). War according to such a formulation indicates that two or more parties have declared their intention to hurt each other, or that those who name a condition "war" wish to evoke sentiments normally occasioned by being at war. Yet there is a perceivable and analytically critical difference between nonviolent coexistence and preparing for and engaging in wars. It seems incorrect to assert that West Virginian farmers are at war because their government is channeling national resources into arms manufacture. It is, however, as incorrect to assert that Americans in the twentieth century have not fought a war on their own territory, for the inner-city gang wars of Los Angeles, Detroit, and Miami as well as the nuclear tests of the 1960s (Stiles 1994) are just as much postmodern wars as were Vietnam and the Lebanese civil war.

To invoke the notion of postmodern war is rather to recognize that there are many more and longer wars in the world than we care to acknowledge and that these wars have sometimes become inextricably intermeshed with war as metaphor. Reagan's War on Drugs began metaphorically as a concerted campaign to wipe out drug abuse in the United States, yet under the Bush administration it became a literal war on the purveyors of narcotics. Warships off the coasts of Colombia signal the transformation. The "war of the sexes" that some claimed second-wave feminism declared in the 1960s is producing its own body count. Right-wing vigilantes shooting doctors who work in abortion clinics justify their actions with the slogan: sacrifice one life to save many lives. In 1988 a white middle-class unemployed man massacred feminists in Montreal whom he considered to be responsible for his own personal and professional failures. This lethal resentment of the growing numbers of women and minorities in professions previously more or less restricted to white men needs to be watched lest it also turn into a war.

During the past forty years violence and its potential organization into lethal encounters has become a global phenomenon. Gangs fighting in downtown Los Angeles are waging urban warfare that the media represent as being equivalent to civil war in Lebanon and the jungle guerrilla warfare being waged in Central America. Many will remonstrate that to call inner-city violence war is to stretch the meaning of the word beyond reason and usefulness. Is there any justification in the appellation? In spring 1994 Stephanie Murn, a student in my War and Gender class wrote a paper in defense of the proposition that to understand what is going on in the American inner city we must face the fact that the street gangs are not just wayward teens who do not want to work. They are organized troops waging war. She observed that the gangs "tag" their space.[13] These "tags" are words or symbols representing the gang, which are splashed over walls in what outsiders understand to be graffiti. These tagged walls become the perimeter surrounding an area that is thus rendered dangerous, and therefore empty except for the combatants. This space becomes their front. Should gang members wear the wrong accoutrements, like beads, or even only the wrong color, which may be as much as is needed to constitute a uniform, they risk death through mistaken identity. Those not directly involved in the fighting, the "civilians," nonetheless have to take wartime precautions: newspapers picture local civilians going to work wearing bulletproof vests with guns in their holsters. They may protest that these measures are taken for self-defense, not for war. But is that not the attitude of all people in a war that has gone on for a while and that is no longer always intense: detachment and denial (see chapter five for a discussion of denial of death in war).

The media have made much of the war-ness of inner-city violence by comparing it with wars elsewhere. The 1988 made-for-TV film

Women and War compared women's involvement in war from Lebanon, Guatemala, Northern Ireland, and the American inner city. In June 1990 children from war-torn countries were flown in to Boston where they met and discussed common problems with children from violent urban areas in America. A Lebanese teenager commented that children from Washington, D.C., might witness more violence than she did in Beirut. On 18 June 1990 *Time*'s lead article, "Child Warriors: The Suicide Machine," compared children in Afghanistan, Northern Ireland, Burma, and Los Angeles. In May 1994 the magazine *Details* published an article on love in war, and the places it focused on were Sarajevo, the Alexandra township in South Africa, and south central Los Angeles.

How is it that one of the oldest of all binary constructs, that of war and peace, broke down? I would suggest that Hiroshima and Nagasaki, the Cold War (which John Lewis Gaddis dubbed the Long Peace), and now the global proliferation of post-Cold War ethnic and nationalist conflicts made explicit what had long been implicit: as long as nations prepare for war—when they conduct nuclear tests, perpetrate "nucleocide" (Stiles 1994)—they are not at peace. Writings about war in the shadow of what Edith Wyschogrod calls "man-made mass death" highlight the continual negotiation of categories within a context that destabilizes dichotomous thinking.[14] In *Maternal Thinking,* her pioneering work on the political potential of the practice of mothering, Sara Ruddick writes: "the curtain is falling on the drama of victor and vanquished, soldier and civilian, hero and villain. Saturation bombing, nuclear missiles, and profiteering in small deadly arms were enough to stop that play" (Ruddick 1989, 247). Nuclear threat makes a mockery of us and them, combatant and civilian, front and home front. William Schwartz and Charles Derber suggest that it is not necessary to be personally involved in a war to be at war. Some states use others to fight their wars for them; the fact that they themselves are not actually fighting and dying does not of course mean that they are not at war. They write that the "restraints of the Cold War in Europe, however, did not apply to the third world. There, the Superpowers have continually used and sponsored enormous violence. . . . In the last few years *every* state known or presumed to have nuclear weapons has fought in the third world" (Schwartz and Derber 1990, 82, 145). Mobilization for war production is only different in degree from mobilization to fight.

To "wage war" is good; it implies purpose, will, and power to enforce. In the United States, the language of government as well as of corporate advertisement appropriates the term "war" and renders it positive. It is good to wage war on drugs, on oil prices, on banks, on taxes. To "be at war" is bad. It is not merely a question of calling not-war war, the converse is also true. Those who live *in* a war often cannot live *with* it. In South Asia the Bengalis, Punjabis, and Kashmiris who continue to battle over their right to self-rule did not call the British partition of the subcontinent in 1947 a war, nor do they now call their regional struggles war. In their eyes, partition was the coup de grâce of the British Raj, as a result of which they are all now living under the constant threat of "riots." The Northern Irish do not call their war with England a war but rather "the Troubles." The Lebanese did not at the time call their seventeen-year-old civil war a war, but "the situation," *les événements,* or *al-hawadith.* The Palestinians and the Israelis describe themselves as having waged six separate wars. So what is the meaning of the 1990s "Peace Process" if there is no war?

To recognize the continuum between war and peace does not mean that they are reduced to equivalence. After all, dodging bullets in downtown Beirut is different from analyzing war fiction at an oak desk overlooking the calm green of some campus quadrangle. It is not that war has replaced peace but that the two must be seen to be linked in a way that includes both at all times.

Victory and Defeat as Discursive Constructions

Just as peace and war must be seen as containing rather than excluding each other, so should victory and defeat. The end of formal engagement in combat is marked by a declaration that victory, however tenuously established, has been won. Only in the unlikely event that one side exterminates the other does it achieve incontestable victory. Its victory translates as having inflicted the greater injury. This is the presumption of what would happen in

nuclear war. But even then there would probably be survivors to
tell their story, to remember or rather to construct a new reality in
the name of which they would seek to injure proponents of an
oppositional reality. Even though incontestable victory is rarely
possible, wars usually end with one side declared the victor, the
other the vanquished. Wars are decisive not because they are so in
fact but because they are *said* to be decisive. The Algerian novelist
Assia Djebar understood this when she described the Algerians'
refusal of the French victory and occupation of 1830: "Even when
the native seems submissive, he is not vanquished. Does not raise
his eyes to gaze on his vanquisher. Does not 'recognize' him. Does
not name him. What is victory if it is not named?" (Djebar 1985,
56).

Experience of war is not a self-evident absolute category that
precedes and exists independently of language. Experience, rather,
is the product of language. The outcomes of wars are discursive
constructions built on the foundations of human pain. Scarry writes
that physical injuring marks bodies and thus records its own activity (Scarry 1985, 115–16). This record provides the material for
a story that gives meaning to experience and constructs it *as though*
that was how it had happened. Scarry writes: "Injuries-as-signs
point both backward and forward in time. On the one hand, they
make perpetually visible an activity that is past, and thus have a
memorialization function. On the other hand, they refer forward
to the future of what has not yet occurred, and thus have an as-if
function. This might be called their 'fiction-generating' or 'reality-
conferring' function, for they act as a source of apparent reality for
what would otherwise be a tenuous outcome, holding it firmly in
place until the postwar world rebuilds that world according to the
blueprint sketchily specified by the war's locus of victory. That this
function entails fictitiousness does not mean that it entails fraud-
ulence: what it substantiates is *not untrue*: it is just *not yet* true"
(Scarry 1985, 111, 121). Reality and representation blur into one
another as "fiction-generating" and "reality-conferring" are seen to
be equivalents. Fiction makes fact.

In 1845, after the French occupying forces had burned Algerian
rebels in some caves, they knew that they had to use the mutilated

bodies to prove the victory. The commander of the operation ordered his men to bring out "their rotting corpses! Then we shall have won, we shall have made an end to it!. . . . The corpses exposed in the hot sun have been transmuted into words" (Djebar 1985, 73, 75). When the black woman student in the 1980s musical *Sarafina* shows her torture scars to her classmates, her body memorializes the wrongs of the South African government and becomes the rallying point for resistance and opposition. In 1993 the Serbs marketed films depicting their mass rapes of Muslim women; they thus memorialized the dishonoring of these women and the people for whom they were made to stand in. In Khalifa's *Wild Thorns*, a man who is trying to survive under Israeli occupation criticizes his revolutionary son: "You can still see the marks of torture on his body, but he still hasn't learned his lesson. What I'm most afraid of is that he'll do something stupid and then they'll blow up our house" (7). And perhaps one day the son will use these scars as foundations upon which to build his version of the outcome.

Wars do not spontaneously generate assessments about who has lost and who has won, as their narrations make them seem to do. Although war is not war without injury in fact or in potential, it also involves a concrete discursive struggle that uses physical injury to feed its debate. In the power vacuum that war opens up, each side tells its story and seizes the right to name itself and its experience and to question the legitimacy and reality of the other's self-naming. War is a contest "to see which one of the two not-yet existing (entities) will be produced as an outcome" (Scarry 1985, 132). During war, cultural constructs on both sides are suspended and deconstructed so that they may become the building blocks out of which the postbellum societies, both losers and winners, construct themselves. Ultimately, consensual discursive practice decides the outcome.

Wars are fought to win definitive resolution to problems, tensions, and conflicts that have exceeded diplomats' skills. They are also fought to establish uncontested control by one group over another. During World War II, just as more recently in Bosnia, attempts were made to "cleanse" outsiders, however they might be defined, and to silence competing discourses. Yet each attempted

genocide had survivors who told their stories. War, far from providing an abiding outcome, has become the pretext for urging the
validity of one story against another. Tim O'Brien eloquently articulates the fictiveness inherent in war stories where "it's difficult
to separate what happened from what seemed to happen. What
seems to happen becomes its own happening and has to be told that
way. The angles of vision are skewed. . . . And then afterwards,
when you go to tell about it, there's always that surreal seemingness, which makes the story seem untrue, but which in fact represents the hard and exact truth as seemed" (O'Brien 1990, 210).
The surreal seemingness effaces the hazy line that separates historical narrative from fictive creation not only for the narrator but
for the audience also and allows the narrative to continue and
evolve. This haziness in language can turn what seemed like certain
defeat into victory. This is what happened after the Vietnam War.

Almost two decades after the American defeat in Vietnam, the
outcome of the war was still being debated. The war that was lost
in 1975 remained lost and invisible for a number of years and then,
in Ronald Reagan's 1980s, it was somehow recuperated. In 1985
magazines and journals like *Time, Life, Newsweek, Cultural Critique,* and *Wide Angle* produced special ten-year anniversary issues
on Vietnam. The articles in *Cultural Critique* are particularly interesting for their self-conscious revisionism. In his "Visions of
Righteousness," Noam Chomsky meditates on the meaning of a
war that he describes as having been both won and lost. Rick Berg
describes the waxing and waning of media interest in Vietnam.
Whereas during the war, Vietnam "rushed into living rooms," in
the immediate aftermath neither the media nor the academy, what
Berg calls the "two contending clearing-houses of information,"
paid attention to the war. He writes that it was "as if TV had
cancelled the war." And then "Ten years after Saigon's fall and
liberation, Vietnam has become, if not a commodity, then a resource for the American culture industry. . . . These ruins and fragments of Vietnam—these mutable, protean images—compose a
history of recuperation that signifies not only our desperate desire
to win the lost war, to conquer and possess it . . . but also Vietnam's
continuing liberation" (93, 95). Michael Clark describes how the

Vietnam vet ceased to be represented as a pariah and became "an idealistic avenger whose mission was to set society back on the right track" (Clark 1985a, 51, 74, 75). Judy Lee Kinney shows how postwar films like *The Deer Hunter* reconstruct the war as having been won: "Somehow we defeated the Other and returned home safe. Vietnam becomes an existential errand into the wilderness" (Kinney 1985, 40).

In 1988 a bimonthly magazine called *Vietnam* was launched. The June 1990 editorial explains the magazine's agenda: a reversal of the assumed outcome. The editors announce that the campaigning of the Vietcong backfired because of "the courage, valor and sacrifice of American combat forces. Instead of the Allied side being weakened by these preliminary attacks, it was the North Vietnamese Army (NVA) which bled itself badly. . . . It can be argued that, indeed, the NVA lost the Tet Offensive. . . . Hawk's contention that the Vietnam War was lost on the battlefield through poor tactics (and by inference, through poor combat performed by our fighting forces) *flies in the face of the editorial position of this magazine*" (my emphasis). The editor is unequivocal about the magazine's desire, intent, and right to reconstruct the story of Vietnam. Titles of the articles include "The enemy's jungle cover was no match for the finding capabilities of the Army's Radio Research Units"; "At Dak To in the Central Highlands, the NVA decided to make a stand. The 'Sky Soldiers' showed them the errors of their ways"; "Hanoi's Paul Doumer Bridge was a tough target. The Air Force's PAVE STRIKE bombs proved even tougher." The 240,000 circulation indicates that the magazine is responding to a widespread need.

Then in February 1991 the war in Vietnam was finally and conclusively won through the American triumph in the Gulf. But this war's triumph was more successful in bestowing victory to another, lost war than it was in holding on to its own successful outcome. Stam writes of the made-for-television mini-series that were designed to convince viewers that the war was truly over. He goes on to say that "now that the victories have largely unravelled, the media still cling ritualistically to the fiction of victory, for it is in the nature of fiction that the text is written once and for all—one does not change the final paragraphs of *Anna Karenina*—and that subsequent facts need not disturb our narrative pleasure" (Stam 1992, 123). Contra Stam, I believe that the stories woven around this war will continue to be written over the already written. The final paragraphs in particular will continually be changed in light of subsequent "facts." America might even end up losing the war, which is precisely what Saddam Hussein claimed, when on 16 January 1992 he celebrated the first anniversary of his victory over the United States. So what will America do for an encore? Klaus Theweleit is of course right to note that all wars, but particularly lost wars, need other wars so as to recuperate any notion of loss (Theweleit 1993).

Postcolonial wars in Asia and Africa and more recently in the former Soviet Union and Eastern Europe have been opened up to public debate, relentless revision, and multiple representations through the media. There is no one version that is allowed to prevail unchallenged. Today's warriors challenge the fictionality of war's "as though" outcome. Victory no longer belongs to those who wreak the greatest devastation on the greatest number of opponent bodies, but to those who tell the most convincing story. To repeat Djebar, "what is a victory if it is not named?"

Powerful Groups, Violent Individuals

The argument thus far is premised on the individual's right and ability to construct and represent the experience of war. There is no longer a white heterosexual male's story to which all of us must subscribe. Poststructuralist discourse reveals the instability of all subject positions that vacillate between the disintegrating universal ahistoric unified subject and burgeoning heterogeneous subjectivities. The literatures of what was previously the margin celebrate the emergence of plural agents who recognize that their othering is necessary to construct the unified hegemonic self. They refuse to remain complicitous with a system that invalidates their experience and expression.

It is in the context of postcoloniality that new discursive fields have opened up in which all can construct and center themselves

as effective agents. Arendt wrote in 1970 about the sixties' separatist movements of the Scots, the Welsh, the Bretons, and the
Provençals a comment that remains relevant in the 1990s as we
watch Europe, the Soviet Union, South Africa, and South Asia
fragment into ethnic, racial and religious groups: "While national
feelings formerly tended to unite various ethnic groups by focusing
their political sentiments on the nation as a whole, we now watch
how an ethnic "nationalism" begins to threaten with dissolution
the oldest and best-established nation-states. . . . Whatever the ad-
ministrative advantages and disadvantages of centralization may
be, its political result is always the same: monopolization of power
causes the drying up or oozing away of all authentic power sources
in the country" (Arendt 1970, 84–85). Nations have become too
big, too impersonal to command the loyalty of individuals who
cannot recognize a special place for themselves in the system. Individuals are forming extended families according to political interest whose space they can cognitively map and in which they hold
a meaningful role (see chapter six). Whether these groups do or do
not aspire to form coercive centralized systems is less important
than is the urge to autonomy at any level.

The case of Lebanon is instructive. Since the outbreak of civil war
in 1975 and even before, the social fabric had so unraveled that any
group, however small, could vie for power on behalf of a Lebanon
it had defined to suit its particular purposes. Jean Said Makdisi
eloquently describes this proliferation of groups: "Just when one
thinks that the war is over, that, for better or worse, one has
understood what it was all about . . . just as one gets one's political
bearings after emerging from the bomb shelter in the latest battle,
and, looking around, blaming this or that faction for its arrogance,
short-sightedness, cruelty, and treacherous alliance with this or that
foreign power; just then the whole picture changes again. A new
battle erupts, and new political realities appear. It is like looking
through a kaleidoscope: Shake it, and a design appears; shake it
again, and an altogether different one replaces it" (Makdisi 1990,
15). Alliances form and transform with the speed of a twist of the
kaleidoscope. Individuals create a community that confers meaning
and self-worth (see chapter six). When the group can no longer

satisfy its members' needs, they reject it. Our best view of this process is at times of conciliation. Just as negotiations seem to be producing progress toward cessation of hostilities, group cohesion often gives. Those who cannot see a significant role for themselves in the new system refuse the second-tier spot assigned to them. The only group that validates the individual is the one that is under stress or under that individual's command. This phenomenon is not unique to Lebanon: as the British were about to set up the structure for autonomy in Northern Ireland in May 1990, the Protestants split. It is in the very space he vacated that the War Story teller may once again find a place—but this time alongside others. Gayatri Spivak celebrates this process: "This is the greatest gift of deconstruction: to question the authority of the investigating subject without paralysing him, persistently transforming conditions of impossibility into possibility" (Spivak 1985, 336).

Nuclear age nationalisms are the outcome of a radically altered relationship between individuals and the collectivity. Newly politicized individuals are making themselves heard where before they had been silenced. They are asserting themselves over against the collective site of anonymous control, what Arendt calls the "rule by Nobody" (Arendt 1970, 38). Individuals are claiming responsibility for and control over their own lives. In the American inner cities, communities, like the Fairlawn Coalition in Washington, D.C., and the Black Panther Militia in Milwaukee, who threaten war before the end of the millennium if the state does nothing to improve the situation for African Americans, are setting up their own residential, anti-crime task forces that are more effective than official law enforcement.

How is it that individuals are able to wrest power? They are beginning to recognize that those in power are no longer fully in control and that to survive they must take over, appropriate the means to make others listen and thus possibly to transform their world. The most effective weapon is physical violence. Never before has there been such a concentration on the invention and production of the technology of violence: "The technical development of the implements of violence has now reached the point where no political goal could conceivably correspond to their destructive potential or justify their actual use in armed conflict" (Arendt 1970, 3). Although Arendt is referring to nuclear escalation in the late 1960s, the fallout into conflict and violence at the national and individual level is obvious. Jean Said Makdisi quotes the Lebanese daily *Al-Diyar* as saying that in a single night of shelling $15 million is spent: "And this war has been going on for 14 years . . . and ours is only one of the dozens of so-called small wars going on around the world" (Makdisi 1990, 240). We need only reflect on images of Iraqi and Iranian preadolescent boys toting submachine guns at the Shatt al-'Arab, of Red Army Faction women heaving hand grenades in the streets of European capitals, of Afghani tribals directing rocket launchers against Russian air might, and of millions of Americans with their guns at the ready to realize that the means to violence at all levels are widely accessible. Juan Corradi describes such anomie as being a late-twentieth-century phenomenon. Today, he writes, violence is different "not necessarily because it is more cruel or brutal, but because it is continuous, total, and undifferentiated . . . [violence] is a narrative of deconstruction . . . [that breeds] a culture of fear . . . terror and terrorism can be seen as the accelerated and generalized appearance of violence in political and social relations . . . a terrifying impasse, horror, a catastrophe of meaning" (Corradi 1988, 10, 14, 17, 18, 26).

Violence is not power, it is the means to empowerment. Although power always contains violence, even if only epistemic violence, the only power that inheres in violence is the power to injure—physically as well as psychologically—and to kill. Power and violence are distinguished primarily by their relationship with the individual. Power is group-related and depends for its survival on legitimacy; physical violence is individual-oriented and depends for its survival on justifiability. Power, Arendt writes, is never "the property of an individual; it belongs to a group and remains in existence only so long as the group keeps together. . . . Power needs no justification, being inherent in the very existence of political communities; what it does need is legitimacy [which it derives] from the initial getting together rather than from any action that then may follow. Legitimacy . . . bases itself on an appeal to the past, while justification relates to an end that lies in the future" (Arendt 1970, 44, 52). Physical violence does not rely on the action of groups of people but on the use of things; its end is the enabling of individual action.

Violence is the resource of powerless individuals when they perceive a chink in the armor of power. Physical violence both given and taken—as when the tortured perceives the torturer's violence to signify loss of power—gives the hope that the powerless can win power. And they can if they are able to justify their accession and gain legitimacy. In July 1980 the Lebanese Phalangists under the leadership of Bashir Gemayel conducted a systematic operation against their chief opponents, another Maronite militia under the leadership of Camille Chamoun. Within fewer than twenty-four hours, they had achieved their objective. For three days, the operation was denounced as a massacre, Bashir Gemayel as a butcher. Meanwhile the Phalangists cleaned up East Beirut, paying special attention to such apparently nonmilitary details as the collection of garbage. They controlled and honed internal violence into an effective weapon to be used against outsiders. Local newspapers began to change their tune. The massacre became "Operation Lina," and its mastermind was eventually looked to by many as the possible architect of a new Lebanese future. When violent action is successful its retroactive justification brings with it a linguistic transformation, a renaming, so that, for example, the terrorist becomes the freedom fighter. Ex post facto justification can gain support for otherwise unacceptable behavior, thereby giving credibility to the agents of violence.

When violence is thus deemed justified and its cause and proponents have become widely credible, the seeds of power have been sown. To transform violence into power, the individual action must gain the support of a group that will give it authority. So as to be able to win authority or the legitimacy of power, perpetrators of violent actions must restrict themselves to short-term goals that, when successful, continually reinforce the justification for such behavior. Violence should not be mistaken for anything but an instrumentality toward the goal of transforming itself into power or the means for maintaining power. Violence dramatizes grievances and may thus help to relieve them. For Frantz Fanon violence did contain the power of its own enforcement. In 1954 the Algerians launched their war of independence against the French within a global context of concern about individual human rights as well as national rights to self-rule. Violence gave them victory; it was justified. Their revolution became the banner under which other African and Asian countries opposed colonial rule throughout the colonized world. More often, however, violence introduces its own practice, namely, anarchy or the rule of the amoral individual or community without regard for the whole. In his analysis of the Iran-Iraq War, Samir al-Khalil writes: "From being a means to an end, violence has turned into an end in itself, into the way in which all politics (finally no politics) is experienced by the public in Iraq" (al-Khalil 1989, xi, 271).

The Lebanese civil war also introduced the practice of violence into the body politic. People used violence as an instrumentality to achieve ends they hoped would justify its use and establish legitimacy for themselves. Yet this violence became its own end. The crisis of power in a confessional system that had long ceased to be representative had already in 1958 sparked a civil war. Within a few months calm was restored but the underlying tensions had not been resolved. In April 1975 tensions once again exploded into tribal confrontations and identity politics. One Maronite clan would challenge the right of another to call itself truly Lebanese. Phoenician roots could become more Lebanese than Arab ones. It became important to identify and exclude the *ghuraba'*, the foreigners. They, whoever they were, were responsible for the war. Samir al-Khalil describes the same process in Iraq where the government became "obsessed with this problem of who is 'in' or 'out' of their polity. In 1968, 1975, and 1976 laws and resolutions decreeing the execution of non-existent categories of enemies—Freemasons and Zionists—were either reiterated, amended, or promulgated." The population was divided into the *taba'iyya 'uthmaniyya* who were in and the *taba'iyya iraniyya* who were out (al-Khalil 1989, 35). These politics of identity, difference, and scapegoating are a commonplace of societies in crisis. The Latin American theater critic Diana Taylor has written that societies in crisis "invent false differences and convert members of society into grotesque and apparently threatening others. Initially, this attack on others also passes as a solution to crisis . . . violence is perceived as a *defense* against crisis, rather than an *effect* of crisis. By participating in the creation of difference and in the politics of segregation and exclusion, people can comfort themselves that they are doing something to solve the problem" (Taylor 1991, 58).

In the postcolonial context, individuals have easy access to the means to violence. Short-term successes to violent ventures lead to other short-term goals, and power becomes a shimmering prize waiting at the end of a long line of crimes. Power beckons alluringly to all who dare to dream of it, but violence is the only certainty.

Civil Soldiers

Violence in civil wars like the one in Lebanon, in totalitarian systems like those of Iraq and Iran, in occupation like that of the Israeli Occupied Territories, in urban guerrilla warfare like that within the American inner city, has become the familiar emblem of everyday living whether we call this quotidian peace or war. Yet, because we usually equate peace with non-violence, this condition of violence must be war.

Late-twentieth-century wars present participants in a new light. Whereas the War Story casts male soldiers as the only participants and all others as civilians, postmodern war stories highlight the combatant role of anonymous participants who wear no uniforms.[15] The postmodern combatant is unstable, changing identity as necessary: now terrorist or freedom fighter; next, guerrilla; then, liberation army activist; finally, soldier in some national army. Written thus the chain is progressive. However, what is critical is the fluidity of this model; individuals who have moved up may just as easily move back and even disappear. Yet this disappearance may in fact be part of a rallying and regrouping. Like a virus, combatants mutate to avoid eradication.[16] How can the state eliminate the guerrilla when she is once again a terrorist and may tomorrow be the loyal soldier of the new state's military apparatus? When is she a friend, when a foe? With the confusion over who can and who cannot be killed it becomes difficult to objectify and dehumanize the enemy, the sine qua non for mobilization. How can we kill "him" if we pity his child or torture "her" if we laugh at her jokes—above all, if we identify with their humanity?

The 1954 Doolittle Report codified for Americans ways in which to overcome the human face of war. The Soviets were demonized as "an implacable enemy whose avowed objective is world domination. There are no rules in such a game. Hitherto acceptable norms of human conduct do not apply." Vietnam became the testing ground, yet their Southeast Asian enemies were not implacable nor were they always recognizable: American servicemen often could not tell the combatants from the noncombatants or distinguish enemy from ally. Yet they had to continue to fight. The American GI who had decided that the Vietnamese in front of him was a fighter could never be sure whether this fighter was friend or foe; yet he had to be ready to kill her. Peter Marin writes that "many of the U.S. commanders and troops attempted to distinguish between civilians and combatants—as difficult as such a task is in the midst of guerrilla warfare—and to observe the ordinary 'rules' of war. But far more often than Americans like to realize, those rules were broken" (Marin 1981, 71). William Broyles Jr. observes: "One of the greatest problems with Vietnam: it was hard to tell friend from foe—it was too much like ordinary life" (Broyles 1984, 57). And W. D. Ehrhart's poem "Guerrilla War" is eloquent:

> It's practically impossible
> to tell civilians
> from the Vietcong
>
> Nobody wears uniforms.
> They all talk
> the same language,
> (and you couldn't understand them
> even if they didn't).
>
> They tape grenades
> inside their clothes,
> and carry satchel charges
> in their market baskets.

Even their women fight;
and young boys,
and girls.

It's practically impossible
to tell civilians
from the Vietcong;

after a while,
you quit trying.

Vietnam predicted other wars in which combatants were scarcely distinguishable from civilians. This is the case both in guerrilla warfare and in highly technologized military encounters. In high-tech offensive actions, civilians become military targets. In grass-roots resistance movements, civilians easily change into combatants. During the Operation Restore Hope in Somalia between December 1992 and May 1993, soldiers "trained to be warriors for national security were sent on an international humanitarian mission. . . . Tension grew because soldiers could not distinguish pro- and anti-U.S. Somalis from one another. One officer said she was concerned that the situation was 'turning into something like Vietnam where we can't tell the good guys from the bad guys" (Miller and Moskos 1994, 1, 8). I am not arguing for the novelty of guerrilla warfare or of civilians as collateral damage or as unofficial fighters because the term "guerrilla"—deriving from the Spanish for little war—is almost two hundred years old. It described the citizen-soldiers mobilized to oust Napoleon during the Iberian Wars of 1811–14. At the end of the eighteenth century the military historian Carl von Clausewitz wrote: "Suddenly war again became the business of the people—a people of thirty millions, all of whom considered themselves to be citizens. . . . The people became a participant in war" (Clausewitz 1976, 591). Civilians as war participants may not be new but what is new today is that the media, writers, and even military leaders are beginning to acknowledge the civilians' changed role in war. They talk about civilians as combatants and not as accidental victims or unwitting participants. In March 1993 General Max Thurmond spoke at the North Carolina Triangle Universities Security Seminar on Women and the Military. He was describing the challenges facing the American military at the end of the twentieth century. Although he granted that women were not yet officially in combat (several months later, the U.S. Presidential Commission for the Assignment of Women to the Military passed a resolution allowing women into a very few combat positions), they had surely performed combat duty. The parents of the woman who was killed by a SCUD in Dhahran during the Gulf War, he said, *knew* that their daughter had been killed in combat duty. Even onlookers become active eyewitnesses in such accounts (Schweik 1991, 150).

Peacekeeping has presented its own set of problems in terms of combat definition. Some believe that when a military is involved in a humanitarian project, the action should be designated combat. Writing of Operation Restore Hope in Somalia, Laura Miller and Charles Moskos write that "veterans of the Gulf War were among those who believed that participants in this operation deserved combat recognition, since they 'saw more action' in Somalia than in the Gulf, where combat patches were awarded. . . . That the Somali mission was not yet defined as combat contributed to soldiers' fear that . . . they might die or be injured in a so-called humanitarian mission and not be recognized as a combat veteran" (Miller and Moskos 1994, 12).

Postmodern wars are not waged in a space where only young men fight. The elderly, the infirm, children, and women are combatants in wars that are no longer waged according to the conventional paradigm of men galloping off in shining armor to glory or death and wan women weeping yet waving them on from a distance. In postmodern wars the battlefield is written as not masculine but rather as that place where gender is most destabilized; it is there that it must be restored. Susan Jeffords shows how masculinity in Vietnam was continually undone through confrontation with an enemy that was often discovered to be female. Le Ly Hayslip's remarkable autobiography of a Vietnamese girl warrior caught between the Vietcong and the South Vietnamese reveals the widespread mobilization of women and girls throughout the war. Jeffords explains how 1980s films and novels tried to recuperate a masculinity that the fighting in Vietnam had destroyed. In Stanley Kubrick's *Full Metal Jacket* the men destroy the sniper who turns out to be a girl. Jeffords speculates that the emasculated are remasculinized through this destruction of the enemy who is after all only a woman. Jeffords points out that the murder is a variant added in this 1987 film adaptation of Gustav Harford's 1979 novel, *The Short Timers*.

The cross gendering of war terrain is anticipated in some World War I accounts. In her postscript to the 1989 reedition of Helen Zenna Smith's *Not So Quiet . . .* (1930), Jane Marcus points out how women's representations of themselves as ambulance drivers in what was officially known as the Forbidden Zone highlights their masculinization. She compares this gender reversal with that to be found in Erich Maria Remarque's *All Quiet on the Western Front* (1929). The soldiers are feminized as they remain "passive, silent waiting for attack, which fills them with fear and makes them into 'women' [just as women] ambulance drivers are equally made into 'men' by the requirements of their jobs. They must overcome their fear of open spaces and the dark and drive long distances in the night with their cargo of maimed men. . . . Each experiences war through the body of the other" (269). Elaine Showalter elaborates on the bending of gender lines during war: "We can also see now that shell shock was related to social expectations of the masculine role in war. The Great War was a crisis of masculinity and a trial of the Victorian masculine ideal. In a sense, the long-term repression of signs of fear that led to shell shock in war was only an exaggeration of the male sex-role expectations, the self-control and emotional disguise of civilian life" (Showalter 1985, 171). Contra Marcus and Showalter, the Australian Ross Poole celebrates the threatening of masculinity in war when he writes that war "is not so much the construction of a new and virulent form of masculinity, as the recovery for masculine identity of that relational form of identity constructed within the family. It is in this sense the return of the feminine" (Poole 1985, 76–77). Perhaps.

The official recognition and acknowledgement of women's participation in war is very recent. Scholars are only now discussing the gendered nature of warfare regardless of where the actual fighting takes place. Where the journal kept by the Southern woman during the American Civil War was until recently considered peripheral to the war experience, the diary notes of the Arab woman living in Beirut in the late 1970s is central to the definition of the war participant as well of the civil war itself. This scholarship is rewriting, and thus changing, history. Those who write about the American and British women who rallied to the home front during World Wars I and II and the Algerian women who participated in the revolution are beginning to change the meanings that have been attached to their wartime behavior. Feminist historians are now describing American and British women's non-military action as being part of the actual war effort.[17]

The reinterpretation of women's experience in the Algerian war of independence is new. During the past ten years scholars have begun to describe their participation as peripheral and untransformative (see Cooke 1989). Yet that was not the way the War Story was told. Frantz Fanon, the first to analyze women's participation in the Algerian war, celebrates women's "immense role" and of their conscription as "an authentic, pure birth" (Fanon 1975 [1959], 20, 32–33). A woman had to learn how to use her new body, how to be "a woman alone in the streets" and perform a revolutionary mission. Fanon explains how hard this was: "the unveiled body seems to get away from itself, to go to pieces. There is an impression of being improperly dressed, even nude" (Fanon 1975 [1959], 42). Women had to learn how to negotiate public space without the veil. Marnia Lazreg criticizes Fanon's dramatization of unveiling. These butterflies were not all fluttering uncertainly out of the chrysalis; many had already unveiled, especially in the French neighborhoods. She protests that "the emphasis on the body caught in the memory of the veil and struggling to adjust to its freedom is overwrought." She goes on to assert that his misunderstanding "of the various ways in which women could move in and out of identities resulted in silencing their unique contribution to Algerian independence." Lazreg writes that for the Front de Libération Nationale (FLN), "the abstract notion of 'freedom,' equated with entry in the war, was seen as the sum total of a presumed change in women's lives." What the FLN created was "a 'myth' of the woman fighter which had little bearing on the actual military involvement of women" (Lazreg 1994, 127–28, 130, 131). However, Lazreg is concerned that readers not lose sight

of women's actual participation. McLuhan and Fiore also discuss
the militarily expedient change in Algerian women's dress codes.
They, too, describe the trauma of unveiling that they contrast with
the later stage "when they resumed the purdah and returned to their
old surroundings, they discovered that they had become utterly
alienated from them and had undergone a radical sensory change"
(McLuhan and Fiore 1968, 157). These "disoriented" women did
not derive the kinds of benefits normally associated with sacrifice
on behalf of the country. Their military participation was quickly
redefined as civilian service that did not merit the rewards meted
out to veterans (see Hélie-Lucas 1990). I cannot agree with Lazreg's
assessment that it was foreign men's poor understanding of Algerian women's lives that in itself obscured the importance of their
participation. In the following chapter I discuss the role of these
women's silence about themselves. At any rate, wherever we choose
to assign blame, it is clear that the War Story was not modified to
include these new combatants except as anomalies, as women
briefly doing what men usually do.

In stories about postmodern wars, women's participation is evident. It is not masquerade. They are fighters and survivors, even
of torture. Although women were tortured in Algeria, as for example in Zohra Drif's testimonial, subjection to torture was not
interpreted as military participation. In contrast, in the Israeli Occupied Territories, Bosnia, and Latin America, torture of women is
represented as a form of military aggression integral to war. Serb
rape camps in Bosnia in the early 1990s were militarily designated
and in some cases U.N.-controlled. These women were legitimate
military targets essential to the prosecution of genocide. Ximena
Bunster-Burotto writes that in Central America "political torture
reaches women as daily terror (i.e., generalized violence). . . . By
contrast, in the countries of the Southern Cone, where a military
government or succession of military governments have been en-
trenched for decades, women are *systematically identified . . .* as
'enemies' of the government." She goes on to talk of the significance
of these women who have fought for justice and endured the un-
endurable without yielding. Self-sacrifice for justice has given them
"an identity of their own; they have become full persons in their

own right and thus challenged the passive, submissive, dependent role assigned to women. . . . They are creating new female models for the younger generations to follow" (Bunster-Burotto 1986, 297–98, 318; my emphasis). These women have turned their experiences as victims into political, even military, participation. This process is not merely a rhetorical ploy, it is a conscious act that has radicalized these women's identities as women.

Women are fighting as women; they are fighting also as mothers, like the *madres* of the Plaza de Mayo in Argentina. What Jean Franco writes of militant mothers in Chile, Argentina, and El Salvador is as relevant to mothers in South Africa since 1977, in the West Bank and Gaza since 1967, and in Iraq since 1980—if we are to believe that Suhayla Salman's "A Horse Bit My Aunt Umm Malik" is more than just a good story (see chapter five). Franco writes that "this resistance would not have been possible if mothers had not behaved as *mothers*. By refusing to regard their children as terrorists, by reiterating their mothering role, their particular regard for the continuation of human life, [they] were able to interrupt the dominant discourse and resacralize the body" (Franco 1986, 74). These women spectacularized their resistance by chaining themselves to fences, carrying their men's photographs on their bodies, by presenting themselves in sacred terms, for example, as Mater Dolorosa.[18]

These women refuse to consider themselves as victims, as mothers and wives who have lost their men. They call themselves active resisters, women who refuse to accept the loss of the men and who demand their return. They are transforming their kin identity within the struggle so that mothering becomes a political rather than a social role. They are in some senses mothers of the new nation that is to emerge out of the struggle. As Sara Ruddick states, "Typically, the point of women's politics is not to claim independence from men but, positively, to organize as women. . . . Insofar as they become publicly visible *as mothers* who are resisting violence and inventing peace, they transform the meaning of 'motherhood'" (Ruddick 1989, 223, 241).

In postmodern wars, women's participation may not seem traditionally military—although it may be—but it is becoming more explicit. Like American urban war zones, the Lebanese civil war implicated all without distinction. It was a war waged on multiple fronts by individuals and their unstable communities. It became part of daily life, not only in its savagery but also in its forging of an eerie wartime normality. Fighting was not everywhere, yet at any moment it could be. The front was anywhere that two individuals, male or female who might or might not represent a community, disagreed. For the duration of their confrontation they were combatants. But by extension we can say that they were combatants as long as they stayed in this environment and ceded to its logic. Jean Said Makdisi writes: "Women, protected by tradition from such practices as kidnapping, often found themselves confronting the violence that their men eschewed. Women grew in the war" (Makdisi 1990, 5). Victimization in the Lebanese civil war as in the American urban ghetto family was renamed survival. To stay in a war zone and to survive meant to resist, to be a combatant.[19]

Postmodern war story writers are inserting others who have been marginalized into the war story. Children are no longer hapless victims or precocious exceptions. They are now being officially enlisted—the new Children Warriors, the 18 June 1990 *Time* lead article called them.[20] According to the article, the United Nations estimate that "200,000 children under the age of 15 are bearing arms around the world. . . . The Mujahidin of Afghanistan have boys as young as 9 battling in Kabul. . . . In El Salvador the FMLN is an equal-opportunity guerrilla group, one of the few to allow young girls to bear arms alongside the boys. . . . History suggests that there is nothing new about child warriors, partly because in centuries past youngsters were looked upon as small adults, and thus the sight of them in combat was less horrifying. But there is a difference between being trained to fight and being used to make a symbolic point" (32).[21] Miller and Moskos describe the Somali children who were sent "to the front lines to shield adults and attack soldiers who would not or could not return the attack." Apparently, flyers were distributed "around Mogadishu telling the people (only the women and the children) to stone/ rock/ attack all U.S. vehicles" (Miller and Moskos 1994, 9, 15). Some Israeli military commentators justify killing children by saying that the Intifada leaders use them as "foot soldiers." An anonymous official was quoted in the 17 May 1990 *New York Times* as saying: "We are faced with a situation where children are among violent demonstrators and it is not always possible for the soldier to discern the presence of children. Children are turned into martyrs and are engaged to confront soldiers."

The following passage taken from Khalifa's *'Abbad al-shams* (Sunflower; 1985b [1979])—analyzed in chapter four—describes a typical pre-Intifada confrontation where civilian children and mothers become combatants and then again civilians: "A young boy walked along, stumbling in his clothes. Then he fell on the ground and started to scream. His mother hurried toward him with a small stone in her hand. When she made sure that he had the stone, she returned to the group of women to listen to the rest of the story. . . . A soldier approached the woman shouting: 'Yallah, yallah! Imshi!' They turned to him blankly and continued their storytelling about stupid Israeli soldiers." When the soldiers interrupt them, they "stuck out their hands and tongues and screamed. The children stood with stones poised, awaiting their opportunity. All they needed was for the women to get away from the soldiers. Then the stones started to rain down and the earth split to spew forth hundreds of children [i.e., combatants]. Some of them were from al-Rakab and some from the nearby camp. *The street became a front.* . . . The children kept on throwing more stones and the camp kept on throwing out more children" (Khalifa 1985b [1979], 248–49; my emphasis; cf. 253–54).[22] *Sunflower* was published in 1979, namely eight years before the Intifada broke out, yet this passage describes exactly the ways in which the uprising was fought. Today, however, when the media cover such an event, they talk only about the young men—ersatz-soldiers—and their stones.

Will the children of Ireland, Bosnia, and South Africa who were born into violence be able to function outside its logic? Writing of the Palestinian Intifada, Joe Stork writes that the "youth have also thrown off the Palestinian leadership embodied in the older generation of "personalities" and notables. They have thrown off the unequal relations that had characterized the role of the outside PLO leadership. They have thrown off the condescension and complacency of King Hussein and other rulers throughout the region" (Stork 1989, 68). Salim Tamari points out that 60 percent of the population of the West Bank and Gaza is under seventeen and that they have begun "to lose fear in facing death or mutilation of their bodies" (Tamari 1989, 127). Can the children of Lebanon who were suckled on war and who have adopted its chaos as their order conceive of another morality that does not condone violence as the sole means to achieving ends? Can the Iraqi children brought up in a war culture help shape a society that does not give first priority to violence?

Or, may chaos be creative? Some seem to think so. Diana Taylor describes the current "inchoate period" in Colombia, Cuba, Argentina, Chile, and Mexico as being "a moment of re-positioning, of transition between negation and re-affirmation" (Taylor 1991, 10). Juan Corradi underscores this hope out of despair when he asks whether terrorism in Latin America could not be perceived as a harbinger of "an honorable form of post-modernity?" (Corradi 1988, 25).[23] Do we not also have to bear in mind May 1994 images of Nelson Mandela thanking Frederik Willem de Klerk for putting an end to apartheid in South Africa as we lament persisting violence in the townships? Had it not been for their unleashing of anger and hatred there is no reason to believe that white minority rule would ever have been challenged. Is the same not true for the Palestinians? Years of struggle and standing fast have forced their presence on to the international agenda and granted them at least a first step along the road to autonomy.

Conquest of Space

There has been a radical change in the imagery of war, of the military, and also of the front.[24] The army used to be the place where boys were sent to become men. Soldiers were assured their masculinity because the physical space they occupied was free of women. They then became responsible for clearing women out of their mental and moral space so as to dominate "the hostile 'female' element within themselves" (Theweleit 1987–89, 1:435).

The masculinization of space has become increasingly complicated. The rising up of the colonized Algerians, represented as the oppressed feminine, against the masculinized French colonizers illustrates powerfully the military effectiveness of geographic gender-bending. The colonizers had established absolute power over their feminized population. Lazreg documents how Algerian men came to see themselves as having been emasculated by the French presence. Her analysis draws on J. Desparmet's 1910 "L'Oeuvre de la France en Algérie jugée par les indigènes." She writes: "The devout Muslim should rarely venture out of his home. If he must he should lower his hood over his face and walk with his eyes averted 'just like a woman wrapped in her veil.' The recurring comparison with women denotes Algerian men's concern with losing all the trappings of masculinity and being rendered powerless" (Lazreg 1994, 53). To confront the French and reassert their own power, Algerian men can be seen to have exploited their feminization: they conscripted a new category of military agent, women; they drew the French soldiers into unfamiliar terrain—the labyrinthine womb of the medina became an Algerian-defined front that compelled the French to fight by new rules. After over 120 years of dealing with Algerian men only, the French had to confront women, not only as veiled presences but also as warriors. Fanon writes that women's inclusion as combatants necessitated a change in the "*conception of warfare* . . . to involve women does not merely signify a desire to mobilize the whole Nation. One must harmoniously link women's entry into the war with revolutionary warfare. . . . The women could not be regarded as replacements but as individuals capable of effectively executing new tasks. . . . The decision to include women and to make the Revolution depend upon her was obviously very revolutionary" (my emphasis). Fanon quotes an article that had appeared in *Résistance Algérienne* of 16 May 1957 that lauds women's role in "the heart of the combat. Arrested, tortured, raped, destroyed, she is witness to the violence and inhumanity of the occupier." Fanon describes these "pure-born" women as signaling to the French the need to "se faire une idee de la *stratégie-femme*" (Fanon 1975 [1959], 30–31, 33). The hyphenation of the term *stratégie-femme* is a curious development that seems to point to women's participation as women and not as substitutes for men and to their role in transforming the nature of the resistance strategies and tactics.But Fanon does not account for reactions to this revolutionary decision. These useful women presented a threat to their men whom long colonization had feminized. How could the men acknowledge women's new roles without further disempowering themselves? In *Qui se souvient de la mer* (analyzed in chapter three), Mohamed Dib describes as a hyperspace the city that was divided between its underground and the new constructions. It became a maze that disoriented the French soldiers but also, apparently, the Algerian men. In Dib's war novel, Algerian men's confusion is exacerbated by the fact that the walls keep moving and changing and so do the people. The heroine, Nafissa, easily navigates the new constructions and the underground city, which, as Woodhull writes "is gendered female by virtue of its figuration by Nafissa" (Woodhull 1993, 63). This novel is emblematic of men's fear of what they perceive to be women's growing power (see chapter three). The men struggled for control over women's transforming bodies that became the site for establishing their power. Thus, we see that the success of the revolution depended on an irony: Algerian men used the women in a revolution that was fought to recuperate a jeopardized virility; yet it was their own feminization and that of their society and consequently of their struggle that gave them their victory.

The representation of the Algerian battlefield—particularly as imagined by male writers—foreshadows the hyperspace of Lebanon as of the Palestinian Intifada while providing a contrast with the manner of fighting. In Beirut, as already noted, the front was anywhere localized tensions burst into flames. There was no constant enemy to use as other in structuring the self. Changes of alliance, therefore, did not threaten existential cohesion. In the West Bank and Gaza, Israeli soldiers trained to fight soldiers had to improvise in the face of the unexpected. They had no rules, only the threat that if they did not act as soldiers they would cease to be soldiers, cease to be completely masculine. The combatant fighting as a non-soldier, as a woman or as a child, threatens the soldier with his (female Israeli soldiers are not allowed into combat) own dissolution should he not keep himself under complete control. He must play the game according to rules he learned before this encounter. In this case, how can he act? He is paralyzed by underaged and motherist militants. Women's writings inscribe the change through descriptions of women's resisting strategies: by everywhere confronting Israeli soldiers with their unarmed women's and children's bodies they throw into confusion all the familiar binaries that structured their expectations of and training for war.

How can soldiers function in wars that do not follow the old rules, that do not even allow for the simple demarcation of home and front? The postmodern battlefield accommodates non-soldiers on an equal footing with soldiers who may be new soldiers, and new soldiers with new soldiers. It has new rules. The introduction of women into selected combat positions in the American military has challenged an age-old fact that Cynthia Enloe articulated more than a decade ago. Women, she writes "*as women* must be denied access to "the front," to "combat," so that men can claim a uniqueness and superiority that will justify their dominant position in the social order. And yet, because women are in practice often exposed to frontline combat, the military has to constantly redefine 'the front' and 'combat' as wherever 'women' are not" (Enloe 1983, 15).

This discursive trick is no longer so convincing. The front, the physical equivalent of the psychic space of the modern male subject, has been invaded and occupied. This move is profoundly disorienting because it connotes a change in tactics. In this newly configured space, the soldier subject has no assurance of integrity and agency except in relation with others, not his cohort others, but different unsoldierly, unmasculine others, sometimes also mechanical, nonhuman others. No one can give him clear rules about the formation of such relationships. He is like the pilot in the hyperspace of postmodern war. "Looking up, he sees the digital display (opto-electronic or holographic) of the windscreen collimator; looking down, the radar screen, the onboard computer, the radio and the video screen, which enables him to follow the terrain with its four or five simultaneous targets, and to monitor his self-navigating Sidewinder missiles fitted with a camera or infrared guidance system . . . the confusion of sensations involves not a panic-stricken terror but a technological vertigo or purely cinematic derealization, which affects the sense of spatial dimension. Tied to his machine, imprisoned in the closed circuits of electronics, the war pilot is no more than a motor-handicapped person temporarily suffering from a kind of possession analogous to the hallucinatory states of primitive warfare" (Virilio 1989, 84–85). The pilot's alienation is an extreme example of what the traditionally trained soldier is likely to experience.

This alienation on the battlefield can be compared with the affect of postmodern architecture. Fredric Jameson describes John Portman's Westin Bonaventure Hotel in Los Angeles as disorienting by deliberate deception. Things appear to be other than they are: the main entrance turns out to be a back door of an upper story; huge kinetic Japanese lanterns are in fact glass elevators. Unlike the grand modernist designs of a Le Corbusier that offered utopian alternatives to a dystopic world outside, the Bonaventure refers to itself in isolation from the outside world with which it seeks no links. The Bonaventure "aspires to being a total space, a complete world, a kind of miniature city . . . ideally the minicity ought not to have entrances at all, since the entryway is always the seam that links the building to the rest of the city that surrounds it." Its glass walls, or its "skin," do not locate the hotel but rather the observers who see not the hotel but themselves reflected in distortion. The instability of the building's location is not restricted to the outside. Once inside, the individual is confronted by a hyperspace that refuses perspective and volume perception. It has "succeeded in transcending the capacities of the individual human body to locate itself, to organize its immediate surroundings perceptually, and cognitively to map its position in a mappable world . . . [this requires] the coordination of existential data [the empirical position of the subject] with unlived, abstract conceptions of the geographic totality" (Jameson 1991, 40, 44, 50). The decentered and fragmenting subject has lost control over his space that turns out to be the space of others also. His project to reconstruct himself without reference to surrounding anomie has become a dystopia for him, a foot-in-the-door for others. The Bonaventure describes other worlds, other battlefields that deny access through normal entrances. Once inside, the disorientation is not alleviated, it is heightened. Curiously enough, Jameson alludes to this deterritorialization in hyperspace as being analogous to the Vietnam of Michael Herr's *Dispatches*. I would extend this analogy to compare the experience of the architectural hyperspace with that of the soldier, the male assured his masculinity because of his soldierliness, when compelled to function in the unfamiliar territory of postmodern war.

The involvement of new soldiers in late-twentieth-century wars has required a new mapping and naming of the battlefield. No one is exempt from the fighting—a child can be a new conscript to a militia, or a well-paid sniper, or a victim of another child sniper. Sometimes fronts are drawn, but even then they may serve more as parodic reminders of classical wars. Artists create the orderliness of conventional combat and assure the memorialization of what will come to be seen as its historical significance because it will have been constructed in counterpoint to history. Saddam Hussein called the Iran-Iraq War Qadisiya in memory of the first war in 637 C.E. between a conquering Arab army under the leadership of Sa'd b. Abi Waqqas and a non-Arab, in fact Iranian enemy. This was not to be a postmodern war, its goal to undo militarized masculinity, but was to be seen and represented as a conventional men's war, despite the enemy's enlisting of "veiled battalions of female Iranian soldiers" who had as their models a mother and a warrior: Fatima, the Prophet's daughter, and Zaynab, his granddaughter famous for her military exploits (Reeves 1989, 2 passim).

The end of the colonial era brought radical change to the ways in which wars in the Middle East have been waged and written. Wars of liberation became a reference point by which to gauge a different experience. Most Arabs, and particularly Palestinians, have idealized the Algerian war of independence as a "proof that a people can organize themselves and successfully build their military power during the fighting" (Hart 1984, 122). The Algerians reciprocated by tying their revolution to that of the Palestinians. In 1982 President Houari Boumedienne announced that "Algeria's independence would be incomplete if Palestine is not liberated."[25] With time, however, Palestinian women began to warn each other to pay attention lest they also suffer Algerian women's postbellum oppression within a neotraditional system. In Sahar Khalifa's *Sunflower* a character asks: "What happened to Algerian women after independence? Women returned to the rule of the harem and to covering their heads. They struggled, carried arms, and were tortured in French prisons—Jamila, Aisha, and more Aishas. Then what? They went out into the light and the men left them in the dark. It was as though freedom was restricted to men alone. What about us? Where is our freedom and how can we get it?" (Khalifa 1985b [1979], 119). While Palestinian and Lebanese women salute the women of the Algerian revolution, they want for themselves participation without the consequent disempowerment.

The classical battlefield has fragmented and scattered throughout a hyperspace that includes the home fronts. There is no longer a special place for men to fight and for women to be defended. But was there ever such a place? Postmodern inquiry into the nature of the front and combatants calls into question the authenticity of the original. Were the wars that King Arthur and his knights of the Round Table waged chivalrous events that touched noncombatants only through deprivation, such as the loss of a loved one? Perhaps they were not so different from medieval wars, when the distinction between battlefield and civilian space was breaking down. The Thirty Years War (1618–48) and the Great Northern War (1700–21) and to an unprecedentedly vast extent the total wars of 1914–18 and 1939–45 involved those who should have had nothing to do with bloodshed. Maybe it has always been the case that all are involved in war though few are acknowledged.

However, as I mentioned at the beginning of this chapter, wars today *are* different. They are different because of the technology of the fighting and its recording. The other major difference that forms the substance of the rest of this book is the changed role of women. Women have begun to realize that what they do in war constitutes war action and that these actions must be publicly recognized as such for social change to take place. But before social change is possible, personal transformation is essential. Writing is key in this process. It is not enough to write afterwards. In war more than at any other time, it is crucial to write at once and then to act in terms of the discourse created. The experience that is immediately encoded retains the play of the conflicting discourses of wartime. Wordsworth and other poets may recommend contemplation and time for the experience to mature into the stuff of great literature. But in this interval the experience is re-membered in such a way that it is created anew to fit the War Story. Whatever does not fit is omitted; there is little room for improvisation.

In what follows I pay particular attention to literary erasures of the boundaries splitting men's and women's spaces and activities during war. Women may have always been in war, but it is only now that they are attracting attention for that participation. I analyze the writings of Arab men and women who have been engaged by war in the second half of the twentieth century and try to assess how postcoloniality has affected the waging of war, its space, its participants, and its representation. I focus on the ways in which women's consciousness has changed and how these changes have allowed women to tell their own *petits récits de guerre*. These little stories have proliferated since Vietnam and they are making it harder for the War Story to survive.

Chapter Three

Silence Is the Real Crime

Not only the arms but indeed also the speech of women must never be made public; for the speech of a noble woman can be no less dangerous than the nakedness of her limbs.

Francesco Barbaro,
On Wifely Duties (1417)

In Algeria many, including myself, kept silent for a whole decade after independence. We gave those in power the time to strengthen and organize and enforce discriminatory laws against women. . . . Of course we congratulated ourselves on the freedom that women had gained during the struggle. We were inside the myth talking about the myth.

Marie-Aimée Hélie-Lucas (1990)

If nothing else is left, one must scream. Silence is the real crime against humanity.

Nadezhda Mandelstam (1971)

I write to record what others erase when I speak, to rewrite the stories others have miswritten about me, about you. To become more intimate with myself and you. To discover myself, to preserve myself, to make myself, to achieve self-autonomy. . . . To show that I can and that I will write, never mind their admonitions to the contrary. . . . Finally, I write because I'm scared of writing but I'm more scared of not writing.

Gloria Anzaldúa, *This Bridge Called My Back* (1983)

These epigraphs talk of the prohibition on women's voices everywhere and at all times. They call for an end to this silence that has been imposed on all women, but particularly on those who have acted and then been repressed. The story of the Algerian war of independence from the French is a story about silencing. Throughout the 124 years of French rule, the Algerian people—both men and women—resisted but did not speak out. Finally in 1954 they mobilized in the cities and mountains and—after over seven years of fighting—they won. They were free to create the government and the society of which they had dreamed. But dreams turned reactionary: revolutionary leaders became conservative rulers. National liberation did not bring social emancipation, particularly not for women. For women, the silencing persisted.

The Algerian cause was adopted by committed revolutionary intellectuals worldwide. The war became emblematic for the struggle of the colonized, cowed but not crushed, against the colonizer. The Algerian government after 1962 fashioned a radical self-image as a "beacon of the African Revolution. For Algeria was the only Arab, African nation to have waged a protracted war against a former colonial power in order to gain independence" (Knauss 1987, xi). Violence was sanctioned. Intellectuals like the Martiniquais psychiatrist Frantz Fanon, who died a year before the end of the war, and the French writers Simone de Beauvoir and Giselle Halimi went to Algeria to witness the uprising and to make what Winifred Woodhull calls "cultural political intervention[s] in a historical process whose outcome . . . remained uncertain. . . . [They were trying] to *enable* the liberation of Algerian women in a form that complements nationalism and simultaneously challenges Western ideologies" (Woodhull 1993, 22).

These foreign intellectuals were as fascinated by Algerian women as had been their colonizing predecessors. In *Fantasia: An Algerian Cavalcade,* Assia Djebar quotes a French woman prisoner deported to Algeria in 1852 who had said of Algerian women that some were "treated as beasts of burden, and others [as] odalisques in rich men's harems" (Djebar 1993 [1985], 223).[1] Marnia Lazreg documents attempts by the French in the nineteenth century to co-opt Algerian women by, for instance, trying to make them wear French-style clothing. Those who could resisted, even if only "passively." Others were less able to retain their distance, and Lazreg explains how the French indulged in "sex tourism, which turned dancers from the South, who had been free to marry men of their choosing, into prostitutes." The practice then became widespread. Lazreg concludes that the "French implicit promotion of prostitution and nationalists' objections to it reveal the extent to which both groups understood the crucial role played by women in maintaining cultural integrity. The traffic in women was a daily reality that gave the colonial administration a powerful tool of social control of the indigenous society" (Lazreg 1994, 45, 55, 59). The Algerians were well aware of the ways in which the French were trying to infiltrate their homes, trying to tear apart the fabric of their culture. Women disappeared from spaces where the French might appear.

Like all colonial adventures, this French one was accompanied by a drive to educate segments of the "native" population who might thus become useful to the colonizers. The question of literacy in French at the expense of the mother tongue become vital. Lazreg writes that by 1954, the first year of the war of independence, there were over 200,000 boys and 80,000 girls attending schools—but among them were no more than 1,014 women in high schools and only 51 in college (Lazreg 1994, 62, 96). She accounts for the comparatively small numbers of girls by explaining that throughout the nineteenth century the French had concentrated on the education of boys, especially those from notable families. Isolated attempts to open French schools for girls were so poorly funded and the curriculum so poorly conceived that few girls went beyond the equivalent of the seventh grade (Lazreg 1994, 63–79). So what kind of girls did get education? Fadhma Amrouche's autobiography, *My Life Story: The Autobiography of a Berber Woman,* published in French in 1968, chronicles her education at the end of the nineteenth century. As an illegitimate child, she was sent away to French schools for girls to avoid the opprobrium of her society. These schools were usually run by some Catholic order and they were often interchangeable with orphanages. School was thus often less a privilege than it was an asylum. Amrouche is clearly grateful to the French for intervening in what she calls "brutal customs," that included honor executions, as well as for providing her with the opportunity to be educated. Although she describes some of her experience as very difficult, Amrouche seems able to talk about the faults of her own society as well as of the French without fear of reprisal. Maybe it was her advanced age at the time of writing that allowed her to conduct this double critique, the privilege of the strong.

This much education for girls would not seem to make much difference, yet some critics saw even this as being the cause of the "underdevelopment of Algerian society" (Mosteghanemi 1985, 31–32). In a situation where it was evident that women were pawns between French and Algerian men, any intervention in their lives was seen as threatening. It mattered little how many women were being educated and to what level since, as Lazreg writes, apart from a small group of elite urban women most Algerian women were illiterate at the time of the outbreak of the war. What counted was the perception. Some men must have feared loss of control at home, others may have felt threatened economically. Fatna A. Sabbah explains that the "invasion by women of economic spaces such as factories and offices, which is an economic fact of development, is often experienced as erotic aggression in the Muslim context, where the female body . . . has been neutralized by the traditional restructuring of space" (Sabbah 1984, 17). Algerians and particularly the men rejected French attempts to modernize women's lives, as Woodhull writes, "women are the guarantors of national identity, no longer simply as guardians of traditional values but *as symbols that successfully contain the conflicts of the new historical situation*" (Woodhull 1993, 11).[2] By the mid-1950s, the French made a last desperate effort to intervene in Algerian family life. Between 1957 and 1959, they passed ordinances and decrees designed to alleviate "women's oppression," as they patronizingly framed their intentions. But these attempts to strengthen women's legal positions by insisting on their right to consent in marriage and to divorce as well as complicating men's ability to divorce came too late. The resistance movement had taken off, and the leadership of the Front de Libération Nationale was outraged that the French should presume to continue to meddle in their most intimate affairs (Lazreg 1994, 132).

War had broken out on 1 November 1954. Norms gave as the war raged on. Many women—mostly rural because much of the fighting took place in the countryside—joined the ranks to fight for their nation. Centuries-old traditions were broken for the space of the war. Frantz Fanon writes, "Fathers no longer had any choice. Their constant fear of shame became illogical in the great tragedy which the people were living" (Fanon 1975 [1959], 94). The commands of the leaders of the nationalist opposition overrode the fathers' authority. Fanon writes that during the war men's attitudes toward all women, and particularly the fighters, changed. The women fighters, like Hassiba Ben Bouali—who died during the 1957 battle of Algiers—and Jamila Buhrayd, were revered.[3] Those who had not only fought but had also experienced prison and torture—like Jamila Boupacha and Zohra Drif—became revolutionary heroines. Fanon seems awed by Algerian women's swift adaptation to guerrilla activities: "The woman ceased to be a mere complement for the man. Indeed it might be said that she had pulled up her roots through her own exertions" (quoted in Horne 1979, 402). In their jointly written book, *Djamila Boupacha* (1962), which traces liberal French attempts to champion the revolutionary endeavor and focuses on the case of one of the heroines, de Beauvoir and Halimi demonstrate what they describe as Jamila's growth in feminist consciousness.

Women's War Stories

These women, who had been so important to the revolution, were swiftly suppressed. How was this possible—particularly if de Beauvoir and Halimi were right to describe at least some of them as having experienced a transformation in consciousness? Novels written in French by Algerian men and women during and after the war suggest an answer. At the time of the war very few intellectuals wrote in Arabic. Arabic had been so long excluded from the Algerian educational curricula that only those seeking a religious formation had competence in literary Arabic. These writers therefore shared an educational background and an existential dilemma: in the revolt against the French the only language they could use was the language of the enemy. (In the 1980s and early 1990s more Algerians wrote in Arabic—novels including *Dhakirat al-jasad*

[Body memory, 1993], said to be the first Arabic novel by a woman, Ahlem Mosteghanemi—but these works do not figure in the following analysis.)

The first novel of this war was *Aziza* (1955) by Djamila Débèche, a middle-class French-educated woman. As Algeria's representative at the 1947 International Women's Congress in Paris, she was one of only a handful of Algerian women to be actively concerned with western-style feminist issues, and therefore her views cannot be considered to be broadly representative. In 1947 she founded the feminist socialist literary journal *L'Action,* stating that her goal was to "look into the conditions under which our least privileged Muslim sisters live" (Lazreg 1994, 199). She also demanded that Arabic be taught to Algerians and that women be given the vote. Débèche was adamant that in Algeria, religion and traditions were not antithetical to modernization. There was no contradiction, she claimed, between wearing a veil and going to school (Débèche 1946, 143). Her novel *Aziza* is her fictive articulation of a plea for the integration of French and Algerian cultures. The French-educated Aziza is married to a poorly educated nationalist lawyer. Like many male revolutionaries in women's literature, he mouths pious phrases about the emancipation of the Algerian woman while keeping his wife, his possession, under lock and key. As his political preoccupations increase, his time for Aziza decreases and he dispatches her to his village. After an initial rebellion that brings immediate retribution from all, even her French-speaking women friends, she submits. Despite Aziza's capitulation, the novel was condemned as antinationalist, since it focuses on women as social problems rather than as symbols of opposition to the French. Nationalists rejected the implication that male oppression is more painful than the biculturalism born of colonial oppression; they demanded that the feminist struggle be subsumed under the revolutionary struggle. They also deplored the focus on upper-middle-class women.

In 1960 Marguerite Taos Amrouche (1913–76), a Kabyle Berber and the daughter of Fadhma Amrouche, published *La rue des tambourins.* Like Débèche, Amrouche is concerned with the struggle of a young woman faced with a choice between her French education and her traditional upbringing (Bamya 1982, 207). She recognized the privilege in her university education, yet she is the first to acknowledge that her freedom is skin deep only. Algerian society is not yet ready to integrate the educated women. Amrouche later endowed a chair of Berber literature and society at the University of Algiers.

This passive pessimism resurfaces in the oeuvre of the leading Algerian woman writer, Assia Djebar (born 1936). In all her works, even those that deal with the war directly, Djebar explores love in the hidden, oppressed world of women. She published her first novel, *La soif* (1957), three years after the outbreak of the war. In June 1956 students from the University of Algiers staged a strike with the Front de Libération Nationale. Djebar participated. Within a month she had written *La soif*. Eight months later it was published and successfully sold. Djebar denies any autobiographical references, claiming that the novel was not supposed to be a reflection of the war but rather the escape from it. *La soif* focuses on the social mandate for sons; it also describes some women's tentative rebellion. When the protagonist Jedla has a miscarriage, she fears that her husband will divorce her. Yet when she becomes pregnant again, she listens to her childhood friend Nadia, who encourages her to have an abortion because her husband would surely not be rendered loyal merely by becoming a father. It is only when Jedla dies from the abortion that Nadia realizes the consequences of her thoughtless words. She repents and reforms, having "lost her thirst for independence." The revolution is not mentioned. Djebar's harsh indictment of a patriarchal system that turns women into their own worst enemies and oppressors was criticized for what was considered to be blatant unconcern for revolutionary reality. Joan Phyllis Monego writes, "Only after independence, when the expected liberation of women was not effected with the liberation of the country was the seriousness of problems raised in the novel appreciated: the affective relationship between spouses, infidelity, women's fear of sterility and of subsequent repudiation, the subordination of the wife to the husband" (Monego 1984, 134). A year later, Djebar published *Les impatients* (1958). This time the writing took three months. Again there is no mention of the revolution. The impatient individuals of the title are cloistered women chafing against their segregation. Instead of attacking the system, they use deceit against one another to gain individual freedom. Djebar has said of Dalila: "I wanted to show how in a calm world, where objectively nothing had yet changed, there was developing a process that allowed one to guess at future upheavals" (Monego 1984, 136).

In 1959 Djebar left Algeria for Tunisia. There she wrote "Il n'y a pas d'exil," a short story she did not publish until twenty-one years later. The protagonist is a young woman, a divorcée who has lost her child. She hears the lamentations of her neighbor whose son has just been run over. She is plunged back into the misery of her own loss. While she is thus brooding, some women come to visit. They are looking her over for their son and brother. She remains aloof during the interview in which she is supposed to participate only in silence. When the visitors demand a decision from her mother, who acquiesces nervously, the protagonist blurts out: "I don't want to marry!" (Djebar 1980, 94). Everyone is shocked and she is hurriedly led away. But her remonstrance has come too late and her mother has agreed; the decision has been made without consulting her. This was normal, even though she was an adult woman who had already been through this ritual before her first marriage. As she ponders her refusal, she seems surprised at the vehemence of her reaction. She was already coming to terms with her fate: "Who cares! I don't know what got into me just then. But they were all talking about the present and about how so much had changed and how unfortunate they were. I said to myself: What's the point of suffering far from our country, when I have to continue doing as I did in Algiers" (Djebar 1980, 95). During the revolution it made little difference whether one was in Algeria or outside; women were still expected to remain silent and to have all decisions made for them. The cynical pessimism of this piece and its feminist tone may explain why Djebar waited until 1980 to publish. But written as it was in 1959 in the middle of the war, it is a vivid depiction of women's continued powerlessness and silence during the war.

From Tunisia Djebar went to Morocco, where she reported on the fate of Algerian refugees. Her journalism gave her a perspective on the war and its participants. Her next two novels, derived from encounters with refugees, were *Les enfants du nouveau monde* (1962), which came out during the last year of the war, and *Les alouettes naïves* (1967). The protagonists have become conscious of their political role in the country's reconstruction. Yet they remain silent: "A body submits silently because the dialogue of mutual contact is missing" (Djebar 1962, 18).

Les enfants du nouveau monde focuses on the experiences of several women and men in Blida (Djebar's home village) during a twenty-four-hour period. For some of the women, love is still a major motivation. French-educated Lila is ready to oppose the nationalist endeavor because she fears the loss of her husband. Participation in the fighting is involuntary, not willed. Such participation serves as an antidote against the boredom of their lives, making it possible for them "to stop thinking of love only" (Djebar 1962, 143).

There are others whom the war shocks awake. When her husband, Youssef, is in danger, Cherifa leaves her house by herself for the first time. She crosses the city, lightly protected by her veil, to warn him (Djebar 1962, 137–50). This foray into the city is presented as a journey filled with significance, almost a rite of passage into adulthood. In the maquis—the area of thick scrubby underbrush where Youssef must go—there are women, as Cherifa knows, but she does not demand to be taken there. It is enough that she has acted and that she has "discovered that she was not merely a prey to men's curiosity . . . but that she existed" (162).

Others weigh their love against the mandates of the nationalist endeavor. Suzanne is a French intellectual married to Omar, the last Algerian lawyer left in Algiers. Omar wants to leave the country and it is the *French* Suzanne who insists that he stay. The following day Omar leaves, saying: "I'll write. I'll give you my address in France" (Djebar 1962, 16). Suzanne's response is that she will stay "even if [the war] goes on for ten years. If I leave you some day I'll only divorce you at the end, when it's all over and the country is free." Her resolution and patriotism are as strong as that of the nationalist Youssef, who as a young man had discovered that "homeland [*patrie*] is not only common land, nor merely shared misery, but blood shed together and on the same day" (194). Suzanne is an anomaly in Algerian writings. Most writers present foreign women as incarnations of the temptations of the West. By presenting a foreign woman positively, Djebar is emphasizing women's steadfastness in contrast with the men's fickleness. (Even male Algerian writers acknowledge women's greater steadfastness; Haddad's war novels each deal with men who have left Algeria during its time of greatest trouble to live in Paris while the women remained to fight or just to stay.)

The illiterate Amna, who has had countless children, is another nationalist without being on the "front lines." She lives next to Cherifa and Youssef and knows of the latter's clandestine activities. One day she finds herself involved, almost in spite of herself. When her husband, who is a police inspector working for the French, asks about their neighbor's revolutionary activity, she lies: "May God forgive me, I lied to him and I don't regret it at all" (86). When she tells Cherifa, the two women sharing in this subterfuge feel themselves strengthened by their opposition to the corrupt law, personified by a husband. She calls Cherifa her sister because it was as if "the same blood joined us, as if we had drunk milk from the same mother" (84). Linked by blood and milk in a powerful sisterhood, these two uneducated women isolated in their homes and far from the action represent a first step toward the identification of a growing feminist awareness.

Then there are the women who seek liberation through military action. There are the heroines. A thirty-one-year-old school teacher, Salima, works as a go-between for resistance fighters and their families and is imprisoned. Although she longs to be married and to be like other women, her motto is, "Act like a man!" (94). She does and finds herself in prison.[4] Her story foreshadows Djebar's later work in which she reflects on women's silence while they were still active in the resistance. For ten days, Salima is tortured and forbidden to lie down. Her courage impresses a guard, who tries to help her. He is concerned for her, but when he asks her how she is, she "notices that she no longer has a voice" (97). The guard calls her "sister" and ironically thanks her for not talking. But the reader begins to suspect this speechlessness. Salima already, while yet participating, is losing her voice.

The heroines are not the only ones to have become actively engaged in the resistance. There were others who did so in a way that many could not understand and certainly not accept. Touma was such a one. It was she who was responsible for Salima's arrest. In a 1987 interview Djebar calls Touma one of the "misguided" feminists who thought that it was enough to look western; worst of all she believed that she had the right to sacrifice the nationalist cause for personal reasons. What could be worse than to work for the authorities as an informant? Djebar explains that she had used Touma to exemplify the ways in which the French were trying to westernize Algerian women. The only outcome of such a program was to turn the seduced women into prostitutes and traitors.[5] The men in their families were "compelled" to kill these women to redeem their lost honor. When I first read *Les enfants du nouveau monde,* I was struck by how partial was the picture it drew of those women warriors and how ambivalent was Djebar in her assessment. In many ways Cherifa, still veiled, still secluded, seemed to embody nationalist ideals more fully than women like Salima who paid so dearly for their involvement.[6]

Ambivalence about the significance of women's mobilization recurs in a ten-page testimonial written by Zohra Drif, a woman who had been a member of the terrorist network of the Armée de Libération Nationale and was later known as a heroine. "La mort de mes frères" (1961) describes Drif's arrest in 1957 and her subsequent detention in the women's section of Barberousse prison. She is coolly realistic about what it meant to have been so intensely implicated. She flatly rejects Malraux's definition of terrorism as a "search for absolute personal realization, pushed to heroism, understood as individual exaltation. [Such a definition] contradicts the reality we are experiencing in Algeria" (Drif 1961, 3). She justifies her attitude by describing the ethos of the Algerian army, which repudiated the value of individual action and heroism in favor of subservience to the group. Like any other soldier, these warriors did not see themselves as individual terrorists but rather as soldiers with a responsibility to the group, and this group ran regular war risks, such as torture and death. She writes: "In this Algerian war in which all, civilians included, are participating in the struggle for liberation, my participation as a young woman student is natural and fairly common" (6). Her insistence on the naturalness of women's military action and of its commonness is reiterated by women writers as well as by fighters.

In 1971 Jamila Buhrayd gave an interview to Walid 'Awad for *Al-Hawadith* magazine. Throughout 'Awad calls her a heroine and glorifies her role in the revolution. Her unvarying response is to downplay what she did and to insist that it was no more than other women had done: "I'm not really sure why all the publicity ended up centering on me. For there were many women in the prison with me, subjected to the worst kinds of torture, and they didn't betray their comrades either. Each of them deserves pages and pages from the poets. All of us, all of us Jamilas were parts in the whole. Individuals don't make a cause you know." When 'Awad deafly persists in idealizing her, she exclaims: "I am not a case. Please. I simply played a small part in one period of the Algerian struggle" (quoted in Fernea and Bezirgan 1977, 257, 259).

The Stories the Men Wrote

While the women were talking and writing uncertainly about their military participation, male writers like Kateb Yacine, Mohamed Dib, and Malek Haddad filled their works with ideal types. They infused all women's actions and their temporary change in status with significance. They wrote not so much out of admiration as of dread. The reader senses the fear that women are gaining control and that the danger they pose to the social order, their *fitna* (an Arabic word that means both women's physical attraction and political unrest), is about to be unleashed.

The first major war novel by a man was *Nedjma* by Kateb Yacine (1929–89).[7] It appeared in Paris in 1956, namely in the year when the Moroccans and the Tunisians gained their independence from the French, and when the British and French attacked Egypt over control of the Suez Canal, and two years after the outbreak of the Algerian war. Kateb Yacine claimed that it was the war that made French publishers realize that Algerian literature might be written by Algerians and was not restricted to what was written by French *colons* like Albert Camus (Yacine 1991, xxxi). The novel is set in Bône, a coastal town in Algeria, between Armistice Day, 8 May 1945, and the early days of the war of independence. The plot involves four young Algerian men, an omnipresent patriarch Si Mokhtar, and the beautiful Nedjma.

Many critics have read Nedjma as a transparent symbol for Algeria. Some are more guarded. For example, Louis Tremaine writes that "the conception of Nedjma as a direct symbol of Algeria is no longer tenable, for the simple reason that the text will not support it. There are too many descriptions of her as sterile, disdainful, false, fatal, and capricious which conflict with such an understanding." Such a caveat notwithstanding, he then goes on to call her "the tribally created illusion of fulfillment and significance, and her continued pursuit only prolongs the group's inward violence and outward 'absence of itinerary' or inability to act meaningfully to restore direction and significance to the world" (Tremaine 1979, 156, 157). Woodhull emphasizes the significance of the name Nedjma, which in Arabic means star. This name, she writes, "evokes the modern 'warriors'—Algerian immigrant workers—who in the 1930s formed the secular anticolonial movement called the Etoile Nord-Africaine [North African star]. Yet as a 'star' Nedjma recalls not only the tribal bond whose renewal in the Etoile Nord-Africaine is to propel the forward-looking nationalist struggle, but also the atavistic aspect of that bond." The convergence of the atavistic and the utopian "functions now to mobilize the male protagonists in their collective struggle, now to immobilize them in endless reverie or condemn them to aimless wandering and random violence." Woodhull may consider Nedjma a symbol of the nation, but she rejects the other common assumption made by critics that Nedjma represents the ideal woman, as though ideal means secluded and silent. She points out that far from being submissive, Nedjma struggles with the men who want to imprison her. She praises Yacine for "successfully stag[ing] some of the processes by which women are constituted as actors in history—and are limited in their ability to act in nationalism's confrontation with colonialism" (Woodhull 1993, 27–28, 30, 3).

My reading goes further to propose that Nedjma—who appears first on page 65 in the naming of her house Beausejour as Villa Nedjma—is better interpreted as representing the new women produced by the revolution. In fact, the men describe her as uncomfortably modern. Mustapha tells Mourad that when he first saw Nedjma, she was wearing "a pale blue silk hood such as recently adopted by emancipated Moroccan women" (Yacine 1956, 72). She is modern in appearance and also in behavior. Mustapha notes that while still in her teens, she was supposed to have asked her cousin Mourad to leave school, marry her, and take her to Algiers so that she might escape Bône and "realize her young girl's dreams of becoming 'enlightened'" (84). But Mourad declined the offer and she had to remain in her native town. Most important for our present purposes, Nedjma is once described as revolutionary. As though in passing, she is called the "amazon of the attic" (78).

Although Yacine does not develop the allusion to legendary military women in this novel, he does do so in his play *Le cadavre encerclé*, which he wrote at the same time that he penned *Nedjma*, that is, in the late 1940s, but which he did not publish until later. Nedjma is heroine in all three plays.[8] In *Le cadavre encerclé*, this other Nedjma leads the women to war, exclaiming: "It's now or never! This is war! Let's take our freedom!" She exhorts these women to throw away their jewelry, material symbol of their worth in a traditional society, and to take up arms. Yacine was also deeply interested in the Kahina, a Berber woman from the Djarawa tribe of the Aurès who in 702 C.E. was killed after organizing a resistance to the Arabs who were bringing Islam from the East.[9]

Nedjma in the eponymous novel is neither nation nor ideal woman. Rather than a Penelope who quietly awaits the return of her men, she is a seductively dangerous woman who sows "discord everywhere . . . the femme fatale, sterile and fatal, a woman worth nothing, through the passionate night ravaging all the blood that was left us, not to drink it and thus to liberate us . . . but just to disturb" (146, 187). Lakhdar, the brave, who had stood up to the French, pursues Nedjma fearfully: "Nedjma is the physical form of the lover who awaits me, the thorn, the flesh, the kernel, but not the soul, not the living unity where I could melt without fear of dissolution" (247). As I shall elaborate below when discussing Mohamed Dib's 1962 work, this fear of dissolution in the feminine terrifies men during war.

She is also the "femme sauvage" who figures so prominently in Yacine's plays.[10] When she is three years old, Nedjma is adopted by Lella Fatma, a Kabyle woman. She grows up a wild child whom "her educators gradually agreed to surround with barriers" (185). She is married against her will to what turns out to be a half brother, lamenting: "They isolated me the better to vanquish me, isolated me when they married me off. Since they love me, I hold them in my prison. In the end it is the woman prisoner who decides" (67). Nedjma demands acquiescence and is cruel to "those who do not play her game." When Rachid meets Nedjma, he is immediately fascinated and frightened, and he is then devastated when he loses sight of her. Si Mokhtar warns him that should he "find her again, you would be scorned, betrayed, and cheated" (68, 110). As though looking for help in his search, Rachid joins Si Mokhtar on the pilgrimage. It is then that he learns that Nedjma is his half sister; their mother was a French woman raped by four men, among whom were Si Mokhtar and Rachid's father, whom Si Mokhtar may well have murdered. Si Mokhtar warns Rachid against ever thinking of marrying Nedjma (129) and then asks his help to kidnap her so as to free her from her incestuous marriage. They want to take her to the Nadhor, the seat of the ancestral Keblout. Their scheme fails. Rachid is torn between desire and dread for his "evil star, the Salammbo who was to give meaning to the sacrifice . . . she was the sign of my loss, a vain hope to escape. . . . I know no one who has approached her without losing her . . . the ogress who died of hunger after eating her three brothers" (176–80).

Nedjma is an unlikely symbol for Algeria. But the four suitors, to whom the largest part of the novel is devoted, may well represent the ways in which the Algerians launched their resistance. Rachid, Mustapha, and the half brothers Lakhdar and Mourad struggle to survive under the unscrupulous rule of the French who have come to Algeria to get rich. They are day laborers in a village working

under the supervision of the mean-spirited Monsieur Ernest. Lakhdar attacks him, is arrested, and quickly escapes. Later, Mourad
kills another Frenchman while the man is beating his maid. Mourad
is arrested and the three others escape the village. Their stories are
fragmented but always linked to the distant, almost silent Nedjma,
to whom Rachid and Lakhdar are related. This is indeed a tight
tribe, bonded by incest. Incest is necessary to their survival but it
is also an unfailing promise of tragedy. They all know that "incest
has been our link, our principle of cohesion since the exile of the
first ancestor. The same blood carries us irresistibly to the mouth
of the passionate river close to the siren whose responsibility it is
to drown her suitors rather than choose among the sons of the
tribe—Nedjma completes her game of a fugitive, hopeless queen
until the husband's appearance." Their only solution is to "link in
their friendship, conjoining their rivalries the better to circumscribe
her . . . they were all planning their vengeance," because they are
afraid of "Nedjma, our ruin, the evil star of our clan" (186–88). No
longer merely Rachid's evil star, she has come to occupy the place
of dread in the lives of all around her.

Si Mokhtar, the hovering ancestral presence, may represent some
aspect of Algeria; after all he was asked to be the representative for
Algeria "tout entière" during the pilgrimage he undertakes with
Rachid (112). This almost legendary figure has fathered countless
offspring, including Nedjma, her husband, and one or more of her
suitors. He knows he has wronged women and that they have
poisoned "his death drop by drop, weighed down his body with the
long, sticky tears that he had blindly scattered" (99). Fadela M'Rabet is referring to Si Mokhtar when she writes, "today—and this
is one of the 'infantile diseases' of decolonization—the ancestors
came back to life; as Kateb Yacine says, 'their ferocity is redoubled.'
Why? because the 'ancestors are in the streets—they are us'"
(M'Rabet 1983, 247). Is it Si Mokhtar whom Rachid targets when
he rails against "the fathers who sold their land to the French, thus
contributing to their ruin of the ancestral creation" (Yacine 1956,
146)? Kristine Aurbakken calls Si Mokhtar a "parodic incarnation
of an identity whirling in the void and an unconscious catalyst of

a future . . . demise of the old order to make room for the new" (Aurbakken 1986, 128). Most of all, Si Mokhtar stands for the corruptness of the past.

Nedjma is no purer. The illegitimate child of a French woman and Si Mokhtar, she is the product of the coupling of the colonial system with local blood. We read here Yacine's implementation of what the Moroccan writer Abdelkabir Khatibi thirty years later was to call a "double critique" (Khatibi 1983). This two-pronged attack simultaneously targets the western heritage imposed by colonialism *and* local patrimony. It is only through such a double critique that we may come to some understanding of how subjects are formed in the postcolonial era. Here already in the first years of the war, we read a man hinting at what was to come in reality as well as in men's later literature: the men formerly terrorized by powerful women, "femmes sauvages" (see Sbouai 1985), would want, indeed need to control them.[11]

Mohamed Dib's *Qui se souvient de la mer*—translated as *Who Remembers the Sea* (1985 [1962])—enacts a woman's transformation from wife into warrior. Nafissa is the wife of the bemused narrator, and it is their relationship and its dissolution that form the plot of this novel. Dib compares his surrealist oneiric discourse with *Guernica*, Picasso's masterpiece on World War II. Held within the rigid frame of the war, the narrative loops a tale of terror and abstraction, as people turn into stone, and stone into snakes.

Whereas in his earlier trilogy, *La grande maison* (1952), *L'incendie* (1954), and *Le métier à tisser* (1957), Dib depicted women as social victims always acted upon and never acting, in *Who Remembers the Sea* women are strong. It is they who initiate action and remain active and alert throughout the anarchy (Dib 1985 [1962], 51). Their action takes place against the background of the sea with which they are often connected. Sometimes as a group they become a sea, they are a "sea of women wrapped in snowy veils" (66). He had at first confused these veiled women with the howling iriace, horrifying mythical creatures that circle above the new constructions. The presence of wild, mythical beings like the iriace intensifies the libidinal atmosphere. Theweleit quotes Freud's *Interpretation of Dreams:* "It might be said that the wild beasts are used to represent the libido, a force dreaded by the ego and combatted by means of repression" (Theweleit 1987–89, 1:194). At other times, they are the gentle life givers, the sea-mother-women who prepare the men for the fight they could not otherwise undertake: "Without the sea, without the women, we would have remained orphans permanently. They covered us with the salt of their tongue and that, fortunately, preserved many a man among us! It'll have to be acknowledged some day" (Dib 1985 [1962], 10; cf. 30, 38). The narrator associates Nafissa, his children's mother (*mère*), with the sea (*mer*) of the title. This homophonous association recalls the male fantasies and anxieties that Klaus Theweleit locates in fascist men's writings of the between-world-wars period. Quoting Sandor Ferenczi, Theweleit writes: "Mothers should actually be seen as symbols or partial substitutes for the ocean.... First comes *la mer*, then *la mère*. First streams, then their lesser equivalent, incest . . . and the coupling of erotic woman and water [happens with] the pure woman without boundaries" (Theweleit 1987–89, 1:292, 420). Clearly such an association is deeply troubling, for it epitomizes the narrator's loss of control. However, beyond the awesomeness of Nafissa's transformation, the alternative reading of the title of the novel—not *Who Remembers the Sea* but *Who Remembers the Mother*—indicates the author's awareness that however strong these women may be, however much the men rely on them and fear them, this association may not last. Already in 1962, Dib was warning Algerians that the mother, the most honored role for women within Algerian society, was going to be forgotten.

Nafissa is never clearly delineated, but as the novel progresses she becomes more and more elusive. Even when all seems to be well between the narrator and his wife, he feels threatened by her simple smile, which is accompanied by "defiance in her eyes" (Dib 1985 [1962], 25). He describes her absences—we presume she is out on some military mission because on one occasion there is an explosion where she is—as "black holes" into which he is sucked. In her association with water, the coupling of erotic woman and water, her strength and power, disguised as fragility, become most evident: "Nafissa's voice overwhelmed me with its water, cradled me. . . . Had the world hardened into one great block of concrete, it still would not have formed such a rampart as we find in this fragile water" (19). Nafissa's voice is at once as fragile as water and as hard as a concrete block. Dib celebrates women's voices as forces of nature, vulnerable and tough.

As the novel progresses, Nafissa and the sea become interchangeable; the growing fear that each inspires is palpable (37–38). Nafissa is more and more "indistinct, peaceful, motionless, and absent. She looks around her and leaves me powerless" (51). The narrator grows dependent on her for survival at the simplest level. He needs her to "transfuse her energy into him" (63). This is not a totally benign energy because it empowers her to conquer "the universe, establishes her dominion over everything, and then uses her smile to put my worries to rest. . . . I will never find out through what channels Nafissa acts upon me" (74). He is out of control, he knows he is out of control, but he does not know how it is that he got out of control, except that Nafissa is responsible. Nafissa, whose name derives from the Arabic word for soul, represents an atavistic impulse, the "soul that designates our line of descent" (80). She is a part that he needs to survive and to function. But a part that he cannot control. Medusa-like, this *femme-soldat* turns him into stone, hardens him. And she alone can depetrify him, soften him, and save him from his paralysis (18). This description recalls Freud's *Medusa's Head*: "For becoming stiff means an erection. Thus in the original situation it offers consolation to the spectator: he is in possession of a penis, and the stiffening assures him of the fact." But he must beware lest, as Theweleit writes, "Contact with erotic women would make him cease to exist in that form" (Theweleit 1987–89, 1:198, 244). Nafissa is just such an erotic woman who plays with her man as she wills. When the city burns, she carries him aloft above the devouring flames. When he suggests that he might accompany her on one of her missions, she refuses. She compels him to play the role that had been hers before the war: to wait passively.

The narrator submits to his new fate and justifies it as a communal necessity: "The guiltiest are those who distrusted the sea, who failed to place their confidence in her" (Dib 1985 [1962], 103).

All have to recognize that the sea, that women, are "preparing the coming of another world" (106). They are the architects of the brave new world that they will shape and cover, as the sea, at the end of the novel, covers the whole of existence. Theweleit writes that such floods do not signify a Jungian "oceanic feeling," but rather a threat that "may be combatted with 'erections': towering cities, mountains, troops, stalwart men, weapons" (Theweleit 1987–89, 1:402). And these are precisely the scenarios that Dib delineates. The coming flood presages the last stage in the narrator's loss of control, his social boundaries are eroded and undermined by a flood of feeling. He can no longer distinguish himself from the woman, the wife as well as the vulnerable feminine within himself. The woman has deprived him of control, of identity, and of life.

The anxiety that informs this novel runs through Malek Haddad's works, *Je t'offrirai une gazelle* (1978 [1959]), *L'élève et la leçon* (1960), and *Le quai aux fleurs ne répond plus* (1961). To discover how Haddad explores the role of writing during the revolution, how the revolution shapes identity, and how women increasingly subvert that identity, we need to read these novels in the order in which Haddad wrote them. In his first novel—a metatext that questions the fate of the book that he is writing as though it were written and submitted to a publisher—his narrator lyrically denies the significance of writing: "Writers who have nothing more to say invent stories or dive deep into the blasé depths of their skills. They have nothing more to say because they have not understood the need for silence, this silence that allows for the contemplation of the other. They exist too much. Their novels encumber them" (Haddad 1978 [1959], 26). Later a friend writes from Algeria assuring him that the fighters could not care less "about your gazelle" (120), namely, his book. While still writing, the narrator anticipates an apathetic reception. In *Je t'offrirai une gazelle*, women play a minor role to the narrator's self-obsession. At will, he collects and rejects women of all nationalities. He describes the veiling of his compatriot women as being "not only modest, it's also very elegant" (123). The ironic tone reveals the author's contempt for this man who still sees women as objects to be possessed.

A year later, Haddad published *L'élève et la leçon*. His portrayal of women has changed. The first line of the novel is: "I did not know that my daughter was so beautiful. Insolent and aggressive." The careless romances of *Je t'offrirai une gazelle* have given way to the intensity of a father-daughter relationship. The protagonist has no power over Fadila who "has come not to explain. She had come to demand her due and to condemn." In a description reminiscent of Dib's Nafissa, the father-narrator compares Fadila to night, dark and frightening and incomprehensible. She smokes and he can do nothing, even though he "does not like women who smoke. Especially when they're Algerian" (Haddad 1960, 13, 16).

The novel is in the form of an interview between father and daughter. The narrator rarely speaks but only dreams in response to his daughter's urgent request. Fadila is a fighter who associated closely with men. She is having an affair. Her father condemns her immoral behavior so as to ease his own guilt—it is better to be in Paris writing than in Algeria whoring. But the worst is yet to come. Fadila has come to him not as a father, the father who left Algeria when her mother died, but as a doctor. She wants him to perform an abortion on her since she cannot have a child "under these circumstances" (18). She has to be fit to fight, and for the first time in her life she has sought his help (63). His daughter's nationalism forces the narrator to confront his own inadequacy. He admits to himself that he was "nothing but a vulgar egoist without a nationalist conscience, without any conscience. Being partial to easy solutions, I took refuge on the other side of the sea, on the other side of History" (19–20). Hypocrite that he is, he chastises Fadila for not caring for the unborn baby's father. Not knowing how to treat a woman who is both a nationalist and a "prostitute" he seeks acceptance while condemning her. When she includes him in a "chez nous" that refers to *their* Algeria, he is almost unbelieving: "So she hasn't completely excluded me from her community" (43). He has given Fadila the right and therefore the power to accept or to exclude him, to make him Algerian or to confiscate his birthright. He cannot understand and can "never forgive that they [Fadila and Omar] had thought of getting rid of that child that they alone had invited. That they asked me the father, me

already the grandfather, me almost the father-in-law, to get rid of
the child" (62). Yet, remonstrances notwithstanding, he agrees. He
understands that his act goes beyond his relationship with his
daughter. By acceding to her impossible demands, he has empowered her and others like her. It is now the "Fadilas [who have] the
final word" (99). The novel ends with the completed abortion. It
is not clear whether performing the abortion has allowed the narrator to feel more Algerian because he is freeing up a fighter for the
war, or whether it has served to exacerbate the loss of control and
dignity.

In *Le quai aux fleurs ne répond plus* (1961), ambiguity about
women who have participated in the revolution gives way to deep
distrust. Like his predecessors, this narrator, Khaled Ben Tobal,
goes to Paris. He has chosen to write and not to fight. In Paris, he
finds himself surrounded by other Algerians, but they do not even
write. Writing becomes his passport. He hopes to become a fighting
Algerian through his Parisian poems that are "read in the maquis,
in the prisons. That gave him no pride, no joy. But fear. Panic. Was
he as good as the men, as their explosions, their historic vocation?
Does he know their fear, can he despise heroism as much as they
who do not acknowledge that they are heroes?" (Haddad 1961,
29). He knows that he is deluded to believe that writing can give
identity, can replace speech, can give authority. The reality is that
writing, which demanded physical separation from Algeria, is a
form of exile.

Throughout his time in Paris and his affair with the French
woman Monique—his best friend's wife—Khaled longs for his
wife, Ourida. Like so many women in this literature, she stayed in
Algeria when her husband left: "Ourida watches the rain, in Algeria. In France, Khaled looks straight into the eyes of boredom,
his own" (35). Why did Khaled leave? Was he afraid? Or did the
need to write override all other feelings? Writing and his love for
his wife—whom he identifies with Algeria—became his bonds
with his country. He dreams of her as loyal and unchanging. He
cannot imagine that his departure could change anything. The
ironic end is prefigured in a report of a hit-and-run accident: "The
car did not slow down. . . . The man and the woman were no

longer embracing. The wild fig tree culled the lovers' blood on its broad leaves" (106). Haddad then flashes back to Khaled who is still singing to Monique of his undying, unshakable love for Ourida. Next day he opens the newspaper, and he turns to the Trivial News section. He reads: "In Constantine, Boulevard of the Abyss, terrorists assassinated a Muslim woman and a lieutenant paratrooper. The unfortunate victim had confirmed her belief in a French Algeria by participating in a tour with General X. Several months before, she had separated from her husband, the pseudowriter Khaled Ben Tobal who is only permitted to continue writing because of the absence of authorities" (116). Two dreams—his love and his self-worth as writer and long-distance nationalist—shattered in an instant, and Khaled realizes that his "only distinction will have been to have believed in shit. To be shit" (119). The fragmentation of the end of the novel into shorter and shorter paragraphs is mimetic of Khaled's own dissolution. His wife and his country had ceased to be his when he left. In this last war novel, Haddad explicitly states that when an Algerian leaves the war zone, he forfeits his birthright. All attempts to construct an identity by claiming to write for Algeria are part of a tragic farce. And although Ourida might be dead, she would live on forever as a testament to Khaled Ben Tobal's incalculable insignificance.[12]

Postbellum Constructions

Between 1962 and 1967 intellectuals began to shape the War Story. It was a great victory. Although many men, particularly those writing in Arabic, produced encomiums to the war and particularly to the women who participated, the women writers remained skeptical. A well-known example is Zoubeida Bittari's *O mes soeurs musulmanes, pleurez!* (1964). Many are quick to point out that this is not a major work; they cite the schoolgirl French and the simplistic autobiographical style. Yet is this not a familiar criticism of any work that unsettles status quo by chronicling women's experience?

Bittari scarcely mentions the war, yet the story—written in exile in France—tells an otherwise almost inexplicable growth in feminist consciousness. The heroine is married at the age of twelve, she is persecuted by her mother-in-law, and then, she is repudiated. Contrary to expectation, she does not feel helpless; her new independent status gives her insight into her situation and a sense of power. She even works for a French couple. When "the husband" comes to reconcile we can read her strength. Whereas until then she had referred to him with the distance of the third person, she addresses him on page 146 with the almost contemptuous familiarity of the second person. Calling him an "imbecile," she mocks his overtures and ends up taking him to court. She is awarded custody of her son, and she warns him that he will "learn how a mother who is separated from her son suffers. . . . You thought that being a man you were strong. But French justice does not allow you to oppress the weaker sex. You must respect it. Obey it" (Bittari 1964, 149). Woman, she announces defiantly is "not born to be a servant, but to be man's equal" (164). She helps others to reach this awareness. Despite misgivings about her stepmother, she defends this woman against her natural father. Written two years after the end of the war, the novel indicts traditional values and calls for awareness of oppression and for women's community.

Bittari's work foreshadows later literature that criticizes the revolution and its reactionary outcome that included increase in polygamy and divorce. The French who had been the enemy are surprisingly recuperated by some writers as being Algerian women's supporters. It is as though after 130 years of colonial rule and French integration into Algerian society, it was no longer possible for the Algerians to divorce themselves entirely from their colonial past. To be authentic no longer equaled conformity to some originary identity. To strip Algerian identity of French influence would not uncover a pure authenticity but rather a multiply layered identity that comprised Arab, Berber, and various tribal elements in addition to the French. Bittari's novel is one of the first to recognize a French participation in constructing Algerian history and identity, a participation that was not always bad.

Soon after the revolution the sociologist Fadela M'Rabet published *La femme algérienne* (1964) and *Les algériennes* (1967). In the first study, she seems to praise President Ahmed Ben Bella for his inaugural speech at the July 1964 Congress when he claimed that the "liberation of women is not a secondary matter to be appended to other objectives. It is a problem whose solution must precede any form of socialism" (M'Rabet 1983, 12). In *Les algériennes,* she quotes another apparently profeminist official declaration. On International Women's Day 1966 President Boumedienne reassured women that the projected Personal Code would not deprive them of their rights, "our policy in connection with women is clear . . . and in the interests of Algerian society. Our revolution will only be complete when everyone, including women, participates effectively" (239–40). M'Rabet exposes these statements as well as the 1962 Tripoli Program and the 1964 Algiers Pact, which claimed to recognize women's contributions and rights, as empty rhetoric: if men are not prepared to change and allow women to act out their potential, all the lovely words in the world will make no difference (86, 246). Why not, she asks, form "brigades of military women to guard over women's peace and security"? (87). Later, she remonstrates with those men who "gliby repeat that Algerian women won all their rights during the war" (237). No woman in her right mind would say such a thing. M'Rabet cites many true stories she has been told and letters she has been sent to convince the reader that these rights are far from won. In *Les algériennes,* she targets an Islam that has been misinterpreted by men as tradition and she asserts that such a tradition is a "collection of prohibitions" (225). Indeed, patriarchy benefited from the revolution.

What is striking about both these works is that they scarcely allude to the war. M'Rabet demands attention to women without compelling a remembering of the war as a time when the women had been needed and had been effective. She is writing about women, not about women's stories with the war and particularly not about the transformation brought about when experience is recorded. She scarcely reflects about the reasons for the suppression of the importance of women's participation in the War Story. Her primary concerns are those of feminists anywhere: education (or the lack thereof), bad and arranged marriages, prohibition on women marrying foreigners, persistent polygamy, overpopulation because of women's ignorance (M'Rabet 1983, 229), the importance of breaking the link between femininity and maternity. When she does refer to the war it is in negative terms: since independence polygamy and divorce have increased (105, 181); no research is being conducted into women's high suicide rates (165–66). Yet she does presage the later writings that decry women's silence when she writes, "If to be human, as opposed to being vegetable or mineral, is defined by speaking [*la parole*], freedom of action, of planning, of deciding, then women are not human . . . women's language, like that of animals is reduced to the expression of emotions. Just as one does not converse with a parrot so one does not converse with a woman. . . . Deprived of speech, of rights, reduced to the state of nature, women . . . find themselves excluded from political action" (14–15). It is unthinkable that such creatures might change. By 1967, in *Les algériennes*, M'Rabet demonstrates that the silencing has become quite virulent: "In February 1965, a week before the celebration of International Women's Day, the only program on Algerian Radio that gave a forum to women's problems was closed down. The director has ordered that the growing number of letters women are sending to the broadcasting station be thrown out" (161).

In the same year that *Les algériennes* was published, Djebar brought out *Les alouettes naïves*, a novel she had written between 1962 and 1965. Flashbacks, abrupt changes in narrator and in type face, volatile tenses, many reflexive verbs—all point to a carefully crafted text. It is a reflection of a "war [which] is often only a life led according to a disharmonious rhythm" (Djebar 1967, 228) and in which what is "essential is not the memory of the fighting but of its rhythm . . . the greatest curse is a kind of torpor" (410). In this novel Djebar writes of those, like Omar, "whom History has devoured" (397). Five years have elapsed since independence and writers are beginning to take stock. Who really won? What did winning entail? What happened to those who fought and sacrificed? *Les alouettes naïves* revolves around the lives of three couples who participated in some way: Nessima and Omar, the intellectual narrator with whom Djebar identifies;[13] Julie and Farid; and, finally, the legendary lovers, Nafissa and Rachid, Omar's brother.

In *Alouettes naïves* we do read of heroines—Lila, Fatouma, and Nadjia (see Cadi-Mostefai 1978, 163)—modeled on women like Jamila Boupacha and Jamila Buhrayd, and politics are indirectly evoked.[14] But the focus of this novel is personal relations. Like their predecessors in *Les enfants du nouveau monde*, all three women are preoccupied by love and their need for a man and an escape from personal failure (Djebar 1967, 334). At university Nafissa meets Karim, falls in love, and becomes engaged at the age of nineteen. She accompanies him to the maquis, where he is killed. Later she meets Rachid and falls passionately in love. Rachid reciprocates but finds himself adored by Julie. Julie's husband, Farid, maintains a low profile as Julie pines for the man she knows she can never have. Finally, Nessima longs for Omar, who longs for Nafissa (as he does for all the women whom Rachid has loved). The declarations of the lovers to the reluctant beloveds are uncontrolled and often banal (240, 254, 280–89, 330). Throughout Djebar reiterates the explicitly erotic bond that holds Nafissa and Rachid together (e.g., 164–88).

The space around these Racinian couples is filled with shadows, most of them veiled. Again and again, Djebar introduces women as veiled, belonging to a world apart (79, 101, 147). This world and those veils are not described as oppressive but rather as seductive and safe: they encompass the one who sees but is not seen (e.g., 102, 104). They evoke a special ephemeral femininity. When Nafissa wears the veil for the first time, she "was proud to demonstrate that she could drape the veil with confidence. . . . Nafissa followed her companions through the dark streets. Her gait became more harmonious: she discovered a hitherto unnoticed *majesty*" (102; my emphasis). The *hammam* (public bath) is a "*kingdom* of whispering shadows" (129; my emphasis). When she leaves the *hammam*, Nafissa feels as though "she had returned from an enchanted world that did not know the others; that is, the men" (132). The veiled women are described as "alone, they glide along in the twilight like translucent goddesses" (194). In each case, the segregated past is imbued with majesty and sanctity. Is Djebar admiring women's strength and solidarity? Structure seems far from meaning, since the context militates against such an interpretation: women's bliss is said to derive precisely from their ignorance. Nessima tells Nafissa that she envies her *un*liberated mother: "You walk on with eyes closed, listening only to your instinct. In the desert, that is the only way one has a chance of arriving" (294–96).

The book ends in despair with a visit to a psychiatric hospital full of "women recently returned from the front" or from the forests of the maquis (414, 415). The women fighters have lost their minds. Djebar develops the theme in the short story "Femmes d'Alger dans leur appartement" (which she published with collected essays in 1980). Djebar revisits the "fire carriers against whose eyes and stomachs the bombs still explode" (Djebar 1980, 61–62). The fighters have become drug addicts and prostitutes. Participation forced women into the public realm so that people could say: "Our women are our men" (230). But then when they return no one knows what to do with them; they are not quite ostracized, yet they are not integrated. They find themselves on the razor's edge, neither virtuous nor dishonorable, while being both. Their families were proud of their heroine daughters, their "real Muslim daughters" (407). At the same time they could not come to terms with these "good Muslims" who were also part of their families. Neither vestal nor virgin, they became marginalized. What had been a strength during the war became a liability in peace. At the beginning of *Alouettes naïves,* Nafissa and some other *femmes-soldats* (44) are ambushed by the French. When the French realize who their captives are they exclaim: "Ah! There they are!. . . . The larks [*allouettes*]!" (39). This line is echoed almost 400 pages later when the reader is told that the *alouettes naïves* of the title are "the prostitute-dancers . . . symbols at once of an external decline and an altogether anonymous internal light" (423). These are the women who participated and about whom Omar mused, as though echoing the sentiments of Haddad's narrator in *L'élève et la leçon:* "I don't know how, but thinking of today's heroines, I remember yesterday's prostitutes . . . maybe because they are unexpected. Yet they are not prostitutes, nor are they part of a respectable harem of cloistered wives. What is to be done with these war heroines? How are we to act with them?" (235). How, indeed can these women be fitted into prewar categories? They cannot. For the time being, they are in the "Heroines' House" (237). In their splendid isolation they are exceptionalized and can eventually be forgotten.

It is not only in literature but also in reality that they were neglected: in 1970 Algerian radio adapted Djebar's play *Rouge l'aube* (written in 1960) and omitted all references to women's struggle in the war. By 1971 women's participation could not only be omitted but also denounced. Moustapha Toumi published a poem, entitled "Femme, femme, femme" in *El-Moudjahid* in which he criticized women whose behavior he considered unseemly and praised those who were conservative. Djebar describes these conservative women metonymically, they are the "veils" that had never before dared to appear in public (Djebar 1967, 424). So that is what happened to the women: the fighters were locked away so as to make room for the "veils." The women who had stepped into the public realm had opened a crack; they had paid the price and now others were beginning to emerge.

At this transitional phase there is considerable ambiguity about women's roles and power. The men in *Les alouettes naïves*, like male protagonists in Algerian men's literature of this revolution, register a loss of authority, even of identity. When Julie asks Omar, "What are you looking for?" using the intimate and singular *tu*, he replies: "I? During this war I've become so used to saying 'we'" (389). When Omar realizes that he has truly lost Nafissa, he is angry: he cannot hope to possess her because she had become "like others of her sex, independent" (329). Si Othman also is disturbed by these new independent women, represented by his daughters. He feels that he who had once been the "master, was today merely a man who trembles" (408). The women, however, do not see themselves in this light. The men's perceived loss of authority is not paralleled by women's growing sense of power. Djebar describes in this novel what can be read in earlier novels by both men and women: there is radical dissonance between male and female perceptions of gender roles consequent to the war. While the men are threatened, the women remain unaware.

During the 1970s Algerian women began to reassess what they had done during the revolution and how they had been treated afterwards. An interesting interim work that links the early unreflective mode with women's later recriminations about their silence is Yasmina Mechakra's *La grotte éclatée* (1986 [1979]). This novel, in the form of a nurse's journal, was written in 1973 but not published until 1979. It chronicles the events of November 1955 (when the author was one year old!) through July 1962. Kateb Yacine's introduction explains that as a child Mechakra had seen her father tortured and killed. It is not surprising, therefore, that one of the first vignettes should be particularly grisly: "I dragged myself to the bloody corpse. My lips brushed the gaping throat, slowly I licked the blood of the beast that had fed off the flesh of a man who was sleeping somewhere in the shade of a rock, his stomach exploded by a shell" (Mechakra 1986 [1979], 17). The narrator has been hiding out in the maquis for a week with two men; they are starving and she finally nerves herself to share with a jackal the fresh blood of a human corpse. She endures the same hardships as the men, and at one point describes herself as "bold, red-eyed from lack of sleep, hard-lipped, and the earrings hanging from her lobes made her look like a real mountain brigand" (26).

The novel romanticizes the resistance as existing beyond the "laws of impure men" (33). It condemns the intellectuals and the pacifists for their cowardice (60). The narrator marries an "authentic revolutionary, an illiterate who had learned the Revolution one night in November 1954, when he watched his mother throw off her veil" (69). There are moments, however, when the reader begins to suspect the wide-eyed wonder of this child of the revolution. When the nineteen-year-old narrator becomes pregnant, she talks enthusiastically of her body renewing the fighters, but then the cave in which they were hiding is blown up. There is little of romance in what follows: she loses an arm and her two-month-old baby son is brutally maimed by the napalm, and in a perversely ironic move the mother turns to the shreds of this tiny body to renew herself (95, 107). The heavy irony continues as we read of the ways in which her contributions to the war have been recognized: stars are pinned to her armless shoulder, while bandages protect her napalm-burned legs; she is promoted to the rank of lieutenant, and she is named "heroine" (100). She adopts Algeria, its mountains, and its cities as her sons. But it is her destroyed son, gradually going mad from his injuries, who is her "Ariadne's thread into the future centuries" (121). The last third of the book is an elegy and a plea that there will be more children (more like her maimed son or more like her adopted country?) to hold on to the memories. Images of explosions recur throughout, as though to emphasize the violent action and the lack of control. The narrator praises the resistance as though men only constituted it, while she is by turns the woman masquerading as male fighter and poet or the mother grieving for her son destroyed by napalm or the wife mourning the death of her revolutionary husband. She acts out all the roles the war demanded of her as though these multiple duties were not in any way anomalous. But the tone of the frame undermines the content. When she returns home after the war, she is hobbling, "my feet cratered with napalm, my naked carbonized feet. I gently embraced the burning earth of my country" (173). The last we see of her is her grotesque attempt to walk as she hallucinates the earlier explosion, realizing that only she and nature survive. Even after reading the novel for the second time, I was not sure what was more important: the sacrifice for the country, or the sacrifice.

Toward the end of the 1970s women were recognizing and condemning their silence during the war. But too late. In 1976 Aicha Lemsine published *La chrysalide: chroniques algériennes.* This novel presents a feminist dystopia. Khadidja is dismayed at her husband's collusion with his mother against her. She is recently married and cannot conceive. When traditional methods do not cure her infertility, Khadidja goes secretly to Marielle, the boycotted French woman doctor. She is amazed to find herself spontaneously drawn to this foreign woman as though "united by the same ancestral evil" (Lemsine 1976, 39). I cannot agree with the Algerian critic Ahlem Mosteghanemi, who idealizes this relationship between two individuals who "have only their sex in common" as being the "struggle for the cause of Woman" (Mosteghanemi 1985, 104). Mosteghanemi also lauds Khadidja's courage and innovation in turning to French medicine in an environment where it was profoundly distrusted (198). Her struggle, however, is unavailing. At last Khadidja gives birth to a son but her husband takes a second wife after discovering that childbirth left his wife barren, unable to bear another son.

Khadidja takes the second wife, Akila, into her confidence. She needs companionship and help in her loneliness. The reader who remembers Celie and Shug's friendship in Alice Walker's *Color Purple* might well expect this friendship to symbolize the beginnings of a community of women. But here again, structure is far from meaning; women's solidarity merely serves to darken the tragic conditions in which these women continue to live. It seems to me that Mosteghanemi exaggerates when she describes Khadidja as a "unique case in Algerian literature." She goes on to describe her as a woman who "has the courage to defend all oppressed women in her entourage, even her rival" (Mosteghanemi 1985, 198). In fact, Khadidja cannot even defend herself; she must rely on her son. She is gratified when he goes off to the maquis to fight. This Patriotic Mother now has the courage to stand up to her husband. When he suggests taking on a third wife, she explodes: "Have you not understood the lessons of this war we're living?" (Lemsine 1976, 108–12). Mosteghanemi reads this passage as a strong feminist statement. She quotes: "Assuming the anger of Akila, Faiza, Malika, and Hamia, the anger of all women, she roared. She became 1,000 women!" (Mosteghanemi 1985, 198). Khadidja manages to dissuade her husband from taking the third wife. But for herself and for all the women on whose behalf she "roared," she gains nothing but the honorific title, Lalla Khadidja. Contra Mosteghanemi, I do not read this demand as feminist: she does not aim to subvert the system in which she lives. She wants, and gets, reward within the status quo!

If there is no hope in the older generation, what of the new? Who is the chrysalis of the title? It is Faiza, Akila's daughter. She teaches herself to read and write. When Mouloud, her half brother and Khadidja's son, returns from the war, he takes her to the university (Lemsine 1976, 163–69). By 1965 she is doing brilliantly in medical school. Although her half brother has been a staunch supporter, he is no feminist. One day he announces his engagement to an uneducated girl. Faiza is amazed, especially when Mouloud confesses that he has always been somewhat afraid of highly educated women (191). Faiza comes to terms with the marriage and moves in with the young couple. She continues her studies and considers herself the equal of any man (213). Then one day Faisal walks into her life and Faiza feels like "the traveler who has finally reached his goal . . . she knew that he was the one she had always awaited" (219). Until this book it was only male writers like the Egyptian Ihsan Abd al-Qaddus and the Lebanese Habshi al-Ashqar who had written so eloquently of the futility of women's education. There is not enough irony in the following exclamation: "Fortunately, there are men in this country. They know how to get rid of the powerful foreigner. They'll know how to control you, my daughters!" (239). The melodrama reaches its climax when Faisal is killed. Faiza is pregnant and she decides to have the baby in the village, where she finds support for what before would have been punishable by death. Such romanticism stretches credulity: can the liberated brilliant woman really prefer to live in a village with the illegitimate child of an impossible love rather than to pursue a career?

During the 1980s Djebar published the first two volumes of her quartet.[15] In *Ombre sultane* (1986) the romance of the harem—a place of female bonding—inexplicably persists. Djebar writes again of the drama of unveiling: how strange it was "to be able to let go of the edge of the material, to look with face uncovered. Even to look up to the sky, as I did when I was ten" (Djebar 1986, 27). How wonderful to unveil, but also how dangerous; it entails exclusion (53). In 1986 she calls militantly for universal unveiling, for an assertion of individuality (42). The protagonist's daughter challenges her mother in the following terms: "No. It's your fault, Mom. Your fault. If only you did not run to him every time he hits the slipper on the floor to summon you. If only you did not even stand up" (143). In this literature, activism on behalf of women's rights seems to be in its infancy.

Djebar hints at the reasons for the neglect of women's revolutionary accomplishments: silence. At the time no one, not even the women, spoke out on behalf of women. It was only in retrospect that awareness dawned. Although in *Les alouettes naïves* Nafissa warns, "I'm forgetting the war" (Djebar 1967, 298), she is alone in her perception. By 1980 this neglect by women of the war and its impact on women has become a leitmotiv. In *Femmes d'Alger dans leur appartement,* a collection of essays written during and soon after the war but not published until 1980, Djebar constantly reiterates the lack of, and the need for, the feminine voice: "My voice does not reach them. It stays inside. . . . I am the collective voice . . . that touches one, embraces another" (Djebar 1980, 15, 145). Women *must* speak, *must* ask if there had ever been brothers, *must* tell the world of their experiences of prison and torture. A young woman muses: "I've always had problems with words" (62–63). Later she tells of her time in the Barberousse prison: "I howled silently. . . . All the others could see was my silence" (65). Yet once she does talk, it is as though talking has made her realize both the importance of talking and the dangers of silence. She announces categorically: "There's only one way Arab women can unblock everything. They must talk. They must keep on talking of yesterday and today!" (68). If they do not talk, they will get nothing. In "Les morts parlent" (written in 1970 and 1978 but not anthologized until 1980), another young woman is described as having "kept a morose silence during the war" (126).

In her autobiographical novel *Fantasia: An Algerian Cavalcade* (1993 [1985]), which is also the first volume of her quartet, Assia Djebar searches through the word-corpses of the past to understand this silence. In a mix of history, fiction, interviews and autobiography, Djebar strives to make some women visible and above all audible, so that they might cease to be "bodies bereft of voices" (Djebar 1993 [1985], 156). This three-part novel, which is primarily concerned with her relationship to her father, is presented as a musical arrangement whose third part is organized as a symphony harmonizing eight of the many lost voices of women fighters. Some clamor, some murmur, some whisper, some dialogue, some soliloquize, and several embrace. The novel is about the Algerians' unremitting refusal of the French colonial presence, the constant role of women in the resistance, everyone's silence about women's participation, and the crime of this silence: she remembers her grandmother with tenderness but also with pain: "Only her former silence continues to hurt me today" (197). How can she change a culture that demands of women that they be resigned and silent, that deprives them of the ability to tell their stories in the first person until they are old when "they use this 'I' against the younger women so as to control them" (15)? How is it that girls must be silent when they have been given the gift of four languages: "French for secret missives; Arabic for our stifled aspirations towards God-the-Father, the God of the religions of the Book; Lybico-Berber which takes us back to the pagan idols—mother-gods—of pre-Islamic Mecca. The fourth language, for all females, young or old, cloistered or half-emancipated, remains that of the body . . . which, in trances, dances or vociferations, in fits of hope or despair, rebels, and unable to read or write, seeks some unknown shore as destination for its message of love" (180). She is celebrating a linguistic hybridity that should empower women to speak and communicate with many; but she is at the same time lamenting the multiple and multilingual silences.

The women in the first resistance to the French were silent in the 1830s, so were their granddaughters in the war of independence, and so had she been. How can she understand her past silence? She compares her experiences with those of women during two periods of Algerian national resistance to the French: the first, during the fifteen years following the French landing on Algerian shores in 1830; the second, during the revolution. Her sources for the nineteenth century are thirty-two flowery, formal chronicles written around the 1830s campaigns by little known French captains; for the revolution, she uses interviews she conducted with women fighters; for her own story, she pieces together written and spoken records with vignettes from her own past. But she finds the truth of her past mixing and blurring with the stories of these other women whom she had actually heard or those whom she had only imagined. She struggles to hold on to a multilingual past that the tyranny of French threatens to reduce to sameness, strangeness: "Autobiography practiced in the enemy's language has the texture of fiction, at least as long as you are desensitized by forgetting the dead that writing resurrects. While I thought I was undertaking a 'journey through myself,' I find I am simply choosing another veil. While I intended every step forward to make me more clearly identifiable, I find myself progressively sucked down into the anonymity of those women of old—my ancestors!" (216–17). How can she, "twenty years later, claim to revive these stifled voices? And speak for them? Shall I not at best find dried-up streams? What ghosts will be conjured up when in this absence of expressions of love, I see the reflection of my own barrenness, my own aphasia" (202). Her silence is intimately tied up with her body and its pathological inability to produce. It cannot produce another body, it cannot produce a voice. The association of body—both living and dead—and voice is a theme resonating throughout this novel. Sometimes the voice is a living being, sometimes it is a stinking cadaver.

After their long silence these women did not know how to speak; their voices were mutilated. Djebar describes a woman, herself perhaps, in the late 1960s walking down a street in Paris. A man is following her and she is surprised by the sound of her own voice that issues as a stranger from her throat after years of imprisonment: "One single, prolonged, interminable, amorphous tear-drop, a precipitate congealed in the very body of my former voice, in my frozen larynx; this nameless coagulate is washed away in a trail of unidentifiable rubble. . . . This nauseating network of sounds seems scarcely to concern me; viscous syrup of rasping gasps, guano of old hiccups and choking sobs, smelling of some strangled corpse rotting within me. The voice, my voice (or rather the voice that issues from my open mouth, gaping as if to vomit or chant some dirge) cannot be suppressed. Perhaps I ought to raise my hand in front of my face to staunch this invisible blood?" (115). This voice is disgusting, putrid because it has lived and died as a separate suppressed entity inside her. The fetus-voice that should have sought its freedom outside her body had died and rotted within. The dead voice manifests itself in numerous forms: it can be *seen* as a congealed teardrop washed away with some rubble; it can be *tasted* like syrup; it can be *smelled* for it is both guano and decomposing flesh; its liquidity can be *touched* as coagulated teardrops, viscous syrup, vomit, and blood; it can be heard as rasping gasps, old hiccups, choking sobs, attempted chanting. The narrator is in shock at what she has involuntarily produced.

But this sound, these cries (*les cris*), are not so different from their homonym, the written (*l'écrit*). I have found it useful to compare this passage with one written by the French literary critics Gilles Deleuze and Félix Guattari to describe Kafka's interest in the notion of sound without meaning, one that signals the straightening of a head bent in submission. This sound, they explain, is "always connected *to its own abolition*, a deterritorialized musical sound, a cry that escapes signification, composition, song, words, a sonority that ruptures in order to break away from a chain that is still all too signifying." The chain in this case is of course the chain of silence, and the cry can be quickly absorbed, abolished. Deleuze and Guattari even use the same language as Djebar does to articulate the process of deterritorialization initiated by the cry: "He [Kafka] will turn syntax into a cry that will embrace the rigid syntax of this dried up German. He will push it toward a deterritorialization . . . even if it is slow, sticky, coagulated. To bring language slowly and progressively to the desert. To use syntax in order to cry, to give a syntax to the cry" (Deleuze and Guattari 1986 [1975], 6, 26). That is indeed the answer: to catch the revolutionary moment in the sound-straightened head and turn it into writing. The constant juxtaposition of these homonyms thus translates into a mandate to turn the cries into writing, *les cris* into *l'écrit*. She must preserve in ink the transient outburst, transfigure uncontrol but also anger and fear into a symbol of power that can be circulated among others. Only thus can *les cris* empower others.

The Frenchman ceases to be a menace in comparison with the fear inspired by the narrator's own voice. Gently, he interrupts her reverie about her "involuntary *lamento*," protesting: "Please, Madame, please don't cry out like that!" (Djebar 1993 [1985], 116). This predator has acquired humanity. How? Ironically, through *his voice* which is described as "warm, vibrant, quavering slightly from the urgency of his request." When he walks away, she describes that strange encounter as a "fantasy embrace." The potential rapist has become the possible lover! But this remains a love that divides her against herself. It is with her people, with her brothers and her lover-friends that "I finally recover my power of speech. . . . At last, voice answers to voice and body can approach body" (129). A stark contradiction? The French gave her writing which then took her voice; Algerian men will be the ones to restore it.

The novel begins in the early 1940s with Assia's hand in that of her father, the teacher at the local French school. It is her father who introduced her to French, he who is thus made responsible for her being cut off from her mother tongue. She is deeply ambivalent about her relationship to her father, an Algerian man who introduced her to the language of the colonizer. He cuts her off from her mother's words, "the rich vocabulary of love of my mother tongue" that is the only language in which love can be expressed (4, 62, 128). This autobiographical project is in some ways her attempt to reconnect with her mother's language.

Writing and voice are constantly juxtaposed and contrasted. Writing, necessarily in French, is "denial of my body," (59) that is connected with voice. But it provides a "relief from deep inner hurt" (154). Writing can enable voice. In this case, her writing of the voices of the silenced, segregated women of her society can empower both the writer and those written: "What if the maiden does write? Her voice, albeit silenced, will circulate. . . . As if the French language suddenly had eyes, and lent them to me to see into liberty; as if the French language blinded the peeping-toms of my clan and, at this price, I could move freely, run headlong down every street, annex the outdoors for my cloistered companions, for the matriarchs of my family who endured a living death. . . . I know that every language is a dark depository for piled-up corpses, refuse, sewage, but faced with the language of the former conqueror, which offers me its ornaments, its jewels, its flowers, I find they are the flowers of death—chrysanthemums on tombs!" (3, 181). Swept away by the enthusiasm of the writing act, she gives herself a license to speak for others until she is suddenly caught by her realization of the cut between French writing and their Arab and Berber voices. She sees once again that the voices have been killed. How can she stop her language, her French, from destroying their Arabic and Berber languages? How can she turn the freedom she gained with French into freedom for others?

Writing defies men's prohibition on women's voices. It is the way to trespass on men's space by annexing "the outdoors for my cloistered companions, for the matriarchs of my family who endured a living death." French offers her ornaments that turn out, however, to be flowers of death. Then, in yet another paradox, she claims these flowers of death as a salvation: they "brought me to the cries of the women silently rebelling in my youth, to my own true origins. *Writing does not silence the voice, but awakens it, above all to resurrect so many vanished sisters*" (204; my emphasis). Writing in French allows her to respond to the peasant woman who had lamented to her: "Alas! We can't read or write. We don't leave any accounts of what we lived through and all we suffered! . . . You'll see other people who spent their time crouching in holes and who, afterwards, told what they've told!" (148).

Djebar writes a reality out of the fragments of the past that will contest those other fragments from crouching cowards by showing their very fragmentedness. Writing re-members what others have mutilated. Writing creates connections. She writes with amusement about the daughters of the local religious leader who wrote love letters to strangers all over the world, hoping that one of them would come to save them from their dark and dreary fates (11–13). Writing is dangerously enmeshed in love; it helps "to lift the veil and at the same time keep secret that which must remain secret. . . . The word is a torch" (62). Later, she intensifies the ambivalence of these "torch-words which light up my women-companions, my accomplices; these words divide me from them once and for all" (142). To write is to have a silent voice. Djebar is rebelling against what happened to women, yet her only route to freedom is the production of this contradictory autobiography, in which she negotiates the borderlands between her two cultures. Writing the body locates the space between memory and language, a space that will always remain removed. Djebar is simultaneously creating and questioning her identity; she is writing to find voices—her own and those of others—that had been silenced. She is writing into the fissures and the gaps that she has uncovered in the French men's colonizing discourse produced a century and a half earlier.

Writing connects, resurrects, creates, but it is always also the tool of those who would dominate, oppress, and silence. Somewhere between these two incompatible instrumentalities, Djebar is looking for a writing location that will allow her to protect her healing words from co-optation while assuring the effectiveness of her contestatory words. As the literary critic Mary Jean Green writes, it is in her style that the author finds such a middle way, in the "narrative constructed by Djebar the texts of the colonizers themselves appear only in fragmented citations, interwoven with her own words: the text itself thus creates the possibility of a dialogue absent from the historical record" (Green 1993, 962). Djebar reads the French failure into their records of "rape" of a "motionless and mysterious" woman "impossible to tame" (Djebar 1993 [1985], 7, 56–57). Contempt rings loud in her description of these messengers of the *mission civilisatrice* as French peasants who "only know how to milk a cow" (24). They wrote to savor "the seducer's triumph, the rapist's intoxication. . . . And words themselves become a decoration, flaunted by officers like the carnations they wear in their buttonholes; words will become their most effective weapons . . . to hide the initial violence from view" (44–45). Djebar claims to be "strangely haunted by the agitation of the killers, by their obsessional unease" (57). She even goes so far as to thank Pelissier, the leader who ordered the massacre of hundreds of Berber villagers in a cave during the 1830s, because he had written of an event she would otherwise not have discovered. He had had remorse and had "looked on the enemy otherwise than as a horde of zealots or a host of ubiquitous shadows" (78). He had demanded that the corpses be brought out, and in the heat of the sun they were "transmuted into words" (75). It is as though Pelissier had personally handed her these corpse-words. These are the words that she is now using against the scribes.[16]

She is looking for the history of her people in the gaps and spaces of these men's writings. Women, too, should beware lest the love that they commit to paper be thus examined and then used against them. Writing should be used rather to disguise love (58) because it cannot express "the slightest heart-felt emotion" (128). Writing means to "travel to fresh pastures and replenish my water skins with an inexhaustible silence," this silence which is as rich and as heavy as "brocaded gold" (63, 109). Writing reveals the fear that it is trying to repress.

Invisible eyes watch these envoys of the French Revolution whose paradoxical project is to deprive North Africans of their *liberté, fraternité, égalité* (16, 39). Djebar may not have access to these women's words but their invisible presence haunts her thoughts about nineteenth-century Algerian history as well as about the revolution. The writer is suspended between these men, whose language will become hers to write, and the "invisible eyes," whose silent voices she is trying to hear across the chasm of more than a century. These women may not have left any written records but that does not mean that they were not there. She writes them into her story as witnesses to the invasion whose eyes plant the vessels "above the glassy surface of the water" (8). She knows they were there, not only because they obviously were (where is the society without women?), but also because she has read accounts of two women who so terrified some Frenchmen that they recorded their actions in a text that otherwise systematically erased all mention of women. These two ferocious tribal women prefigured the "future Muslim 'mater dolorosa'" (18–19). One had ripped out a Frenchman's heart and the other had crushed her baby's skull when she was hit lest the French capture it. During the revolution the *voyeuses* are "allowed into the party as spies." But what happened afterwards was that these women, like their daughters, "in their own domain, began to impose the veil on others" (204–5). Above all, amongst themselves they told and continued to tell tales that allow Djebar to question the women-erasing French written record. In the first section entitled "Capture of the City," Djebar mixes the Frenchmen's historical narratives of naval blockades of Algiers and the Battle of Staoueli with her personal memories of going to school for the first time and of visits to a village in the summer. She thus reframes the colonizing text in a subversive collage that draws on testimonies of actual women who had fought during the 1950s and 1960s.

The women fighters were tough, tougher than the men who gave in to pressure and especially to torture (138, 147). A peasant woman who had been taken a prisoner of war reported that the men had told her: "Come back here with one of your sisters; we need you up here!" (118). She escapes to them in time to see her brother shot. When she comes back at night after helping the *maquisards,* her mother says nothing. This war allowed transgressions of social norms of segregation; the most nubile of women could wander freely among men in the dark because they were fighting for their country. Djebar calls this peasant woman Cherifa, like the Cherifa of *Les enfants du nouveau monde.* The choice of the name connects these two novels written about the same subject but at an interval of twenty-three years. In 1962, the veiled Cherifa timidly ventures out of her house when her politically engaged husband is in danger and she is the one who must inform him. She has done her duty and does not feel that this act has changed her. The 1985 Cherifa reminisces about the men's expressed need for the women. She is there in the melee, sees her brother killed, and makes sure, Antigone-like, that his body is washed so that it will not remain unsanctified, even if she cannot bury it. She knows that she was needed and remembers what her special contribution was.

Djebar contrasts revolutionary women in the war of independence with the nineteenth-century men, particularly the *goumiers,* a term used to designate the Algerian men who had enlisted with the French. She is critical of those who merely mouthed the party line. A peasant woman complains: "All the men I used to depend on, all those men have gone" (200). A woman in Paris with her fiancé insists on returning to Algeria to fight. Like the French Suzanne in *Les enfants du nouveau monde,* this is an Algerian woman who feels the draw of the land. Her bourgeois revolutionary boyfriend objects that there are no other women student fighters, only "peasants used to the forests and brambles." She counters, "were not the Nationalist leaders anxious to make it known that all were equal in the struggle?" But her boyfriend is no socialist; he is unwilling to mix with the peasants in a "homeland [that] seemed no more real than a sunken city or a desolate ruin" (103–4).

Djebar's writings of the late 1970s and 1980s betray a cautious, highly fraught attraction to the French. She seems to feel that since Eugène Delacroix—whose painting gave her the title for her 1980 collection of short stories and showed, Djebar believed, unusual understanding of Algerian women's circumstances—French men have understood Algerian women in a way that the Algerian men never did, perhaps because they could not. Djebar is less concerned than Palestinian women to dance through the minefields of competing allegiances to nation, culture and gender. She is not afraid to admit her fascination: "For me, these French homes gave off a different smell, a mysterious light; for me, the French are still 'The Others', and I am still hypnotized by their shores" (23). Yet these men can also be called the "vilest of men from the dominant society" who could never assume "the cloak of seducer in women's eyes" (128). So what of the Frenchman who had pursued her and with whom she had exchanged the fantasy embrace? And what of Eugène Fromentin, whose painting helped her to fit another piece into the puzzle of her past? In 1853 he visited an oasis where a massacre has taken place and "picks up out of the dust the severed hand of an anonymous Algerian woman. . . . Later, I seize on this living hand, hand of mutilation and memory, and I attempt to bring it the *qalam*" (226). The last unglossed word means pen. It was Fromentin's vision that put her in touch with an unknown heroine. A French orientalist painter actually presents her with a dead woman's hand that she can imagine herself reviving and empowering to record its experience. She can give this unknown soldier a silent voice.

Women's texts on the war of liberation indicate that strong, self-conscious heroines during the war were more or less a fiction. Even critics like Mosteghanemi, who try to portray the blossoming of feminist consciousness, admit that the revolution "did not shake the social structures" (Mosteghanemi 1985, 222–30). Hélie-Lucas writes that "even in the hardest times of the struggle, women were oppressed, confined to tasks that would not disturb social order in the future. Although these tasks were essential, they should not have absorbed all female energy. One woman bore arms, none was in a decision-making position! sixty-five dealt with bombs in the urban sectors [probably carrying spare parts!], and there were two political commissaires!" (Hélie-Lucas 1990, 107). So much for Fanon's and others' myth of Algerian women liberated along with their country. Only later did women acknowledge the participation of other women and perceive its potential significance to feminist consciousness.

Interviews with women fighters from other parts of the world suggest that involvement in some aspect of war does not necessarily entail raised feminist consciousness. D'Ann Campbell explains that after World War II women were not "coerced *en masse* to 'return' to the home: most of them had never left it to begin with, and those who had shared the domestic dreams of those who had not" (Campbell 1990, 7). A Jewish woman who fought the British in Palestine said: "And anyway, we girls weren't fighting to prove anything. . . . I have no hang ups about feminism. I fought when there was no choice, but when I was no longer needed in that role I was happy to move on to something else" (Saywell 1985, 189).

In Algeria novelists like Débèche, Amrouche, Djebar, and Lemsine as well as poets like Nadia Guendouz, Anna Greki, Danièle Amran, and Leila Djabali wrote during the war, but they wrote alone and without commitment to a women's cause that could stand side by side along with, but not under, the nationalist cause. Unlike the Beirut Decentrists who wrote as a "group" on the Lebanese civil war (Cooke 1988), or the Palestinian women who wrote of the need for a women's agenda as they saw the Intifada erode their roles (see below), the Algerian women writers did not share a sense of moment. The war was not so much a consciousness-raising event as an exciting interlude in the gray monotony of an unchanging routine. In *Les alouettes naïves* Djebar describes the women who fought feeling "as though they were playing a game." Nafissa exclaims: "In the maquis I was alive. Here I'm dreaming" (Djebar 1967, 37, 110). As though anticipating this sentiment, Jean Bethke Elshtain quotes a French woman who said of World War II: "You know that I do not love war or want it to return. But at least it made me feel alive, as I have not felt alive before or since" (Elshtain 1987, 10). The fictive Algerian woman and the real French woman both recall the war as an experience of alive-ness.

A brief survey of men's writings after the revolution indicates a change in male portrayal of women who participated. The anxiety of the war years has dissipated. Mouloud Mammeri's *L'opium et le bâton* (1965) is a highly acclaimed dramatization of the revolution that was written three years after independence. Characters are reduced to stereotypes who act out highly determined roles, even including a male Touma who rejected his own culture and religion in the hopes of profiting from the French. The anguished self-questioning of Malek Haddad's intellectual in Paris has given way to formulaic rejection of writing and advocacy of militancy. Bashir, Mammeri's intellectual who is a doctor, is shown at the beginning of the book and the revolution as being almost trapped into marriage by Claude, his conniving French girlfriend. The revolution is his salvation. The threat posed by women is restricted to a dream in which Bashir sees his mother with her cold eyes and her right hand "furiously spurring on her horse" and her left hand "furiously shaking a rattle" (Mammeri 1965, 46). Nevertheless, Mammeri does include women who stayed in Algeria while husbands and sons left for Paris (80).

The women fighters are no longer frightening. Farroudja—her name means chick (!)—is used as a decoy. She is shown to be dumb and innocuous since under torture she has nothing worth telling (125, 130). Women are army prostitutes (204), and stereotypes of bitch goddesses are returning en masse (211). Itto, the activist, no longer cares what people think of her: "Tomorrow I shall be gone . . . with you . . . or alone . . . or with some other man. You're crazy! You're married! Do you believe that? Well, take it easy, everyone! I don't plan to abandon him. In a month— no, in 29 days I'll go back to him" (226–27). She is less heroine than camp follower (295). The veil commands everyone's respect: "In the tram the Europeans gave up their seats for veiled women. They used to call them Fatmas, now they said: Please, Madam" (249). Women's attachment to nature, to the trees, is almost mocked (258). Yet it was this very attachment that had made them stay. Then there are women like Titi who have lost their sons and who accept their fate with the stoicism of a Spartan mother by Henri Rousseau dit le Douanier (266). In *L'opium et le bâton*, women are once again helpless victims of men's craving for power.

In 1969 Rachid Boudjedra wrote *La répudiation*. The war is merely alluded to, glimpsed in the interstices of flashback, memory, hallucination, and in the violent staccato of its language. This memoir of a crazy, disillusioned fighter traces through the development of misogyny in the son of a woman repudiated at thirty by her hypocritically religious husband. In an often gratuitously obscene language, Boudjedra documents the sexual experiences and fantasies of a boy born at the end of World War II. This Oedipal tale illustrates the fine line that Algerian women once again walk— the line between lust and disgust. The only woman to be granted a measure of humanity is the repudiated mother. In her moment of greatest pain and with "death on her face" (Boudjedra 1969, 63) she prepares the marriage of her husband to his second wife, and her son finally relates to her not as a sexual being but as an individual. Otherwise women are contemptible: "All the women in the country were organizing clandestinely to march on the seat of government" (242). So they must be threatening! What was their plan? To "Suffocate the president with their farts!" (242). So much for women's power and threat in 1969! Yet tension remains, for the obscene fantasies of women's unbridled sexuality finally drive the protagonist into a psychiatric hospital.

What is the reader to make of the contrasting images of women found in men's and women's writings both during and after the Algerian revolution? Is it possible to claim that any one of them is more correct than another? I think not. The crucial difference lies in perception. In the women's wartime writings, female protagonists are focused on love. When they recognize their oppression, they fight in nonthreatening ways to assert themselves in a traditional world. During the war, and even after, the women seemed oblivious to the import of their actions, unaware that they were challenging the social fabric. The only woman writer to indicate awareness of this dissonance is Assia Djebar. In *Les alouettes naïves* she hints at the gap between men's and women's perceptions of the significance of women's participation. For the men who wrote during the revolution, the specter of radical change overshadows a new world in which male protagonists lie in anxious wait for what the future will unfold. Their women are no longer theirs to control. This incongruence in men's and women's perceptions of women's power during war can be seen in post-World War I English and American writings. Sandra Gilbert and Susan Gubar reinterpret English and American literature of the late nineteenth and twentieth centuries as a battlefield where women and men are fighting for literary primacy. They argue that the increasing numbers of women professionals constituted a threat men tried to parry through their writings. They maintain that the fact that "women have been less confident may seem paradoxical, in view of the resentment with which such men as W. S. Gilbert, T. S. Eliot, D. H. Lawrence, Ernest Hemingway, and Norman Mailer reacted to what they perceived as unprecedented female power. Yet when we turn to works by women who were contemporaries of these men, we find that the female writers have often felt even more imperiled than men did by the sexual combat in which they were obliged to engage. For as is so frequently the case in the history of sex relations, men view the smallest female steps toward autonomy as threatening strides that will strip them of all authority, while women respond to such anxious reaction formations with a nervous sense of guilt and a paradoxical sense of vulnerability" (Gilbert and Gubar 1988, 66, 72).

Since the Algerian women did not recognize the men's trepidation and the impact of their new roles, they did not exploit their opportunity. When the war was over, the men imposed neotraditional demands as part of national self-assertion. They encountered no resistance and quickly patched up their tattered egos. The moment was lost.

> You weren't
> a symbol
> Fatiha Iratni
> weapon in hand

dressed in khaki
that should have been
white
as your purity
you are the forgotten one
from the days of glory
you will be the reminder
of happy days
19 years
without a cry
without a tear
in the maquis
you fell
dead in the village of honor
dead and forgotten
but during this feast
a friend of yours
gave me your name
it's so easy
to render you homage
in our hearts
. . . .
I salute you Fatiha Iratni (Guendouz 1968)

In 1968 Nadia Guendouz was lamenting women's silence. In the 1980s Algerian women are asking themselves why they did not speak and write while they were still active and needed. How was it that over two decades later the women finally spoke up? My hunch is that they were listening to women in comparable situations elsewhere, women who saw and refused the familiar pattern of marginalization. Palestinian women in the Occupied Territories in particular were beginning to speak out in an unprecedented manner. They were demanding attention to the fact that since 1967 they were the ones who had invented a special way of resisting the Israelis and that it had worked. By 1982, with the removal of the Palestine Liberation Organization headquarters from Beirut to Tunis and away from contiguity with Israel, the resistance moved to the Occupied Territories, where women had long been "shaking off" the Israelis. Their sporadic unorganized confrontations had minimized the impact of what would otherwise have been a crushing occupation. By the mid-1980s their proto-intifadas became a magnet for the international press. Algerian women, poised on the edge of civil war, heard their Palestinian sisters insist that they must learn the Algerian Lesson, a lesson that they themselves had absorbed: Speak while you are on the stage—silence is the real crime.

Chapter Four

Talking Democracy

For it is implicit that to speak is to exist absolutely for the other.
    Frantz Fanon (1952)

Our political struggle, for us women, gives us a greater possibility of liberating ourselves from that given to other women in Arab countries at present; but we feel that the liberation of women will only come about within the framework of a socialist society, an authentically social-ist one, since the fate of women is bound with that of society as a whole.
    Mai Sayeh (1986)

For this rise in the political status of women's committees [during the Intifada] was accompanied by an even firmer shelving of the "feminist agenda" than before.
    Rita Giacaman (1988a)

With or without duress, to be silent is to acquiesce to exclusion from the political process. Silence signifies capitulation and abdication of all rights to participate in the construction of a democratic society. The historian Barrington Moore defines democracy as "a long and certainly incomplete struggle to do three closely related things: 1) to check arbitrary rulers, 2) to replace arbitrary rulers with just and rational ones, and 3) to obtain a share for the underlying population in the making of rules" (Moore 1967, 414). How can individuals control their own destiny and then play a part in the ordering of their society? One answer is to construct a political-linguistic forum in which different constituencies with their different languages can communicate *with respect*. Beyond listening to and hearing one another, all constituencies by democratic practice must actively develop their own language and ensure its reception.[1] Women writers are key agents in this process, yet until recently they have not known how to impose and hold on to their voices. Literary history is full of women whose writings reached a small audience and no farther. How do I know they exist? Because of the fragments that somehow survived, even if hidden for centuries.

Contestation over access to discursive space is at the heart of democratic practice. Arab women have long participated in their societies' politico-literary debates. The first example of Arab women's literature to be uncovered so far is the poetry of the sixth-century Khansa' bint Tumadir. Although an entire anthology, or *diwan,* of poetry by al-Khansa' has been pieced together, it comprises elegies primarily. Does this mean that this woman who lived through the earliest, and some of the most exciting, moments of the rise of Islam wrote only of death? What of love and politics? The Tunisian critic Raja Ben Slama provides one possible answer to the question about love when he suggests that pre-Islamic women poets in the Arabian Peninsula, like al-Khansa' and Layla al-Akhyaliyya, waited for the death of the beloved to express their passion (Ben Slama 1991, 17–23). Political commentary is apparently absent. Does that mean that women did not participate in the political life of sixth- and seventh-century Arabian society? This is impossible. Contemporary sources document women's public activities that extend even to military encounters. So does their absence as political commentators mean that there was some kind of prohibition on their *literary* participation? Pace Stetkevych, this too seems unlikely in view of the fact that the Meccans chose al-Khansa' to be a judge of their poetry competitions, the most prestigious cultural events to be held in the city (Stetkevych 1992, 161–205). Clearly, something has been lost. The reasons for the disappearance of early Arab women's writings with the exception of elegies are yet to be revealed. I suspect that the elegies survive because they deal with a woman's relationships with her male relatives, particularly those who have been killed, and whose deaths probably need to be avenged. Such writings are safe: they support the system and reveal no internal rifts as women retain their shadow roles, urging their men to do what society expects them to do. Such writings can survive, they can even be celebrated. When women wrote about themselves, however, their works were pronounced dull because autobiographical or out of bounds. Yet when men like the ninth-century Baghdadi Ibn Taifur and the nineteenth-century Cairene Qasim Amin pontificated endlessly about women, their opinions were carefully considered and then bound in Moroccan leather. This dichotomization of society between those who could and could not write changed in the modern period.

During the first half of the twentieth century, the Arab world was thrown into turmoil as nationalist movements began to challenge colonial powers in the region and to search for models of self-rule. The woman question took center stage as men and women debated what women's roles and status in their changing societies should be. Could a society develop and flourish if it drew on only half its human resources? Women like the Palestinian-Lebanese Mayy Ziyada who had found acceptance among male *littérateurs* wrote circumspectly about women's needs. She celebrated women's contributions to Arabic literature. Ziyada wrote biographies on Warda al-Yaziji, 'A'isha al-Taymuriya, and Zaynab Fawwaz and then, in their turn, Rose Ghurayyib and Widad Sakakini produced biographies of Ziyada. Together they were constructing a women's literary tradition that would draw attention to women and their rights as citizens. These writings were not threatening to status quo but merely supportive of women in a pro-feminist political climate and they were in general hailed as politically correct and quietly shelved.

The establishment of Israel in 1948 galvanized literary and political attention throughout the Arab world. Just as Arab countries were beginning to seize their independence from European colonizers, the Palestinians confronted a new period of colonization. The Palestinian community split between those who left and those who stayed within the green line (the 1949–67 borderline between Israel and Jordan, on international maps). Whereas women in exile, like Samira 'Azzam, wrote angrily of the need for resistance, those inside Israel, like Najwa Qa'war Farah, first tried to negotiate a livable future with the Israelis. Since women wrote about national and not women's issues, they were allowed to say what they wanted.

After the June 1967 War, Palestinian women in the Gaza Strip and the West Bank of Jordan, the territories that Israel occupied, but not inside Israel proper, wrote about women. Quietly at first but then with growing insistence, these women pointed to the need to balance their activism and their writing about what they had done with what was labeled almost antagonistically as national interest and popular cohesion. More than most, Palestinian women in the Occupied Territories have been politically active, and they have written about their activism despite pressure from within and from without to remain silent. They have understood the importance of what the Moroccan Abdelkabir Khatibi calls a "double critique," or the simultaneous criticism of the colonizer as well as of one's own cultural patrimony. For women in a colonized society, such a critique is particularly hard for there are many waiting to condemn as cultural betrayal what they consider to be a demurral from a hardline, single-focused nationalist stance. External and internal pressures notwithstanding, women from the West Bank like the poet Fadwa Tuqan and the novelist Sahar Khalifa have simultaneously criticized Israel, America, and their own society, calling for what some term a women's agenda but *all within the context of the nationalist movement*. They argue that just as the liberationist struggles to free themselves from Israel will succeed only if they transform gender relations, so the social-feminist revolution must include a political victory for the Palestinian nation.

Palestinian women writers emphasize that equally indispensable elements of the nationalist revolution are women as actors and feminism as an ideology of radical social change. Mai Sayeh explains that women are not asking for liberation for themselves alone, but as part of "a revolutionary transformation of society. . . . We are living at a time of revolutionary struggle and we are determined to assert the need for the presence of women" (Sayeh 1986, 88). Khalifa calls for a real nationalism, not what she calls a "naive" version. Real nationalism "means to know and to love the nation with its rights and its wrongs, its sweet and its bitter, because without diagnosis there can be no prescription."[2] The Syrian critic Bouthaina Shaaban interviewed a Palestinian woman whose articulation of the dilemma of the feminist activist in the nationalist struggle reveals its paradoxical nature: "However deeply I empathise with the women's issue, I can't give it priority in a society which is rife with social and political problems and whose very identity and existence are in question. . . . I fight to break the fetters of femininity which cage my soul and mind; at the same time I fight ferociously for the restoration of my homeland to its own people. . . . My struggle for emancipation as a Palestinian is inseparable from my struggle for genuine liberation as a woman; neither of them is valid without the other" (Shaaban 1988, 160– 64).

These women are demanding to be heard. They see little recognition of what women have done and said, despite the dozens of books and hundreds of articles in several languages that have been written about Palestinian women's participation in the resistance.[3] These women are fighting to hold on to their words and the meanings they have assigned to these words, so that they will not be left out of the democratic process.

Contextualizing Erasure

Palestinian women were the first among the Arabs to organize themselves politically. The earliest institutions that they established were in general charity-oriented and helped foster a pro-feminist climate at the very beginning of this century. In 1903 Christian women in Acre set up an association to look after destitute children. Sixteen years later Muslim women in Jerusalem organized a parallel group called the Palestinian Arab Women's Congress. In 1921 the first Muslim-Christian women's unions were formed in both Jerusalem and Haifa when the Christian Milia Sakakini and the Muslim Zulaikha Shihabi joined forces to found the Arab Women's Union. Momentum gathered and then, in 1929, the union convened the first pan-Arab women's conference—the Arab Women's Congress of Palestine—which demanded the establishment of a national parliament, rejection of the Balfour Declaration, and boycott of Zionist products. In 1933 a Christian woman delivered a political speech inside the Omar Mosque and a Muslim woman made a speech in front of Christ's tomb in the Holy Sepulcher (Antonius

1983, 63–64; Mogannam 1937, 55–70). By 1936, the date of the Arab Revolt against British rule, there were thirteen women's associations in Palestine, even including secret paramilitary cells like Uqhuwan. The war and the establishment of Israel slowed women's activities until the founding and formal recognition of the Palestine Liberation Organization (PLO) in the early sixties. In 1964 women participated in the PLO's first conference that included a resolution calling on women to struggle side by side with the men to liberate Palestine. The following year the General Union of Palestinian Women grew out of politicized charitable organizations. During the twenty years following 1967, women became more politically active than they have ever been. Suha Sabbagh, director of the Institute for Arab Women's Studies in Washington, D.C., says: "Before the intifada broke out in December 1987, there existed between 200 and 400 social service agencies on the West Bank, all run by women" (quoted in McMahon 1991, 32). Between 1988 and 1990, namely during the Intifada, five women's research centers were opened in Nablus, Gaza, and Jerusalem and in 1993 plans were developed for an institute of women's studies at Birzeit University on the West Bank. Nadia Hijab considers these centers to be important "in setting the agenda of the future Palestine. They are tackling hitherto undiscussed issues related to women's legal and economic status, such as violence in the family, inheritance, school dropout rates for girls' and women's economic activities in the informal sector." She goes on to talk about the Technical Committee for Women's Affairs, which is deliberating "a bill of rights for women, and it is reviewing the personal status laws issued by other Arab countries in order, as they put it, 'to avoid their mistakes.' The Committee is also working to prepare women to participate actively in elections" (Hijab 1994, 13–14).

Although there is relatively little research available on the women's associations and their participation in nationalist programs, it is clear that men were aware of them at the time and acknowledged their importance to the nationalist movement.[4] In January 1955 the writer Emile Habibi (b. 1919), one of the founders of the Israeli Communist Party and longtime editor-in-chief of its paper, *Al-Ittihad,* responded to six articles about women's rights that had appeared in *Al-Mujtama'*. He celebrated women's resistance during the war of 1948. He went on to demand that "they may fight side by side with the men to destroy the chains of oppression, suffering, and hunger that bind their people. . . . Withholding this freedom disempowers society. . . . To defend the right of the ordinary peasant to stay in his village and on his land, the women of Kafr Munda stood by their men, not inside the house but in front of the bullets of the police" (Habibi 1955, 6, 50).

In 1967, when Palestinians on the West Bank and in the Gaza Strip came to share the fate of those who in 1948 had stayed inside the green line, the cultural logic of the Palestinian resistance changed. There was greater understanding of what the Palestinians who had stayed in 1948 had endured, and of the importance of collective action. Women mobilized. Their weapons were not guns but stones, weapons of the weak that often disarmed their soldierly opponents. But sometimes did not. Many on both sides were killed, especially in the 1970s.

By the end of the 1980s, when the informal skirmishes were organized and named Intifada, women's roles had entered the realm of legend. In 1993 the folklorist Sharif Kanaana published his study of the emergence of what he calls Intifada Legends. Within his collection of about two hundred fifty independent versions and several hundred variants, he finds that the male characters are generally young men "restricted essentially to one kind of role, that of direct confrontation with Israeli soldiers." Curiously, there are virtually no fathers—the legends have done away with that troubling vestige of patriarchy. The women are mainly older and they "are given a much wider range of roles . . . [and] they appear to be the strongest figures—the pillars of the Palestinian Arab family" (Kanaana 1993, 42, 43, 58). These legends strip away the complicated intergenerational relationships to concentrate on men's and women's ways of fighting. Explicit in this necessarily stark story is that the ones to devise effective forms of resistance were the women. Ghassan al-Masri in his introduction to Akram Abu Samra's book on Palestinian women's roles during the Intifada cites the thousands of women prisoners and dozens of women martyrs, including Fathiya 'Awad al-Hurani and Lina Nabulsi, who were killed in what he calls the two intifadas of 1974 and 1976–77.[5] He holds them out as proof that the Algerian heroine "Jamila Buhrayd has not died and that all Palestinian women are like Jamila the resistance fighter." He credits the women with daily acts of resistance that stopped Israeli attempts to cut off life lines; when necessary, they sewed new flags to replace those that had been confiscated. Echoing others, he praises mothers of martyrs and Patriotic Mothers who particularly in the recent period have been giving birth at abnormally high rates (Abu Samra 1989, 8, 87–90). He lauds women for informing the international media of what was happening during the uprising despite Israeli attempts to block news. He points out how international gatherings convened by women made the Palestinian cause an item on other countries' agendas.

So it would seem that this time at last women will not be forgotten in the aftermath. These legendary characters will surely be included in the democratic process of constituting a state out of the nation that they have worked so hard to maintain and for whose survival they can take a large share of the credit. Unfortunately, evidence from within the Occupied Territories indicates that this is not necessarily the case—maybe legends, like symbols, consume their subject when that subject is a woman. Moreover, there are some women, particularly those who are married, who are not learning from the Algerian Lesson because the multiple pressures are too great to focus on the women's agenda (see Mani and Ghazawneh 1993, 68–75). Yet a significant few are recognizing and already struggling against the impending erasure of their voices and, therefore, of their experience.[6] They are articulating their concerns, formulating new strategies to memorialize their contributions, and engaging in what the sociologist Rita Giacaman calls "a process of self-criticism": "Rather than working through committees, where gender is used as a means to recruit for factional ends, we are convinced that women should enter politics as agents of change. . . . I believe we can only realize a truly independent agenda for Palestinian women if we set about forging alliances and coalitions with these other oppressed groups, around these issues of democracy and equality. . . . For us, feminism is an ideology that calls for the social integration of women, and so is a part of a wider ideology calling for equality across all spheres and for all sectors of political and civil society" (interview in Usher 1992, 33, 35, 36).

In 1988 Giacaman with the writer Sahar Khalifa established a feminist association and sociopolitical training institution called Women's Affairs to safeguard women's political roles during the Intifada as men took over the leadership of the neighborhood committees. These committees, often formed by women, had served in place of the generally absent civil administration. The men described women's roles throughout the 1967–87 period as social rather than political.[7] This attempt to minimize women's importance to the uprising can be seen in subtler strategies also. Giacaman points out how men's increasing focus on the importance of women as prisoners and martyrs obscures what women *have done* behind the screen of *what has been done to them* (Usher 1992, 42). Najah Manasra emphatically underscores Giacaman's concern: "To count the number of women martyrs, and speak about their important role in the fighting, without mentioning the negative developments is a dangerous policy" (Manasra 1993, 19). These "safe nationalist issues" drain the meaning out of women's oppositional practices. Is this perhaps how the non-elegiac poetry of al-Khansa' was lost?

The subtle and not so subtle erasure of women's centrality to the uprising and their omission in plans for reconstruction can be found in men's writings as well as in the ways women writers describe men's reactions to women activists. One of the best known male Palestinian writers living in Israel is Emile Habibi. During the 1950s he wrote little fiction, and what he did write might be described as accomodationist (see the discussion of "Mandelbaum Gate" below). After the war of 1967 his attitude changed. In 1974 he published his first novel that garnered him much fame, *The Secret Life of Saeed, the Ill-Fated Pessoptimist*. It goes back to the early days of the new Israeli state to tell the story of Saeed, a wise fool who returned to Israel illegally soon after being compelled to leave. His story is presented as a wild picaresque seeming to draw on traditional genres. I believe Saeed's predicament can be best understood in terms of the father figure in Deleuze and Guattari's scheme of the Exaggerated Oedipus who has "to be enlarged to the point of absurdity, of comedy." This man lives with "head bent," trying to compel his son to do the same. Saeed, like other characters in a minor literature, is trying to find a way to survive in a culture that strives to exclude him, or at least to push him to its borders.

Saeed's reterritorialization entails complicities, betrayals, collaborations. His two sons, Walaa (loyalty) from his wife Baqiya (a verb-name meaning "he stayed" and indicating a relationship to the land) and Saeed from his lover Yuad ("it will be returned," namely another verb-name related to the land), must find a new path, one the father was not able to find: "The hypothesis of a common innocence, of a distress shared by father and son, is thus the worst of all hypotheses. In it, the father appears as the man who had to renounce his own desire and his own faith," and who demands the same of his son. In the intervention of 1967 the sons escape the impasse of the triangulation of the exaggerated Oedipus between father, son, and mother (Deleuze and Guattari 1986 [1975], 10). Saeed goes to prison, where he meets his unknown son Saeed, who has become a guerrilla fighter. When he learns that he has a son who has become part of an effective revolutionary force, Saeed can raise his head from the generations-old attitude of men who searched for treasure on the ground. But when he looks up, he sees that his other son named Loyalty has chosen to become Palestinian also; he rejects his father's becoming-Israeli desire. In each case, the sons are empowered by their mothers, women who are not afraid to say no and who consider loyalty to the Palestinian nation more important than citizenship in the Israeli state. The sons and their mothers—a foreshadowing of the Intifada trope—cannot, and do not wish to, reterritorialize themselves there where their father seems so invested. They deterritorialize absolutely by diving deep under the sea or by escaping the territory. Saeed cannot learn from them, and so at the end he finds himself the only possible space for survival: on top of a tall, blunt stake surrounded by a terrifying void. The epilogue announces that this story was told by a madman who is living in a fantasy world with extraterrestrials—the dream of reterritorialization but from outside—in fact from a psychiatric hospital, as well as a one-time prison, shrine, and museum. The women instigate what Deleuze and Guattari call the proliferation of new series, each promising escape from an impasse, but Saeed cannot benefit from the openings they create. The women disappear with their sons after having put up a resistance, a resistance that cannot function effectively within such a context.

Widad Barghuthi intimates that such disappearing of women's political presence and importance is not new. She scans men's poetry of the twentieth century and finds that male poets do not incorporate women as sociopolitical actors into their discourse. In the 1930s, namely during the Arab Revolt in which women took a significant part, poets like Ibrahim Tuqan addressed women as muses (Barghuthi 1990, 155). She claims that the wars of 1948 and 1967 mark a change in men's representations of women. Mahmud Darwish, for instance, reduces women to symbols of the nation, or of struggle and loyalty, so that the one is indistinguishable from the other. They are also mothers (who lost their children, who give without taking, who are martyrs or prisoners or struggling peasants) and lovers awaiting the return of the beloved knight. For a short time, poets like Nayif Salim and Samih al-Qasim wrote of women as resistance fighters and Rashid Husayn invoked the Algerian Jamila. But this does not last. Barghuthi concludes with a quick overview of men's poetry about the Intifada that she says once again erases women's achievements. In fact, it indicates no change in women's social status, as men continue to write longingly for their lovers. At best, women are Spartan Mothers (Barghuthi 1990, 158). She ends with a call to women poets to correct the omission and offers as models unnamed women from Latin America and Cuba. Ironically, even she does not acknowledge that Palestinian women have written of their own political involvement in national liberation.

Mai Sayeh was marginally optimistic in the early 1980s, writing that "the younger writers and poets, like Khalid Abu Khalid, Yahia Badaw, and others, now depict two faces of woman: the strong woman, symbol of the home and the land, who encourages her son to fight, and the young woman, the beloved, who is herself a fighter and active in the struggle. These are new depictions of woman: to be loved she has to fight actively for her country" (quoted in

Antonius 1983, 67). This optimism is tempered by Ilham Abu Ghazaleh, who has analyzed men's poems composed between December 1987 and May 1989. She finds that poets stress women's physical appearance and not their actions, their roles as kin and not as activists. Although women are out in the streets, men write of them waiting at home to be told stories about what had happened as though it were utterly remote from them. She observes that "women are either totally negated by their absence, or they are depicted as incomplete beings. . . . All this passivity in depiction took place at a time when women in every neighborhood were more active than they have ever been" (paraphrased in Najjar 1992, 260–61). Kristin Brown's survey of popular Palestinian poetry and songs during the Intifada finds that if anyone is to be highlighted as having fought for the nation, it is going to be men who can be cast in mythic molds, especially of classic heroes such as 'Antar and Abu Zayd al-Hilali (Brown 1990, 3). Perhaps women cannot be sung because there are no mythic models for women warriors in Arab history? But then what of Zaynab, the Prophet's granddaughter famous for her exploits on the battlefield, who has become central to postrevolutionary Iranian women's construction of an acceptable woman fighting side by side with her men? By 1992 Hanan Mikhail Ashrawi, the former spokesperson for the PLO, points out that men's writings about women's resistance and the uprising have erased women's political and social agency; they have once again been reduced to "the embodiment of the unattained, the perfect goal: fertility, lush land, the womb of society, Palestine itself" (Najjar 1992, 260). Women are turned into symbols of national integrity and renewal and in the process they are denied oppositional agency (see page 214).

Many Palestinian women insist that they and their sisters must record what they have done outside the home and demand what they want. It is not enough to say that the women's, or the social, revolution and the national revolution are mutually dependent for their success, that the one fails with the failure of the other. As Giacaman asserts, echoing a growing chorus, women have to overcome their reticence at drawing attention to their specific needs and goals; they must publicly articulate and pursue a women's agenda.

In the preface to her volume of edited essays on women's roles during the Intifada, Ebba Augustin writes that "the gain of the uprising is an increased consciousness and practical understanding of gender issues on the part of the middle class leadership and the intellectuals. With a women's agenda being worked out and a leadership pushing for political representation while closely working with the grassroots, it is to be hoped that women will have their voices heard when there is a political settlement" (Augustin 1993, xi). In the same volume, Najah Manasra underscores the point when she says that "an increasing number of them are taking up the fight not just against the Israeli occupation but also against the restrictive norms of their own society. . . . During the Intifada the pressures on Palestinian society have increased. For many people, one method of coping is to 'go back to the roots'. . . . The victims of this trend are Palestinian women. . . . We need to see that many forces are at work attempting to curtail our existing rights, not to mention the rights we are fighting for" (Manasra 1993, 18–20, 20). This emphasis on the women's agenda should not be seen to conflict with the nationalist agenda. Rather it seems to be the only way to hold on to the necessary simultaneity of women's allegiances to gender, nation and culture. These allegiances are not contradictory but they will seem to be so if one is favored over the others. If, for instance, women prioritize "political and national considerations" they will not gain the confidence and strength that will allow them to become full citizens in the new society that they want to build with the men. Palestinian women are fighting for a democratic nation.

Radical and new? No, just a sharpening of rhetoric already out there. Sahar Khalifa, the best known woman novelist working in the Occupied Territories, has written four novels that compare men's and women's ways of resisting. Muhammad Batrawi quotes Khalifa as saying that Palestinian women writers "are progressive already, to pass the obstacles of 'to want to write' and 'to write', while men writers—even leftists—are still bound by the traditional role of women. . . . Real-life women are never represented [in their work]" (quoted in Augustin 1993, 118). She knows that women must constantly talk and write about what it is that they have done, show how what they have done has shattered the myth of a men-only space; they must not allow the men to forget. Once they have made their voices heard, they must demand inclusion in the new body politic. She provides a model in her 1981 dramatized response to critics of her novel '*Abbad al-shams* (Sunflower). One woman in the resistance complained: "But they do not hear us!" To which her companion replied: "How could they, when we do not open our mouths?" "But if we open them, they say it is silliness." "The important thing is that we open them *while we are on stage*" (*Al-Katib,* September–October 1981, 83). Yes, women must speak and write while they are still in the public eye, when their actions are still visible. Women like Rosie the Riveter in America and the Algerian Jamilas learned too late that actions do not carry their own rewards, but that they must be re-membered and repeated so as not to be erased. Khalifa heeds Cassandra's warning about what happens to women fighters when the "chorus of female speakers has vanished, swallowed up by the earth. The woman can now become the object of masculine narrative, in the role of heroine. . . . Do people suspect, do *we* suspect how difficult and in fact how dangerous it can be when life is restored to an 'object'? When *it* has to say 'I,' as a woman? We see a landscape generations wide where the writing woman still tends to get lost: lost in the man, the male institutions, federations, churches, parties, states" (quoted in Wolf 1988, 296–98).

Palestinian women like Sahar Khalifa are determined not to vanish, not to become the object of a masculine metanarrative because they already know that if they do why then it will be, as always, as heroines, martyrs, or some other idealized category that will erase what they have done by turning them into national symbols. She is saying "I" as a woman and refusing to get lost in male institutions, federations, churches, parties, and states.

1948

Let us now turn the clock back a half century and ask what role, if any, a woman's agenda played in the writings of women who experienced the war that was to lead to the foundation of the Israeli state. Women's issues then, as always during national crisis, were relegated to secondary importance. The women like Najwa Qaʿwar Farah, Asma Tubi, and Thuraya Milhis who wrote in the late 1940s and 1950s rarely raised women's specific problems. Their writings resemble those of their male counterparts like Emile Habibi and Hana Ibrahim. Like the Algerian women under French colonial rule and then during their war of independence, Palestinian mothers, daughters, wives, and sisters did not demand radical changes. In fact, they advocated traditionalism, especially in the family. Education and professionalism were luxuries to be postponed indefinitely. Women like Najwa Qaʿwar Farah who wanted to be heard had to suppress feminist expression.

In general, Palestinians writing within the new state were cautious. In his analysis of the "Jewish neighbor" in early Palestinian fiction, the Israeli critic Sasson Somekh distinguishes two categories of writer: those who were close to the Communist Party, and those who threw in their lot with the Israeli regime. Although they all wrote about "Arab-Jewish brotherhood, peace, and co-operation," Somekh cautions that such writings were often coerced. The Communists wanted "their Arab comrades to write in the spirit of internationalism and to describe the common Jewish-Arab struggle against imperialism and chauvinism [in both nations]." The government demanded praise for its democratic achievements (Somekh 1989, 113, 114). Such pressures notwithstanding, the 1950s stories do reflect the harsh realities of life in Palestinian communities in Israel. Authors describe the struggle to survive with dignity and to establish a just, if patriarchal, society. Many seem as concerned about the persistence of injustice and oppression as they are about political violence. Somekh describes their writings as bitter but not accusatory: "At most there is an evil institution that is called Zionism or The State, but this is a meta-structure which is not identical with the simple human being. The Jew who appears in these stories is generally not ugly, and sometimes he is human and even likeable" (Somekh 1989, 119).

One of the very few Palestinian women writers of the earliest period who stayed in Israel was Najwa Qaʾwar Farah (b. Nazareth, 1923). She published her first collection *'Abiru al-sabil* (Passersby) in 1954, *Durub wa masabih* (Paths and lanterns) two years later, and *Li man al-rabi'*? (For whom is the spring?) in 1963. The dates of publication of the collections rarely indicate when the stories were actually written. Despite its 1954 publication date, *Passersby* contains only stories published before 1948; of the eight stories in *Paths and Lanterns* only two are post-1948; most of the stories in *For Whom Is the Spring?* are from the early and mid-1950s—the last two collections are relevant here because they contain stories written in the immediate aftermath of the war. After leaving Israel in 1967, Farah continued to write and in 1981 she published *Rihlat al-huzn wa al-i'ta'* (The journey of sadness and giving) and in 1991 *Intifadat al-'asafir* (The intifada of the birds). I focus on Farah's writings between late 1940s and early 1960s because they demonstrate the development in nationalist consciousness from accommodation with the Israelis to rejection.

Unlike most Palestinians who remained after the establishment of the Israeli state, Farah was educated. She graduated from Dar al-Mu'allimat, a women's teacher training college in Jerusalem, though she decided not to attend university because of parental pressure.[8] In her midtwenties she became a member of the Arab Women's Union for which she lectured about women's issues. At the same time, she wrote plays and stories that were broadcast on radio in Israel, England, and Holland and then were published in journals like *Al-Adib*, *Saut al-Mar'a*, *Al-Muntada*, *Al-Qafila*, and *Al-Ghad*. Like the men who wrote just before and after 1948, she criticized social values and indicted the excesses of the rich and nouveaux riches, men and women alike. Society had to be reformed from within. But unlike the men who often criticized the national leadership, Farah did so only by indirection (Peled 1988, 202).

In her introduction to *Paths and Lanterns*, Farah spells out her vision of the role of the writer. It is threefold: "sometimes to portray life, sometimes to criticize and often to forge a better path. . . . Sometimes the writer must portray truthfully, sincerely, and precisely and then keep silence. Truthful portrayal is more eloquent than criticism because it is in itself revolutionary" (Farah 1956, i). Although many of her stories are socially motivated, dwelling on class and gender issues, Farah was among the first of the Palestinians who stayed to write political stories.[9] The critic Ibn Khaldun, who describes her *Passersby* collection as "cautiously revolutionary" (Ibn Khaldun 1956, 53–54), writes that in *Paths and Lanterns* the author has changed "from onlooker to participant in a struggle necessary for development" (Ibn Khaldun 1957, 22). Mattityahu Peled claims that her 1948 story "Inspiration from the Holy War" is probably "one of the first attempts to reflect the national struggle in prose literature." The story was published in *Al-Adib,* September 1948. Peled writes that men before 1948 did not deal with political topics (Peled 1988, 154, 182). Revolutionary is thus an adjective that not only she but also others use to characterize Farah's writings. But revolutionary here connotes political rather than social action.

When asked about her identity as a woman writer, Farah replies, as do many other Arab women writers, that it is not gender but personality and literary style that differentiate one writer from another. There is little of the feminist in her public persona. Her writings connect with men rather than with women. For example, she allowed a committee of three men, 'Isa al-Na'uri, Sami Habibi and Taufiq Qa'war, to select the stories for her first collection that al-Na'uri introduced.[10] Whether this was a conscious strategy or not, it worked. He praises her works for their dramatic atmosphere, their psychological range, and their rhetoric against hypocrisy and arrogance: "Any religious person who reads her will feel her writing has more influence than 1,000 priests' sermons" (Farah 1954, 12). Unlike Algerian male critics of women's early writings on the revolution, he does not condemn a woman's critique of her society from within as subversive. In fact, her critique was not so different from that current among men. She was read with the men, her gender did not signal the need for another reading.

The frequent choice of male narrators is another tactic that allows Farah to expose corruption in society without risking trivialization as feminist carping. In her pre-1948 stories, male narrators criticize rich men and women, who unscrupulously exploit the poor and those who trample all over each other in the struggle to the top.[11] They mock the older generation's cultural and political blindness. For example, in "Which of the Two Paths?" a young man rejects his father's advice to accept the inevitability of corruption and withdraws into ninth-century literature and starts to write. His mother exclaims: "As though all those books with which he stuffed the house were not enough, he had to add his own. His poor father! While he is knocking himself out all day long, this one sits around and writes." The father adds: "And we have to pay. . . . People are flying to the stars and he goes backward to write about the Abbasids!" Neither parent can see the relevance of the past to the present, much less its potential as "fuel for the revolution" (23, 24).

As she wrote in her introduction to *Paths and Lanterns,* Farah does not merely attack miscreants; she also describes and thus penetrates the tragic world of the poor. "The Newspaper Vendor" is a boy who, in the face of tough competition, must earn enough to provide his sick mother with her medicine. One of his battles lands him in reform school where he learns not reform but crime (26–37).

The war does not put an immediate end to Farah's social criticism. In her 1950 story "Two Beggars" a boy, brought up to be a beggar, is suddenly struck by the reality of his misfortune. He overhears conversations as the people leave a cinema-house and he realizes that they were *born* into different expectations. Far from disabling him, this realization empowers him to change his fate and leave the city. The story ends with him getting his first paid job and exchanging his first flirtatious moment with a woman. Although Farah scarcely alludes to the radically different political reality, she does suggest that the time has come for people to take their destinies into their own hands (Farah 1963, 5–11).

Get active. Do something. But is it too late? Have the Palestinians lost their direction and their compass also? "The Story of a Generation" describes the *angst* of those who cannot fit into the new world and whose only solace may be found in the land. A farmer on his way to market in Haifa runs into a wheat agent who had once been in his debt. He had offered to defray the debt by giving his creditor four dunams (each about one-quarter acre) at the foot of Mount Carmel. The protagonist had refused because at that time the land on which Haifa was built was worth nothing. How times had changed! This once-destitute wheat merchant had flourished under the new system: he lived in a splendid new home with his silk-clad wife and his children, each of whom had a French name, spoke French, and had western table manners.[12] The farmer, embarrassed by his own lack of "sophistication," escapes. At the bus station, he realizes that he has arrived too late for the buses. Although Farah does not say so explicitly, the reader assumes that it is Friday: the Muslim protagonist had attended the noon communal prayer, there is no bus after sundown because of the Israeli prohibition on driving during the Sabbath. Even at this point, she does not mention the Jews and the specific nature of some of the changes they instituted. In consternation, the protagonist returns to find the house full of gamblers, bare-armed women, and blaring music.[13] He escapes again and after many ordeals on the road returns to his village from which he feels that he has been parted for a lifetime. He picks up a piece of earth that "embraced a whole life, many generations even. Then he threw it away slowly, lovingly, reverently. It was sacred" (Farah 1954, 184). "The Story of a Generation" broaches a major issue of post-1948 Palestinian women's writings on their wars: the existential importance of staying on the land, of being true to oneself and above all of not profiting from a situation that brings misfortune to others.

Earlier than most writers, Farah warns of the dangers inherent in commingling with the European immigrants. Although like many of her contemporaries, she differentiates between the people and their military administration, she is less sanguine than most about the prospects of mixing with the Israelis. She urges caution as she extols traditional bonds, even if at the expense of women's freedom of action. Her pre-1948 "When Nairuz Returns" (Farah 1954, 185–225) is a prognostication of the pains and dangers to come. One day, villagers awake to find Polish and Russian women walking through the streets. Whereas the Palestinian women recoil from these libertine women, the men are attracted. Ibrahim is one such. He throws himself into a relationship with some of these new women, even on one occasion driving off to Tiberias with them. Samiha, his fiancée, tries to keep faith but has to acknowledge finally that he has become "mean, stubborn, selfish, and indifferent" (204). Ibrahim is not evil, merely weak. Just as Samiha is about to be married off to a class mate, he comes to his senses. They are reconciled, but on the wedding night Samiha dies. Ibrahim loses his reason. This melodrama compels Samiha's family to recognize the depth of his devotion, and they forgive him. The story ends with a striking vignette of Ibrahim and his to-have-been brother-in-law walking toward the grave. So strong are the ties that bind these Palestinian villagers that nothing, not even the foreign femmes fatales, has power enough to undermine them. As Somekh points out, this description of Jewish women's freedom and Palestinian women's dependence on "the will of the man" is a topos of the literature of the 1950s (Somekh 1989, 116).

Six years later, Farah wrote what might be considered to be a sequel. Yet this story neither criticizes foreign women nor affirms Palestinian solidarity as critical to survival. Like many men's stories of the period, "Layla and the Fragrance of Oranges" (Farah 1956, 72–80) proffers the hope that Palestinians might be able to communicate with the Israelis.[14] The protagonist is a Bulgarian gold merchant who came to Palestine after the failure of the *suq shakhur* (Hebrew for black market); note the use of Hebrew vocabulary which Farah must assume her readers will already understand. Yaqub Ibn Yusuf—whose name is oddly Arabic-sounding—is one of the very few explicitly Jewish protagonists in Farah's works. He is not an expropriator but a family man who bought the land he now loves. One day he notices an "eastern man" in his garden, and he asks him his name using the Arabic he has already bothered to learn. The man runs away. Yaqub remains wary and that night when the man returns he is ready to shoot him. His Iraqi son-in-law stops him; an Arab Jew intervenes to save a fellow Arab. The Palestinian is called Ahmad and it transpires that this was Ahmad's house and that his bride, killed by loose shrapnel on their wedding night that was also the first night of the 1948 war, is buried in the garden. After establishing a measure of rapport, he begs them to make sure that she is properly buried should he come to harm. They sit together and talk about his eight years in refugee camps, and of his longing for the land of his birth. Ahmad mirrors Yaqub's language when he describes his feelings for the plantation: "Yaqub could understand how Ahmad loved the plantation because he too

had experienced and fallen under the spell of its magic because this
was his homeland just as Vaudeville had once been his home" (80).
While they are talking they hear sounds and they try to hide Ahmad.
When Ahmad hears them turn on the radio, which they had agreed
would be the danger signal, he escapes. However, "a few seconds
later a shot was heard. The next day's paper mentioned that soldiers
had fired at an audacious infiltrator who had burst into a plantation
at Rehovot and had killed him. It was an almost commonplace piece
of news." The Israelis are not to be confused with their military
administration. The reader assumes that the two Jews will honor
their promise to give Ahmad's bride a proper burial. But what kind
of a burial will it be? Will it be Jewish or Muslim? And once they
have performed the ritual, how will they feel about the land whose
former owner their government has killed? In this story the humanity of both sides becomes apparent to each. It leaves open-
ended what the outcomes of such an interaction might be. This
story joins others of its period in which Jews appear as fully
rounded characters.[15]

Despite her political and social involvement in women's issues
prior to the war, Farah advocates that women should now control
personal desires and ambitions. Women should not move out of
their traditional, narrowly circumscribed roles. The following two
stories are among the few that Farah seems to have written for the
female reader. In "Baha" (1951), Farah criticizes mothers whose
only interest in their daughters' education is their beautiful teachers
who may serve as brides for their brothers. The lovely teacher Baha
and the protagonist's brother marry according to the mother's plan.
But then the couple throw the ambitious mother and the narrator
out of the house in which both had been born. Farah is warning
Palestinian women against exploiting the situation lest it lead to
their expropriation by their own men who know no better than to
obey their wives just as they had previously obeyed their mothers.
Women are participating in their own exploitation; they should
turn their energy to positive ends so as to create a different future
for society as a whole.

"Stumbling Block" (1953) is another cautionary tale for foolish
women. The story is ostensibly concerned with women's chastity

but in fact it is a warning against meddling with traditional values. An older woman urges Basima to elope with her lover and not to submit to her brother. The following day, with her lover in the hospital and her brother in prison, Basima is in terrified hiding. The well-meaning Salma al-Mubarak is horrified at the results of her words and somewhat abruptly and unexpectedly dies. She is a warning to all who would interfere in traditional codes of behavior. At such a time of cultural and political vulnerability, Palestinians should adhere to tradition even if at the expense of women's freedom and right to self-fulfillment. This warning against involvement with or emulation of Jewish women's freedom again echoes men's literary concerns (Peled 1988, 184–85).

By the mid-1950s and early 1960s, Farah's writing becomes more radical in content as in form, as she includes extended passages written in Palestinian Arabic. Recognizing the effects of expropriations, the humiliations of living as a stranger, a hireling on one's own land, she seems less and less committed to negotiating a future in Israel. In "The Call of the Ruins," she expresses doubts that coexistence is at all possible. All that remains of a prosperous Galilee village is a convent that seems to wish that it too had been destroyed so that it might now be spared its daily witness to the surrounding devastation. Yet it is not the Israelis alone who are blamed: "It is better to be wronged than to do wrong. . . . You may ask yourself and those close to you who is responsible for the refugees' plight. They'll say the English or the Arab or the Jewish leaders. Doubtless they are all responsible. But I must teach you something else. The one responsible in a deeper sense of the term is the human heart, the source of good and evil, the progenitor of crime and compassion, the nurturer of love and hate. The human heart is the workshop out of which even atomic and hydrogen bombs explode because when love and hate appear they need to express themselves. . . . I don't want to teach you revenge. How miserable is the life of the vengeful. I want to teach you forbearance because it precedes goodness and mercy. When I have done this I shall not fear death" (Farah 1963, 68–69).

This exhortation to recognize individual responsibility ends on a bitter note because, as some claimed, responsibility is not the message of the story.[16] The protagonist's daughter hallucinates her dead mother's voice and follows its sound into no-man's land. There, when she sees her "beloved earth," she squats. She does not resist the police who arrest her because she has no papers; "after a short trial the girl was fined 50 liras" (Farah 1963, 71). She was arrested for being on her own land. This end provides an immediate ironic commentary on assuming responsibility. For no matter how much the Palestinians accept responsibility and try to work with the Israelis, if they so much as step on no-man's land, which may in fact belong to them, they will be swiftly punished.

"A Hired Hand on His Own Land" (1958) tells the familiar story of wave upon wave of colonial rulers whom the Palestinians have endured. A poor farmer who had survived the Ottomans and the British finds himself deprived of the land he had worked so hard to buy. Yet, being an easy-going and unresentful fellow, he is happy to work the land for another. Anticipating calls to *sumud,*[17] or steadfastness, that mark post-1967 Palestinian commitment to resistance, she creates a character who is determined to remain on that land whatever the costs of such a remaining. The Jewish owner respects him and heeds his agricultural advice. Just as he is beginning to feel a measure of control, however indirect, he gets a mortal blow. The owner announces in broken Arabic that he has been compelled to sell the land to someone who was bringing his own workers (Farah 1963, 87). Within ten years of the establishment of Israel, the first generation of Jews with whom it had been possible to live and work was being replaced by another who rejected interchange.

By the late 1950s Farah's stories are about the need to leave. "The Bitterer Choice" (1957) tells of the difficult decisions that old people have to make. Abu Ibrahim dies in exile consumed by longing for the land he had left. As the family goes through his belongings they come across a note: "If some day you return, take my bones with you" (Farah 1963, 80). In 1957 he did not have the relative freedom of the Lebanese Radwan in Emily Nasrallah's *Al-iqla' 'aks al-zaman* (Flight against time), who in 1980 could leave his children living in exile to return to die in his own country. Abu Ibrahim did not die with Radwan's smile of satisfaction that could only come to those who had followed their hearts to their land (Cooke 1988, 156–60).

"The Call of Damascus and the Pomegranates' Censure" (1959) is the first story to refer to the Israelis explicitly and negatively: workers can neither get permits without work nor work without permits; Histadrut inspectors catch those who try to outwit the system. The Palestinian men do not know how "they can remain steadfast and be proud of being Arab and survive." When the male protagonist despairs and decides to leave, his brother tries to bring him back, but "as he was crossing, he heard shots from the Israeli side. He tried to hide behind a stone. But he was caught and taken to prison" (Farah 1963, 96–97). One young man was probably killed and his brother captured. The decision to leave the land is disastrous but so is the staying.

The two stories Farah wrote in 1962 just before leaving Israel mix nostalgia with bitterness. "Granny's Things" describes how outcasts forge links that derive from love for a common past. The younger villager, trained as a lawyer, feels alienated in the city. It is only when he gives protection to the son of a blind man that he finds solace because the boy shared his love for his grandmother's things. This story is reminiscent of the pre-1948 "Café Wise Man" in which Farah narrates the alliances that the marginalized and the oppressed forge.

"Mandelbaum Gate" (1959) describes the excitement of Palestinians on both sides as they anticipate meeting in Jerusalem and then their pain at parting. Written eight years after Emile Habibi published his own story under that same title in the widely read *Al-Jadid,* these stories demand comparison. Both focus on a grandmother who is meeting with a son who has left. Habibi's protagonist is herself leaving to join her family, presumably in Jordan; Farah's grandmother is going to the gate to see her son Halim who has come from Kuwait. Halim bears gifts and stories of another life that make his mother's life with her ailing husband even more unbearable than it already is. Habibi's story ends with the grandmother crossing no-man's land, and her granddaughter, unaware of political frontiers, rushing to hug her. The Jordanian and the Israeli guards are equally moved as they "hang their heads and dig their feet into the ground." Whereas Farah's 1959 story portrays life in Israel as unbearable, in 1951 Habibi is still concerned to show that Israelis, even the military administration, can be touched by a show of tenderness. Farah left Israel after writing this story; Habibi is still there.

How should we read Farah's writings? What are the connections between her activities as a member of the Arab Women's Union and her writings? Despite the conservatism of Palestinian society in the young Israeli state, feminism was on the rise.[18] As in all societies in transition, for a feminist to be read and heard, she had to write in a way that made her criticism palatable. Was this what Farah was doing? Certainly in her interview with Mahmud Darwish, she complains that the "women's cause is a cause in which women are absent." Like Algerian women, she is aware of the difficulties of biculturalism for women: education opens the doors to new horizons whose attainment entails compromise between intellectual needs and cultural duties (Darwish 1962, 61). However, and this is crucial, Farah does not deal with these problems in her stories. Indeed, the men seem to feel freer than she does to write about the impossible conditions in which women found themselves in the aftermath of 1948.[19] Her concerns in the later stage reflect what Khalifa calls "naive nationalism": criticism of the Israelis with less advocacy of internal reform in class and gender relations so as to strengthen society. Except when she wanted to urge women not to rock the boat, Farah wrote for men and as long as she remained in Israel she used their language.

1967

Whereas 1948 distracted Farah from internal criticism as she turned her attention to the political crisis through which she and her people were passing, 1967 inspired women intellectuals in the Occupied Territories to mobilize and to write about mobilizing for social change. Because coexistence was not a real prospect, writers did not have to imagine ways in which individuals might forge relationships with the Israelis. They wrote about the hardships of work in Israeli factories, women's struggle, prison life, and the problems connected with persisting social and gender stratification.

In the wake of the defeat of 1967, writers all over the Arab world questioned in fiction and poetry what had gone wrong. Many conducted a "double critique" that targeted Israel and America while looking in on their own societies. They asked themselves how might they have changed the outcome had they been more politically committed, perhaps even more religiously observant? Some women writers in the Occupied Territories suggested that a social revolution in gender relations might have strengthened the society and made the nation less vulnerable. They began to insist on internal reform and change, while calling attention to their particular experiences and oppositional practices. Unlike Farah, they were not isolated, individual voices but were forming a chorus made up of writers, readers and activists. They wrote to transform relationships so as to create conditions in which individuals might respect and therefore empower one another in a situation where everyone was needed for the resistance to be successful.

Post-1967 women's writings hark back to Farah's pre-1948 criticism of society and particularly of class. As Rosemary Sayigh writes: "The reality of being a minority has produced a mood of acute rebellion among young people against class and family structures that are seen to transmit Israeli oppression . . . rebellion against Israeli oppression and the patriarchal family are refused" (Sayigh 1992, 202). The tone is urgent: if men do not heed this socioeconomic and of course patriarchal critique they will not succeed. They are their own worst enemies by alienating half of their population and accusing of vulgarity women who try to function alone. These women affirm that if all accept responsibility and participate in the restructuring and strengthening of society, they will themselves be restructured and strengthened.

Nablus has been the center for women's literary activity in the post-1967 period. Three women stand out as having attracted international attention: Raymonda Tawil (b. 1940), Fadwa Tuqan (b. 1917), and Sahar Khalifa (b. 1941). Each of these women witnessed the events of 1967, the violence as well as the human displacement. Tawil recounts the story of her collaboration with Khalifa on a dangerous mission. They confronted Israeli soldiers who had taken over the social welfare department and demanded food. They got what they wanted, but upon their return escorted by a soldier, some of the refugees became angry. Khalifa in her turn became angry with them, exclaiming: "We have suffered enough from slogans and ideologies! Baathism, Marxism, and all the rest. Now we have thousands of mouths to feed, hundreds of wounded to care for. We've talked enough! Now let's go to work and save what we can of the Palestinian people!" (Tawil 1983 [1980], 98).

Raymonda Tawil's work has been the most criticized, for it has been interpreted as a form of cultural betrayal. Her many acts of defiance, her attempts to inform the world of the Palestinians' situation in the Occupied Territories, have been largely overlooked in the outrage at her condemnation of her husband and other Arab men in *My Home My Prison* (1983 [1980], 253–55). In this work Tawil recounts her life from the moment an Israeli policeman knocked at the door of her childhood home in Acre to question her mother about her involvement in the resistance of 1948 through her own activism and its costs; it ends with her 1978 imprisonment and torture in an Israeli jail. Tawil is calling for a strengthened resistance movement, yet the tone of her criticism of Arab patriarchy is sometimes so shrill that it overpowers the overall nationalist message. Why, for instance, does she end her story comparing the Israelis' ill-treatment favorably with Palestinian men's oppressiveness (Tawil 1983 [1980], 257)? Finally, the fact that the book is written in Hebrew and was published first in Israel creates the problem of audience. It is one thing to write about pressing internal problems for the Palestinians in Arabic, quite another to write for the Israelis in a language accessible to few of her compatriots about issues that would seem to render her society even more weak and vulnerable than it already is.

Fadwa Tuqan, the poet born into a well known and highly respected literary family, also wrote of Palestinian women's double burden but her language is Arabic and its tone is more moderate. She is always balancing her allegiances to culture, nation, and gender, catching herself when a conflict threatens to emerge, when one loyalty seems about to overwhelm the other two. Her work *A Mountainous Journey,* serialized in *Al-Jadid* in the late 1970s and published as a whole in 1985, recounts her life in Nablus from childhood in the 1920s through 1948 and ending with 1967. This is the first time that this premier Palestinian poet writes in prose. She tells of personal difficulties she encountered as a woman in conservative Nablus. She details the trials and restrictions that she endured as she brushed up against patriarchal authorities—many of them weak men whom she sarcastically refers to as "lords of the family." Tuqan asserts throughout that the Palestinian woman faces a double struggle: "to assert her liberation as a woman and the struggle to assert her and everybody else's national liberation. What I am sure about, however, is that once the inevitable national liberation is achieved, our feminist liberation will also prevail and there will be no relapse of the kind that can happen after national revolutions" (Tuqan 1990 [1985], 204–5). Su'ad Qaraman claims, though not quite correctly in view of what Tawil and Khalifa had already published, that Tuqan is the first woman "to express frankly and truthfully the problems of the Arab women. Arab women before had only referred to such problems symbolically and by means of allusion. Tuqan said everything openly and in an exquisitely sweet style" (Qaraman 1990, 8).

As a child, Tuqan had been deeply hurt by her family's indifference toward her: no one could even remember when she had been born. For the month, she decided to place herself "under the sign of Pisces" (14). For the year, she asked her mother to give her an approximate date. Her mother tells her cruelly that her birth inauspiciously coincided with the death of her mother's favorite cousin. Again and again she criticizes her mother as though trying to free herself of this debilitating biological bond. Her politicized mother, who had been a member of the Society for Women's Welfare, which in 1929 became affiliated with the General Union of Arab Women, should have provided her daughter with a powerful role model. Yet it is probably this very fact of her political activism that led her to want to abort what turned out to be her daughter Fadwa. She was rejecting fecundity as a raison d'être, and her daughter cannot condone this feminist gesture without bringing her own existence into question.

The only happiness and freedom Tuqan ever experiences is with other writers and when she is writing—a trope in Arab women's writings: "My ability to separate myself from reality and to dive into daydreams began to grow. These dreams helped me to escape my prison bars and to venture forth into the streets alone. I travelled to lands unknown where I met strangers who loved me and whom I loved. I would always leave the family out of my imaginary trips because they were the prison out of whose locked gates I wanted to escape" (58–59). But the greatest freedom of all was when her father died in 1948. She no longer had to escape the family because the heavy patriarchal presence was gone. She gained a sense of herself "as a social being. It was during the Occupation only, when I gave poetry recitals and met the people, that I learned the value and true meaning of poetry that matures and ferments in the popular earthen wine jug" (109).

The style of the autobiography underscores its function. The circular narration gives Tuqan the freedom to arrange her life according to her own desires and needs. Again and again, she returns to events in the past to add layers upon layers of experiences that thus come to assume their full significance. She ends with twenty pages, divided into twenty-seven diary entries, that chronicle the year before the 1967 war from a political as well as from an apparently personal perspective. The last page is broken up into four sections in which she lives through the period after the occupation; feverishness, silence, and then finally five poems that are harbingers of many more. The autobiography awaits completion to cover the post-1967 period when Palestinian women in the territories became so active in the resistance. The fact that it does not go beyond 1967 is significant for this section of the autobiography. This is the period that precedes Tuqan's composing of committed poetry. She is reconstructing herself at a time before and during the formation of her identity as a poet, not as a woman poet.

The Intifada

Like many other Arab women poets, Tuqan wrote elegies. She describes her initiation into poetry and adult identity through the memorization of an elegy. She explains how hard it had been for her to write at first, particularly to write political poetry when her experiences were so far removed from the realm of politics. After 1967, however, her poetry became politically engaged. She celebrated the ways in which children were resisting the occupation. Her "Song of Becoming," written after 1967, was—to quote her—prophetic, describing "the *intifada* before it started, which proves how absolutely inevitable it was" (Tuqan 1990 [1985], 204). Others point to the importance of this poem that foreshadows the shape of the resistance to come, for example Khalifa uses it in 1979 as an epigraph for *Sunflower*. After wandering through the streets, and watching the military settle in, Tuqan writes about the jumping, whistling, kite-flying boys who have suddenly "grown more than the years of a lifetime. . . . They're now the voice that rejects / they're the dialectics of destruction and building anew / the anger burning on the fringes of a blocked horizon / invading classrooms, streets, city quarters / centring on the squares / and facing sullen tanks with a stream of stones" (Tuqan 1990 [1984], 10). In an interview I conducted with her in Nablus in December 1982, she told me that she had started a salon in 1968 that the military soon banned. She explained that they feared that "each reading will give birth to ten fedayeen." In general, because of the moral authority of poetry in the Arab world and because of the wide appeal of Tuqan's work, it has drawn more censorship than works by other women, including Sahar Khalifa. The Israeli authorities have allowed Khalifa's subtly subversive literature to circulate, though they screen out from others' writings obvious symbols like "paradise," "olives," and "wild thyme growing on hills," "snake," "dark clouds," and "predatory foreigners."[20]

Throughout her oeuvre, which is also set in Nablus, Sahar Khalifa traces women's growing politicization and effectiveness. By evoking the tensions underlying nationalist as opposed to feminist struggle, she shows how women can name, control, and extend their own actions. In a letter she wrote to me in August 1991, she explains her conception of the role of the writer. It is "to understand human behavior rather than prescribe it. What drove all those women to do what they did at the beginning of the Intifada was not the love of Palestine, but rather the pain of losing their sons, husbands and brothers, or even the idea of losing them . . . from what I have witnessed, women are motivated (at least at this point) by their blood ties rather than by conceptual, abstract, nationalist thinking." Echoing the General Union of Palestinian Women's slogan that it was established not so much to liberate women as to liberate Palestine, she demands that women balance their multiple allegiances so that culture, nation, class, and gender remain in tension with one another. Like Tuqan, and more effectively than Tawil, she argues that the successes of the nationalist and social revolutions are interdependent.

Khalifa speaks out of loyalty to her nation and her culture, but because she focuses on gender roles and relations her works have been charged with being feminist only. Although I was at first surprised at such a misreading, I have come to believe that this judgment has a great deal to do with her location. Writing from within the Occupied Territories, she is expected to represent her nation uncritically. Self-criticism is out. What critics overlook is that writing from inside, Khalifa does not have the freedom of Palestinian women from elsewhere who can write with impunity about the Israelis and the hardships of separation from the homeland. Equally important, she does not have the distance to overlook the damaging effects of a persisting bourgeois patriarchy.[21] In 1989 Khalifa told Sibylle and Shraga Elam that she "has been accused of being like the Israelis and of wanting to undermine the Intifada since I was raising to the forefront a secondary matter, women." She complains that people do not know how to read her works that talk "for the first time of women's ways of fighting that are not recognizable as fighting" (quoted in Bunzi and El-Masri 1989). Self-criticism is urgent for survival.

Khalifa often contrasts men's and women's ways of fighting the war against Israel. In her Intifada novel, *Bab al-Saha* (1990a), she criticizes the strategies and tactics of Palestinian men's resistance, as she did in *Wild Thorns* (1985a [1976]), the first volume of her second novel that she wrote between 1972 and 1974.[22] In the earlier period the men saw themselves as having only two choices: to leave and plot revolution, or to stay and compromise. In the later

period they invited military retaliation by throwing themselves
against the Israelis without thought of the consequences. Khalifa
demonstrates the bankruptcy of both ways of fighting.

In *Wild Thorns,* those who remain suffer a kind of internal exile,
as they work for the enemy. Zuhdi works "inside," as does 'Adil
al-Karmi. He knows that he and his family cannot survive if he
refuses to compromise. Unbeknownst to his father, he joins the
workers "inside," while trying to survive with a modicum of de-
cency. How bitter are the words of Abu Sabir, who loses his fingers
in a factory accident in Israel: "Israeli cash is better than starvation. . . . I've tried hunger, but all it did for me was to wear me
down to a skeleton, weak in body and mind" (Khalifa 1985a
[1976], 52–53). Outsiders are quick to judge and condemn. When
Usama arrives in the West Bank from Kuwait, he asks his taxi
driver: "Where's the resistance then?" the latter jokes: "With those
who are paid" (21).[23] He has not lived under military occupation
and so he can continue to be dogmatic: "They've stuffed you full
and made you greedy. They've absorbed you. And I see no sign of
shame in your eyes." To which 'Adil responds: "Ah, Usama, I said
the same thing when I first arrived from Amman. . . . Do you measure man only by his deeds of glory? What about his weaknesses?
The harshness of his life?" (27, 65). His cynicism foreshadows the
futility of armed resistance from within.

Khalifa criticizes Usama, the revolutionary in exile, in even
harsher terms. When Usama ironically accuses 'Adil of forgetting
his country, the latter retorts: "The proof that I haven't forgotten
my country is that I haven't left it," and he accuses Usama and his
cronies of wanting "*us* to bear all the burdens of risk and sacrifice
on our own" (98). Usama does not appreciate the complexity of the
issues involved, believing "that there was no longer more than one
dimension to the issue, not after the 1967 defeat and the occupation
that followed" (88). His myopia misdirects his challenge to the
occupation onto fellow Palestinians whose murder he claims is not
a crime (94). His operation, the attacks on Israeli buses carrying
Palestinians to work in Israeli factories, killed Palestinians only,
among them a friend: "The individual was of no importance when
the fate of the community was at stake" (86). Let them, like him,

"be martyrs to the land, to the cause" (181). In the end, the exiled revolutionary is killed, desperately trying to recuperate a measure of pride in his senseless behavior and declaiming: "And me, I'm a real lion, mother; tell everyone I died a martyr, a martyr to the cause. A martyr to the land" (185).

In *Wild Thorns*, men embody political positions and attitudes. They are fighters and martyrs, but also compromisers and inveterate conservatives whose bourgeois values seem the more heinous when compared with stark statements by workers like Abu Shahada, the old retainer of the al-Karmi farm, who scoffs at Usama's zeal for the land: "Why should we die for it? Don't give me that! Nobody ever came and asked about us when we were nearly dying of starvation" (42). On another occasion, Abu Sabir reminds 'Adil that "doors will always be open to you, the doors of the rich, the doors of the banks. And the gates of heaven, too" (51). His father comes in for particularly severe criticism. The patriarch is weak and dependent on a dialysis machine that is in turn dependent for its proper functioning on the family members. Yet, undaunted, the old man continues to curse "the workers right back to their ancestors" (55). He entertains foreign journalists and dignitaries, hoping that help can come from outside. 'Adil bursts out in frustration: "He hangs on to life as . . . a virus to a living cell. And I'm that cell" (95). Like other protagonists of Palestinian literature, particularly that by men, 'Adil rejects his father and above all his complicity with the occupation. At the end when the Israelis blow up the al-Karmi mansion for having been the storehouse for guerrilla arms, 'Adil leaves behind the dialysis machine. He must liberate himself of the burden of this father if he is to move on. This death, like that of other tyrannical bourgeois fathers in stories written in the Occupied Territories between 1967 and the outbreak of the Intifada (al-'Alam 1991, 1), signals the hope that the reactionary values of a sick patriarchal bourgeoisie will also die.

The women are stronger if less prominent actors in this first volume. During the five years Usama had been away, things had changed for women: "The servant girls were servants no more, and the class ladder was less steep" (Khalifa 1985a [1976], 27). The situation was opening up what had previously been closed doors for women; they were less anxious to marry. Some, like Lina, were joining the struggle, even being incarcerated. Although individual women are not portrayed as fighters, Palestinian women as a whole are. When the mothers are annoyed with their children, they send them into the streets, the new front, to "pester the Jews." The children laugh at the Israeli soldiers when they curse them. When an Israeli soldier beats a child, the mothers in unison "let loose a stream of curses on all who'd had a hand in the creation of the state. Their husbands blinked in surprise at the volley of oaths. . . . The children's chanting and clapping rang through the empty streets, a crescendo of rhyming slogans about God, Palestine, Arab unity, the Popular Front, the Democratic Front, freedom, dedication, self-sacrifice, and Yasser Arafat" (104–5). While the mothers and children are defying the soldiers in this proto-Intifada confrontation, other Israelis are exploding condemned houses in the neighborhood. At the sound of the explosions, the women once again break into shouts: "Palestine! Palestine!" In 1976 during the second year of the Lebanese war when Palestinians in Beirut were coming under growing pressure to leave, it was not clear whither, Khalifa—like Tuqan—predicts a new way: the revolution had to be accomplished from within and by a new cadre—women and children.

These women know that there is no hope of resolution as long as action is male-driven and full of compromises. Unarmed, they confront the Israelis. Usama's mother remains cool while the soldiers search her house for her son. She reaches "out to the machine-gun, push[es] it out of her way," and sits quietly playing with her prayer beads and silently repeating verses from the Qur'an (164–72). Umm Sabir sells her bracelets, her dowry, to sustain her family while her husband is out of work. The women are grounded and suspicious of rhetoric. The woman in the taxi bringing Usama to his home in the West Bank for his first visit in five years mocks his empty slogans. Later when Usama warns his mother of a Kissinger conspiracy, she mishears and asks: "Singer? You mean there are still imported sewing machines in the country?" (31).

Women have another way of seeing the conflict, they may have another way of addressing it. *Wild Thorns* highlights one aspect of women's ways of fighting that recalls the writings of Farah and other early Palestinian authors in Israel: recognize and negotiate with the humanity of the enemy. In a powerful scene, Umm Sabir and her son witness the murder of an Israeli officer and the distress of his wife and daughter. She uses her veil to cover the little girl, who has fainted, and calls her "my daughter." She turns to the widow and calls her "sister." At the moment of their loss, this Palestinian woman draws the Israeli woman into her family in a profoundly human gesture that recalls Virginia Woolf's declaration: "As a woman I have no country, as a woman my country is the whole world."

Khalifa does not restrict this recognition of the human in the enemy to women. By learning from women's ways of knowing and acting, men may cease to fear and reject the feminine, the tender, in themselves. When 'Adil then enters the murder scene, he, too, is moved by the woman's tragedy. He holds her briefly, then raises the girl onto his shoulders (157–60). His compassion is immediate and unthinking. Later, after Usama is discovered to have been the murderer, he muses over the irony: "My cousin kills a man and I carry off his daughter" (171–72). Another man to acknowledge an Israeli's humanity is Zuhdi. Just before dying, he says that Shlomo, the Israeli worker he had tried to kill and because of whom he had been imprisoned, "wasn't all bad. Just an ordinary man, like you, too, Usama, you bastard!" (183). The novel ends with the women standing on the roofs of their houses, helpless as they watch the bus explode.

Because *Wild Thorns* focuses on the relations between Palestinian men who have stayed in Palestine and those who have gone to Kuwait, it bears comparison with Ghassan Kanafani's best known story *Al-rijal fi al-shams* (Men in the sun, 1963). His protagonists also have chosen between these two specific places. Kanafani condemns escape from Palestine; he does not confront and weigh the merits and risks of remaining, because in 1963 he does not yet have the hindsight to deal with the paradoxes Khalifa raises. The answer, Khalifa writes, lies neither with Usama nor with 'Adil who each consider the other responsible for action as well as for failures. Her pessimism questions the earlier male-authored text that posits one way as superior to the other.

The second volume, *Sunflower* (1985b [1979]), also anticipates the Intifada.[24] The novel is written in a lyrical style with characters repeating themselves in insistent refrains that satirize and condemn the one who speaks. This novel chronicles the lives of three women. Each is without a male protector. Each is, therefore, socially suspect. Rafif, the journalist, struggles with her need for 'Adil. The peasant Sa'adiya, Zuhdi's widow, works inside. Khadra is a prostitute.

Sunflower reiterates a central concern of *Wild Thorns:* it is great "for people to dream of a better world, but it is greater for them not to lose contact with the facts of their present world so that they should not float like bubbles on the surface of stagnant water" (Khalifa 1985b [1979], 40). The men in this book are the bubbles: the journalists—'Adil, Badi, and Salim—are mouthpieces for ideologies that range from a pure Arabism through an idealized internationalism to a romanticized collaboration with the Israeli intellectual left. 'Adil, in particular, has become self-important, "contradictory and vacillating, making generalizations without applying specifics" (17). These leftist intellectuals have no program, just the need to identify and exclude all who are not "politically correct." Those who have kept "contact with the facts of their present world" are the women. From the first page they appear as strong and rebellious. Rafif, 'Adil's colleague and lover, calls for a women's revolution that "is not a people's revolution against another's exploitation, nor the revolution of the oppressed majority against the oppressing minority, nor a revolution against a ruling system. Rather, it is a revolution against a social, economic, religious and ethical system" (211).[25] Rafif may be right, but her defiance remains abstractly theoretical: an entreaty to take women seriously and to include them in the political process. Khalifa criticizes feminists like Rafif who are as simplistically ideological and programmatic as the men. Rafif's claim to speak on behalf of what she considers to be voiceless women is exposed by Sa'adiya: when the journalist wants to interview her after she has lost her land, Sa'adiya refuses, asking her how she thinks she can understand when she has "no children, has not lost a husband, land, sewing machines, or needles" (268).

Rafif recognizes Sa'adiya's charges as identical to those she her-self makes to male colleagues, and this realization renders her believable and vulnerable. She is not a transparent symbol, but rather an individual torn between political agendas, social realities, and personal weakness. Her mood depends on 'Adil's treatment: when he is cruel and indifferent, she is anguished but rebellious, when he is loving she is seduced. She knows that "all her decisions were made subject to him. . . . Where was her freedom as an in-dependent woman?" (108, 112). Love presents her with a paradox: she has to balance the need to be free of her slavery while holding on to the power of her emotions because revolution, she says once, "is impossible without emotions" (256). Rafif never does manage to balance her love with her political goals, which include intro-ducing a women's page into *Al-Balad,* their failing newspaper. Her feminist scheme is no better than those of her male colleagues.

Is Sa'adiya's untutored, instinctive feminist behavior more ef-fective? 'Adil refers to Sa'adiya as a "strong woman who could challenge her circumstances and her environment and stand on her own two feet" (23). After Zuhdi is killed, she has to fend for herself, while guarding herself against suspicions directed at single, par-ticularly beautiful, women. Widowhood for Sa'adiya means be-coming the "land without a guardian" (30). Independence means freedom from male ownership and therefore openness to suspicion of immorality.[26] Sa'adiya has to learn how to survive in what had until then been a man's world. To that end, she constructs herself outside the mold, and this exceptionality has to be seen as male: "She sees the women in the accursed windows looking at her with envy. She feels as though she had become a man, or half a man. So her step became firm . . . [she] was no longer merely a woman. She was the mother, the father, and the miserable woman moving between home and Tel Aviv" (35, 66). Since becoming a "man," Sa'adiya sees clearly for the first time with her own eyes. Recon-structing the past in light of her new awareness, as do the protag-onists of other women's war fiction, she discovers that her late beloved husband had always tried to possess her. Society sanc-tioned his mastery because he was a man and for no other reason: "I'm a man, Woman." he had once said. "Women are for the home and that's it" (25). The absence of a male to define her as his other shakes this rigid categorization. When Shahada—a peasant-made-good business colleague—propositions her, she immediately rejects the familiar urge to control (69, 73). When he calls her Saʻadiya, she retorts angrily: "First of all, I'm Umm Hamada and not Saʻadiya. Second, I'm not a woman. I'm like you. I have a business. Third, no one is responsible for me but God and I. Understand?" (73). She invokes a female and a male identity: as Umm Hamada she commands the respect due a mother, as a business person she demands equality. In this melding of her two gender identities she escapes the control of her society. Only God is responsible for her now.

Saʻadiya is no simple symbol of *sumud*. She dreams of a house on a plot of ground that she can call her own and where she can live, but it must be away from people. Her need to be alone on the land subverts accepted notions of "non-departure"—a form of behavior more fully elaborated by Palestinian women in southern Lebanon in the wake of the 1982 Israeli invasion. Staying on the land is not enough, as her son assures her, she must stay with her people. Saʻadiya's masculinity is not consciously constructed to create an alternative model for women's participation. It is a survival mechanism that does not affect her socialized attitude to other women without male guardianship. When she meets Khadra the prostitute, Saʻadiya ironically wishes her a *mahram* (a male guardian) to control her excesses (71–72), giving no thought to her own ambivalence in regard to male-female relations.

The political situation forces Saʻadiya to become involved. Her land that she had planned to be the site for her dream home is confiscated. She joins her people in their communal struggle. She can no longer remain alone on the margin. During the Nablus demonstrations, Saʻadiya fears for her son whom the Israelis have detained. She joins a group of women who have lost their sons and who are training their children to throw stones at the Israelis: "Stones, Pebbles. Clods of earth. Shrapnel. Glass. Women's screams. Beatings. Stones. Slings. Children climbing up and down the wall" (278). Together the women advance on the walls of the schoolyard where the young men are being held. When an officer appears, Sa'adiya breaks away from the women and rushes toward him. He beats her but she does not give up, "clinging to his chest: 'My son!' A second blow. A third. She drew back a few paces and then . . . the attack. She kicked him between the legs with all the hate and bitterness and anger of a pained heart" (278). Inspired by her example, the other women start to throw stones and glass. The sons take advantage of the turmoil their mothers have caused and they climb over the walls. When the collaborationist mayor tries to stop the women, telling them to go home so that he can work, the women attack him also. Their ultimate insult was to call these men "women." Yet these revolutionary women were not in any way like the women these collaborators had become (279).[27] The world may not have heard of the Intifada until 1987 but it is clear from this exposé by a twentieth-century Arab Cassandra that its roots had already sunk deep.

If there is a model revolutionary woman in this novel then it may be Khadra, the prostitute. She is afraid of nothing. Khadra has been so thoroughly beaten that she has nothing more to fear. She has her own set of moral rules that sanction dishonesty and theft (92, 99). She teaches Sa'adiya to kick all men between the legs even if she can see no immediate benefit. As we have already seen, Sa'adiya puts this lesson to good use. Khadra's daring is not empty bravado, it empowers women so that they do the undoable and attack the Israelis and collaborators and they can say the unsayable: "They say that we women are each worth five shillings. By God, each of us is worth ten men" (166).

The social outcast–revolutionary Khadra poses a dilemma: how can a Palestinian woman act independently, fight, survive *within the community*, and make sure that her actions will continue to count? In her next novel, *Mudhakkirat imra'a ghayr waqi'iya* (Memoirs of an unrealistic woman, 1986), Khalifa explores how individual transformation can take place and what the consequences might be.[28] What happens to women who create themselves outside the norms of social expectations? How can they deal with their intense self-awareness and yet continue to function effectively? In this lyrical novel written as an internal monologue, Khalifa joins other postcolonial writers—Gloria Anzaldúa, an

American of Mexican descent, is another—who are trying to construct an oppositional consciousness and borderlands practice that
may be safe from co-optation by the dominant discourse. As they
do, Khalifa uses the female body as the site for an experiment that
would melt the boundaries rigidly dividing what is said to be
distinct but is in fact mixed and ambiguous. *Memoirs* is what
Anzaldúa would call "a new story to explain the world and our
participation in it, a new value system with images that connect us
to each other and to the planet" (Anzaldúa 1987, 81).

This new story is about connections: "There is no fixed boundary
between people, animals, plants, and inanimate objects. All are
things in my opinion. People are things? May God forgive me, but
things are people. I mean things are worlds, people are worlds. The
world of people, the world of cats, the world of apples, the world
of stories and songs, all are worlds" (Khalifa 1986, 9). The old story
had been about separation and clear categories: "I am the daughter
of the supervisor and remained thus until I became a merchant's
wife. Sometimes I'm both. When the husband mocks me, he calls
me 'the supervisor's daughter,' and when the father gets angry, he
calls me 'the merchant's woman.' The truth is that I was happy to
be the supervisor's daughter because the supervisor is a symbol of
knowledge, dignity, and authority over all teachers" (5). 'Afaf,
whose name means chastity, is a commodity whose identity changes
with its owner; the only difference that marriage makes is to prove
that she is a "salable commodity" (40). But it is only in the preface
that she unemotionally accepts such reification, for this is the frame
structure that the rest of the narrative serves to subvert.

'Afaf rejects such notions of femininity that allow her no agency,
because a thing cannot act. She tries to learn how not to be a girl,
both physically and socially, and how to become an androgyne: "I
am a girl but because of my anxiety at their anxieties I behaved like
a boy and so became something between both. Because I wanted
to gain respect, I refused my fundamental characteristic and became
an 'androgyne' [*khanata*]: neither male or female. That's what I
heard the old women of the family say about me as they smiled and
frowned, encouraged and warned. . . . My identity became more
and more confused" (6).[29] She has become what Anzaldúa calls

the "forerunner of a new race, / half and half—both woman and man, neither—/ a new gender." This new race, this new gender is ahead of its time whether its habitat be the West Bank or the American Southwest because both are borderlands where life is war, "where enemies are kin to each other; / you are at home, a stranger / . . . you are wounded, lost in action / dead, fighting back" (Anzaldúa 1987, 194). How hard it is to fight back when at every instant the complex self that 'Afaf creates is flattened back into the woman-body equivalence that makes her a "criminal who has committed no crime" (Khalifa 1986, 49). To prevent such an eventuality, like Sa'adiya she acts like a man, pulling back her hair severely and adopting a military step (24). But however hard she tries, she cannot always prevent people from noticing her: her body has turned her into a prey, sometimes paralyzing her so that she "stays in bed sick without sickness" (15)—the allusion to Betty Friedan is unmistakable.

'Afaf tries to create a new self that will escape the prison of easy labels. This new self is not dyadic. In a world that recognizes black and white only, she is neither female nor male, revolutionary nor bourgeois,[30] free nor bound, married nor unmarried, active nor passive. The self-authored 'Afaf inhabits the borderlands that link the oppositions defining her life. It is there that she can "dream different stories" (17), like the ones her grandmother had told, stories whose heroine she might become. Stories, paintings, and dreams are the escape valves from a harsh reality. 'Afaf tries to make sense of her new identity that is splintered between socialized construction, self-perception, and self-production. Recognizing her body to be the source of social censure, she changes it. At one point, it turns into "a human envelope" curled around a red apple—later referred to as religion (218)—her father insists she eat. She refuses because she cannot consume herself. No one can understand how she and the apple-religion had become inextricably intertwined, and their destruction of the apple necessarily destroys part of her: "They skinned the apple from me. I saw a huge knife slaughter it and cut it to pieces. I saw my mother strip off the apple's red skin and I pictured blood and was afraid and hated" (10–11). She finds renewal in another thing, this time in a cat she finds in a garbage can. The cat is not merely a companion, it becomes part of her to the extent that she calls herself half-cat, half-woman: the androgyne becomes Egyptian goddess! Addressing her image in a mirror, she says: "They say you are deceitful and cunning. I say something else. I say that I know you because I know myself. I know myself in you. The self that is revealed in the night mirror. My imagination that lives in the unconscious. My freedom lost in the conscious and unconscious. I am you. So let me begin to draw. A woman with a cat's imagination" (43). 'Afaf uses this real/reflection cat to construct herself other than others expect. But this mythical construction does not affect reality. As long as the context remains unchanged, her own transformation will have no impact. It is not enough for her to change, she must learn how to apply art to life so as to transform reality.

The contradictions of living in the borderlands may become too much to bear unless a way is found to make them less raw. 'Afaf accommodates her new gender by ironically creating another binary between body and mind: "The body was exploited, but the mind was escaping. . . . I knew that in the darkest hours and in the smallest prison cells I could open the window in my head and escape through it into a world full of joy, dancing, singing, and smiling faces filled with emotions. Storybook people came alive and I interacted with them to the point that I became a complete part of their world. . . . Through art I loved people more" (131–32).

In this artist's biography we witness a woman choosing the route espoused by a number of women writers during the Lebanese civil war (Cooke 1988, chapter 8). 'Afaf discovers art as a political tool. Whereas the women in Lebanon used art as a raison d'être that supersedes that of wife and mother so as to find a way to prioritize self above selflessness, Khalifa shows 'Afaf turning to art in an attempt to change reality as she changes herself. While painting she disembodies herself and creates herself and those with whom she comes into contact as being interdependent: "I have my own world on whose colors, melodies, and perfume I fly. At night, when people sleep I draw dozens of drawings and create dozens of faces" (Khalifa 1986, 18). Real people offer less companionship than do her creations: "I exchanged the living for dead, empty canvases which my imagination filled with humans" (60).

'Afaf's relationship with art remains ambivalent. It gives her freedom from convention, while alienating her from those whose loves she craves. At school, a friend turns from her in jealousy because of it. At home, her parents and then her husband misunderstand and despise her creations. They condemn her talent as madness, exhorting her always to be realistic. But theirs is not a reality that she cares to share. Others may despise and even try to destroy what she produces, but she knows that she must continue to create, to fashion herself and by extension her universe too, however imperfectly, in terms of her fluctuating needs. It is this self-centered and self-conscious process that gives her the only possible control over her life.

Self-control entails rejection of social norms. She laughs at the women who ululate with joy when the new-born boy urinates his "cologne" onto all and sundry. She determines to "be a woman who gets her way exactly as men do. A woman who wants, desires, and feels. Who uses her husband the way husbands use their wives. Who treats him the way men treat prostitutes" (30). Above all, she refuses to be quiet even though "speech was forbidden" (27). 'Afaf knows what she must do but not how. When she becomes pregnant she quickly arranges an abortion, hoping that ridding herself of her husband's child would also rid her of the man and her own complicity in the perpetuation of the cycle (33). For her motherhood, especially in war, is destructive.[31] Her family subverts even this decision: so as to ensure her remaining within society, her deed had to be reconstructed as involuntary and above all passive. They announce that 'Afaf has had a miscarriage; she did not do anything to her body, her body did something to her. Like other women protagonists of Arab war fiction, 'Afaf's reaction to such pressure is silence.[32] This silence is called madness: "I was always afraid of crying in front of people. Yet I did. . . . A thing I learned during those years in prison was to control my sobs until I reached the bathroom. I didn't learn shame but fear. Fear of the word 'mad'" (12), even when uttered by a despised husband's whiskey-laden tongue.

Madness is the label for behavior that cannot be categorized or, better, controlled. With time art becomes her madness: "I became drawing crazy and took refuge in my colors. It was said that drawing was the secret of my madness so I increased my madness by drawing. . . . I was convinced of my madness because I constantly heard them apply that word to me" (58). Jane Marcus explains that this labeling of madness is often applied to women in war and she calls those spaces of silence and cleansing into which such women retreat the "asylums of Antaeus." The asylums are "the real and imagined places where the contradictions of her state-enforced roles drive woman mad (where she fights fetishization and fails). She speaks out of the confusion and fear derived from this condition in a doubled voice" (Marcus 1989, 135).

'Afaf had always been called mad. As a child, she changed the meanings of others' labels. When her father called her *hawa'iya*, meaning capricious and lacking in respect, she returned to the root of the word and, finding *hawa'* meaning "air," translated his criticism into praise: she was light as air. But with time she learned that subversive translations were not effective when they remained uninstitutionalized into dominant discourse. For the others, *hawa'iya* lies midway between two poles of unacceptable behavior for women. In a typical stringing of adjectives, Khalifa lays out the natural progression in society's condemnation of women's power: "strong, obstinate, capricious [*hawa'iya*], freakish, mad" (Khalifa 1986, 58). 'Afaf's strength is dangerous and must be curbed with the label of *hawa'iya*, which is only two steps removed from madness. The act of naming empowers the namer. 'Afaf cannot ignore the power of the name and finds herself caught in her own act of defiance. As a "mad woman," she exists in a freedom that is ineffective because it is a freedom to act *outside* society. She has gained control of her body but cannot find a space beyond herself in which, thus transformed, she may act effectively. Finally, she has to face the fact that whether she constructs herself as masculine, feminine or androgynous, society treats her as a woman. Her urine will never become "cologne"; she must marry, even though marriage is a prison, and remain married; she must play the domestic game to the end: "Is there no place for a woman outside her house?" (22, 45, 47). There is a hint that she may not be willing to tolerate this domesticity indefinitely when she links "laundry, dishes, kitchen" with "knife" (60, 70). Stringing them together reveals a deadly desire. How long will she remain within her society's prison and consider it home?

Why should she want to keep such ties? Why not put herself outside a society that she recognizes as harmful to her humanity? Because she loves her country with the love of a child for her mother (74, 80, 99–100). In an extended passage, she describes her mother and herself and the land as coextensive. Her mother retains the spirit of Palestine "before the Occupation, the arrests, and the prisons [when] things were better, or, perhaps, we thought they were better." By remaining thus frozen in time, steeped in tradition and the perfume of cardamom, her mother takes her to a time when dreaming was not escaping and therefore not abjuring responsibility. 'Afaf can remain a child of this mother, this land, or she can grow up and escape the cozy cocoon. She challenges women's implication in the preservation of a reality destructive to women. Reality for 'Afaf is the tension between perceiving her mother as symbol of the land—the highest good—but also of unchanging values destructive to women as well as her desire to remain such a woman's daughter. This reality drives her to madness. Yet she must not submit to this madness lest she lose political effectiveness. She realizes that exercising her freedom to be other than people expect and opting out of the gender prison seems to imply rejection of the political struggle. Hers is not a passive decision—in war no decisions are passive—but an active decision to do nothing. Everything she does has impact on her society and on its ability to act and react appropriately to outside threats. She must continue to search for a way to be who she wants to be and to achieve a fully integrated identity, while retaining the power to act in her society. 'Afaf's introspection provides a multifaceted model for a woman's self-construction during war. This model mirrors a new fragmented reality, a new vision of the future.

But it is only a vision. Instead of closure to the quest in the next novel, *Bab al-Saha* (1990a)—appearing fourteen years after the publication of Khalifa's first war novel, *Wild Thorns*—returns to the theme of men's unsuccessful ways of fighting.[33] The intervening years have changed nothing. The men have not learned from the martial models offered by the women and the children. They must

recognize that the women had managed to keep the Israelis at bay
for twenty years and that they may still hold the key to success. It
is at their own peril that the men are not attending to women's ways
of resisting. Yet they do not; they still leave for the Gulf and the
United States with promises to return and restore Palestine. Their
parents still condemn their staying as folly. They continue to score
small victories that the Israelis quickly undo. Again, they are killed
in ideological actions. Like 'Afaf's father in *Memoirs,* they care
more about *sharaf* (honor connected with women's chastity) than
they do about *'ird* (honor pertaining to dignity).[34] They consider
loss of *'ird* by working in Israel to be less heinous than loss of *sharaf;*
a brother is more concerned to kill his sister who has been forced
into "prostitution" than he is to recognize her contribution to the
struggle. Despite all that the women have achieved, the men cannot
see them except as transgressing bodies. It is not that the women
in *Bab al-Saha* are any less strong and assertive than Khalifa's other
women protagonists, it is just that the transformation in the social
context has not taken place.

    The Intifada that in its 1967–87 phase epitomized the hyper-
space of the postmodern battlefield was already in its waging being
reformulated in the image of the conventional front. Khalifa demonstrates how the binaries that had been shown to be false were
being reinscribed, and how some women were resisting this reinscription: "The women fought with their hands and with pots.
They exchanged insults. They fought with the soldiers in their
nightclothes, their hair unkempt" (Khalifa 1990a, 135). As in *Sunflower,* there are three women protagonists: another prostitute,
Nuzha; another intellectual of sorts, Samar; but instead of the
self-sufficient businesswoman Sa'adiya, who lives on the margins
of society, the third woman, Zakiya, is a pious midwife who is
described as the "alley cornerstone and everyone's mother"
(26). This somber and ironic novel proclaims that the Intifada—
despite widespread claims concerning women's involvement and
empowerment—has changed nothing in women's lives except their
level of anxiety: "Their previous worries remained unchanged and
countless others have been added" (20; cf. 73, 126).

    Nuzha, the so-called prostitute, is again the strongest character
in the novel. After comrades kill her mother, who was suspected of

being a collaborator, and her brother apparently leaves, Nuzha has to sustain herself. Her options are limited: first, in a bakery; next, at Studio Zizi; finally, marriage at age fifteen to a loathsome man (94–107). She becomes politically active with her boyfriend, but after an assignment he escapes and she is incarcerated. In the Ramallah prison she finds herself "lost among Israeli women criminals and Arab women politicians. Yet she was neither a Jewish prostitute nor was she an Arab politician" (148–49). Upon her release everyone, including the pious Zakiya, rejects her. She is thus a double victim, first of the Israeli jailers and then of Palestinian men. As Samira Haj writes, Israelis have long known how to use the values attached to Palestinian women's sexuality to intimidate the society as a whole. Even before the Intifada, but especially since its outbreak, Israeli soldiers were reported to have sexually harassed and raped women in order to "pressure and neutralize Palestinian activists. As of last summer [1991], there had been an alarming number of reports of 'fallen women' who had turned collaborators; women who had been sexually assaulted were then threatened with exposure, forcing them to cooperate with and report to Israeli intelligence on political activists in their communities" (Haj 1992, 771). Sisters are particularly useful targets because of the code that demands of a brother that he avenge the family honor, even at the cost of his sister's life. It is not surprising, therefore, to find that Nuzha's brother Ahmad returns to the square of Bab al-Saha not to take his sister to America, as she had expected, but to discharge his duty.

Nuzha's character and behavior give the lie to people's accusations that she is a prostitute, daughter of a collaborator. Even had this been true, Nuzha's perspicacity shows that such labels serve only to divide the community against itself and to undermine its ability to resist. As long as women continue to be valued for the sexual purity of their bodies and not for their effective participation in the resistance, the nation will remain at the mercy of outsiders who know how to manipulate the culture against itself.

Nuzha saves Zakiya's nephew, Husam, when he is wounded and has no safe house (Khalifa 1990a, 109–10). One by one, the women come to her previously shunned house, and it seems that Khalifa is preparing a utopian scenario. Illusions of a women's community dissipate when Zakiya's sister-in-law arrives. Umm 'Azzam's search for Zakiya forces her to enter the prostitute's house. She begs for help against her husband. This is the turning point. Zakiya remembers her own similar pleas to Umm 'Azzam years ago; she also remembers her sister-in-law's repudiation of her, and she returns to Umm 'Azzam the advice the other woman had given her years ago: go back to your husband, it was probably your fault (159–67). Attitudes have not changed, therefore social relations also cannot change.

The women in *Bab al-Saha* are not as independent as the women in *Sunflower*. They may live alone but everything they do is in terms of others, particularly men. Nuzha laments her brother's departure and longs for him to return so that they might leave (147). When he does return it is not to save her but to kill her (179–81). She escapes him and then he is shot. At that point, she openly embraces him and mourns his loss. She tends the wounded fighter Husam with care and affection. He has been the first man to acknowledge her humanity, even though only when he was weak and dependent. After initial gratification, especially at receiving a second poem dedicated to her as "symbol of the land," she bursts out: "Even in this house I'm a human being. I have a heart and a soul and I'll do a lot for those I love. . . . Yesterday I was Mother. Now, I'm the Land. Tomorrow, of course, I shall be Symbol. I'm a human being. . . . I'm not a symbol. I'm a woman" (176). Nuzha may be angry to be reduced to a symbol, but something has happened between her and Husam. Husam realizes that during his time with Nuzha he has grown up (171). This recognition of a possible change in himself through his relationship with a woman who has fought in her own way is the only glimmer of hope of a change in societal attitudes that *Bab al-Saha* holds out.[35]

Samar is a tough fighter who has stood up to Israeli soldiers but she cannot stand up to her brother (136). Even when she is in a position of power she does not exploit her advantage. As Sadiq is dragging Samar back home after curfew forced her to spend nine nights at Nuzha's house, a patrol passes. Sadiq is afraid because he does not have his identity card on him and he turns to his sister, suddenly gentle in his hour of need. Samar is first gleeful, then sad, and finally protective: she stands in front of him so that the Israelis should not see him. The man is saved by the woman's body, yet he will not remember because he did not understand. When Nuzha's brother Ahmad comes to take Husam to the mountains, Samar wants to accompany them, but Ahmad snaps at her that she will become like his sister. In other words, he cannot think of the woman fighter except as a camp follower (196).[36]

But it is this despised sister who is the heroine, even if an unconventional one. When he is shot and the women see that Ahmad is dead, they emit ululations as though at a wedding. Nuzha remains silent, in shock. The women ask her: "Why are you quiet? Where are your ululations?" Nuzha stares at the women in confusion: "Get them away from me! Get them away!" A peasant woman shouted, "Congratulations, Palestine. Congratulations on your new groom!" (209). The women are furious when Nuzha angrily refuses to celebrate the marriage of the cadaver with the earth.[37] At Ahmad's wake, Nuzha sits frozen next to the coffin, staring at the ceiling, and all pronounce her mad. Madness, as we have seen before, is a woman's reality in war. Madness is a state for which society has no name.[38] In this case, however, it allows her to function effectively because she has an audience to witness what she is doing. They, like Husam, are compelled to learn that women's ways of fighting are also ways of surviving for everyone.

The novel ends with a riot. Some young men decide that they want to break into the square, Bab al-Saha, take over the Israeli command post, and burn the flag. One by one, they climb to the top of the wall, where they are predictably shot down. After twenty have climbed to their deaths, become "grooms" to Palestine, Nuzha quietly suggests a better way to enter the square. She leads them through her kitchen—a powerful domestic symbol—to an underground passage that leads into the heart of the square: "Within a few moments, crowds of women poured out of the earth" (222). The young girl who was in the lead with the flag in one hand and a Molotov cocktail in the other is shot. Nuzha, as though in a trance, goes to the girl's body. The novel ends with her lighting the cocktail, "not for the *ghula* [Palestine] but for Ahmad" (222). She will probably share the fate of her predecessor, but she will have had the time to light and then cast the explosive. Why does Nuzha turn this heroic suicide into an act of revenge for a brother who wanted to kill her? Is it that family, however bad, matters more to women than politics? Or is there another explanation? Nuzha knows that women's activism is doomed to co-optation, and that her blowing up of the command post must eventually be called personal revenge. She keeps control of the naming process, and then, perhaps, others may see that the personal is also political, and that the political is doomed without the feminine personal.[39] But maybe she is lighting the Molotov for Ahmed because, whatever his intentions, he was a Palestinian fighter and his death demands revenge. She, a woman, thus takes on the role quintessentially that of the Arab men, to avenge a kinsman's death. Another interpretation is that this novel bears out the growing belief that once the scattered intifadas coalesced into an organized movement led by men, it lost much of its momentum.

After *Bab al-Saha*, Khalifa published a short story entitled "Our Fate, Our House," which tells in a few words but in graphic detail what happens to a family that determines to stay in the downtown of Nablus. They refuse family and friends who urge them to leave for safer places. What matters is to remain in their house. Finally soldiers break in and demand that the sons be brought forward. Umm Samih tells her husband to go to the kitchen so that she may take care of the soldiers; meanwhile, her daughter is blocking access to her brother's room. Finally, the soldiers throw caution to the winds and they beat the women. While they are thus occupied, the son escapes. The story ends with Umm Samih bruised but triumphant.

Contrasting Resistances

Writing at two different times of national crisis, Najwa Qa'war Farah, Fadwa Tuqan, and Sahar Khalifa each imagine ways in which the society might become stronger. Each of these writers is concerned at the poor status and situation of women, yet each carefully chooses her moment to articulate that concern. Each recognizes that women's disadvantaged positions have a negative impact on Palestinian society and its ability to resist. Although Farah criticized the class and gender hierarchy of pre-Israel Palestinian society, after the war of 1948 she writes to express solidarity in crisis. She tries instead to understand what is happening to her people. Such writing gained her literary acceptance—an important consideration at a time when cultural conservatism seemed to be the best, if only, form of political action. In contrast, Tuqan's autobiography and Khalifa's post-1967 novels are less concerned with solidarity than with change; how to change readers' expectations of how men should behave in society and at home.

These women of course write for women also. Whenever Farah does so her intention is to control change. Like the Algerian women during their revolution, Farah does not see the war as an opportunity for women. Indeed, she warns against its temptations. When Khalifa targets women her goal is changed. She wants to teach women how to transform themselves. *Memoirs* in particular subtly leads the reader through the minefields of oppositional agency and self-construction. Its clear, abiding message is not to accept a black and white world. Conflicts will never be resolved by a violence that pits opposites against each other. The solutions are in the hands of women who have invented a new kind of fighting. Now they must create a new kind of writing that might participate in the resistance.

Sahar Khalifa goes beyond the reflection of experience in war to script the female body as the site for the struggle to establish the possibility of women's literary agency in the time and space of war. As a woman, she appropriates a discursive space presumed to be closed to her. In that appropriation, she shows the hollowness but also the relentlessness of men's attempts to create for the war a structure, that of the War Story. Because she is not expected to write, she does not have to mold her experiences in terms of a necessary preexisting form. She is free to represent the war as lived and not as prescribed. She can even describe this chaotic space as productive. Like the women who wrote of the Lebanese civil war, the Beirut Decentrists, she reacts to the chaos by producing new discursive structures. The Beirut Decentrists challenged male writers' description of the war as a revolution, in other words, as one group's organized refusal of another group's imagined community.

They offered instead descriptions of the minutiae of normless survival. Because they understood that experience is meaningless until it is given expression, they were able to transform meaning. They labeled anomie war, postcolonial war. They described the waiting woman (the noncombatant) in a Beirut apartment (home front) as a combatant at the front. They demonstrated that survival in war was no longer a passive fact but a resisting act (Cooke 1988). The Beirut Decentrists' literary mapping of a postcolonial war is reflected in Palestinian women's writings on the Intifada. They pen the breakdown of binary structures in the individual and in society. They demand that the notions of private and public under military occupation be imagined anew to accommodate the new battlefield that is neither home nor front but both and neither at the same time.

Khalifa's work paints the canvas of postcolonial warfare in which men and even some women fight ideologically, fragmentedly, and schizophrenically. Some women, however, offer new cognitive maps. Khalifa is adamant that women should not be separatist or in any way ideological, for that would be a way of emulating the men. She advocates a politicized domesticity and motherhood that keep women in their traditional roles that they thus transform. Her writing exemplifies what Rita Giacaman and Penny Johnson describe in the political arena: "Women, and particularly those not already originally identified with a political movement or group, have enlarged or extended their traditional role rather than adopting a completely new role . . . particularly defense of family. . . . These aspects of women's roles have become a source of resistance because women have transformed their family responsibilities to encompass the entire community" (Giacaman and Johnson 1989, 161).[40]

Khalifa resists the power of male war discourse that constantly strives to recuperate a threatened masculinity by co-opting women's agency. She warns that without a revolution in men's attitudes nothing will change. Women will have invested much in return for little. The women's revolution must work hand in hand with the nationalist revolution because *neither can succeed without the success of the other.* Khalifa takes note of what women in Algeria and Lebanon have and have not written. She is confronting both Algerian and Lebanese models: fear of the Algerian women's post-conflict disempowerment; aspiration to the utopian inscription of feminist mobilization into Lebanese war discourse. Yet Khalifa shows that Lebanese women's discursive activism, fashioned to counteract the debilitating effects of Algerian women's voiceless-ness, was just that: discursive. Khalifa's novels ask what is appropriate, effective resistance. How may activism be connected to its interpretation so that discourse itself can become an agent of change? How can literature become a nonviolent way to participate in the nationalist movement as a feminist activist?

The challenge to hold on to the memory of what they have done and to retain the right to express this activism and to assign it meaning is an on-going struggle for Palestinian women. But does it really matter if women's writings on national resistance are suppressed? Of course it does. Writing is more than an affirmation of having done something. Writing is a self-constitutive practice. As much as the act of standing up to tanks, of throwing stones, of languishing in prison, writing contains and produces its subject, linking the resister with the resisting writer that she always already is. As Roland Barthes wrote in his pioneering essay *Writing Degree Zero* (1978 [1953]), writing is not merely a transitive verb that mediates the act and its expression; it is intransitive in that it describes the underlying possibility of its own and its author's coming into being. Writing "represents the writer's descent into the sticky opacity of the condition that he is describing" (Barthes 1978 [1953], 81).[41] Writing is central to democratic practice. When it is neglected, worse when it is actively suppressed, not only the words are erased and the writer is denied, but the citizens as subject, object, and pretext of the writing act are disenfranchised.

Chapter Five

Flames of Fire in Qadisiya

Dear husband, you died young, and left me your widow
Alone in the palace. Our child is still tiny,
The child you and I, crossed by fate, had together.
I think he will never grow up . . .
For not in your bed did you die.

Homer, *The Iliad*

In the summer of 1991 *Al-Raida*, the quarterly journal of the Institute for Women's Studies in the Arab World at Beirut University College, published an article asking what had happened to Iraqi women after their war with Iran ended in 1988. What, the anonymous author asked, "has become of powerful women's groups like the General Federation of Iraqi Women?" Although researchers at the institute knew and had approached women who were more recent refugees from Iraq to Lebanon, they found them reluctant to speak. It remains difficult to assess what the repercussions of the war have been on women many considered to have been the Arab world's most educated and highest trained, employed, and paid population.[1] In comparing Iraqi and Lebanese elite strategies for state building, the anthropologist Suad Joseph talks of the importance of women "to the Ba'th agenda for state construction: the need for labor and for re-aligning the allegiances of the population." In the decentralized pre-Baath state, women's allegiance was particularly important. As the state worked to industrialize and bring heterogeneous groups under its control, it targeted women for resocialization into new Iraqi women and "included general vocational and political education for participation in the formal economy and the polity." In this connection in 1968 the Baath Party founded the General Federation of Iraqi Women (GFIW) as a "female arm of the party." By 1980 the GFIW had 256 centers and 177,000 members, and women's literacy rates went up 300 percent. Literacy centers appeared everywhere and Iraqis who did not go or barred others from attending were penalized. Child care centers were built everywhere and women were given generous maternity leave. Women were given the right to vote and to run for public office. Joseph describes a high level of loyalty among women for one another, for the party, and for Saddam Hussein. She points out that the state's support for the family in some ways undermined its goal of resocializing the individuals to absolute loyalty to the state (Joseph 1991, 176–200). How did the war affect women?

Iraqi women supported the war; they were "enlisted in the army during the Iran-Iraq War. It is said that at one point, Iraqi women were selling their jewelry to support the army." Why? Did they believe in the war? Were they acknowledging a debt to the state? If so, why did the state suddenly revoke some of the many rights it had originally lavished? I ask this because what is known is that with the outbreak of the war, women found many of their freedoms curtailed. For example, laws were promulgated forbidding women to travel without husbands' or fathers' permission. They were told that it was their patriotic duty to have five children for the war; in 1986 "birth control devices disappeared from the market; even condoms were declared illegal" (Lorenz 1991). At the same time and typically for a state at war, women were filling in for the men who had left for the front. Officially we do not know, and may not find out for quite some time, what happened to Iraqi women during and after the war. But we do have the words of a few of them that give us fictionalized accounts of what we may assume were their experiences.

I met Daisy al-Amir, one of Iraq's best known women writers, in Beirut in 1980. Since before the outbreak of the Lebanese civil war in 1975, she had been working as press attaché in the Iraqi Cultural Center. She stayed until 1986, when the Iraqi embassy in Beirut was blown up. She lost friends and her ten-year conviction that she should stay in Lebanon, however difficult things became. She returned to her native Iraq, only to find herself in another, but very different war.

Rather than civil war al-Amir found an apparently conventional war between two sovereign states, Iraq and Iran. In his *Republic of Fear,* Samir al-Khalil called the war, whose casualties—between five hundred thousand and one million deaths—amounted to more than the total number of those in all Israeli-Palestinian wars, even including the Lebanese civil war, "the first completely indigenous 'great war' of the third world" (al-Khalil 1989, 274). Both the Iranian leader, Ayatollah Khomeini, and the Iraqi president, Saddam Hussein, eventually claimed that they were fighting a jihad; the Iranians even brought their own coffins to the front in hopes of martyrdom. For each nation this mode of total warfare had a major problem: it was "singularly unsuited to their equipment and completely at variance with their training" (al-Khalil 1989, 280). If the two militaries were fighting an epic war for which they were not prepared, it seemed at least that its space was that of the great wars of Europe: trench and air combat was taking place at various fronts along the border dividing the two neighboring countries. The cities and centers of concentrated populations appeared intact, calm.

The illusion of wartime calm, when lived, was almost harder to bear than the chaos al-Amir had negotiated in Lebanon. The Iraqi critic Matti Moosa called me on al-Amir's behalf and I arranged for her to come to lecture at Duke University. After jumping through various bureaucratic hoops, she arrived in March 1990, relieved and—to my disappointment—not at all anxious to talk about this most recent war experience. Ironically, only ten months later our two countries would be at war with each other in the Persian Gulf.

I had organized a conference on the theme of the journey in Middle Eastern literatures to coincide with her visit. When al-Amir heard that two of the papers were to be on premodern Persian literature, she announced summarily that she could not take part, could not in fact even stay for the event. Why? How, she retorted, could she be associated with Iran? But the papers were about poetry written centuries ago. She was not to be swayed. Before her premature departure, we had time for a hilarious mishap at the hairdresser's and several long rambling conversations. I told her of my project on war fiction in the Arab world and asked her who was writing what in Iraq. She was dismissive of my interest. She could not understand why after writing *War's Other Voices* I was still interested in such a topic. Al-Amir had written *Wu'ud li al-bay'* (Promises for sale, 1981) and *Fi duwwamat al-hubb wa al-karahiya* (In the vortex of love and hate, 1979), her two collections of short stories on the Lebanese civil war, and then a slim volume, *'Ala la'ihat al-intizar* (On the waiting list, 1988), which she had written in Iraq and published in Beirut. The stories are filled with anxiety and dread but say nothing about the war. The mood that haunts the stories is one of unbearable aloneness and heaviness and mistrust as people wait, unwillingly, for the unknown. Each story grapples with the problem of time and how to escape it without destroying the self. In "Thaman bakhs" (A bargain), al-Amir writes of a woman who buys an anonymous family album: "I bought a heavy past at a time when I had decided to escape it" (al Amir 1988, 32). After leafing through others' memories, the woman throws the album away only to be plunged back into her anxiety about her own past and future that in their dialogue with each other always eliminated her present. This woman might have been the author herself.[2]

Several days after al-Amir's departure, the postman delivered two gunnysacks sent by the Iraqi embassy in Washington, D.C. They were filled with novels, short stories, and volumes of literary criticism produced by the Iraqi Ministry of Culture and Information during the last four years of the Iran-Iraq War. One by one, I took the books out and glanced at their imprints: "On War and Culture" and "Qadisiyat Saddam—Under Flames of Fire." As I browsed through these volumes, I kept noticing this name Qadisiyat Saddam, meaning Saddam's Qadisiya, in connection with literary activities surrounding the war. It was attached to a book series, to a literary competition, even to an entire museum. Qadisiya refers to the 637 C.E. battle that marked the first victory of the Arab Muslim forces over their Sassanian Iranian enemy. To announce the significance of the Iran-Iraq War even before the outcome was known, Saddam Hussein already in 1980 named the war Qadisiya.

He was thus comparing and linking his adventure in the Shatt al-'Arab with one of the most significant turning points in the expansion of the Islamic empire beyond its Arab heartland. This naming, representing, and memorializing of an event's importance, often before its actual occurrence, became the hallmark of Saddam Hussein's strategy in prosecuting this war.

I wasn't sure what to do with this treasure trove, wondering whether writings that a government at war commissioned could be anything but propaganda. Despite my misgivings I took a pile of these books with me when I traveled north later that month. I was to spend a term at Dartmouth College as a fellow in the War and Gender Humanities Institute. The first person I met upon my arrival in Hanover, New Hampshire, was the senior fellow in the same institute, Klaus Theweleit. We immediately started to chat about the institute and our own projects. I told Klaus about the Iraqi books and my concern that I probably could not use them. He countered that the very fact that they were state-sponsored, fully censored by others made them particularly interesting. The writings of the Freikorps men he had analyzed for his *Male Fantasies* were also mainly propaganda items. With their own and their censors' attention beamed on particular political themes, tropes, and words, they were paradoxically free to write what they liked about their feelings. My curiosity was piqued.

Qadisiya Against Itself?

Most of the books were by men, only three by women. Since my original interest was in what women were writing on the war, I had thought that most of the novels and short stories would be good only for leisure reading. After speaking with Theweleit, I decided that I should see what works by Iraqi men could tell me about the psychological concerns of writers who had decided to put their talents at the disposal of their government, works someone at the Iraqi embassy in Washington had chosen for me. Later, and thanks to 'Abd al-Hamid Hammudi (1986), I came across the names of writers like 'Abd al-Sattar Nasir, 'Ali Khayyun, 'Abd al-Khaliq al-Rukkabi, and a few other writers who are better known than most of the ones whose books were delivered to my door in gun-nysacks. Nevertheless I decided to limit my data to these books because of the special circumstances surrounding their acquisition.

I was also curious to know whether social and literary critics had been right to condemn writers for complicity with the Iraqi regime. Without knowing for sure, I questioned their view: the writers had a long history of aligning themselves with the people against the state. In discussing Shakir Khusbak's short story "Years of Ter-rorism" (1952), Muhsin Jassim al-Musawi notes: "The narrator associated rejection of involvement with the state with the ability to establish a sense of personal security and peace of mind." In the 1970s the new oil wealth did seduce some writers to sell their services to the state; many, however, withdrew from public life. Then came the war and its literature that al-Musawi describes as "a channel for projecting internal modes of feeling and experience" (al-Musawi 1991, 203, 210). Was this true of the fiction sponsored by the Ministry of Culture and Information that the embassy had sent me?

Attracted by the title, *Imra'a min al-nisa'* (A woman among women), I first read 'Ali Lufta Sa'id's title story. It is a monologue by a son to his beloved mother. She preaches patient acceptance of God's will and tolerates no expressions of grief or pain. Then comes the war, indirectly alluded to as a "wicked time infiltrating the cells of the house . . . coming from the East" (Sa'id 1988, 61–62)—from Iran.[3] First, her two oldest sons come home on a bier and she is a model of constraint and steadfastness because they had done their duty, struggled "to remove the plague so that our house and other houses might be proud" (61). Next, her husband, who had spent time as "a guest on the hills overlooking the central borders," returns on his bier. This time, she does give way to grief. Briefly. When she has torn at the shroud and discovers that he was laughing, she stops her tears. Her youngest son, the narrator, has understood nothing except that as the last male, the last "wall of the house" he is responsible for keeping love and happiness in the "nation that is you" (63). This was a good patriotic ending for a story that verged on the critical.[4] The war had not been described as great, but rather as a wicked time, and the loss of the three men had not been presented as serving a cause beyond pride, the pride of the house.

Spartan to the end, the mother controls her grief because she is glad
to have been able to exchange sons for pride. She is a harsh woman
who demands that people around her be happy and that they not
break down. In a proleptic paragraph, the narrator describes living
with this mother after the rest of her men had died. He dares not
weep in her presence lest she look at him with those "glances that
carried a thousand and one meanings and that would be intermin-
gled with your well-known words: that I should be a man to
confront circumstances, life would not be compassionate to me if
I continued to be so lacking in patience, so weak-willed, so emotional. In fact, I would be consumed and crumble into the first pile
of dirt" (59). This exacting woman he then calls the nation. I read
this passage as a criticism of the nation symbolized by the mother
who consumes her men for no good reason and does not even allow
the survivors to grieve.

Next I read Faysal 'Abd al-Hasan Hajim's novel *Al-layl wa
al-nahar* (Night and day, 1985).[5] I was intrigued because it had won
the first prize in the 1984 annual state-sponsored Qadisiyat Saddam
Novels Competition (the novel was completed in November 1983
but not published until 1985 and was, I assume, submitted to the
competition in manuscript form). I expected propaganda but found
blackness and jolting disjunctures between contiguous passages. A
cheerful song—"We'll have something to tell our kids / Tralalala-
lalala / Scary things, /Happy things / But we'll never forget to teach
them / That there's nothing better than peace"—is interrupted by
"the camp exploded into limbs, heavy dust, and black smoke.
Earcracking thunder followed. Wild screams rose, boulders and
torn sandbags fell. A fierce fire. Red shrapnel like fiery butterflies,
heavy black smoke. A real hell of fire and screaming. Explosions
everywhere" (Hajim 1985, 69). This Remarquesque novel begins
and ends with landscapes of destruction and decay: "Were it not
for the darkness the soldiers could have seen the skin of the soldiers
who had been killed months earlier in no-man's land and which had
yellowed and then become pinkish. Their swollen stomachs were
light green, their backs dark green" (25–26).

The plot revolves around three soldiers who are called the Fire
Soldier, who has had extensive combat experience, the Other Sol-

dier, who is a poet, and the Lute Soldier, who is a musician.[6] The Iraqi critic 'Abdallah Ibrahim writes that many fictional warriors are described as being absorbed in writing; he understands this recurrence of warrior-poets as being a way for the writer to express himself more directly (Ibrahim 1988, 116–20). The Lute Soldier is killed when their shelter is struck; the other two are wedged together under the weight of the debris. They start to talk about their painful pasts that they are mortified to discover they share. It transpires that the wife of the poet is a nurse who was brought up in an orphanage with the Fire Soldier. They fell in love but she refused to have anything to do with him lest he turn out to be her brother. During a moment of passion and frustration, he raped his orphanage sister. Further, her mother had had an affair with the grandfather of the Lute Soldier, who thus might well be the nurse's nephew. These three men, one of whom gave his life for his country, are caught in a ring of incest around a woman who dedicates her life to healing the war's wounded. If Ibrahim is right and the Other Soldier speaks on behalf of Hajim and the identifying reader-warrior, then the danger of cuckoldry, of losing personal honor on the battlefront, becomes a more significant theme of the novel. So much for patriotic duty and male bonding under battle duress. The men are unable to defend their women even from their own countrymen, how much less so from a determined enemy. Had the two young men not been immobilized by the ruins of the shelter they might have killed each other. At the end the Fire Soldier, the singer of the song, declares the war to be "cursed and totally immoral" (Hajim 1985, 83). Already in 1983 Hajim was articulating criticism of the war that was actually financing his writing project and would confer on him the 1984 Qadisiyat Saddam prize.

Five years later Hajim published *Junud* (Soldiers, 1988), a collection of short stories that ends with "'Asha' akhar" (A last supper). As its title indicates, it is full of foreboding and ritual. A mechanic has just received permission to leave the army and he is to spend his last night with his companions. They eagerly await the supper when they expect him to distribute among them the contents of a box he had safeguarded throughout the years he spent in the unit. They want to know what are the things he carried.[7] They watch the Last Supper Man, who no longer seems to belong in their world. They warn him about his wife and how difficult it will be for him to help with the children's problems. When he replies that he did fine before the war, one retorts that now things have changed and that he will "not be able to do a thing," and that he had better leave everything to his wife and not do anything without consulting her because with all that had happened—the war—he could no longer function effectively in civilian society (Hajim 1988, 90, 92). When he finally opens the precious box, out come odds and ends like an almost empty perfume bottle, some black shrapnel, a worn towel, a small shaving mirror chipped in a corner, a needle in a ball of thread, a rusty pair of shaving scissors. Although each item held an important memory for him, for them the most valuable object was an unused can of shoe polish. Finally, the soldiers do find something intriguing: a matchbox-size talisman carefully wrapped in cloth. He remonstrates that they should not touch it because his mother had given it to him. But they have to know what is inside. They open it to find a blank sheet of wrinkled, yellowed paper. The Last Supper Man is astonished: "A blank sheet of paper protected me all these years. I can't believe it" (93). The story ends with bombs exploding close to them.

The other stories in this collection underscore the sometimes angry, always despairing mood of "A Last Supper." Soldiers relate their experiences at a front that was the antithesis of glory. The narrator of "Dhubul" (Withering) is a sensitive young man who learned from his girlfriend, a flower vendor, that flowers are "a method of philosophical, spiritual, and aesthetic communication between nature and humans. They are the path of peace about which Buddhist philosophy teaches." She told him about how "the Fascists had stopped Emile Nolda from painting his flowers, but he painted several canvases in liquid colors that represented other hidden flowers and his harsh guards noticed nothing" (Hajim 1988, 65). Are these harsh guards standing in for Hajim's censors who cannot read subversive messages calling for peace? Then the narrator had gone to the front to learn "the meaning of attack and martyrdom. I spent some dark hours and some so bright they

blinded me. In the trenches my feet got soaked and my toes dis-
integrated in the military boots. . . . My clothes became salt and of
one piece as though they were made of cardboard; they stuck to my
skin, lacerated by the salt water in which I had been wading waist-
deep for days" (66). When he came home on leave, he wanted to
tell her about what he had been through, but he could say nothing
and he no longer enjoyed her conversations about flowers. The war
had withered his link with the one who taught him the meaning of
peace.

Two of the stories are about men's need to be in touch with their
loved ones at home, but with a bitter twist. After we have read
through the letter of "Risala mu'ada" (A returned letter) as though
we were the addressee, we discover that we are in fact three engineer
colleagues. They have opened this letter because it had been sent
back: the wife had just been "martyred" during the bombardment
of Basra. The front no longer has any meaning when the home front
is being targeted; the combatant can no longer define his acts in
opposition to the calm domesticity of his woman. The other letter
is in a story entitled "Ma'an wa ila al-abad" (Together forever),
which earned an honorable mention in the 1987 Qadisiyat Saddam
novels and short stories competition. The soldier is writing to his
wife of his dreams for peacetime, of cultivating with her the land
that his father left on the Shatt al-'Arab even though it is full of
shrapnel. The letter ends: "I shall whisper to you after drawing a
rose in the air with my finger soaked in blood. You and I together
forever . . ." and the letter ends with ellipses. Did he die as he was
writing?

Was this propaganda? Might these short stories and novel serve
the interests of the state? How did the censors read this literature?
As A. Peter Foulkes writes, literature functions "both as propaganda and anti-propaganda." It should be studied both "as a set of
documents" and as "a set of aesthetic objects. For in effect it denies
the validity of such a distinction by assuming that the propagan-
distic or demystifying moment of literary communication may be
inseparable from its aesthetic function. This point of intersection
will be historically determined but it should not be regarded as a

frozen act of past communication" (Foulkes 1983, 106). Propaganda is like censorship in that it is driven by a dynamic that is constantly changing. The Russian critic Lev Loseff, who analyzes Aesopian language as the technique that Russian writers used for two and a half centuries to overcome state censorship, explains that censorship works within the author-reader-censor triangle. It produces a "special literary system, one whose structure allows interaction between author and reader at the same time that it conceals inadmissible content from the censor" (Loseff 1984, x). The role of the censor is not necessarily content-oriented. Censorship may become "an end in itself, necessary as one attribute of the myth of power" (Loseff 1984, 223). The censors must be kept on their toes; the critics must learn how to read Aesopian techniques and to recognize the moment when they have been so thoroughly understood that they have been institutionalized and have lost their resistant meaning and force.

I have never set foot on Iraqi soil or met anyone who knows about the ways in which the government controlled information and knowledge during the war. Yet these few stories persuaded me that there were writers who knew what they were doing, that they were critical of the military enterprise and they wanted to package their message in such a way that it would get through to the targeted audience. I was curious to read on.

Martial Simulacra

As in most wars, the control and manipulation of culture and history, of knowledge, was an essential component of the war. Culture past and present became frontline ammunition. Saddam Hussein situated himself in history: he was the last link in a chain of Iraqi luminaries that stretched from Nebuchadnezzar through the Prophet of Islam to today. Otto Friedrich writes that "Saddam Hussein had himself photographed in a *replica* of the chariot of Nebuchadnezzar, the Babylonian king whom Saddam apparently reveres as his hero" (Friedrich 1990, 23; my emphasis). Samir al-Khalil writes that the problem with inventing lineage and a heritage,

or what he calls *turath,* is that "there is actually no continuity with
a historic past. When the Ba'th finally came around to realizing a
twenty-year-old dream to rebuild Babylon . . . , they built the five-
thousand-year-old capital of Nebuchadnezzar out of thermalite
blocks 'in the style of the Barbican,' according to one English observer." Whereas Nebuchadnezzar had ordered all bricks to be
inscribed with the words "Nebuchadnezzar, King of Babylon from
far sea to far sea," Saddam ordered these bricks to be inscribed:
"Rebuilt in the era of the leader Saddam Husain [*sic*]" (al-Khalil
1991, 70–71).

Saddam then turned to the history of Iraq and, without any sense
of humor, systematically rearranged it under the aegis of his project
for the rewriting of history (Davis and Gavrielides 1991, 132). In
his *Hawla kitabat al-tarikh* (On the writing of history), which the
aforementioned Ministry of Culture and Information published in
1979, he explains that he had to do this to correct all the mistakes
perpetrated by Western orientalists, adding that "history should be
written to serve the interests of Iraqi society as defined by Baathist
ideology" (quoted in Davis and Gavrielides 1991, 139).[8] A year
before launching what was supposed to be a Blitzkrieg into Iran,
Saddam Hussein is declaring his intention: possess history lest it
possess you. The past could, in fact should, be rewritten, the future
should be created to precede and thus to transform an always
already malleable present, the perfect simulacrum. Lyotard describes this interaction between time and the creative artist as the
formulation of "rules of what *will have been done.* Hence, the fact
that work and text have the characters of an *event;* hence also, they
always come too late for their author, or, what amounts to the same
thing, their being put into work, their realization [*mise en oeuvre*]
always begins too soon. *Post modern* would have to be understood
according to the paradox of the future (*post*) anterior (*modo*)"
(Lyotard 1987, 81).

Iraqi civilians became responsible for the success of this cultural
construction, of this invention of *turath.* When the war broke out,
the fighters were the most burdened because they could only come
into their own after winning the victory already said to be won. If

God willed that they should die, why then their names would be added to the monument already constructed in memory of their martyrdom!

How could this anticipatory representation be effected? Artists and writers had to be mobilized to sculpt, paint, write, and sing the glories of the war that, even if they were not yet quite glorious, might in time become so thanks to pens, brushes, chisels, and lutes. During the first year of the war, the Qadisiyat Saddam publication series had already published two anthologies of short stories, which must have been written during the very first days of the war. In the mid-1980s Shakir Hasan Al Sa'id was sent with a group of artists to paint Mandalay after a victory had been won. He published a book of some of the drawings entitled *'Inda masharif khandaq al-istishhad* (Overlooking the martyring trench, 1988). The reproductions are poor but what can be made out does not seem particularly glorious. I was caught by one image that shows the commander's vehicle safely tucked away into a military shelter by the side of a slope and surrounded by sandbags. A few steps away is a sign that reads "Iraq will never bow its head and will continue to fight heroically and courageously." The absence of the courageous heroes speaks volumes (Al Sa'id 1988, 62). The other images are at times so minimalist as to be incomprehensible. Are they as subversive? They may well be and yet these ambiguous drawings were accepted and published by the Ministry of Culture and Information, but, needless to say, with an introduction that talks about the privilege of being permitted to "participate in Saddam's Qadisiya through art."

Fiction, art, but also—and more dramatically—monumental architecture. The huge triumphal double arch of arms—replicas of Saddam's own—crossing swords in Baghdad "was erected shortly after what the regime deems to have been a 'victory' in the Iraq-Iran war, and it was erected to commemorate that victory. Yet it was commissioned several hundred thousand lives earlier, in 1985, when no victory was in sight. Its conception therefore precedes the reality it is meant to commemorate, which is most uncommon in the history of monument making" (al-Khalil 1991, 10). The Martyr Monument also was planned before the object to be memorialized existed: "The war began in September 1980 and on-site construction started in April 1981. The project would have been planned, drawn, managed and detailed many months before" (al-Khalil 1991, 23). In other words, the martyrs were being commemorated before they even knew that there was going to be a war in which they were going to be killed.

At first glance, some of the Iraqi men's war fiction sent to me as well as works about which I later read seemed to function like this monumental architecture: it was anticipatory and glorifying. Stories glorified men's heroism, humanitarianism ,and patriotism and women's jingoism. Perhaps the first story on this war to be translated into English is Abdullah Abdul Razzaq's "Voices from Near and Far." A mother dictating a letter to her son at the front is critical of all men who do not volunteer, including the scribe who is doing her this invaluable service. She idolizes the fighters, even investing in a radio so that she may hear her son's voice should he ever get to a microphone to send home greetings. But even if he does not, it is enough for her that she can hear other soldiers' voices: "The voices would scatter and coagulate. . . . What is it that gives their voices this similar tone? Is it the love that binds them together? Or is it that great shared thing that unites them?" Her son's voice is brought to her through these other voices, and she loves their voices, she loves them all because "those are my sons" (Abdul Razzaq 1983, 114). Her jingoism is an inspiration to all: if mothers are for the war, who can be against?

One of the most striking examples of patriotic writing that I have read is *Al-maudi' al-turabi* (The dusty place). This collection of short stories that Makram Rashid al-Talibani translated from the Kurdish was published in 1987 (in which year, ironically, the government began its systematic purging of the Kurds). It comprises seven stories of exemplary heroism, of undying loyalty to the Iraqi regime and its just cause and certain victory, of Iraqi soldiers' humanity to their barbaric, pseudo-religious, cowardly enemy. Even women write this way. The soldier in Khalida Khadar Ibrahim's "Tears of Joy" is rescuing a wounded comrade when he sees an Iranian keel over and sink into blood and mud. Recognizing this man's greater need, the soldier gently drops his Iraqi comrade to pick up the Iranian enemy. He delivers him to an ambulance as a prisoner of war but one who should be given special medical attention. From a distance, as the camera focus softens and music gently plays, the briefly abandoned wounded Iraqi soldier looks on, his eyes overflowing with tears of joy at the sight! (al-Talibani 1987, 36). There is no evocation of pain or fear, just heroism, camaraderie, and melodramatic compassion for the enemy.

In 1985 at the annual Marbid Cultural Festival, the American-Iraqi critic Matti Moosa delivered a lecture entitled "Love, Death, Honor: Major Themes in Recent Iraqi Short Fiction." It deals with the preoccupations of Iraqi writers between the outbreak of the war in September 1980 until 1982 (literature to which I have not had access).[9] Moosa restricts his analysis to the 452 (!) short stories that had been produced during the war's first two years. Perhaps because the lecture is part of a state-sponsored festival, Moosa limits his taxonomy to expressions of patriotic sentiment and the writers' avowed intent to play their part in counteracting "cultural destruction" by the Iranians. He singles out three major topics: heroism, humanitarianism, patriotism.

Heroism, at both the individual and the collective level, is depicted in the army, the air force, and the navy. The compassion of the protagonist for the enemy, which can already be read in the early literature, has by the late 1980s become a topos, even for some women. Moosa summarizes Balqis Ni'mat al-'Aziz's "Swing of Fire," which lionizes an Iraqi soldier who refrains from killing an Iranian boy because he recognizes in him his own son. Reading Moosa's account, I cannot assess whether this evocation of humanitarianism is in praise of the soldier or a criticism of the war. Some of the early 1980s stories go beyond praise of the Iraqi soldier to adulation of the Iraqi leader. 'Ali Khayyun's "Time Has Three States" and 'Adil Kamil's "The Symbol" extol Saddam Hussein's compassion for the families of martyrs.

Women, Moosa intimates, are reduced to patriotic symbols. We have already seen an example in Abdul Razzaq's "Voices from Near and Far." 'Abd al-Sattar Nasir's patriotic "A Fighter's Wife"

(1982) traces the transformation of a woman's rejection of the war to its hearty espousal. The woman in Raja' al-Buhaysh's 1982 "Tales of Iraqi Suns" incites her grandson to enlist so that he may have the chance to be as heroic as his grandfather had been during the 1920 Iraqi revolution against the British. In 1983 the prolific Lutfiya al-Dulaymi wrote her didactic "A Dinner for Two." A pregnant wife awaits her husband whom she expects to come home on leave from the front. A knock at the door. It is not he, but two unknown soldiers. She fears the worst, but no, he is not dead. He has generously given up his leave so that a companion may get away to marry. The woman shares her would-be romantic dinner with the fighters. No one counts personal sacrifice. Moosa concludes his lecture with a paean to writers who have produced stories "written in the noble spirit and conviction that Iraq is fighting a decisive war for its very existence and national well-being . . . there is no more appropriate vehicle to portray the sentiment, hope, and bravery of the Iraqi people than fiction."

Critics at the Front

These pious concluding remarks echo the tone of most of the literary criticism on the voluminous Iraqi war literature produced on the eight years of the war. Indeed, the criticism, probably more than the fiction itself, became an exercise in proving patriotism and unquestioning support of the war. The critic Basim 'Abd al-Hamid Hammudi quotes a remark by the writer Salah al-'Ansari: whereas the "world wars were inhuman, our war against the Iranian enemy was human because it sought to restore rights" (Hammudi 1986, 97). Numerous literary competitions, cultural festivals, conferences, seminars, debates, and monographs embrace the study of this literature. All critics emphasize the importance of asserting that the war was not only militarily but also culturally significant (Hammudi 1986, 43; and Ibrahim 1988, 5). Thus they justify the political importance of their own roles as bridges or mediators between these two complementary aspects of the Iraq-Iran War. 'Abdallah Ibrahim introduces his monograph on the structure of fifty-seven war novels written in Iraq between 1980 and 1985 with quotations from major French philosophers like Roland Barthes, Michel Foucault, and Tzvetan Todorov arguing that the work of the creative writer and of the critic are utterly intertwined (Ibrahim 1988, 11). Hammudi believes that criticism should precede and encourage the production of literature—a criticism meditating on a not-yet-written literature whose realization it is thus fostering (Hammudi 1986, 15). This criticism literally "pre-scribes" its subject.

Many critical events and publications begin with some discussion of the term "war literature," often also called *qissat al-harb,* or the War Story. Some write as though they were the ones to coin the term (e.g., Ibrahim 1988, 5); others recognize that such literature exists elsewhere. These latter often compare Iraqi war literature favorably with international exemplars of the genre, for example, Hemingway, Dos Passos, Remarque, and even the Argentinian Julio Cortazar. Others, including the internationally esteemed Palestinian-Iraqi writer Jabra Ibrahim Jabra, talk of its importance to modern Arabic literature. Jabra claims that this war—along with the Palestinian resistance and the Algerian war of liberation—inspired many great works: "this war added the figure of the 'real combatant facing death' to the social, emotional, and political themes of modern Arabic literature." Those works by authors who have had actual battle experience are described as particularly important, and they "will remain in communal memory in a way that no other writing can; it is these stories with their emphasis on the tragic and nobility in its overcoming that have made such a special contribution to modern Arabic literature" (Hammudi 1986, 205–10). Hammudi describes this literature as forging a link between literature on traditional Islamic wars and "Arab resistance literature, e.g., Algerian and Palestinian dramatists who wrote about the struggle between the Arabs and colonialism" (Hammudi 1986, 37). Ibrahim points out the uniqueness (*tafarrud*) of the parallel structure of the Iraqi war story and the use of personal or subjective narrative that before had only been successfully implemented by giants like Najib Mahfuz, Jabra Ibrahim Jabra, and Fathi Ghanim. He celebrates also the creation of a new literary character: the warrior with his physical strength, his specialized skills, his battle experience, his ability to confront danger and to submit to the military system. This character embodies at once the individual and the collective consciousness; its role is to "represent the society during a historical period when it was defending values and ideals." Such a description may be a reflection of reality but much in it smacks again of pre-scription. Almost as though to deflect attention from this prescriptive aspect, Ibrahim praises this new literary personality as making an important contribution to Arabic literature in general. This Iraqi hero has a sense of belonging and commitment that has overcome the alienation dominating Arabic literature in the 1960s (Ibrahim 1988, 63, 192, 86, 111, 115).

Some critics assert that the mere fact that the literature is about glorious victories—some of them yet to come—in itself creates aesthetic value. In his 1981 introduction to the first volume of the Qadisiyat Saddam series, Salim 'Abd al-Qadir al-Samira'i wrote that the war had "marked the beginning of a new artistic life" (Hammudi 1986, 58). Seven years later, in his preface to Nu'man Majid's *Fi al-ghasaq 'adat 'arus al-bahr* (At dusk the mermaid returned), a 1988 collection of twelve stories selected for inclusion in an anthology on the liberation of Fao Island, the critic Khudayyir 'Abd al-'Amir echoes the sentiments of al-Samira'i and adds that the war had brought Iraqi literature to a maturity it would not otherwise have enjoyed: "The war inflamed the writers' imagination and provided them with rich material that, combining with artistic vision, produced a writing whose ground was the reality of inspiration and whose structure was formed by the deeds of the fighters at the fronts. . . . War literature in Iraq became a phenomenon that attracted the attention of Arab readers and critics. They referred to it as a rich substance that produced a literary movement. . . . The more the battles raged and the victories multiplied, the surer and maturer became the fiction to the extent that there emerged short stories and novels that could stand alongside international war fiction. . . . Iraqi fiction today is mature and its maturity is due to its having lived with the fighting, politically and militarily" (quoted in Majid 1988, 6, 8). Nu'man Majid, the editor of this collection, elaborates to claim that the mere fact of documenting the wondrous liberation of Fao lent the writing artistic value (Majid 1988, 13). Hammudi enthusiastically endorses such a sentiment by claiming that even journalistic accounts of glorious events can have literary merit (Hammudi 1986, 106).

These critics were not oblivious to the Wordsworthian caveat against the writing of literature without reflection. They discussed the issue in terms of *takhzin,* or storage. Far from agreeing with the Lake District poet and critic, Majid argues that such *takhzin* would detract from the urgency and literary merit of immediate documentation. 'Abd al-Sattar Nasir, a fiction writer and critic, maintains that war literature must be written *at once* and not ten or twenty-five years later, it must record "now—and not tomorrow— the extraordinary heroisms of the Iraqis. If the Iraqi pen did not speak today about the martyrs and the sacrifices and the legendary battles, when will it speak and participate in the defense of the land and children of Iraq?" He goes on to describe this literature as not needing time to mature because the inspiring experience is already mature. He calls for utter clarity and directness because this literature must communicate with as many people as possible, for example "a martyr, a family all of whose sons have gone to the front, an old man who goes daily to the train station to ask about his son who has not yet returned, a woman whose husband is in prison or who is lost" (Hammudi 1986, 213).

All, however, are careful to state that, of course, no one has a role that begins to approach that performed by the fighters. Nasir calls his stories "no more than a handful of bullets in soldiers' belts, a drop of water in a desert noon that a patient fighter may drink" (Hammudi 1986, 215). The more writers create role models at the front as well as at the home front, the more will their work approach the significance of the warrior's work. This is probably why so many of the critics talk of their own experiences at the front (Hammudi 1986, 17–18). In one of her rare writings on the war, Daisy al-Amir reiterates this sentiment in a few prose poems that compare the pen unfavorably with the gun.[10] "Al-asatidha wa al-talamidh" (Teachers and pupils), published in *Al-Jumhuriya,* on 5 April 1986, includes the following lines:

> Fighters and heroes forgive us
> God forbid that your heroic deeds be compared with our words

God forbid that your ammunition be compared with our pens
God forbid that your pure blood be compared with our ink
You are the ones that urge us to write
You are the ones to teach us how to serve our country
You are the teachers, we the pupils.

Basim 'Abd al-Hamid Hammudi's *Al-naqid wa qissat al-harb* (The critic and the war story, 1986) surveys the mass of *critical writing* on five years of literary production. Hammudi sets out seven rules for the writing of the War Story. These rules are: (1) do not conform with the run-of-the-mill; (2) use actual events to increase impact; (3) do not rely on skill alone in the search for effect, find a way to turn the ordinary into something unusual and new, that is, turn the event into a literary event; (4) interact with the raw material; (5) like a journalist, enter no-man's land carefully to reproduce the event but do not use "journalese"; (6) culture [he does not elaborate this point]; (7) destroy the ordinary and escape monotony (Hammudi 1986, 28–29). Hammudi explains that the War Story makes room for what in other literature might be considered weakness, for example, too many coincidences. He concludes that it is time that the world recognize that this war has produced excellent literature and that negative comparisons with other literatures are no longer appropriate. Whenever a writer seems to veer toward criticism of the war, Hammudi will pan the style, the mastery of language, the skill in plot construction (e.g., 34, 106, 185). When a critic does not like a story that was written about a front experience, particularly when the writer may have had the experience he is describing, Hammudi is stern. He seems angry with Muhammad 'Abd al-Majid for his attack on 'Ali Khayyun's prize-winning "Mourning Is Inappropriate for Martyrs." This is a story published in the first year of the war that tells of a martyr who returns to his village to see how family and friends are reacting to his death. Hammudi accuses al-Majid of being unable to appreciate a story about combat because he has not had the experience; he suggests condescendingly that in future al-Majid should write "with love and objectivity because that will be more useful for us and for Iraqi literature" (189–92).

If monuments are built before the realities they are supposed to commemorate have happened, and if criticism pre-scribes stories that have been commissioned to laud heroisms that are yet to be played out, what are we to make of the artist's and writer's responsibility? Is it possible for women and men whose livelihood depends on the government's pleasure to retain a sense of mission, of a special role as the people's conscience? How can I respond to Samir al-Khalil's accusation? He says, "An entire generation of Iraqi intellectuals collaborated with the Ba'thist regime in Iraq. . . . From within the world of fear, opportunism rules behaviour; from within the world of hopelessness, cynicism rules intelligent thought. Never is there a justification for art in itself; survival is all that counts. . . . The peculiarity of the Iraqi regime therefore is to have involved enormous numbers of people directly in its crimes over twenty years, while making the rest of the population at least complicit in their commission. Yet everyone inside the country, including the opposition outside, denies all responsibility for what they know has been going on" (al-Khalil 1991, 116, 117, 129). One of the goals of this chapter is to find some response to this blanket condemnation.

The Stories Women Wrote

As my prefatory remarks about the fiction of Faysal 'Abd al-Hasan Hajim and 'Ali Lufta Sa'id suggest, not all men's and women's war stories are as ideologically driven as this criticism. Sometimes the preface and the contents of a book may be at odds with each other so that the critical commentary, the most transparent genre, is patriotic and the plot is not. This is the case for the Fao collection, *At Dusk the Mermaid Returned*. The triumphalist introduction does not spill over into all the stories. Their message may not be explicit, but it colors the deliberate ambiguity or irony of the language. In the male writer Natiq Khulusi's "Al-diya' al-awwal li al-fajr" (The first light of dawn), an intellectual joins up. His encomiums about the war are interrupted by the death of his companion and then the appearance of the Iraqi flag. In a farcical passage reminiscent of Michael Herr's *Dispatches* out of Vietnam (see the chapter two epigraph), the narrator says: "I raised my hand in a salute and suddenly I remembered what the heroes of the film *Burning Borders* had done. I thought that Mas'ud would do as they had done, and he did not disappoint me. I saw him raise in salute a hand that was dripping blood" (Majid 1988, 84). Reality and representation fuse in the ironic juxtaposition of death description and filmic prescription.

My reading of the women's writings on the war that were published in these two government-sponsored series reveals considerable courage. "Sama' al-Faw min jadid" (The sky of Fao again) by Layla Karim 'Amran plays with the humanitarian topos. Her use of a male protagonist serves two purposes: it signals that this is a "war story," even if written by a woman; and it overcomes the common objection to women writing about experiences at the front (Higonnet 1993). The protagonist has been mortally shot, yet he tries to help an Iranian who is in even worse shape than he. As he is tearing off his shirt to stanch the bleeding, the Iranian dies. The protagonist's mind wanders from the killing field to Jinan, his beloved who died when he left for the front, and then back to his own dying. Although the content of the story accords with a very popular theme, the bitter tone does not. Neither man dies for a good reason.

'Aliya Talib's 1988 collection entitled *Al-mumirrat* (Corridors) goes further than the one by 'Amran. The horror of the front and the pointlessness of death in such a war haunts each story. More than most, Talib parodies this war. Like 'Amran, she often chooses male protagonists. Beyond overcoming the prohibition against women writing about combat, she can portray through their eyes war's unglorious side and its charade of heroism. Talib's most trenchant criticism is reserved for the martyrdom-heroism ethos that the fathers propagate and that the mothers diligently instill in their sons—no one talks about girls!

In "'Uyun ukhra" (Other eyes), the reader follows a soldier who is determined to win glory during his first assignment. His tank has just destroyed four tanks after advancing painfully through mud and rain—a scene worthy of Wilfred Owen. He is shouting for joy when "friendly shrapnel" blinds him! The story ends in a red fog as the hero tries to remain standing, to maintain his dignity as he makes his way, despite impossible odds, toward "heroism, the most important goal" (Talib 1988, 21). This young man has accomplished tremendous feats of military skill and bravery on behalf of his country and yet it is his countrymen who by mistake and stupidity reward him with blindness. The incongruence of the end—the greenhorn less concerned about his sight and pain than he is about heroism—is almost comical. The disjuncture between content and tone is a good example of Aesopian writing.

In "Al-ikhdirar" (Greening), Talib ridicules another male fighter who holds on to his hollow values even when facing death. He is shot first in the arm and then fatally "below the waist." Talib constantly repeats how the soldier is fighting his weakness (Talib 1988, 67), for he must return to his pregnant wife before she gives birth. Before leaving, he gave her strict instructions that he "must be the first to see *him*"—the possibility that his wife might give birth to a daughter does not even cross his mind. The narrative switches from first to third person and back, and then between the wife's agony as she tries to prevent the child from coming and the soldier's agony as he realizes that he is mortally wounded. In a staccato exchange of vignettes, the reader is presented with the two stereotypical associations of the apogee of pain thought to be specific to men and women, a soldier dying on the battlefield and a mother giving birth. Each needs to prevent the inevitable outcome. But the pain has to end, and in both cases it produces death: the baby is stillborn, the father martyred. The final scene lampoons the mother's satisfaction as she presses the dead infant's lips against the dead father's brow. She at least keeps her promise that the father should be the first to "see" his son.[11]

In "Al-nawaris" (The gulls), yet another man is wounded in the mud. He is not sure whether he is alive or dead, unaware of the moment of his dying. Images flash across his mind's eye and sensations through his body as he struggles to understand what has happened. If he has died, why then he must assure himself that the death was glorious. He remembers the hordes of enemies and the explosions, but above all he hears his father's words boom out of the past: "Even if you feel you're dying, do not buckle under! How splendid is death when we welcome him standing!" To which the boy had replied: "My feet shall not waver, Father. I promise." As he forces himself to remain upright after being fatally hit, his father's red, flashing eyes observe his determination (Talib 1988, 43). Finally, he can no longer stand and he hears his father's voice screaming: "Don't fall! Shame on you!" This story is an example of ironic intertextuality. It comments on and satirizes a preoccupation in men's writings: parents' expectations of and prescriptions for men's behavior in the line of duty. "The Gulls" recalls the mother in Sa'id's "Imra'a min al-nisa'" (A woman among women), who instilled the values of masculinity in her son and who insisted that death in battle, regardless of how and why, was to be celebrated.[12]

When choosing a woman protagonist, Talib is no less ironic. In "Al-'inaq al-madi'" (The luminous embrace), she enters the deranged mind of a young woman being dragged toward the coffin of her martyred lover. Her life has been ruined, all that she has left are memories. The heroine of another story entitled "Intizar jadid" (A new wait) has abandoned all her education and training and is awaiting her husband's return. As in "Greening," war imagery serves to link this woman's story on the home front with men's experiences at the front. She is holding the baby that was conceived on the eve of his departure. She has turned the boy into the image of the father and will not be satisfied until she has "made him exactly like him"—only then can the father return (Talib 1988, 38). He does, dead. The message is loud and clear: if a mother insists on perpetuating the destructive cycle of the War Story, she will turn her son into a corpse. The other message of this grim story is equally clear: to sacrifice all for the men at the front is to sacrifice all for nothing, for the men are dying. Women who buy into the war rhetoric will end up losing not only their men but personal resources as well.

Suhayla Salman is less concerned with individual psychology than she is with the government and its attempts to control women's bodies, for example, that women must bear sons for the war. At a time when the war effort was being underwritten by the Soviet Union, she dared to write a stinging critique of the benefactors. "Lara" tells of an Iraqi woman's visit to Moscow and Leningrad under the guidance of Lara, a fat, jovial Russian divorcée. The protagonist watches in amazement as Lara inhales vast quantities of food, much of it, symbolically, from the protagonist's plate. But she does not only take, she offers the protagonist *pork and vodka!* Lara is so oblivious of the needs and practices of her protégée that she does not even realize that such food and drink are forbidden to a Muslim. She is also shocked when the narrator tells her that she should lose weight and stop eating off another's plate. Lara had not realized that the other woman had noticed. Lara's greed and self-indulgence extend to her sexual morals. She allows herself to be picked up by complete strangers and is surprised that her Iraqi charge will not do the same. The story ends with the protagonist's effeminate but insistent admirer, who turns out to be an unscrupulous government official, latching on to them. These Russians are not nice people.

More subversive are Salman's stories about life in Iraq. The first story in her 1988 collection, *Al-liqa'* (The meeting), is entitled "Mashhad." Mashhad is the holiest city for Shiites in Iran; it is a pilgrimage site to the tomb of Imam Reza, yet Salman does not once mention this fact. The reader is supposed to know that the women in the story are on a pilgrimage into enemy territory. There is the young, pregnant woman who has had five sons, the exact number that the government had proclaimed to be necessary for a woman to prove herself to be a Patriotic Mother. In contrast with 'Aliya Talib's stories that talk only of male offspring, this one introduces the possibility that even in times of war women's wombs may rebel and produce girls. All the women pilgrims wish the pregnant woman a daughter, and not another piece of cannon fodder. In fact, they think that she will probably have a daughter because she is so beautiful—beauty in pregnancy is a sure sign that the baby will be female. The young woman is even more vehement in her desire for a girl: "I'll kill myself if it's a boy!" (Salman 1988, 8). She had not had those five boys for the war, as it would have seemed at first, but because she had kept trying for a girl! The focus then turns to the older woman who is going to visit her martyred son's grave. While chatting at length with his ghost, she reflects bitterly on the many ways in which the war had destroyed all their hopes and ambitions (14). This concern with the destruction of the future reappears in "Khayt ma'qud, khayt mahlul" (A knotted thread, a loose thread), a story that was written in 1984. Two sons return to their mother on the same day: the one, a surgeon, had been killed by loose shrapnel as he was saving another's life. The other son was killed on his way to join his brother.

The aunt of "Khalti Umm Malik 'addaha hisan" (A horse bit my aunt Umm Malik, Salman 1988), also written in 1984, was a feminist before the war, which she calls "this disaster that was forced on the country," and this "vicious war against a stupid enemy." She gave up her activism to be with the women in their time of trouble. Whenever a son came back from the front or a letter was received from a prisoner of war, it was "as if he were the son of all the women in the neighborhood. How many martyrs, how many lost men had all of them wept with pain and anger *as though each one of them had lost her own son*" (60–70; my emphasis). This description would seem harmless enough until we start to compare such group consciousness with the *madres* of the Plaza de Mayo and the Palestinian mothers in the Intifada and those in South Africa. These women collectively claim each man as their own. They may eventually challenge the authorities' right to "disappear" young men. Salman's hint at the politicization of the domestic is important because it announces readiness to confront state terrorism.

Lutfiya al-Dulaymi's *Budhur al-nar* (Seeds of fire, 1988) is an example of subversive writing from the pen of a woman whose earlier works were hailed as impeccably patriotic. Her heroine in "Returning from Abroad" (1974) glorifies Baghdad's "streets washed by justice, joy upon the faces, the city no longer rejects its dwellers" (Davis and Gavrielides 1991, 224). Her "Fi al-ghasaq 'adat 'arus al-bahr" (At dawn the mermaid returned), which gave the Fao collection its title, tells of the return of the mermaid to Fao Island after an absence of two years during which period "savages," that is, Iranians, had occupied the island. As soon as she hears shots from the Iranian coast, she slips back into the sea. She leaves behind the sound of her "tender, maternal voice" that promises her return. Then, during the last year of the Iran-Iraq War, al-Dulaymi published *Budhur al-nar* (Seeds of fire).

Seeds of Fire appears to be a conventional home-front novel about two couples on the margins of the war whom circumstances have separated.[13] In fact, this is a novel that traces through the transformation of Layla, a woman working with the system, into a dissident as she uses art to forge an oppositional discourse. Layla had already been politically active after 1967 and had then withdrawn to become a graphic artist for an advertising agency. Layla's director tells her that her job is to convince "people to do what you want" (al-Dulaymi 1988, 42). Layla understands but she needs to create beautiful objects. Her desire to embellish the message makes her director very nervous. Consumers must not be aware of the message; they must be incited to buy without knowing why. He warns her that once consumers become aware of the art in the message, they will become aware of the artist, of the intention underlying the work of art, and of the result in their own actions. At that point, they will be less likely to continue doing what they have been doing. This prescription for the creation of subliminal messages in advertising recalls Foulkes's definitions of "integration propaganda." In both cases, awareness of the message will depend on maintaining "the ideological distance which separates the observer from the act of communication observed." Therefore, the real power of advertising, as of propaganda, "lies in its capacity to conceal itself, to appear natural, to coalesce completely and indivisibly with the values and accepted power symbols of a given society . . . propaganda which is the most elusive, and which for that reason is most in need of detection, is not the one we observe but the one which succeeds in engaging us directly as participants in its communicative systems" (Foulkes 1983, 5, 6, 3, 107). Layla's art makes explicit what was meant to remain hidden, but in the very same process it hides another message that is the story of its purpose. Her art demystifies the information the company is disseminating and changes consumers from unconscious participants into observers.

The director knows how dangerous this can be; Layla's designs had already lost them an important contract with an insecticide company. This reference to insecticides within a war context is very

significant. After all, there is a well-known precedent: Hitler ordered the development of gas for the extermination chambers of his
World War II concentration camps from a substance that had been
used as an insecticide. Then there is the fact that Layla's art appeals
to women in particular. The director knows this fact and tries to
use it against itself: "You are copying pagan arts; our ancestors,
despite everything, were pagans in the way they regarded women.
Women will attack you. Please avoid such situations. I'm concerned
about your reputation" (al-Dulaymi 1988, 165). He has identified
an audience that he evidently fears Layla is targeting and that will
create dangerous meaning out of her nonconformist art. The reader
makes easy, obvious connections with other passages referring to
women's legendary power and status in pagan times. In one of
Yasir's sections, we read of a tradition of strong women that no one
remembers. They were leaders in battles and of tribes. They themselves took revenge for the killing of their men. Their stories were
not told by "travelers or passing historians or legend tellers. Their
exploits were told by hired female mourners, by letters carved in
stone and on sword blades" (56). The director fears Layla and her
targeted audience of strong women who threaten to disrupt and
subvert the system he has put into place. Is it not possible that this
passage about Layla's role in losing the insecticide company contract is an allegory for women's role in exposing the Iraqi government's policy of using chemical weapons against its own citizens,
particularly the Kurds?

Does Layla know what she is doing? Are we reading of subversion by Layla or by Lutfiya al-Dulaymi? Might this state-sponsored
book about an artist who uses her art against those who pay her
be a work against the state? Loseff writes of the Aesopian writer—
which I believe al-Dulaymi to be—that she "alludes to information,
or rather a body of information, which is already known to the
reader by experience, rumor, or other channels as foreign radio
broadcasts" (Loseff 1984, 219–20). She turns this information into
a story she can readily defend as pure fiction, knowing full well that
"art and literature are capable of producing a counter-vision which
in turn creates the sense of ideological distance which renders

propaganda visible . . . fiction [can] subvert the very processes of general ideology, and not merely express its sense of disinheritance from it" (Foulkes 1983, 6, 39–40).

Death and Desire

Some writers are critical of the war and the role they are expected to play; others are critical also of the ways in which the war and their role are represented. I am interested in how this critique is conducted. My readings of some of these novels and short stories indicate that the connections writers make between desire, love, and death during war reveal profound opposition to a war that was destroying their society.

Most people most of the time function as though Eros, or the sexual instinct as the embodiment of the will to live, and Thanatos, or death as libidinal sublimation, were completely separate. Yet Freud insists, only "by the concurrent or mutually opposing action of the two primal instincts—Eros and the death instinct—never by one or the other alone, can we explain the rich multiplicity of the phenomena of life" (quoted in Boothby 1991, 4). Gray elaborates the consequence of this interplay when he writes that Freud's belief in the eternal enmeshment of Eros and Thanatos made him "pessimistic about ever eradicating war as an institution. Men are in one part of their being in love with death, and periods of war in human society represent the dominance of this impulsion" (Gray 1970, 53–54). War provides opportunities for such close, charged encounters.

Freud claims that war produces three reactions to death: anxiety, fear, and fright. Anxiety "describes a particular state of expecting the danger or preparing for it, even though it may be an unknown one. 'Fear' requires a definite object of which to be afraid. 'Fright,' however, is the name we give to the state a person gets into when he has run into danger without being prepared for it" (Freud 1961 [1919], 6). To these three categories I now add a fourth: denial.[14] Denial manifests itself in two ways: a reckless embrace of danger; a pretense that control has not been lost. Denial of death is a crucial aspect of wartime behavior because it accounts for the ways in which individuals function in an otherwise impossible situation. War—in preparation and in metaphor—has become part of everyday life, another, if more extreme manifestation of systemic violence become ordinary. War can be war without feeling like war. It is best survived, for a while at least, if it is denied. More concretely, combat pilots deny death in war lest fear and anxiety make them impotent.

Combat pilots in postmodern wars fight alone, seeing the enemy only as an electronic target. In a death-charged landscape they must overcome this alienating distance so as to remain alert and effective. Many pilots, actual as well as in films and novels, speak of an intense aliveness that translates into erotic fantasy. Wendy Chapkis describes the language that pilots use in the film *Top Gun* as eroticized and she quotes one as saying that viewing training films of F-14s in action gives him a "hard-on." Another pilot remarks that the enemy aircraft "'must be close, I'm getting a hard-on'" (Chapkis 1988, 109–10). They fight virtually alone and with the illusion of power and immortality because of their distance and situation above the enemy. They must not focus on death lest they lose their effectiveness. They must tap into what is most alive in them. Eros—desire for life experienced as sexual desire—is the body's most resilient resource against Thanatos.

The novels and short stories of men like Salah al-'Ansari and Dawud Salman al-Shuwayli interweave desire and death. The eroticism of fright confirms the appropriateness of such a death. Men who die suffused with love and excitement without fear and anger are real men who have not given in to the feminine within because they have directed the masculine out on to a feminized other. These two writers depict several men, often officers directing rather than engaging in combat, at the moment they realize that they have been mortally hit. They almost invariably hallucinate or project images of their beloved. Jabra Ibrahim Jabra labels this use of flashback, nearly always to a woman, a simplistic escape from dealing with trauma (quoted in Hammudi 1986, 208), whereas I read such flashbacks as serving an important function within this literary economy: death is enmeshed with fantasies that provide a libidinal sublimation. Stanley Rosenberg quotes a U.S. Air Force pilot who had done duty in Vietnam: "First, just flying the airplane is a thrill. Then, you need to be dropping bombs. Then, you have to see what you're dropping bombs on. Then, to feel the thrill, you have to see that you've hit what you're dropping bombs on. Then, you need to be getting shot at while you see what you've blown up. Then, you have to be getting hit to feel the thrill, and the last thing is, to get dead" (Rosenberg 1993, 62–63).[15]

Sexual arousal is associated with risking death. Gray tries to theorize away the connections between death and desire as though afraid that such a connection might dilute the greatness of communal participation, of the loss of the ego in moments of ecstasy. Yet later in his analysis of erotic love in war he describes the soldiers' preoccupation with the need for women that derives from the desire for conquest of an interchangeable partner or enemy (Gray 1970, 45, 67). War writers like the Algerian Mohamed Dib and the German Freikorps of whom Theweleit wrote emphasize the connections between fear of death and erotic arousal. They create combatants whose fright is accompanied by erotic fantasies that counterbalance the threat of disintegration, physical as well as psychological, by producing an illusory unity, a reinforced masculinity so as to withstand the threat of dissolving into the feminine. Desire is good as long as it is not allowed release.

Dawud al-Shuwayli dedicates his 1988 novel *Ababil* (Flocks) to the heroic pilots, officers, engineers, and technicians of the 29th Air Unit, "emblems of Saddam's glorious Qadisiya."[16] This novel places in high relief the Eros-Thanatos construct. Yasin, an ace pilot on his mission over Iranian territory, is the hero. The planes take off in perfect flying formation, reach their target, drop their payloads, and then turn back. Yasin's plane is hit. Defying commands to bail out, he keeps on course and steers back home. Spartan warrior to the last, we assume that he will not risk being taken prisoner, perhaps even being raped or dying on enemy land. He will return dead or a hero (al-Shuwayli 1988, 74, 84, 92). The novel ends with Yasin's ecstatic dying utterance: "God is great!" This war cry, which has become emblematic of Islamic holy war, seems to mark the author's approval of death in a just war such as this one is for this man.

His inspiration for such bravery is Sausan. The echo of this woman's words reassures him not only of his masculinity but also of his potential heroism. For had he not been a hero she "would not have accepted to be related to you" (75). Then there is Amal, who is not merely inspiration, she is also an erotic presence from the moment that he is about to drop the bomb until his realization that he is going to die. The narrative fragments into a staccato alternation between descriptions of the present operation and flashbacks to encounters with Amal that become increasingly physical. He conflates signifieds as he interchangeably calls his plane and his fiancée his beloved (*ya habibati*). As the crisis climaxes, he hears Amal again urging him to hold her tightly: "O, Yasin, embrace me . . . ! Stretch out your hands! Hold me close to you! Don't leave me like this! Without hope! Hold me to you!" (93). Frantically, he tries to grab hold of the *'atala*. Although the reader assumes that what is referred to by *'atala* is the pilot's "joystick," its actual meaning (according to Hans Wehr's *Arabic-English Dictionary*) is a "crowbar" or (according to E. W. Lane's *Arabic-English Lexicon*) a "large, or thick, rod of iron, having a wide head. Or, a thick staff of wood." Since the term is left imprecise, it is hard within this eroticized context not to assume a phallic referent. Yasin finally gives up, frozen with fright that, as Freud describes it, is "a lack of hypercathexis of the systems that would be the first to receive the stimulus. Owing to their low cathexis those systems are not in a good position for binding the inflowing amounts of excitation and the consequences of the breach in the protective shield follow all the more easily . . . the mechanical violence of the trauma would liberate a quantity of sexual excitation" (Freud 1961 [1919], 25, 27). Yasin has lost control of himself and of his plane. He swoops so low over the earth that he can see everything clearly. Then, at the height of the trauma, he is overwhelmed by a sense of dissolving: "The earth welcomes me. I see her opening her arms . . . she is calling to me" (al-Shuwayli 1988, 94). The association of danger, death, desire, and release in union is at once orgasmic and Oedipal—the son returning into the embrace of the mother.

In August 1993 I was interviewed by Wayne Ponds of National Public Radio's "Soundings." He was asking me about *Gendering*

War Talk, a collection of essays that I had edited with Angela
Woollacott and that Princeton had just published. The following
week, the Southern author Clyde Edgerton contacted me in connection with the program. He sent me a copy of a story he had
written about his experience in Vietnam, a story he had never liked
enough to publish. I was startled by the parallels between it and the
Iraqi men's stories that I had analyzed. Briefly, "Search and Rescue"
is about what a pilot believes to be his last moments. Fact is
interspersed with fantasy. At the critical point, he flashes to a
pornographic film he had once seen. A woman enters a room, takes
off her long white robe. She sits naked on a couch, rubs her breasts,
and "wets her lips. . . . The woman gets down on her hands and
knees in front of the couch and looks behind her. A pig walks on
screen from behind her and sniffs at her butt, which she wiggles
back and forth." After a flash back to reality, the narrator returns
to the pig, its penis, and the woman it is mounting.[17]

Not only male protagonists experience arousal in war, women do
also. For women the stimulants are different. Wendy Chapkis notes
that women in real life may be as susceptible as men to the eroticism
of the military myth, but for different reasons. She writes that when
women become combatants, the military myth provides "an avenue
to personally transgress gender boundaries or as a means to project
the eroticism of power on to male objects of desire" (Chapkis 1988,
111).

Although women were involved in the war—in 1976 Iraqi
women were enrolled into the popular militia forces that, by 1982,
had 40,000 women combatants (al-Khalil 1989, 92)—the novels
and stories I have read do not describe military women. Military
service is not necessarily key. As I have already argued, war literature can be the site for the transformation of a woman into a
combatant. These women challenge gender norms by refusing society's rules of proper conduct for women. The change from observer to combatant is often erotically marked, strikingly so in the
literature on the Lebanese civil war. After bidding her husband
farewell, Nuha Samara's protagonist of "Two Faces One Woman"

(1980) finds herself alone in the war. It is the first time that she has ever had the opportunity to think for herself, to make her own decisions. From this new vantage point, she begins to assess her situation rather differently. It is suddenly unacceptable that her husband should have left her in this dirty war, suddenly evident that she is not waiting passively. She is expected to cope alone in the chaos. Although at the time she had not objected to his decision to go, people's comments make her realize that staying alone involves responsibilities and self-defense. She cuts her hair, a literary convention that marks women's assumption of control over their lives, and enrolls in military training. The metamorphosis is erotically marked: looking at her newly masculinized image in the mirror, she masturbates. She then determines to find a lover and calls up her husband's best friend (Badran and Cooke 1990, 304–13).

The heroine of Hanan al-Shaykh's *Story of Zahra* also experiences sexual pleasure as she moves from the margins of the war to its center. When her neighborhood is plunged into a violence over which a sniper reigns supreme, Zahra begins to move out of her shell of pain and madness. Seeing others in pain makes her feel less alone, more willing to be touched. With time she adopts responsibility for those around her. Despite warnings, she ventures out into the menaced streets and makes her way to the building out of which the sniper is said to be functioning. If she can distract him even only for a while she will have saved one innocent person's life. Day after day, she trudges back to the building and up the stairs for a ritual reenactment of the first encounter. Finally, one day it is as though the sniper is actually making love to her, and he gives her pleasure. Zahra, like the woman in "Two Faces One Woman," has become a combatant who has found erotic pleasure in that role. She has not witnessed death while being constantly in its presence. She can thus imagine that the emblem of war's senseless killing is not a death machine but rather Sami, a man she would like as a husband for herself and as a father for their unborn child.

Likewise when Layla in al-Dulaymi's *Seeds of Fire* (see below) turns her job in the advertising agency into a site for the construction of a dissident discourse, she feels powerful and able to love Yasir. It is at the moment that these heroines recognize that participation in the war always under the shadow of death gives them freedom, self-control, and the chance to affirm themselves as *other* than expected that they experience erotic desire and pleasure. These non-military women combatants bear out Chapkis's contention that making themselves into warriors allows women "to project the eroticism of power onto male objects of desire."

The difference between men's and women's erotic reactions to death in war is that whereas men's desire is activated by battle participation that *confirms* gender identity, women's desire marks the assumption of a role that *contradicts* social expectations of how they should behave. Each is in some ways overcoming the feminine condition that disables the warrior spirit. For men, the fantasies dissipate in the light of reality. For instance, the soldier in Salah al-'Ansari's "The Two Walls" tells his wife, "I loved a woman other than you" and it seems that this other woman was in fact her, but only when she was not who she was then (al-'Ansari 1988, 82).

The Binary Mandate

Men and women usually write of war heroes and heroines in gendered spaces. Out of these spaces, men and women talk about absent women and men. When they write of men and women *together* during war, the only love they invoke is a sick love. In women's writings, death brings the loved men home and reveals the emptiness, the destructiveness even of that love that required distance to survive. Remember 'Aliya Talib's young woman who is driven crazy by being dragged toward the coffin of her martyred lover; and the waiting wife who grimly plans to turn her son into the image of the father who is brought home on a bier; and the pregnant woman who prevents the birth of her fetus until her husband returns, and when he does, dead, she can finally release the dead baby from her body.

Lutfiya al-Dulaymi's *Seeds of Fire* is the only novel on the Iraq-Iran War I have read to present both men's and women's perspectives on the war and on each other. It discusses their fantasies and representations of each other from three perspectives: Yasir's in the desert—a place that is not the front yet is described in terms that always recall the front—and Layla's and Asila's in Baghdad. This assigning of sections to a man on an ersatz-front and to two women on the home front allows the author to establish as though self-evident gender-specific spaces and roles. Yasir, like the military men, is associated with spheres of death and war: the arid, life-devouring desert and the front with its risks of death and imprisonment. While in the desert Yasir reads about poetry, he even writes a book on the subject. The critic Ibrahim comments that beyond writing, many warriors in this war literature read "books specialized in literature, history, and culture" (Ibrahim 1988, 116–17). Hence, this hobby seems to link Yasir to other poet-warriors, including the aforementioned Hajim's Other Soldier, whose story subverts any possibility that this war might be considered glorious. The women are associated with life and peace: nature and doves and olives (al-Dulaymi 1988, 28) and lush greenness; they ripen "like fruit on the tree of waiting" (40). This marking of the man's absence as being "not at the front" allows al-Dulaymi to describe men's experience without trespassing on what was said to be male writers' turf. Yet the war is always there: explosions are heard in the distance (43); Yasir describes plants that survive the heat and the dryness as *samid,* or steadfast, a term that Palestinian usage fills with political and even military resonance (17); families are fragmented by the conscription of sons (114); mothers wait (43); martyrs are announced; aunts adopt war orphans; brothers are imprisoned; even the home front is hit; above all, women and men organize their lives around the "end of the war" (e.g., 27, 29, 225).

Yasir went to the desert mines to replace someone who had been conscripted to the front. The desert may not be the front, but he tells his wife, Layla, that she should think of it as though it were. Hence, she should not think of joining him because his co-workers, as though they were soldiers, will not respect her for who she is but will regard her as a body only (39). His experiences in the desert so parallel those of the soldiers (105) that the war becomes part of him: "The night winds of the desert had sown seeds of fire beneath his skin and in his blood, small seeds that the hand of time had scattered over the earth of his body. . . . When he feels the burning of the flames, distant and recent memories are churned up and for a while he forgets this hell that pervaded his world and left in it fires, the stench of corpses, and the ghosts of the dead" (131). Rather than life at a mine, here is life on the battlefield: privation and nightmare but also oneiric escapism and heightened sensuality. On a furlough home, Layla tells him that she sees "seeds of fire" in his eyes (143).

During his times of loneliness and crisis far from home, Yasir, like the men discussed above, longs for a woman. His fevered imagination conjures up Layla. But this is not Layla the wife, this is Layla, a woman, Woman, who fuels his fantasies (17–20, 117).[18] By calling the fantasy Layla, he can convince himself that his adventures with other women are not betrayal (122–27). Conversely, he calls one prostitute Laylayana so that he might imagine the affair as one with his wife. His acknowledgement of his misdemeanor involves an unspoken apology to Layla and the assurance that when he is with other women he feels himself to be with her (126–27). When he comes home, however, he loses his fantasy of Layla the lover and cannot tolerate Layla the wife. He wants her to be devoted to him and to his needs. He resents any sign of independence or lack of respect or admiration (191).

Outside the advertising agency, Layla plays her war role as waiting woman: pregnant, she awaits her unborn child; sister, she awaits her brother from the front; wife, she awaits her husband from the mine. She tells her friend Asila that women's lives are devoted to "waiting in which there is pleasure at combating death" (91). The possibility of combating the threat of death gives pleasure and feeds love. At the beginning of the novel, the waiting role predominates, though with immediate caveats as she contextualizes her fantasy within reality. When she hears an enemy bomb explode her first thought, spurred by the baby's kick, is that of the mother: she wants to give birth to the fruit of her love for Yasir before dying. A political reflex relieves this saccharine moment: thinking of her own motherhood makes her think of other, less happy mothers "as they awaited the return of their sons from the front" (43). In war, women give birth to death either as a product, a killed son, or as an instrument, a son who will kill. Then she is the waiting wife worrying about her husband's welfare as he confronts danger and death. She can talk about love as "wanting someone for his sake and not for the sake of our happiness with him. . . . Love is giving happiness and joy without counting the cost. It is then that the loved one gives us what we would never have expected" (227).

When Yasir is home on a brief leave, his presence shatters illusions his absence nurtured. He is so self-absorbed that he does not even notice that she is pregnant (31–32). The mirage of connubial bliss dissipates in the bright light of reality. Involuntarily, she thinks back to the time of their engagement and his delight at being the possessor of so much "beauty, femininity, and gentleness" (38).[19] This memory brings back others. They had talked "three years ago about putting on her first show and he had written the introduction to a few of her new canvases. However, his introductions were never published, and her show never happened" (184). When she tells Yasir that an art critic has taken an interest in her work and published an article about one of her paintings, he is annoyed: "I read the article. ʿAbd al-ʿAziz al-Qadiri didn't say anything new. He only wrote what I've always thought about your style and technique because I know your background and experience. Haven't I already told you everything he repeats in his article? . . . al-Qadiri is not an art critic. He merely flatters women painters" (184). Not only is Layla remembering an unfulfilled promise, she is again confronted with his jealous possessiveness. It should be enough for her that her husband admires her painting, irrelevant that another bothers to put into print and therefore bring to public attention what he merely thought. Eager to put his competitor down, Yasir loses himself in a paradoxical discourse. First, he establishes himself as the more credible critic because of privileged information; then, he turns his argument against himself by discrediting as flattery the criticism that he compared with his own. Another memory is of her director rebuking her for not asking him to intercede on her behalf so that Yasir should not be sent to the mines (167). It does not occur to him that Yasir may have chosen to go, that Layla may have been happy to let him do so.

Layla recognizes that her life is a struggle not to become a victim, "the worst role for women or for any human being" (61). She must resist her husband's indifference to who she really is, her friend's need for Layla to suffer in love as she did (96, 101, 235), her male colleagues' fear of the power of her painting, and society as a whole. She can never be alone in public without suspicion of immorality. One day she is in the streets, enjoying her independence, when a woman silently hands her a jasmine flower and a soldier accosts her without respect for her pregnancy (173). Denied her own independent space, she turns their son into a "new independent island" (253). The future will be different if the next generation can be spared the influence of the fathers.

The other plot of *Seeds of Fire* involves the unscrupulous Rashid, the unrequited lover Riyad, and the sculptress Asila. Asila despises her soldier admirer and obstinately holds on to her love for Rashid, despite his marriage to another. Asila describes her love for Rashid as a "sickness" (100) and then later she describes his occupation of her thoughts as a "rape" (235). This is no soldier in danger of his life, he is a philanderer. Yet Asila is determined to love the man who jilted her as though he were a hero at the front. The loyalty she reserves for this man who abandons her but who yet wants to retain control over her is truly "madness." Asila has the choice between a conventional wartime relationship with Riyad and one with Rashid that goes against the grain: to love a non-soldier with the love reserved for the man at the front—passive loyalty. Rashid exults in Asila's misplaced love: "I know how to pull the strings and make the puppet dance. I have my ways that a dreaming lover like you, Yasir, who is satisfied with the love of one woman, does not know" (119). He mocks Yasir's loyalty that the reader learns is self-deceptive at best, hypocritical at worst.

Asila is not like other women who prefer education to marriage unless it be to richer and younger men than the divorcés and widowers who are currently presenting themselves (202–4). She pursues an old and hopeless love as far as the westernized neighborhood to which Rashid moved. Here his assistant Victoria presents her with another version of how to succeed as a woman: "I'd never have done well in my work if it hadn't been for you, Mr. Rashid. No woman, however talented, can succeed without a man's support" (213). Asila's life and friends are proofs of the contrary, yet because she made her choice in wartime to love someone who opted out of the war, she finds herself in an impossible situation. During the last scene that Asila and Rashid share, bombs and death break into the meeting. This independent woman artist—who assumes the role of martyr's wife by adopting her nephew, a war orphan (90)[20]—is driven to love a selfish man who hopes to use the war for his own purposes. Her love is always a "sickness," always a "madness." She does not need the return from the front to reveal her self-delusion. Her love is inappropriate; she loves a civilian, and a rascal at that, with the love reserved for the soldier. When the lover is not in danger of death, but rather is exploiting a situation of danger for others, such a love becomes destructive for both subject and object. Yet even under such perverse circumstances, during wartime a man is shown to be redeemable. Asila's love earns Rashid the title of martyr when he dies in the explosion. For he did not die, *mata,* he died as a martyr, *istashhada.* Asila, of course, also died; however, as a woman she could only die, *matat!*

When characters challenge the spatial and behavioral binaries proper to war, they destabilize identities and roles. Rashid refuses the war except for personal gain. While family and friends are dying at the front, he convinces his brother-in-law to finance his furniture and perfume factories. Soon his marriage falls apart, his businesses collapse, and he tries to lure Asila back. Just as he is about to succeed, they are both killed by a couple of explosions. Rashid brings the killing home. Layla, in contrast, uses the war and the consequent absence of men in Baghdad to establish a space of action for herself. She paints subversively. From the heart of the war machine, she is combating the system. Her methods are so subtle, so subliminal that even she does not seem to know what she is doing. Yet her art creates an alternative for others—particularly women—and for herself. It gives her the courage and self-assurance to confront the men who want to control her.

This artist's biography is reminiscent of those women have written out of other wars, for example, Sahar Khalifa's *Memoirs of an Unrealistic Woman* (see chapter four). Layla finds release from personal crisis through art: she constructs a world outside the one in which she was compelled to live. After hearing of her brother's capture at the front, Layla returns home and starts to paint. She places his photograph on the table and begins to paint in "hot, staccato [*mutaqata'a*] colors." Out of the colors emerge the shapes of lovers intertwined. She paints on "until the painting turned into a strange star freed from the bonds of existence and she hurried to give the man the features of Yasir. Contemplating the painting, she felt the satisfaction one gets after plunging into something beautiful. She felt relieved to have unloaded the weight in her head and body into the sudden, brilliant colors of her painting" (237). When reality becomes unbearable, she transforms it through art. As long as her husband is away, he can be her inspiration and her ideal.

The novel ends with Yasir returning home for good. He finds Layla slaving over a hot kitchen stove, the baby boy slumbering, and delicious smells wafting out of the kitchen. Who is she expecting? Why, him! Every night, she says, she prepares his welcome. Saying which, they fall woodenly into each other's arms. She is *not* the Layla of the preceding 260 pages, a woman who resists all the men who try to control her, Yasir in particular. Yet this ending provides the censor with a "happy ever after" sense of closure and the reader with the need to read beyond the ending. Indeed, the conclusion puts into question all those moments when Layla expresses any form of domestic delight. Hence, we anticipate beyond the ending to a month hence when Yasir will leave for the front, but we also return to page one. As long as Yasir is far away, at the ersatz-front, Layla loves him perfectly. She can daily charade the happy homecoming. When he is there, her love melts into frustration and anger. As long as he is gone, Yasir loves Layla, even if only as a fantasy he realizes through other women. Back home, he is annoyed at any sign of independence she may show.

Love and desire thrive only when men and women retain their gender-specific spaces as mandated by the exigencies of war. For men, as writers or characters, women are back home as Spartan Mother, castrating wife, or erotic fantasy. For women, men at the front are much loved heroes-in-the-making. When these men come home alive, reality effaces dreams. When they come home dead, the absurdity of the meaningless death—for that is how it is often described—strikes at the heart of constructions of masculinized patriotism. Literature becomes the site of a struggle over the interpretation and definition of the war. Is it a manly war? Or does the war, as al-Dulaymi suggests, unman its men? As long as a man and a woman do not cross into each other's space, the Eros-Thanatos construct holds. When they do cross into each other's zone, which by being the other's is forbidden, they disturb what are seen to be "natural" social arrangements. Although it is not mentioned explicitly, for in patronized, patriarchal literature it cannot be, their crossing into that forbidden zone shows how fragile are the foundations on which that segregated society is based. If men discover that during their absence women enter public, that is, male, space and are there negotiating power relations that the men thought to be essential and unchanging, then the reasons and motivations for going to war are destabilized. How manly is the soldier whose wife is independent and perhaps stronger than he? If an unpatriotic man can elicit the same devotion in a woman as one who is prepared *pro patria mori,* of what value is that love? Once notions of militarism as the quintessential domain of masculinity, and of this masculinity as inherently superior to femininity are questioned, stable gender relations so necessary to the peaceful waging of war are undermined.

As I read this literature, I felt like the protagonist of Jihad Majid's short story "Al-dhikra al-mi'awiya" (Centennial jubilee) who must orchestrate an event to celebrate the Fao victory in the year 2088. He has no contact with any of the participants and little access to the archives. He, the city historian, knows, as does the "administration" who set up the centennial committee, that something happened that should be memorialized. The committee, headed by the protagonist, includes an artist, a poet, a military analyst, and some administrators. Curiously enough, the artist and the poet are the only ones to question the appropriateness of their presence on such a committee—they implicitly reject the immediate connection between culture, or, rather, its manipulation, and war. The others find the connection to be self-evident, the reconstruction to be essential (in Majid 1988, 27–38).

My project is reconstructive also, I hope not as manipulative. I know almost none of the players. I may not be a hundred years removed from Fao, but I might as well be. I am piecing together a history that creative artists chronicled or, to be more precise, were paid to chronicle. I have acquired only a few dozen novels and collections of short stories out of a total output that at this point must exceed several hundred. I have seen only reproductions of drawings and monuments. Yet I maintain that among all the toadies who worked away during the government drive to whitewash and glorify the war there are some, many of them women, who risked much to tell the truth as they see it.[21]

On a daily basis, the media bombard us with images and stories of a ruthless tyrant who will stop at nothing to eradicate dissent. By decoding their Aesopian symbols and subversions, am I endangering the lives of those who managed to survive their manipulations of the system? There will be those who argue that these writers used imagery and metaphor to veil their meaning so that they might continue to write in safety. Loseff poses the "ethical dilemma" of the investigator of Aesopian language thus: "to what extent has the critic the right to expose a writer's anti-censorship tactics when in Russia [but which is also the case in Iraq] ideological censorship has not only not been abolished but, on the contrary, is patently on the increase?" Loseff's solution is to look only at the works of those who left the country or of those who had "already been unmasked and branded or have repented." That decision, he laments, compels him to exclude some "highly relevant material in favor of less impressive examples," because "discussion of anti-censorship tactics is impossible in a state of censorship." Yet he quotes L. J. Paklina's *Iskussto inoskazatel'noj reci: Èzopovskoe slovo v xudožestvennoj literature i publicistike* (1971), where he writes that "to decipher an Aesopian image is not to put one's finger on that fact of reality which occasioned the allegory, but to interpret the life of this fact in the artistic world of the writer." Such is the case because Aesopian language does not translate facts directly into fiction; it is rather "a product of relationships which are formed on the surface of cultural life, in the political sphere" (Loseff 1984, x, xi, 13, 19, 51).

The question for me has been, should these Iraqi writings remain veiled? Should I have limited myself to the writings of Iraqi expatriates like Samira al-Mana so as not to endanger the lives of those who have written from within? I think not. I believe that the critic has a double role. First, to identify writing that interacts with its context in the hope, however forlorn, of transforming it. Second, to map a new terrain where the unspeakable can be read. Silence is not an option. As long as we remain silent about what these writers are doing, as long as we shy away from analyzing what and how writers are articulating their dissent in a totalitarian system, we collaborate with the silencers. We must study these sponsored-censored works in such a way that we reconstruct "the relationship between textual structure and reception . . . [so as to] transform the critic [and, I insist, the reader] into the observer of an actual sign process, it may also lead to a clearer understanding of the ways in which literature functions as propaganda," both for *and against* the government (Foulkes 1983, 107).

What I can read through, so can others. This transparency is essential to make us realize that even under the most coercive circumstances, consciousness and conscience do survive. These brave writings challenge damning contentions that state-sponsored literature is necessarily propaganda. We must not accuse all writers of opportunism and therefore of dubious aesthetic merit merely because of literary and artistic patronage. Where would that leave Mozart and Michelangelo? Loseff even supports the contention that censorship can improve a text because it necessitates recourse to metaphor that "renders a work structurally more complex and leads to additional stratification of the text." He credits Aesopian language with the "rise of new genres" (Loseff 1984, 9, 119). Is the new genre in this case the "War Story" that the critics had been celebrating in the late 1980s? Who knows? What is sure is that sponsorship is no surer a guarantee of quality of cultural production than is its obverse. Writers who are state-sponsored may write well or badly. They may obey the rules of the game or play with these rules. Those who play the rules against the game begin to undo the atomization of state terrorism. These writers are opening up a space in which lateral links can exist and where new voices can resound. These writings are only a beginning, a glimpse of a vision of a nation that would engage its citizens in shaping a future that would include all equally. Above all, they undermine the

Mephistophelian contract that Saddam Hussein tried to impose on each Iraqi citizen.

Gulf War Postscript

In April 1995 I received three accounts of the 1990–91 Gulf War written by women. There was a collection of short stories by the Kuwaiti Layla al-'Uthman, a novel by the Iraqi Ibtisam 'Abdallah, and a journal by the Iraqi poet Dunya Mikha'il. Each book told of the shock of the beginning of the war and the subsequent brutalities.

At a feminist conference that we were both attending, Layla al-'Uthman gave me a copy of her *Al-hawajiz al-sawda'* (Black barricades, 1994), a collection of short stories she had written during and shortly after the Iraqi invasion of Kuwait. She describes the shock of the invasion, its brutalities, the rape of mothers witnessed by their sons, and the small acts of resistance and defiance performed by Kuwaitis who refused to be cowed by the Iraqis, and finally the refusal to leave the land and, even more important, the sea that defined their existence. The collection ends with nine sections, each entitled Barricade. Each barricade has the narrator conversing with an Iraqi soldier. At Barricade Two, she meets a soldier who seems sympathetic to her and almost apologetic about his presence, assuring her: "I curse the hour that my feet stepped on this ground!" When she asks him why he came, he replies:

"Orders!"
"Oppressed?"
"More than you."
"Do you smoke?"
"I'd love to. Do you have a cigarette?"
"Aren't you afraid it might be poisoned?"
"We've already drunk poison over there."
"Where's there?"
"During the Eight-Year War [referring to the Iran-Iraq War]."
"So you came to participate in a new war of liberation!!"
"You didn't need anyone to liberate you. You were free and we were envious."
"Do you know the truth?"
"I know it very well . . . I wish . . . Ah . . . "

"What do you wish?"
"That Iraq might be liberated."
                    (al-'Uthman 1994, 149–51)

Layla al-'Uthman adds her voice of dissent to those already echoing within the Iraqi state. Her sadness at the loss of the country and her anger at its devastation at the hands of the filthy soldiers and their co-optation of some of her countrymen give way at the end to a realization that not all of these men are in Kuwait of their own free will. Saddam Hussein is one thing and the miserable creatures that have found themselves far from home and doing the unspeakable are quite another.

Ibtisam 'Abdallah's *Matar aswad . . . matar ahmar* (Black rain . . . red rain, 1994) provides the obverse of al-'Uthman's stories. We read of the invasion but from Baghdad.[22] Riham, whose name means gentle rain, is a thirty-year-old upper-middle-class woman who recently divorced her husband. She buys a flower store, hoping that owning a business will allow her to pull her life together. She has planned a trip for 10 August 1990, but then 2 August intervenes. Kuwait is not mentioned by name. The American government and its military are the enemy. Five months and twenty-five days later, after the night of bombing that marked the beginning of *umm al-ma'arik* (the mother of battles), Riham opens a curtain and looks out: "The sky was multicolored, a panorama of yellow and red explosions, *like a video game*" ('Abdallah 1994, 66; my emphasis). We read here an Iraqi woman responding to what became cliché in North America during the Gulf War. She recognizes that this is "a world war, a modern war with the United States and the world." Later, she describes that orange-red sky as looking like *Gone with the Wind,* only worse. In an amusing exchange between an older woman and some men who are jostling for a place at the front of a line for fuel, 'Abdallah questions whether this war will allow men to remain men, let alone prove their masculinity! The narrator realizes that "this war is different from those preceding it. They are going to drop an atomic bomb on Baghdad." While that did not happen, it was certainly a commonly held fear. Civilians in Najaf came close enough to the

Americans that they could see the pilots flash victory signs at each other when they made a successful strike. And for those who wanted to believe in the smartness of these bombs, why all they had to do was to survey the damage and to whom it was done. The novel ends with the devastating assertion that the bombs that were dropped on Iraq were "six times what was dropped on Hiroshima" (72, 91, 82, 75, 90, 98, 135).

Dunya Mikha'il's *Yawmiyat mawja kharij al-bahr* (The journal of a wave outside the sea, 1995) is published by the Iraqi Ministry of Culture and Information, the ministry that sponsored publication of the books analyzed above. It thus forms a perfect last link in the chain of this chapter's story.[23] This journal is written as a series of prose poems that trace through, sometimes with the help of a time machine, the poet's reactions to the events of the war with a particular focus on 17 January 1991, the "night of nightmares." The episodic, fantastic, sometimes mythic, generally macabre nature of the pieces are reminiscent of Ghada al-Samman's 1980 *Kawabis Bayrut* (Beirut nightmares) that chronicled the days in which the hotels battle of autumn 1976 took place. Mikha'il describes the Iraqi people cowering in their houses like sardines in their cans, while "they [unspecified, but clearly the Americans] sit calmly in front of their electronic screens, pressing a button to shred our torn wings just before our low flight above our devastation." But those for whom she feels the greatest sadness and bitterness are the children who ask the difficult questions: "What did the twentieth-century Santa Claus feel when he brought the children of Iraq sacks full of shrapnel? What did he feel when they returned him the sacks full of gifts that included an amputated finger, a red hair plait, the guts of a book, a smashed doll, and a ticket of protest for Christopher Columbus." But as in all wars, there are also the war merchants, those who sell air (Mikha'il 1995, 12–13, 21).

These are only three of what I assume will turn out to be a stream of writings that will be produced over the coming years. The Gulf War may not have lasted long but it introduced into the Arab world a postmodern war that threw into question all the certainties surrounding preceding wars.

Chapter Six

Reimagining Lebanon

We must resist the formation of national, ethnic, and other myths, as they are being formed.
Eric Hobsbawm (1993)

In this chapter I turn to Lebanon in the wake of the Israeli invasion of 1982 to see whether its literature can answer the question: what is this concept of the nation that the Algerians and Palestinians fought for and that some Iraqi writers tried to imagine despite the blinkers their government placed on their eyes? It is a difficult question to answer at the end of the twentieth century. We are confronting paradoxical global phenomena that suggest the need for a new approach to defining the nation. First, macroeconomic forces are aligning groups that see no other reason for unification beyond economic expediency. Within this overall drive for realignment, differences are highlighted, even created, and then used to forge new alliances that often conflict with the interests of the larger socioeconomic group. The establishment of multinational companies and supranational coalitions coincides with the proliferation of multiple political identities, each demanding autonomy and recognition. Second, the transport revolution scatters people in search of a haven or of economic advancement all over a shrinking world. Mass migration thus coincides with affirmations of political attachment to particular parts of the world even if from afar. How are we to address the apparent contradictions between global unification and local differences, between world citizenship and parochial identities?

To address them I propose degree-zero definitions of "nation" and "nationalism" that will allow us to span the spectrum between individual and collective identities. For many, the nation is that geopolitical entity from which nationality derives. Whereas the use of nationality as an identity marker is not in itself subject to debate, the nation that gives rise to particular nationalities is. Eve Sedgwick defines the nation as a "set of discursive and institutional arrangements that mediate between the physical fact that each person inhabits, at a given time, a particular geographic space, and the far more abstract, sometimes even apparently unrelated organization of what has emerged since the late seventeenth century as her/his national identity, as signalized by, for instance, citizenship" (Sedgwick 1992, 239). I refocus that more abstract concept of national identity on three very specific ways of understanding the nation.

Algerians, Palestinians, and Iraqis who write about the wars they lived have helped me to understand that the nation is at once concrete and fluid. I have come to think of the "nation" as an emotional space in which individuals feel rooted and to which they feel they belong. This space can be, but need not be, coterminous with a political entity, a piece of land, a human collectivity organized around a culture, a religion, or a language. "Nationalism" is action motivated by that feeling of connectedness. In general, its goal is to foster a conceptual community that shares an understanding of what constitutes a given nation. Thus construed, nationalism may be primordial, a sentiment that has always driven human beings to fight together as members of a chosen people to assert or defend their right to and control over a piece of land promised to them because they spoke the language of their god. What is different about today, the expanded today of the post-Enlightenment, is that nations are imagined, and nationalisms are played out within the context of nation-state ideology. In other words, each nation, once imagined, is almost obliged to agitate for a state that will give it political autonomy. This context must shape our considerations of nation and nationalism.

Lebanon has long been a site of contestation over the meanings attached to nation and nationalisms. Although some claim that its civil war renders Lebanon an anomaly, I am not persuaded of that. In light of the developments since 1989 in the former Soviet Union and Eastern Europe, and especially in Bosnia, it seems rather that Lebanon encapsulates a global, postcolonial situation. As the poet

Rashid al-Daif puts it: "The whole world is Beirut/Lebanon" (quoted in Takieddine-Amyouni 1993, 5). Providing a special lens on the rest of the world, Lebanon reflects trends that are also manifest, but less visibly, elsewhere.

Like other colonized people, many Lebanese have seen emigration to be a solution to economic necessity. Since the late nineteenth century Lebanese men in particular have opted to make physical homes for themselves outside their country even while attempting to carry with them their cultural homes. Current estimates put the number of Lebanese living outside the country at five to six times the number remaining on the soil of Lebanon. The poet Henri Zghaib succinctly articulated the fact that the expatriate understanding of the Lebanese nation was not only its *soil* but was, most importantly, its *soul*.[1] Yet for those living on the soil of Lebanon—especially after the ravages of a seventeen-year war—the sense of nation has been less mystical. As demonstrated by the writings I analyze, the soul of Lebanon has been tightly bound to its soil. It was for hegemony over this stretch of land that generations of combatants fought to the death. Lebanese nationalism was invoked under the different banners of competing ideologies that were generally organized into autonomous groups, militias, each claiming to represent the best interests of a Lebanon that, in fact, often served only their individual interests. The labels attached to these groups might be political (such as Marxist or Nasserist), religious (Maronite or Shiite), or feudal (Zghorti or Jumblati). However particular these identifications might be, they always had a nationalist connotation. Only members of the Kataib (an extreme right-wing Maronite militia) or of Saiqa (a left-wing Palestinian group) or of the Ahrar (another Maronite militia) or of Amal (a moderate left-wing Shiite militia) or of Hizbollah (a pro-Iranian, Shiite fundamentalist organization) could really understand and therefore be qualified to respond to Lebanon's needs and to represent its aspirations.

Women's literary constructions of the nation in post-1982 Lebanon emerged in response to a sense that not only had these nationalist-ideological projects failed but that they had been responsible for the carnage of the civil war. Such constructions challenge the generally accepted use of nationalism to denote advocacy of the principle that a state should conform to the wishes and beliefs of the majority, however that majority may be defined. This kind of nationalism can be called "statist" because of its insistence on the overlap between an imagined community, the nation, and a public entity, the state.

Political scientists, historians, and sociologists name the various forms of nationalism popular, romantic, racist, cultural, authoritarian, ethnic, religious, or official.[2] Yet these classifications are in general subsumed by the broad canopy of what I am calling *statist nationalism*. In the nineteenth century and up to the end of the Second World War, nationalists movements in Asia and Africa grew out of popular dissent and provided the mobilizing rhetoric for peoples who recognized—and found unacceptable—the fact that their states were under foreign rule.[3] In the second half of the twentieth century, statist nationalisms have proliferated globally. Some, like the Palestinian and the Kurdish nations, have struggled long to win autonomy in and control over their own lands. Not every nation has its own state. John Hall writes of the 250 minorities worldwide who are now seeking states and, quoting Ernest Gellner, of the 8,000 "natural" languages that "could be used to put forward nationalist claims" (Hall 1993, 22). In its extreme form, statist nationalism can become maniacally xenophobic, with all foreigners—whether they are in power or not—fair game. But who are these foreigners? Foreignness is a matter for negotiation and even construction. The fragmentation of centers in the post-colonial era gives the possibility of autonomous ethnic purity to groups who never thought of themselves collectively before and highlights differences—some might say, invents differences—as it opens up divides in what once seemed to be homogeneous communities. New myths of origin allow groups to remember or discover or create a uniqueness that "spontaneously" produces a shared identity and promises the fruits of a common destiny. These then segregate themselves and exclude those who do not fit, those who threaten their freshly constructed and thus fragile group ethos.

This process is inherently violent because it involves imposing ideology on geography. Statist nationalists place the state first and the nation second—but always as though the nation were at once primordial and immortal. Since, as Gellner notes, "nationalism emerges only in milieux in which the existence of the state is already very much taken for granted" (Gellner 1988, 4), statist nationalists are usually involved in a conflict with the state's existing power structure that may escalate into a war. Wars ensure that nationalist sentiment receive an outlet, that it may serve as the bedrock for the foundation of the new nation-state. Anthony Giddens observes that "the advent of the nation-state stimulates divergent and oppositional nationalisms as much as it fosters the coincidence of nationalist sentiments and existing state boundaries" (Giddens 1987, 220). Ross Poole sees war as "important for national identity, not so much because individuals have shown that they are prepared to kill for their nation . . . but because men—and sometimes women—have been prepared to suffer and die on behalf of their nation" (Poole 1985, 77–78). Vaclav Havel goes even further, calling nationalisms "the instigators of modern wars" (Havel 1993, 3). Here is the danger of statist nationalism: it is inherently violent.

Statist nationalists claim to represent all the people comprising their imagined community. In general, however, these nationalists have been indigenous male elites who invoke, without listening to, others' voices, which is not to say that statist nationalism is either evil or inherently masculine. Globally, women are as much at the forefront of violent statist nationalist movements as they are advocates of nonviolence. Three examples of what Jean Bethke Elshtain calls the Ferocious Few are the women of the Shining Path fighting peasants in Peru, Serb women blocking aid convoys to Muslim civilians in Bosnia-Herzegovina, and Israeli women establishing Zionist settlements on Palestinian land. Yet women rarely, if ever, lead these movements. Highlighting the gender of nationalist groups and their leaders reveals what is at stake for each group in advocating a particular identity. Once such stakes become transparent, we see individuals who are talking not so much about and for others, but about and for themselves—those who dominate the group that aspires to dominate. Such decentering of a particular nationalist discourse assigns it a place alongside others.

If we give equal consideration to all competing nationalist ideologies of all groups within the confines of a single state, then nationalism emerges not only as a collective ideology, but first and foremost as an individual state of mind, a way of expressing a sense of belonging to an entity that people choose to create. This complex of emotions is what I call *humanist nationalism*. Whereas statist nationalism is absolute and requires a binary framework of differentiation and recognition, positing the nation "out there" from time immemorial and awaiting discovery by those who "naturally" belong to it, humanist nationalism construes the nation as dialectic, as both produced and productive.

Humanist nationalism is a program of action that people may pursue without reference to a state. It unites individuals and accounts for the subjectivities of several communities: those who are usually lumped together as anonymous "nationalists"; those who are not, strictly speaking, nationalists at all because they do not belong to a group that designates itself, first and foremost, as nationalist; and those who call themselves nationalists but whose individual needs have been marginalized, such as some women's groups. R. Radhakrishnan notes that faced "with its own repression, the women's question seems forced either to seek its own separatist political autonomy or to envision other ways of constituting a relational-integrative politics without at the same time resorting to another kind of totalizing umbrella. . . . Nationalist totality . . . is an example of a 'bad totality' and feminist historiography secedes from that structure not to set up a different and oppositional form of totality, but to establish a different relationship to totality" (Radhakrishnan 1992, 78, 81).

In outlining my definitions of nationalism, I am mindful of the neglect of individual motivations that Terry Eagleton deplores, saying that the "metaphysics of nationalism speak of the entry into full self-realization of a unitary subject known as the people. . . . If subjects have needs, then we already know what one at least of these needs must be, namely, the need to know what one's needs are. The metaphysics of nationalism tend to obscure this point, by assuming a subject somehow intuitively present to itself" (Eagleton 1990, 28–29). The 1980s poetry and fiction of Lebanese women allow us to connect the first stirrings of nationalist sentiment in the individual psyche—the identification of individual need—with its mobilization and organization as a collective movement when the nation imagined by the individual requires its invention by the collectivity.[4]

Lebanese women's writings redefine nationalism and extend it to reveal its humanist dimensions. They reveal the individual's construction of links with a piece of land, the geopolitical dimensions of which are rarely defined, that then becomes instrumental in an individual's self-definition. This focus on individual agency in constructing political selfhood makes it possible to see nationalism as a meaningful and dynamic way of belonging and caring, rather than a way of dominating what Gellner calls an "anonymous, impersonal society with mutually substitutable atomized individuals."[5] Redefining nationalism from the perspective of the individual subject position would seem to vindicate Fredric Jameson, who claims that throughout the twentieth century third-world writers have produced national allegories. For him, citizens of this so-called third world cannot write of themselves except as metonyms of their nations. Some critics question Jameson's totalizing narrative and suggest that it is dependent on the omission of all literature except that written by indigenous male elites.[6] But if we accept the premise of humanist nationalism, then it may well be that twentieth-century literature, and particularly that written by postcolonial male and female writers of all classes and all nations—not only those of the third world—may be engaged in a nationalist enterprise. Their project begins in the individual imagination and may in some cases ally itself with others and evolve into some form of statist nationalism. They are inscribing a sense of belonging in the face of a global economy that is less and less hospitable to the individual and within a world that is increasingly fragmented just when it seems to be more unified; their goal is to accommodate, reintegrate, and empower its alienated citizens.

Humanist Nationalist Allegories

Since 1982 Lebanese women have produced several humanist nationalist allegories: some critical, others constructive; some political, others mystical. In *Hajar al-dahak* (The laughing stone, 1990),

Huda Barakat examines the ways in which nationalism drives human beings to reject their blood kin so as to create new families out of a military matrix. There is the merchant whose wife is convinced that the Virgin Mary will reappear to her, for example. Ostensibly to give her some rest, but really to free himself to take over the leadership of a militia, the husband sends her to his family village. The fact that a neighboring country, and not some local political or religious group, sponsors the militia allows him to claim "irrefutably that belonging was not to the confession but to the nation [*watan*]" (Barakat 1990, 103). Barakat may ridicule this nationalist husband, but she does not trivialize the compelling attraction of statist nationalisms.

Khalil, Barakat's anti-hero, describes his first brief membership in a nationalist group as empowering. He recalls the joy he experienced in being part of "a group, even if only on its margins." He recalls how comrades dropped by whenever they needed anything and confided their fears and their dreams: "In front of you they strip off their family to choose you. . . . When you leave the group you become a real orphan because you have lost your chosen family to whom you gave birth because you had become a man. Your friend becomes your ultimate father and you forget the first one. You have relegated him to the edges of childhood memories so as to be able to create new loved ones" (122–23). In addition to these companions, Khalil creates other surrogate fathers, who include Dr. Waddah. This doctor successfully operates on Khalil for an ulcer, and, when Khalil comes out of his coma, he turns his savior into both father *and* mother. In the recovery room he feels the touch of Dr. Waddah's hand, "the warmth of which gave me more than the umbilical cord that had connected me to my mother. . . . While I slept, he looked at me more than my mother did when I was a child. . . . Like my father when I recovered, he was happy with me." Later, leaning his head against Dr. Waddah's chest, Khalil finds himself nestling between two large breasts, and he realizes that this man is "more than my mother and his eyes are more than her milk" (204–5).

These created parents are more real and loving than are the natural ones. Khalil is particularly repelled by his beautiful mother.

Toward the end of the novel, when Khalil has come to terms with his homosexuality, he thinks about his mother, whose beauty makes him hate her "because beautiful mothers cannot be mothers for us. . . . When we grow up and become leaders [*zu'ama'*], we hate them and completely destroy their beauty" (243). He compares his mother unfavorably with the women of Carthage, who cut their hair and melted down their precious metals for the national fleet; his mother, shame of shames, "laughs a lot. . . . Khalil began to hate his mother a little, and her laughter a lot, and he came out top of his history class" (133). It is almost as if despising his mother and her foolishness garnered him academic rewards.

Through Khalil, Barakat demonstrates how the nationalist group displaces the individual member's family by means of a reconceptualization of birth—men's birth at both the passive and the active levels. To give birth to the new family, the boy must become a man. So how does the boy become a man? In the passage describing how companions become fathers, Barakat glosses over the transformation of the boy into a man with a simple causative conjunction: "because he had become a man."

Looking elsewhere for elucidation of masculine birth in a nationalist context, we find Klaus Theweleit's *Male Fantasies,* an analysis of German Freikorps writings from the era between world wars. Theweleit claims that all military formations provide a womb for the gestation and birth of the properly masculinized man, the only person qualified to be a citizen. The military corps renders the mother's body irrelevant and redundant. The mother cannot give real birth to real men, real citizens. This real birth must be out of the all-male fighting, killing corps, whether it be an official military unit or a civilian militia. The mother must be eliminated (Theweleit 1987–89). Barakat takes this transferal of the birthing function further than Theweleit does. She proposes that the real birth, with its attendant militarized masculinity and right to citizenship, relegates not only the mother, but *also the father,* to the margin of memory. Khalil does not even long for a better father, he wants to imagine new bonds that are based not on kinship but on ideology.[7] Masculinization gives birth to new beings. The masculinity of these new men is proven by the fact that they kill. Barakat presents this lethal masculinity through Khalil's necrophiliac desire: whenever he reads the paper, he becomes excited by photographs of dead militiamen laid out, "their firm, naked bodies affirming without a shadow of a doubt that they are men and that the acute igniting of their masculinity was what had led them to kill" (Barakat 1990, 170).

How are we to recognize real nationalism? It is to be found in those who exhibit nationalist feeling (*hiss watani*). How can we recognize such feeling? Tongue in cheek, Barakat announces that there are telltale signs, like the censure of laughter. Only extreme seriousness and a consorting with death are truly indicative of nationalist feeling. Hence, Khalil spends most of the novel preoccupied with death—that of the men he has desired, that of their families and his own, and his illness and death: "Nationalist sentiment suffers when it is far from death. History is constructed by death alone, full of hatred and contempt for laughter. Khalil had known two history teachers. He remembered them well. Neither had laughed. Both were infatuated with nationalist sentiment and with death" (131).

Laughter is a sure sign of nationalist inconstancy, if not betrayal. The list of those who laugh is telling: those involved with militias laugh a lot; they tell terrible jokes at parties and burst their sides laughing. Laughter rings loud when the bombing starts because this is the signal that a holiday has started. Women laugh because they can meet to chat. The shopkeeper and the baker laugh because everyone is panic-buying. The restaurateur also laughs because people care less about their safety and they risk dining out. The gas station owner laughs because suddenly he is powerful and may even become a political leader. The money changers laugh because remittances start to pour in. Poets laugh because their moral authority is renewed by their elegies for the newly dead. Foreign correspondents laugh because they are sure of a good story. Everyone in real estate laughs because bombs are good for business. Worst of all, "even the mothers of the dead laugh because new delegations will join their sons and thus lessen the loneliness of the mothers." But the ones who laugh the most are the armed elements, "blue-blooded laughter turns black from laughing . . . dies from laughing. You,

Khalil, who coldly drink your tea, why do you not laugh?" (145–50). Khalil, it seems, is the only one in this carnival of laughter, of antinationalism, who retains dignity and composure, his nationalist sentiment.

Khalil can easily control his laughter, but in the early stages he has no stomach for that aspect of nationalist sentiment that is obsessed with death. When he sees the fountain of blood at the Ministry of Tourism exhibition, he faints (130). This is a fountain that he will later revisit in his dreams. Yusuf, the object of his passion, has been shot to death and appropriately buried, but here he is again being led to the fountain by the wife of the President of the Organization (without further precision). She attaches two wings to his back that are held in place by white silk bands threaded through his bullet wounds. After embracing him, she seats Yusuf on the fountain and the blood starts to flow from the top of his head, but without discoloring his wings. Dream blurs into reality as Khalil vomits blood because his ulcer has become irritated. Mortified that he cannot be a better nationalist, he thinks of the people of Tyre, who had immolated themselves for their nation, and weeps "for love of his nation and for sadness at its miserable fate" (132).

Khalil loves his nation and understands its prohibition on laughter, yet after meeting Yusuf he always laughs, and with "nationalist feeling," when Yusuf once returns home alive from some mission (135). Knowing that nationalism demands seriousness and the affirmation of death, Khalil nonetheless laughs when his beloved is not killed, explicitly naming what he does and what he feels "nationalist." Although both laughter and the affirmation of life are antinationalist, Khalil's love defiantly redefines them. Has his love for Yusuf turned the negative mandate of nationalist feeling into something positive? Or is his desire a threat to his nationalism?

Yusuf, like Khalil's earlier infatuation, Naji, is killed. Khalil even fantasizes, as Yusuf lies dying in the ambulance, that it is he who has pumped Yusuf's body full of lead. Khalil mourns deeply and painfully for a long time, cutting himself off from everyone until his bleeding ulcer compels him to go to hospital. After recovering from surgery, Khalil suddenly sees the world differently. Instead of pondering death, he begins to feel that he deserves to live and to live well and happily. He gives in to his old friend Nayif, who has been trying for weeks to convince him to start working for his militia's newspaper. Khalil goes to a party thrown by the militia and discovers that the editor is interested in him sexually. Although Khalil does not reciprocate the editor's interest, he becomes involved with him anyway, knowing that such an affair will change his life. It does. Now he can convince himself that morality and nationalist sentiment are meaningless in this city, and that what really matters is to love oneself even if that love means hating others. By the end of the novel, Khalil takes this new philosophy so far as to rape the woman who lives upstairs from him. He succumbs to the temptations of the drugs and arms trade and to the lure of the group—the real family—that makes him one of the boys. He laughs with the others now when black jokes are told (219).

On the very last page, the narrator intervenes wistfully, saying, "How you have changed since I described you in the opening pages! You have begun to know more than I do. Alchemy. The laughing stone. Khalil has gone and become a male who laughs. And I remain, a woman who writes" (250). Khalil is now the laughing stone, the polar opposite of his own conception of how a nationalist should feel and act. As a stone he feels nothing, but he laughs nonetheless. Khalil joins a nationalist unit, but in defiance of what he had believed to be the necessary conditions for nationalist sentiment.

When I reached the ending of this novel, I was shocked. Relentlessly optimistic up to its final pages, I hoped to read of a man who could stay in Lebanon during the war and not become involved in the fighting, not give in to the immorality and violence. I immediately wrote to Barakat asking her why. Why, having started to do so, could she not create a model for humanist nationalism that would not be undone by its own project? Less than two weeks later, I received her reply. She was happy the novel had made such a strong impression, but I had to understand that this war was different from any other war, even the Spanish civil war that had two clear sides. In other wars, in which the enemy is clear, "nationalist feeling can develop as a kind of defense of identity and belonging. But what I wanted to say was that in the Lebanese civil war, all the fighters were corrupt, and violence and hatred had reached the point of absolute evil, so that all claims to defend a cause—whatever it might be—became a lie and a crime." In such a situation, Barakat's letter continued, individuals had the "choice between being the executioner, which Khalil rejected at the beginning, or the despised victim. In the latter case, the outcome is *madness,* drugs, or escape. I wanted to write an accusation, a complaint. I wanted to understand how an entire people turns into criminal fighters. What human resources do we draw on when legal protection is withdrawn and the body consumes itself from within? I wanted to convey the deepest impact of the civil war on human society and how it changes and rots when the only enemy is ourselves" (letter from Paris, 28 October 1992; my emphasis).

Barakat's next novel, *Ahl al-hawa* (People of passion), was written in 1993, a year after the war ended. It explores one of the outcomes of victimization: madness. The narrator is a man who had been kidnapped and tortured. His sister, Asma, commits him to a psychiatric hospital run by nuns, whom he upsets with his singing and his crazy perspective on the world outside. At times of danger, the patients flock to him, "believing that I was their father. They would crawl under me as though I were a great hen" (Barakat 1993, 19). This description is reminiscent of Khalil's reaction to Dr. Waddah; in other words the main character is both mother and father to the other patients.

The narrator talks about "them"—other inmates, people outside—thinking he must have been driven mad by his torture and his failure to end the war. But he thinks that his real problem is his obsession with images of the woman he had captured during a bombardment and whom he imagines he has killed. He rehearses again and again the sensuousness of her body and tries to convince himself that he was indifferent to her, did not really care that she had tried to leave him. But perhaps the real reason for his madness is that he has lost his ability to function morally in his society. The reference to laughter may provide a key. He and his friends are uncontrollably amused—antinationalist?—whenever they hear the word "society." The doctor tries to calm them down by suggesting other words, like "people of the family" (*ahl*) or "people" (*nas*) or "the outside" (*al-kharij*). But their preferred words are "state" (*umma*) or "nation, tribe" (*qawm*) or "populace" (*sha'b*). The patients do not like these alternatives and assure the doctor that there is really no need to find another word because they like the word "society" very much. Finally, "we agreed to a neutral phrase like the ones used by the doctor and we began to say 'the people outside'" (95). The people outside were part of a "society that gave rise to much mirth while laughter was tearing itself apart with anger and violence." It was a society that expected men to prove themselves by killing. The hero cannot relate to such a society and its gendered expectations, so he becomes fascinated with androgyny, "jealous of animals and plants reproducing themselves because they have male and female organs. This sex is freed from torment" (88). Since he cannot satisfy his society's demands in connection with masculinity, the narrator finds that he has become one of those "who do not fight in these wars. We have no sex to bring to our women. . . . Because we are no longer any good to fight or fuck they are taking care of us and not even asking our families for money" (154, 165). He cannot—perhaps, will not—do all the lethal things that a real man is supposed to do, and so he has become useless to his nation, sterile, and thus unable to survive. He is fit only for a psychiatric hospital.

Women in the War

What place do women occupy in such a system? Few are the stories of women joining nationalist movements, despite the fact that recent research mentions the presence of women in several militias—in some cases, in combat roles (Shehadeh 1993). As we have already read in Iraqi literature, joining a military unit or a militia is not the only way to be a nationalist. My reading of women's writings during the civil war indicates that their conceptions of nationalism were no less strong than those of the men, but that their writings expressed them differently. In tandem with women's global politicization and invention of women-specific strategies of resistance and opposition, women, and particularly the school of writers whom I call the Beirut Decentrists (Cooke 1988), propounded a nationalism that was rooted in an individual, nurturing relationship with Lebanon. It was through a dynamic, reciprocal relationship that they belonged to the Lebanese nation, one they defined sometimes as the extended village or even family, because they adopted a quasi-maternal responsibility for the people and, above all, for the land of Lebanon.

Yet women's nationalism also excluded. Like the militia men, women discriminated between those who were qualified to assume Lebanese citizenship and those who were not. These qualifications did not pertain to membership in political, religious, feudal, or what Etel Adnan calls "tribal" groups (Adnan 1978). For the women writers, citizenship in the Lebanese nation accrued through individual evidence of loyalty to the land, an entity at once concrete and amorphous, because it had no natural boundaries. As long as people, usually men, left the country and allowed it to self-destruct, the war would continue. To stay Lebanese, people had to stay loyal to the land. The Beirut Decentrists called for a collective sense of responsibility rather than an insouciance that put the blame on others, for, as Ghada al-Samman writes in *Kawabis Bayrut* (Beirut nightmares, 1980), "there are no innocents in an unjust society" (315). This sense of responsibility demanded that each person make the impossible decision of loyalty to the land and participate in the effort to end the violence. Through fiction writing, women came to understand their decision to stay. Their discourse then became part of the new social and civic contract between the Lebanese and their nation, as defined by these same texts.

From the beginning of the war, Emily Nasrallah was creating maternal prototypes of the ideal Lebanese citizen. Nasrallah's citizens were not necessarily and essentially women, but they were capable of what Sara Ruddick calls "preservative maternal thinking" (Ruddick 1989). Even the devastation and despair wrought by the Israeli invasion did not undermine the contract between the women and the land. Post-1982 women's writings reaffirm the need to stay and to redefine nationalism as a positive force. Some imagine writing itself as that space in which the nation can be constructed. When Barakat contrasts the man who laughs to the woman who writes, for example, she seems to be privileging discourse as the site for constructing the nation: "Khalil has gone and become a male who laughs. And I remain, a woman who writes" (Barakat 1990, 250). Nasrallah makes the connection between writing and the nation unequivocal when she writes: "The word has become a refuge and a life boat—the poem or story a substitute nation" (Nasrallah 1992, 12).

Nasrallah wrote prolifically in the wake of the Israeli invasion, publishing two collections of short stories in 1984 and 1985. The later collection, entitled *Al-tahuna al-da'i'a* (The lost mill), deals with the difficulty of communicating nationalist sentiment, or what Barakat's Khalil calls *hiss watani*. In one story, "Kulluhunna um-muhu" (All of them are his mother), she offers empathetic grieving as a form of nationalist sentiment, which is an ineffable feeling packaged, paradoxically yet inevitably, in words. Her narrator, the only audience member in an auditorium, assumes that the masked, screaming players on stage are acting for her alone. Yet they "seem oblivious" to her presence. When she tries to leave, she find that she cannot: the theater has no exits; she must stay, compelled to observe passively and uncomprehendingly. Then one of the players raises his mask. How long has she been there? "Since the curtain went up." Briefly, the boundary between stage and audience, between fiction and fact, is sketched in. So she is in a real theater. "What did you see?" the player asks. "What I see now." "What did you under-stand?" She is relieved at the question: maybe the anonymous masked players were just screaming and there was nothing more to understand. Her relief is short-lived: since she understood nothing, why had she stayed? There are no exits. He pulls down his mask, plunging her back into confusion and frustration. Her illusion of communicating and understanding—that the screams were just screams—shatters (Nasrallah 1985, 197–99).

Next, a woman separates herself from the mass of actors. How, the narrator wonders, does she know that this is a woman? "From the voice. Yes. It was a wounding voice, erupting out of the depths of creation and fluttering off into space, spreading fear and pain. 'She's weeping for her son.' A voice from nowhere reaches me" (198). The woman's voice is distinctive. Even though it utters no words, it imparts meaning by creating spontaneous empathy.

Then the father (inexplicably recognized as such) joins the mother, and they scream together. At this point, when the parents' voices melt into a single scream, the narrator feels the foggy barriers that surround her understanding dissipate. She begins to weep, to share the feelings of those people with whom she could not otherwise communicate. She has tapped into the core of the others' intensity. Although Nasrallah is not explicit in her description of this shared emotion, it is suggestive of grief for the nation, especially in the context of contemporary women's writings on the civil war. This grief is not the proscriptive seriousness of nationalist sentiment demanded by Barakat's Khalil and his comrades in *The Laughing Stone*. To grieve during this war is to feel with, to belong and only then somehow to communicate nationalist sentiment.

At that very moment of identification with that grief, the same disembodied voice tells Nasrallah's narrator that, unlike the rest of the actors, she is not "his mother." The narrator insists: " 'But I am his mother.' The voice replies: 'Your tears are outside the theater. Remember, you're the audience.' 'But I'm the participating audience.' I was delighted with my courage. The voice was silent, or maybe it had left me to watch the scenes. Then I saw the mother's shape separate for the second, third, and fourth time. Then that recurrent mother began to form a wide circle and the others became a dot to that circle. All of them are his mother" (199–200).

The symbiosis of dot and circles, of mother and mothers, is assured through the maintenance of the scream. The story ends when one of the mothers approaches the narrator with arms outstretched, "ropes of unearthly light," beckoning her up on to the stage. The narrator is about to react when the mother turns into a huge tree, and the voice explains that she has "taken root in the soil" (204). The materiality of the soil is vivid.

It is as mother that she unites with the soil. When the voice becomes silent, the narrator realizes that the theater has become a forest. All of the mothers are now trees whose roots reach down to the "living principle" (204). This ending, the transformation of a mother into a tree, echoes a topos in other works about women's growing strength during the Lebanese civil war. All who wish to consider themselves Lebanese must stay in the country and become an organic part of its regenerative soil. But who can plant such roots? People who feel together and intensely for something that is at once their child and, paradoxically, their parent, the source of their communal identity.

Nazik Yared has been more tentative than Nasrallah in prescribing nationalist action. In 1986 she published a novel, *Al-sada al-makhnuq* (The stifled echo), which examines the consequences of emigration. In contrast to earlier literature that portrayed men who leave and women who stay, Yared's protagonist in this novel, Najib, is a man who stays, while his wife, Amal, emigrates to Paris, "for the sake of the children." As in most fiction about Lebanese war emigrants, the one left behind does not censure the one who leaves. With time, though, and particularly after a sojourn in France, where the Lebanese live easily and distantly from the war, Najib becomes embittered. No longer feeling guilty about the tentative affair he has begun with Nuha, he justifies having cut himself off from the wife who left him. All but one of the characters in this novel have been corrupted by the apparent necessity of leaving Lebanon; the exception—and the only person to elicit sympathy—is Najla. She has done the right thing, having stuck by her husband when he decided to go to Paris. Yet she can never banish her country from her mind. When friends rebuke her for not taking advantage of the joys of Paris, she responds: "My nerves may be tired. But I feel as though people here are looking at me with some contempt because I enjoy safety and contentment while my country burns and my compatriots are dying. I feel ashamed. . . . I envy those who are in Beirut. How can you enjoy living here, Amal, when you could be at home?" (Yared 1986, 160–61). Not only does Najla remain firmly loyal to Lebanon, but she fosters in her children the same kind of loving loyalty. Unlike Benedict Anderson's "long-distance nationalists" (Anderson 1992), who buy their peace of mind and their citizenship with money, Najla remains connected to her nation through love and loyalty. By teaching love of nation to others, in this case to her children, Najla seems to be involuntarily becoming a long-distance yet still humanist nationalist.

An anthem to the Lebanese nation is Nur Salman's 220-page poem, *Ila rajul lam ya'ti* (To a man who did not come, 1986). The title immediately signals its tone and message: a love poem filled with blame and pain. Salman's dedication indicates its audience: "To my mother, Zahiyya, and to my sisters, Najla and Widad and Saqala." On behalf of the women in her family, she is writing to the men who did not come to Lebanon, without being explicit about who or when. Yet, put into the context of women's literature on the Lebanese civil war, it is likely that she is referring to the expatriates, many of them men, who watched the war from a safe distance. The accusation directed at absent Lebanese recalls criticisms by Aijaz Ahmad and Benedict Anderson of emigrants who claim exile status. Both insist on the importance of clarifying the terms of what Anderson calls "long-distance politics without accountability [among] émigrés who have no serious intention of going back to a home, which, as time passes, more and more serves as a phantom bedrock for an embattled metropolitan ethnic identity" (Anderson 1992, 20). In an era of mass migration when a hundred million people are wandering the globe, it does make a difference if this wandering is forced or chosen. Economic migrants will have a different sense of attachment to the country to which they may return than exiles who know that their chances of returning are slight. Statist nationalists in London, New York, or Paris who send regular remittances to relatives fighting the enemy back in the home country do not necessarily intend to return to the land for which they are paying others to die and to kill. The publicized contributions they make serve rather to assure them of a securer space wherever they are now. Choosing to settle in a land that is far from the nation that continues to shape their identity pushes against international frontiers and forces the frontiers to serve as national boundaries.

Throughout Salman's elegy to a man who did not come, the poet summons and then immediately repels Ya Baidi, "my distant one." The use of *ba'idi,* from the root *b-'-d,* recalls the elegiac formula *la tab'ad,* meaning "do not be distant," but also "do not perish" (Stetkevych 1992, 169). While the speaker's lover may not in this case be dead, he would have done better to die than to remain distant from the war. The woman grieves for his distance, but never so much as to compel her to escape to him (Salman 1986, 7). Again and again she calls to him, even begging him, "Be a man for my nation!" (17). And almost in the same breath she warns him not to come (7, 133, 139). She fears for him "the narrowness of the pavements . . . / I fear for you our wailing, our lamentations / Our screaming in small valleys. / I fear for you our confusion. Our wretched delusion" (124, 190).

As the poem progresses, the speaker's warnings, always sad and never angry, escalate. He, like the others who left (88), is not safe in this land of martyrs, prophets, and poets who live the terrors and who learn to break down the barriers between death and life, and between life in death and life in life. There is in them a life that death cannot touch. These martyrs who are "the creators of the single echo / They are the ones who remain . . . / All that remains of the body of the nation are its martyrs" (100, 104). These martyrs, human vestiges of the nation, are the prophets whose lives were cut short, so that "we might live" (89), yet these are martyrs who do not die. They are the bedrock of the new nation. How can others become like them? By staying, especially if they are sons of the new nation: "A thousand woes to a nation whose *sons* are not where they should be!" (129) and "My nation without its sons. They are the babies of orphan births" (161). It is the absence of the men that is so painful, and she mourns "my house without a boy, my nation without its sons. They are the babies of orphan births" (166). They must stay but they also must write, because the poets "plant the nation in the earth / Master creators. They fertilize our history with fire / . . . The earth holds its head high because of them and is called nation" (103). The poets will return "my nation to its land" (104). These people who have stayed, these martyr-prophet-poets "are united by the fact that / their dream is one with their waking. Death with life. / Thirst with its quenching. Love with love" (167).

These martyr-prophet-poet-survivors are dangerous for those who have not shared their experiences. The speaker is threatening her lover, while claiming to be protecting him, as a mother, against the harm that will surely befall him. She is warning him, somewhat ominously, against herself: "I fear for you the voracity of my fading / I fear for you the voracity of my loneliness" (169, 172). Finally, Cassandra-like, she intones the prohibition: "Beware of coming! / Do not come to our grief [nation], Ya Baidi . . . / I longed for you. Do not come tonight!" (189–90). The only relief lies in this final, pro-tem prohibition, namely "tonight." Is the woman offering hope for an ultimate forgiveness? There is a possibility that he can find a niche in this dangerous place if, once he returns, he can learn to love the land.

The speaker's feelings for Ya Baidi are fraught with paradox. She loves him and wants him to return, yet she needs him to remain distant. His absence creates a longing, and this longing defines her: "I loved your distance because I was the path to it" (205). His absence makes her productive.[8] She fears his return lest "my body end in a blocked pulse. . . . We are doomed to miscarry we / who are caught between our own wombs, the wombs of time and place / A dead fatherhood and a crippled motherhood" (221). She is trying to survive in a death world that destroys the possibility of parenting. The dream of Ya Baidi enables her to hold on to her own individual power of reproduction, in fact to be at once both mother and father. She dreads his return lest his presence render her body sterile. She manages to retain her fertility because of her dream of him, the dream that makes her a mother: "How this distance brings me close to your absence / I cling to you and sleep in a dream / The dream has made me into the mother of a child . . . / This is our child, Ya Baidi / . . . O the poverty of a love that does not beget life / Before me is my child . . . my boy . . . my son / He is the most important. Indeed, he is the axis planted in the deepest depths of existence / He is the one who joins the 'I' of the masculine with the 'I' of the feminine" (94). This child who is the product of her dream of her love is at once feminine and masculine; above all, he is *her* child. As in *The Laughing Stone,* the new social formation cannot survive unless it excludes the father, for the father may become destructive: "I am afraid of the days that will change me against my will into a frightened, bereaved Sheherezade. / And turn you into a tyrannical, careless, and possessive Sharayar" (79).

The absent presence of Ya Baidi remains the muse of Salman's poem and of the speaker's love, which is creating the nation. Her love for him feeds and is in turn fed by, her love for her nation, with each of these loves made possible by the greatest love of all, that

of the nation for its people: "Your love brought me love of nation /
My love for you would be worth nothing if my nation did not love
me / My love for you would be worth nothing without a nation for
me to love / . . . Our love is not enough for my nation / It loved me
more, more, more / I dissolve into the earth" (15). What is the
nation? For Salman as for Nasrallah, the nation is the grief of the
people who stay and survive and whose staying allows them to push
down roots into the soil, the earth of the nation. This grief of the
survivors is an empathy that links and creates a community out of
those who experience it. Women have the greatest share of grief,
of the nation: "I am a woman whose only right is to grieve" (134).
The earlier association of grief with nation allows us to read the
woman whose only right is to grieve as the humanist nationalist
writ large. This nationalist, this grieving woman, is powerfully
creative because grief, when it overcomes the body of a woman, is
"fertile with the mercy of childbirth" (120, 205). Indeed, the grief-
nation—like the anguished dream of the beloved—makes a woman's body fertile. Salman anchors her hope in the notion of intellectual fertility: as long as the land-woman is fertile, the nation will
survive because blood alone will not beget blood.

Who is this fertile woman? She is both mother and writer. The
mother who nurtures and the woman writer who sows fear. The
poet's father, "the man who was jealous of the thin pen" (41), had
warned her mother when the child was small that her pen would
"turn into nails in the coffin of her happiness" (38). How is the
reader to understand this mother-writer who represents both an
ethic of care and a symbol of terror? Through the transformation
of the meaning of the nation, which becomes the product as well
as the source of the citizen's love. The mother-writer is the source
of the new nation, she is the one who has "no choice but to love
because [she] constantly give[s] birth" (43). Her work, and by
extension her being also, is at once productive and the product of
the nation. Each needs the other to exist and to survive.

A recurrent image in this poem is that of the womb. This quintessentially female organ becomes in Salman's hands the symbol of
renewal. As such, it no longer resides in a particular body or gender,
but rather becomes generalized. How does it work? Twice, Salman
repeats verbatim that the woman writer has many wombs: "A

woman's body has more than one womb / My hands are a womb /
My heart is a womb / My eyes are a womb / My lips are a womb"
(153, 159). In a move that I read as strategically essentialist, Salman
extols woman's body as powerful in its pride, seclusion, pain,
creativity, and freedom (156). She then goes on to declare: "Woman's body has no sin. It has no sin. / It was squeezed into the mold
of sin so that it should become the body of sin. / It is free, proud,
the knots of civilizations have shackled it with brass rings. / In
civilizations it is their conscience, their feeling, and the *qibla* of their
birth" (157). This woman's body recreates "a nation that has left
her" (11), defying the blades of male logic to release "the glorious
labor pains that weave the body to the soul for constant childbirth"
(159). Again, the poet insists that women writers give birth not just
to people, but to nations, which constantly regenerate themselves
through the mother-poet's many wombs. She, the poet, prophet and
thus martyr, must write the abandoned nation back into existence
by giving birth to sons, replacing the sons who are where they
should not be.

Is Nur Salman excluding men from citizenship in a nation for
whose production everyone should be responsible? What is she
saying with her emphasis on the woman's body and on the sons of
the nation whom women must produce? Does the womblessness of
men's bodies disqualify them from producing new sons and creating the nation? Does she deny that men are capable of producing
alternative communities? Surely not, and I believe that her focus on
the woman's reproducing body is key. For just as Salman seems to
be connecting the production of a nation to the physicality of
women's bodies, she undermines the gender-specificity of the connection. She displaces the womb from its natural position so as to
allow it to proliferate throughout the body and to function in
systems that are not gender-specific. This dislocation and multi-
plication of a woman's reproductive organs extends an invitation
to men to join in this process of self- and nation-regeneration.

The writings of Huda Barakat, Emily Nasrallah, Nazik Yared, and
Nur Salman engage the nation in such a way as to produce what
Radhakrishnan calls "a critical and deconstructive knowledge

about nationalism. . . . It is on the basis of such knowledge that postcolonial subjects can produce a genuinely subaltern history about themselves and not merely replicate . . . the liberal-elitist narrative of the West" (Radhakrishnan 1992, 86). The nation that these women write into existence is not an ideological construct, despite its discursive nature; it is, rather, an individual sense of belonging and then of responsibility, which radiates out from multiple centers. It is first of all personal; it *may* become collective. This nation is the context within which each individual constructs a self, a center, to become the new citizen. Citizenship is neither a birthright nor a reward for military service; it is an affective identity that becomes a building block in the construction of the nation, the center for each humanist nationalist. The process is circular and keeps renewing itself in terms of itself. For those who are humanist nationalists, there is no single polity but multiple fragmentary projects that continually disassemble and reassemble and regenerate themselves because, above all, they foster survival.

Conclusion

July 1995

Dear Reader,

Please read these epigraphs.
They are the real conclusion to *Women and the War Story*.

Yours in peace,
Miriam

PS. What follows them is a postscript.

All efforts to render politics aesthetic culminate in one thing: war.... Marinetti says in his manifesto on the Ethiopian colonial war: "War is beautiful because it initiates the dreamt-of metallization of the human body.... War is beautiful because it combines the gun-fire, the cannonades, the cease-fire, the scents, and the stench of putrefaction into a symphony. War is beautiful because it creates new architecture, like that of the big tanks, the geometrical formation flights, the smoke spirals from burning villages, and many others.... Poets and artists of Futurism!... remember these principles of an aesthetics of war so that your struggle for a new literature and a new graphic art ... may be illumined by them!" ... Mankind's self-alienation has reached such a degree that it can experience its own destruction as an aesthetic pleasure of the first order.
    Walter Benjamin (1969 [1936])

It may be that enlisted women, who have little at stake in being manly, who are embarrassed about being protected, and who have not been part of the death lottery that requires a belief in substitutability, are in the best position to discover what truly makes a society secure. It may not be violence; it may not be national boundaries impervious to migration; and it may not be allowing men to hold a monopoly on the means of violence.

Judith Stiehm (1989)

Women, and others who occupy different positions in the world than do the producers of dominant discourses, may be therefore especially able to recognize and articulate exactly what gets included and excluded from those discourses. Discovering the absences and gaps and understanding how these silences function to structure and make patriarchal discourse possible are crucial elements of the strategy of feminist theory and ones with exceedingly important policy implications.

Carol Cohn (1989)

The answer to the problem between the white race and the colored, between males and females, lies in healing the split that originates in the very foundation of our lives, our culture, our languages, our thoughts. A massive uprooting of dualistic thinking in the individual and collective consciousness is the beginning of a long struggle, but one that could, in our best hopes, bring us to the end of rape, of violence, of war.

Gloria Anzaldúa (1987)

The existence of third world women's narratives in itself is not evidence of decentring hegemonic histories and subjectivities. It is the way in which they are read, understood and located institutionally which is of paramount importance. After all, the point is not just 'to record' one's history of struggle, or consciousness, but how they are recorded; the way we read, receive, and disseminate such imaginative records is immensely significant. It is the very question of reading, theorizing, and locating these writings . . . the practice of remembering and rewriting leads to the formation of politicized consciousness and self-identity. Writing often becomes the context through which new political identities are forged. It becomes a space for struggle and contestation about reality itself.

Chandra Talpade Mohanty (1991)

> *Every place the United States has been involved militarily*
> *has brought its offspring, its orphans, its homeless, and*
> *its casualties to this country: Vietnam, Guatemala, Cam-*
> *bodia, the Philippines. . . . Third world populations are*
> *changing the face of North America.*
> Cherríe Moraga (1993)

This book is about postcolonial wars and the space that they provide for women; it is about the authority of experience, and the permission to write. Above all, it describes transgressions and the new realities they create.

It is the focus on the role of women in late-twentieth-century wars that best displays the epistemological difference that postcoloniality makes. Women's articulation of their various participations in these wars as "combatants" and their urging of the national importance of women's agendas compel our new understandings of the experiences and stories of war. Beyond pluralization, these stories complicate the instinctive, conventional framing of the war event.

Women who choose to write about wars they have lived are defying an age-old silencing code. Their speaking out now and in knowledge of their transgressions allows us to read back into the gaps and silences of the War Story. Their stories threaten the privilege assumed proper to the right to tell the War Story. As the right to tell diffuses among all who may claim to have had a war experience, however unrecognizable as such by the standard conventions, the masculine contract between violence, sexuality, and glory comes undone.

When I was halfway through writing this book, the Gulf War broke out. I had been reflecting on the nature of wars in the nuclear age, wondering how important was the role of technology, and here I was watching a cyberwar, to use James Der Derian's formulation. It was a war that pitted machines against other machines, hypermodern machines against old ones. We enjoyed the spectacle and were spared the bodies. It was only later, after Americans had congratulated themselves on the low casualty count, that there was a little outcry about the massacre of Iraqis. The clean war turned out to have been dirty, and after the last clash of cymbals from the last homecoming parade subsided, so did triumph fever.

The Gulf War highlighted what has been the case since the 1960s. The traditional time, space, organization, and representation of war are changing. Like all postcolonial wars, this fantasy war parodied conventional warfare and aggressively shored up destabilized gender identities. It revealed the constructedness and hence negotiability of binaries such as friend and foe, combatant and noncombatant, victory and defeat, women's and men's space—demarcated, ironically, by the "line in the sand"—that allow us to manipulate the names of sites and events. Above all, the war confronted the world with a reality that had long been in existence but that the war myth had glossed over: mothers' presence in the theater of operations. The recognition of the fact that mothers can be soldiers broke down the archetype of soldiers as being by definition male. A major debate ensued about whether women who functioned successfully as soldiers had in fact engaged in combat. Could that last frontier of male soldiering remain impregnable? Try as they might, the crusty old generals and the macho young grunts could not explain away women's effectiveness in what most had to admit were combat roles. At a loss for rational arguments for continuing the prohibition on women's induction into armed combat, they ironically resorted to emotion: they felt . . . they liked . . . they didn't like. . . . Just as these military men were trying to reestablish clear gender lines in warfare, they were obliterating them in war discourse. An amusing example can be found in the March 1992 pages of *Soldier of Fortune,* where First Sergeant Charles W. Sasser vented his frustration. (Some readers may judge the magazine to be dubious material for serious analysis such as this, but it is effective and, perhaps, more representative than some military historians might like.) Sasser railed at the thought of women in uniform, let alone in combat. His frustration at the official injunctions to reform military language so that it might become gender-inclusive exceed articulation except in Old Speak: "I don't think there's anybody left in the military with a working pair left." Thrashing around for rational arguments to disguise his panic, he produced facts and figures on pregnancies that allowed him to fantasize about orgies in the barracks. His parting shot, aimed at the big brass, warned: "The feminization of the American military was destroying its ability to wage war" (Sasser 1992, 74, 41).

Women are going to war, are writing themselves into war. How will they be integrated into the War Story? Will any integration that may happen affect the ways in which masculinity has been linked with qualities necessary to enable the waging of war? We might say, it is not that men are aggressive, courageous, and heroic because they were born with a pair but rather that, if they wish to be clear about an identity that will distance them from the dreaded feminine, they must strive to be aggressive, courageous, and heroic. The arena that allows them to affirm these qualities without threat of the emergence of the feminine is one that traditionally excludes women's bodies except in their role as other: present as nurses or camp followers, women are the noncombatants, and men must be the combatants. The tight, organized body of the military, as Klaus Theweleit writes, allows men to be reborn out of the military's masculine womb; they need not be limited to their mothers' wombs. The mere presence of women's bodies in combat space complicates the connections that previously were so easy to make between bodies and the ways in which they are expected to behave. The biological and the social then slip into new connections between the space and the way that those who function in that space are supposed to behave. Can women in the theater of operations be called aggressive, courageous, and heroic without this naming having an impact on notions of masculinity?

Postcolonial war space holds increasing numbers of women, as targets of bombs and rapes, as guerrillas, as subjects of debates about the gendering of the military, of combat and of war stories. Along with the rest of the world's subalterns, women are beginning to speak out as survivors. Their embodied presence complicates the persistence of masculinity-reinforcing speech and behaviors. As women are compelled to experience war more or less equally with men, they have to make sense of the confusion, just as the men have always done. However, women have much less at stake in distorting

their messy experiences into the neat, tidied-up War Story mold.
Their stories contest the blind acceptance of a dyadically structured
world and make a mockery of such notions as Defender and Defended. If women describe and write themselves as having had a war
experience at home then they deny two critical binaries: home
versus front and civilian versus combatant. The breakdown of those
binaries then allows us to see the cracks in others such as victory
versus defeat, fact versus fiction, action versus writing, experience
versus recording, war versus peace. What more powerful proof do
we need than the obvious persistence into the mid-1990s of the wars
I discuss as though they were over? These binaries, these women
seem to say, were never real.

Women's new and different war stories show us that wars are
being waged now in what are called peace zones, that there were
pre-Intifada intifadas, and that violence in the American inner cities
and at abortion clinics are wars. In my Fall 1994 War and Gender
class, a student chose to focus on what she called the Abortion
Wars. The other students were at first skeptical. They were not
military conservatives who could recognize a war only when it fitted
the frame of its story, because they granted that there were certainly
wars being waged in many North American inner cities and that one
might agree with another student's choice of the neo-Nazi wars
raging in Germany and exported to the United States and Canada.
But Abortion Wars!? As the semester progressed, and Mae Rogers
presented weekly reports on the violent confrontations at abortion
clinics, on the bulletproof vests the doctors were beginning to wear,
on the police cordons around the clinics, their skepticism gave way
to a stunned realization that wars today are being fought over
motherhood. Like combatants in other postcolonial wars, these just
warriors are not fighting to protect women in a somewhere else but
are targeting them at home and physically.

In April 1995 a group of ex-military men dissatisfied with the
U.S. government launched an assault in a war they declared on a
system that is failing them. The 2,000-pound bomb they exploded
outside a federal building in Oklahoma City killed more than 160
people, including the children in a day-care center. Isolationist
crowing about there having been no war on U.S. territory in this

century is giving way to the realization that this view no longer fits reality, that in fact it may never have done so. The means to violence have become so widespread that anyone who cannot find "peaceful" means to achieve a goal will use lethal ones.

Some readers may protest at the way I stretch the term "war." In response, I have to ask: how would you name what we are witnessing in southcentral Los Angeles, in downtown Boston, in Detroit? What of the events happening outside abortion clinics? What of supremacist mobilizings? How are we to name these violent confrontations and the context in which they happen? Clearly, this is not "peace," but then again it is hard for most to recognize such apparently random, sporadic violence as "war." So we usually rely on others' namings. When the Oklahoma City militiamen called their action "war," they compelled the sort of attention that neither individual psychosis nor small group terrorism draws. The naming of the massacre of civilians as war allows connections to be made with other wars at the end of the second millennium c.e. The stories about these wars approximate less and less the glorious War Story with which many of us were raised.

I've given a great deal of thought to the naming of these wars, vacillating between postmodern or nuclear age or postcolonial. Each designation seems to work, yet at this late stage of writing I am inclined to favor "postcolonial wars." Why should naming matter? In fact, might it not be better to leaving the naming open? I have come to believe that naming matters. Wars have always been named and usually by those in power. Governments have called wars civil, revolutionary, genocidal, low intensity, high intensity, total. And this nomenclature has served their purposes. For example, if the government of the United States of America calls what is going on in Bosnia and in Rwanda "civil wars with roots sunk deep in centuries-long, ethnic hatreds," it does not have to interfere; it is not bound by the Geneva Convention that mandates interference in cases of genocide. Conversely, if it calls Iraq's 1990 invasion of Kuwait "aggression against democracy," it can intervene and, apropos, vouchsafe its oil supply.

To call wars postcolonial serves another kind of purpose. It forces an acknowledgment that there has been a fundamental change in the global situation, and that the end of this stage of European colonialism affects the previous colonizer and not only the colonized. More important, to call wars postcolonial is not just whimsical usage, as for example that the unsettling of binaries is a neat phenomenon to theorize. It involves the recognition of a continuum linking the classical oppositions that constituted war and its story, and this recognition has disabled a central process of warfare: the transformation of meanings attached to actions *because of the place in which they occur*. If it is no longer clear when and where we are at war and with whom, then it is no longer clear when it is safe to assume that normative codes of morality have changed. It is no longer clear when it is legitimate for men and women authorized by their uniforms to murder, rape, and pillage for the sake of the nation or some higher cause. Glory gives way to the awareness that for the duration men and women have official sanction to think and even do the unthinkable: kill massively and more or less randomly. The line separating the repellent psychopath from the charming bomber pilot melts, and now all that separates them is the social outcome of their actions: the first is executed, the second is honored. These troops are not acting out natural, biological, or even moral tendencies but patterns that, they are told, will make them better "men." Women who write their experiences in war expose such manipulative patterns because they have no stake in preserving a myth that must exclude them to survive.

In the Arab world, women's war participation creates a space in which a new speaking subject can insert herself. As Algerian, Lebanese, Palestinian, and Iraqi women attach their own meanings to their actions, they inscribe themselves into their wars; their multiple stories about their experiences in war rearrange the possibilities of voicing that in turn open up new configurations of identity. They begin to see a role for themselves—not masquerading as men, but speaking as individuals who have something special to offer precisely because they are women—aware now that silence itself is the worst crime. When these Arab women approve of the war's goal, they show ways to make the fighting more effective. When they oppose the war, they devise ways to reveal the gap between rhetoric and reality, the rhetoric of the leaders who would have their people believe that it is a great war and the reality that it is not.

These women belong to a worldwide movement of writers who are speaking out against silence. Their resistance takes place within a context of multiple oppressions. They create their works and themselves from the places where their multiple identities—biological, linguistic, cultural with its mix of pre-precolonial, precolonial, colonial, and neocolonial—intersect. They are constantly creating themselves anew, always struggling to free themselves from the kind of oppressive thinking that marks off the bad, barbarian others from the good, civilized self. This postcolonial writing is fraught with contradictions: it threatens the self with loss as it falters between competing identities while also offering the opportunity of imagining and creating new, in-between identities, discourses and agencies that can escape co-optation in a flattening global system that would subdue and homogenize differences as ludic.

These Arab women who write about the wars they have experienced are rarely pacifists; they are most often believers in their nations for whose sake and welfare they are taking responsibility as women. It is their taking responsibility that offers them the possibility to rethink the meaning of the nation as that entity that needs everyone, including its women, to talk, to dialogue, to debate, and to function as active citizens for it to be able to survive. They are creating possibilities for a civil society where individuals feel responsible to the collectivity and where democratic institutions are linked to economic development and nonlethal management of conflict. Their stories describe alternative ways of resisting injustice and oppression that will simultaneously call for social transformation. Above all, they point toward the possibility of constructing a discourse that unsettles identities without disabling the author.

In April 1995 I presented the thesis of this book to the conference, Discours sur la femme, held at the Muhammad V University in Rabat, Morocco. After I finished, a woman in the audience stood up and asked me what I had been asked before but in a more forceful way. Surely, I did not believe that Arab women had gained anything from their often forced participation in their countries' wars? Just look at Algeria! How could I equate fighting with writing, the weaponness of the body and the pen? Was I not essentializing women's writings in my attempt to undo the neat categories of the men's War Story, and did that essentializing not run the risk of reinscribing the stories and structures I was questioning? These were valid questions, ones that my brief talk invited. It is my hope that this longer version, even if it does not give definitive answers, will stimulate the reader to ponder such issues anew after closing the book.

Notes

All translations of foreign languages are my own, unless specified otherwise.

1. Subvert the Dominant Paradigm

1. David Harvey on the geographical imagination quoted in Gillian Rose, *Feminism and Geography: The Limits of Geographical Knowledge* (Minneapolis: University of Minnesota Press, 1993), 18.

2. For an excellent discussion of the military's attitude and policies concerning men and women's comparative strength see Judith Stiehm, *Arms and the Enlisted Woman* (Philadelphia: Temple University Press, 1989), 198–205.

3. Thanks to Jody McAuliffe for this insight on the book's presentation.

4. Sontag writes, "Photographic seeing has to be constantly renewed with new shocks, whether of subject matter or technique, so as to produce the impression of violating ordinary vision" (Susan Sontag, *On Photography* [New York: Farrar, Straus and Giroux, 1977], 89). The "lust of the eye," states Gray, "requires the novel, the unusual, the spectacular. It cannot satiate itself on the familiar, the routine, the everyday." His description of the burning bombed villages on the French Riviera as "magnificent" must strike us as obscene, despite the explanation that the aesthetic appeal of war is not beauty but awe in the face of power that produces a "feeling of the sublime." Part of the satisfaction is survival, as "spectators we are superior to that which we survey . . . the self is no longer important to the observer; it is absorbed into the objects with which

it is concerned" (J. Glenn Gray, *The Warriors: Reflections on Men in Battle* [New York: Harper, 1970], 29, 33, 34, 36).

5. As the less euphoric half-page preface to the second edition acknowledged in 1980, other wars followed the two-year war. The preface continued to urge the importance of living the war through its images, concluding: "Whoever suffers, learns."

6. Michael Mezzatesta, director of the Duke University Museum of Art, brought to my attention the startling resemblance between this image and the classical Greek statue of the sleeping hermaphrodite. R. R. R. Smith describes this hermaphrodite as lying in "a long spiral posture. The back view is the more effective and clearly the principal one. . . . The proportions and forms from behind are clearly female; only exploration round the figure revealed its bisexuality. . . . The figure is certainly asleep, and the raised lower leg must be rightly interpreted as 'troubled sleep'" (R. R. R. Smith, *Hellenistic Sculpture: A Handbook* [London: Thames and Hudson, 1991], 133–34).

7. Sontag writes: "Instead of just recording reality, photographs have become the norm for the way things appear to us, thereby changing the very idea of reality, and of realism. . . . Cameras miniaturize experience, transform history into spectacle. As much as they create sympathy, photographs cut sympathy, distance the emotions. Photography's realism creates a confusion about the real" (Sontag 1977, 18, 79, 99).

8. The photography historian John Tagg writes, "The Real is a complex of dominant and dominated discourses which given texts exclude, separate, or do not signify. If the text or picture is going to represent a reality which is different from, and perhaps determinant of, the picture itself, then this representation will be possible through an act of negation, through a demonstration of the incoherence of the system of dominant images. . . . We must not allow ourselves the expedient of imagining something existing 'before' representation by which we may explain the representation away. . . . We must begin to analyze the real representational practices that go on in a society. . . . We must describe the function of 'specific' individuals within them. . . . Only in this way will we come to understand how ideologies are produced in real representational practices" (John Tagg, *The Burden of Representation* [Amherst: University of Massachussetts Press, 1988], 101–2, 211).

9. "Peace will never occur as a consequence of weakness, exhaustion, or fear," writes Gray as he comments on Nietzsche's assessments of military power (Gray 1970, 226).

10. Many women were first brought into the American military during World War II and challenged, D'Ann Campbell writes, "prevailing norms on practical and symbolic levels" (D'Ann Campbell, "The Regimented Women of WWII," in *Women, Militarism, and War: Essays in*

History, Politics, and Social Theory, ed. Jean Bethke Elshtain and Sheila Tobias [Savage, Md.: Rowman and Littlefield, 1990], 108). Some claim that resistance to the Equal Rights Amendment in the late 1970s raised awareness of women's systematic exclusion from those parts of the military that allowed promotion and therefore access to decision-making positions where they might make a difference to the declaration and waging of war.

11. *American Bar Association Journal* (December 1991): 52–59. Christine Chinkin, an international lawyer, writes about the difficulty of defining war crimes: the Geneva Convention was designed around World War II crimes, and the extrapolation to other kinds of wars is difficult (conversation between the author and Christine Chinkin, 15 April 1994). Another international lawyer, Winston Nagan, ascribes the confusion to the fact that the "labels 'war' and 'peace' hold different meanings for different participants in these processes. For the lawyers, war effectively means a breach of article 2(4) of the U.N. Charter involving state-to-state armed conflict. Civil 'wars' in failed states have a more ambiguous characterization" (Winston Nagan, "Human Rights as a Negotiating Tool in Peacemaking," manuscript, 10).

12. "Eritrea: The Kitchen Calls," *Economist,* 25 June 1994.

13. See Diana Fuss, *Essentially Speaking: Feminism, Nature, and Difference* (Routledge, 1989), for an illuminating discussion of the tension between constructivist and essentialist language and the political expediency of essentialism upon occasion. Biologists are divided about the role of gender in aggressivity as also about whether aggressive behavior is innate or learned.

14. Bettina Musall, "Women at the Front," *World Press Review,* March 1994, 49.

15. Amy Swerdlow describes the 1960s Women Strike for Peace (WSP) as "a disorganized band of middle-class housewives pleading for the children in the domestic terms they had been taught since childhood. . . . In their concern for the fate of their children, the WSPers were no different from millions of other American women. However, they did differ in their broader perception of motherhood as a social and communal function. . . . The WSPers were not concerned with transforming sex role ideology but rather with using it to enhance women's political power" (Amy Swerdlow, "Motherhood and the Subversion of the Military State: Women's Strike for Peace Confronts the House Committee on Un-American Activities," in Elshtain and Tobias 1990, 23, 24).

16. Kanaan Makiya, *Cruelty and Silence: War, Tyranny, Uprising, and the Arab World* (London: Jonathan Cape, 1993), 287, where he reproduces an Iraqi soldier's ID card on which his occupation was marked "violation of women's honor." This book has enjoyed a mixed reception.

17. Dorothy Q. Thomas and Regan E. Ralph, "Rape in War: Challenging the Tradition of Impunity," *SAIS Review* (winter–spring 1994): 81–99.

18. Elshtain suggests that the dichotomized constructions of war and peace are reinforced by Kant's absolute segregation of public and private. It is in the former that Perpetual Peace can reign for "genuine peace must nullify *all* existing causes of war" (Jean Bethke Elshtain, "The Problem with Peace," in Elshtain and Tobias 1990, 264).

19. Alexandre Bloch, "Culture of Peace," paper delivered at Opatja Conference on Peace, Human Rights, and the Responsibility of the Intellectual, Croatia, 1 October 1994.

2. Culture Degree Zero

1. On 27 June 1969 the police raided Stonewall Inn, a homosexual bar in Greenwich Village. For the first time, the patrons resisted what had become a pattern of harassment. Their resistance drew support from the New York homosexual community, which erupted into a three-day rebellion.

2. Jacques Derrida, "Beyond Marx," lecture given at Duke University, 4 October 1993.

3. Walter Benjamin writes that the "destructiveness of war furnishes proof that society has not been mature enough to incorporate technology as its organ, that technology has not been sufficiently developed to cope with the elemental forces of society . . . Mankind's . . . self-alienation has reached such a degree that it can experience its own destruction as an aesthetic pleasure of the first order" (Benjamin, Illuminations: Essays and Reflections [New York: Schocken, 1969 (1936)], 242).

4. "Hollywood directors went to work for the government and injected a sense of drama into documentary formats" (Springer 1985, 151).

5. When I asked the NBC anchor Tom Brokaw during the Journalists at War conference held at Duke University in November 1994 what triggered media interest in war, he answered instantaneously: "Testosterone."

6. For an analysis of the role of the media in the war in Bosnia, see Mark Thompson, *Forging War: The Media in Serbia, Croatia, and Bosnia-Herzegovina* (International Centre against Censorship, 1994).

7. Robert Block, "Killers," *New York Review of Books,* 18 November 1993, 10. The American journalist Martha Gellhorn, who covered the Spanish civil war and World War II, wrote that cowboy films were "more thrilling to the audience than a mere convoy of bombers flying at a great

safe height and sending down indiscriminate, expensive steel-cased death and destruction" (Gellhorn 1988, 46).

8. The "Top Gun" incident was reported to me by Kathy Wilkes, honorary Octopus in the Croatian navy, during the conference Peace, Human Rights, and the Responsibility of the Intellectual, 29 September–3 October 1994, Opatja, Croatia.

9. Interview with General Westmoreland in Jonathan Mirsky, "The War That Will Not End," *New York Review of Books*, 16 August 1990, 29. Detail on CBS motif from the author's conversation with Lynda Boose, who served in Vietnam for two harrowing years.

10. Edward J. Epstein, *News from Nowhere,* quoted in Rick Berg, "Losing Vietnam: Covering the War in an Age of Technology," *Cultural Critique* (1985): 97. Frances Lindley Fralin writes: "Since before the American Civil War, scenes have been rearranged or created for the camera . . . Depending on how the picture is used, any war image can serve as successful propaganda—overtly or covertly" (Fralin 1985, 9).

11. There has been speculation about the connections between the Intifada and the war in Northern Ireland. Did the Palestinians copy the Irish when they first used stones and burning tires? And now in the 1990s the Northern Irish are calling their troubles the "Irish Intifada." Like the Palestinians, the Irish considered international media coverage in the wake of the 1969 Bogside Marches to be their first political victory (conversation between the author and the Irish cultural critic David Lloyd, Santa Cruz, 27 April 1995).

12. The Cable News Network called the Gulf War the "first 'real-time' television war which created instant history" (Gerbner 1992, 71).

13. See Adrian Nicole LeBlanc's account of the life of a gang girl called Tamika, where the practice of tagging is described. The language used to describe the gangs is distinctively military, e.g., "the boys treated United We Stand girls as an auxiliary unit." And she writes that the members "depersonalize the victims of their crimes in the same way the military and policemen depersonalize their targets" (LeBlanc 1994).

14. "The death event constitutes a new grid through which all experiencing now takes place . . . the death event, not as a string of facts that together form the basis for historical generalization, but as a structural alteration in the character of all experiencing which has crept up on us without our realizing it" (Wyschogrod 1985, 63–64).

15. Civilians have long been targeted despite rhetoric about concern for their protection. It was only with the Hague international commission in 1920 that their protection became international policy (see Walzer 1974, 94).

16. Conversation with Albert Eldridge, political scientist and my colleague at Duke University, 20 June 1990.

17. Angela Woollacott argues that World War I British women munitions workers thought of themselves as combatants and were proud of their yellow-stained hands that demonstrated to the world their involvement with dynamite (Woollacott 1994).

18. Ann Snitow discusses the tensions that split the Madres: some claimed that their sons were innocent, others embraced their sons' political activism as their own: "They thought their bereavement was not only a moral witnessing of crime and a demand for justice but also a specific intervention with immediate and threatening political implications to the state . . . Surely a mother's grief and rage removed from the home, suddenly exposed to publicity, are powerful, shocking" (Snitow 1989, 49).

19. In October 1987 the Arab League in Paris convened a conference of women of all confessions from Beirut entitled "La Femme libanaise témoin de la guerre," namely, the woman as eyewitness participant. On 20 April 1990 Muna Hrawi, the wife of the president, was reported by *Arab News* as having called on "Lebanese women to help stop civil war."

20. "Child Warriors: The Suicide Machine," *Time,* 18 June 1990, which contrasts with the 1982 *Time* article that highlighted the role of children as victims. See also "Iraq's War on Its Children," *Amnesty Action,* March–April 1989; and *New York Times,* 5 March 1989; *Human Rights Watch* (Human Rights in Iraq), 1990. On 15 December 1995 the *New York Times* editorial was entitled "War's Children." It noted that within "the last decade, child victims of war include 2 million killed, 4 to 5 million disabled, 12 million left homeless, 10 million psychologically traumatized, and more than a million orphaned or separated from their parents. Children are often conscripted at a young age, and are forced to commit atrocities or witness brutalities visited upon their families and communities."

21. Other guerrilla groups such as the Vietminh and Vietcong considered girls to be as enlistable as boys (see Hayslip 1989).

22. To indicate my translation for many of the works—Khalifa's '*Abbad al-shams* among them—at first mention in a chapter's discussion I give its title in the original language. And if my source is a later edition, I add the original publication date in square brackets for readers' convenience.

23. Elsewhere he writes: "Terror aims not only to control but also to change social actors . . . Terror may appear as a distinctive phase in a process of revolutionary transformation of society" (Corradi 1982–83, 63).

24. "Some believe that the war college (Carlisle) is preparing its students to fight the wrong war" ("Conventional Warfare," *Atlantic,* January 1990).

25. *Palestine,* vol. 11 (Beirut: PLO Press, 1982), 5.

3. Silence Is the Real Crime

1. Marnia Lazreg indicates that discourse about Algerian woman succumbs to a "prevailing paradigm [whose] ultimate effect is to preclude any understanding of Algerian women *in their lived reality*: as subjects in their own right. Instead, they are reified, made into mere bearers of unexplained categories" (Lazreg 1988, 94).

2. During the nineteenth century Algerians who resisted the French, as Ibn Badis did, "selected biographies of women who fought alongside men during the heroic period of Islamic history, and presented them to women as role models to emulate. Thus, in the 1950s, women were rekindling a tradition that had been established before them" (Lazreg 1994, 137).

3. The French tried to exploit these women's leadership roles. Ben Bouali and Buhrayd had unveiled and others were following their lead. The French assumed that this unveiling represented a victory for their culture, and on 16 May 1958 they assembled some village women and brought them into Algiers where they arranged for the women to be publicly unveiled. As a result, many women who had long since unveiled chose to reveil as a symbol of nationalist solidarity. As Lazreg notes, this demonstration orchestrated by the French had a long-term negative impact on women's self-awareness, as women were pushed further into subsuming their needs and desires to those of the nation (Lazreg 1994, 135).

4. Another heroine, the sixteen-year-old Hassiba, marches off to war with Youssef (see Dejeux 1973, 250). In a factual account, an ex-prisoner described her time in detention as follows: "The Oran prison was very tough. We had organized classes. Each did what she could. A seamstress revealed her secrets. . . . We taught all the Europeans Arabic, and to those Muslim women who were not too old we taught reading and writing. We also had philosophy classes. There were lectures on all sorts of topics, particularly politics. . . . There was complete solidarity among the women. There was no distinction between us, no difference of opinion about the future as though we had belonged to the same milieu for a long time" ("Femmes algériennes dans la guerre," *El-Moudjahid,* 72/3, 1 November 1960).

5. Interview by the author with Assia Djebar, Paris, October 1987. Cadi-Mostefai claims that Djebar's *El-Moudjahid* articles on the war (perhaps because they are propagandist) have no instances of such women traitors. These are "women who have found themselves. They have a job to do, a mission. For them the situation is clear. There are no problems" (Cadi-Mostefai 1978, 175, 185).

6. One of the first reviews interprets the novel quite differently, commending it for highlighting the "tragic complexity of a war between two peoples who have lived closely together over so long a period. Symbolically, during a night together, a young rebel and his cousin read and recite the poetry of Hugo and Rimbaud. It is implied that out of the disruption of society brought about by the revolution, and out of the new responsibilities undertaken by women as well as men, a world of greater intimacy for both is emerging" (*Jeune Afrique*, 3–9 December 1962, 26–27).

7. Lazreg recounts—without making the connection—what appears to be a source for this story. She quotes Hubertine Auclert's 1900 *Les femmes arabes en Algérie* where an unnamed French administrator "caught sight of a beautiful woman, Nedjma [even the spelling is the same], wife of a Mr. Lakhdar [who is Nedjma's half brother and lover in Yacine's version], and fell in love with her. On the advice of his friend Chaya, a money lender, the administrator framed Lakhdar . . . and exiled him to Noumea, Niger. Nedjma was thus appropriated along with Lakhdar's thoroughbred mare, Rihana" (Lazreg 1994, 49). In quotations from *Nedjma* I translate from the 1956 French edition.

8. He first published *Le cadavre encerclé* in *Esprit* in 1954 and 1955; four years later it appeared with two other plays in a volume entitled *Le cercle de représailles*. The French director Jean-Marie Serreau (1915–73) put on the play in Carthage, Brussels, and Paris, even as the war in Algeria was raging. In the third play, *Les ancêtres redoublent de férocité,* Nedjma is widowed and crazy like her mother, but also like the heroines of the war about whom others, like Assia Djebar, would later write (see discussion below). As early as the mid-1940s Yacine had written a poem entitled "Nedjma ou le poème ou le couteau." In his introduction to the English translation of *Nedjma*, Bernard Aresu describes the poem as evoking "separation and death but [also] ancestral memory" (Yacine 1991, xxxiii).

9. He wrote a play entitled "La Kahina" that was performed in 1985. He titled his preface to Yasmina Mechakra's *Grotte éclatée* "Les enfants de la Kahina." These descendants of the early woman warrior included women like Mechakra, who had "le don de la parole" (Mechakra 1986 [1979], 8).

10. Yacine entitled the first part of *Le polygone étoilé* "La femme sauvage." This section was published in Tunis in 1961 a year after Yacine had read it out over Zagreb radio (see Aresu's introduction to the 1991 English ed. of *Nedjma*, xxiii).

11. This is not to say that Yacine was himself afraid of or ill disposed toward Algerian women fighters. His enthusiastic preface to Mechakra's *La grotte éclatée* echoes Emile Habibi's praise of women's participation in the Palestinian resistance (see chapter four): "Now that the Aurès insurrection has given birth to a new Algeria, this book must be read and reread so that there be others, so that others raise their voices. Right now, in our country, a woman who writes is worth her weight in gunpowder." (Mechakra 1986 [1979], 8).

12. In 1993 Ahlem Mosteghanemi published *Dhakirat al-jasad* (Body memory), a novel that contains several intertextual references to Malek Haddad's war novels (see Mosteghanemi 1993, 30, 310, 375) as well as to Kateb Yacine's *Nedjma* (see 324–28). It is as though the author were establishing a direct link with the men's war stories. The language of the text is very important, and the heroine, who is herself a novelist, says: "Arabic is the language of my heart, it is the only language in which I can write. We write in the language in which we feel" (91). *Body Memory* is about an Algerian artist and his anguished relationship with an Algeria "that is exploding and we are no longer able to avoid uniting with the embers flying out of its mouth and to forget our own little fire" (23). The reality of this Algeria, with its religious extremism (306), destroys the dreams of those who live in exile (283). Algeria since the 1980s has suffered from the violence perpetrated by militant Islamists who killed Khalid's brother when he dared finally to dream (395). What difference, Khalid asks, is there between the French, the Israelis, and the Algerians? (396). Khalid is a veteran of the war of liberation who lives in Paris. He was imprisoned on 8 May 1945, the day that 50,000 other students were taken prisoner, among them Kateb Yacine. Later Khalid was wounded in the fighting, lost an arm, and began to paint as a form of therapy. The daughter of his martyred commander attends the opening of one of his shows and he becomes infatuated with her as a woman and particularly as a symbol for what Algeria has become since the war. The novel ends with her marriage to a corrupt Algerian official who stands in stark contrast with her former lover, a Palestinian poet. Khalid is invited to the wedding; he surmises that they need him to counteract the "plague of corruption" that has infected them all in the police state that Algeria has become (188, 272), where the government uses funds designated for religious purposes, for instance the pilgrimage to Mecca, to sponsor unethical business deals (305).

13. Interview with Djebar, Paris, October 1987.

14. For example, the Arabic teacher "denounced by his djellaba that seemed to retain in its folds his dusty theology" (Djebar 1967, 386).

15. The third volume, *Vaste est la prison,* came out in 1995 just as this manuscript was going to press. Djebar said of this volume that it was about relationships with mothers, whereas *Fantasia* was about relationships with fathers (telephone conversation with the author, 17 April 1995).

16. Anne Donadey describes Djebar's method as "mimicry" as the French feminist Luce Irigaray uses it: "Irigaray posits that it is first through their deliberate repetition of a male discourse of female representation that women will be able to reappropriate language. This repetition will be subversive because of its difference: spoken from a different position, it might extend into the realm of parody. . . . For Irigaray, mimicry is a conscious strategy of resistance to hegemonic discourse, one which must be taken up 'délibérément,' and which points to a feminine elsewhere. . . . Djebar reappropriates the French archives on Algeria by using them as the palimpsest upon which she deciphers the trace of her people, especially the women" (Donadey 1993, 110–12).

4. Talking Democracy

1. John Brenkman recently wrote: "Citizens can *freely* enter the field of political persuasion and decision only insofar as they draw on the contingent vocabularies of their own identities. Democracy needs participants who are conversant with the images, symbols, stories, and vocabularies that have evolved across the whole of the history. . . . By the same token, democracy also requires citizens who are fluent enough in one another's vocabularies and histories to share the forums of political deliberation and decision on an equal footing" (Brenkman 1993, 89).

2. Interview by the author with Sahar Khalifa in Nablus, 29 May 1991. Rosemary Sayigh indicates that the "special difficulty of the Palestinian struggle, its imbalance of forces, means that women's part in institution building, artistic and literary production, professional work, or *sumood* (steadfastness) takes on a national importance. To limit our focus to 'organized' women is to miss another kind of struggle. . . . The slogan of 'organic unity' between the women's and the national movement was fundamental in legitimating women's political activism in the '60s and '70s" but then she adds, "it also repressed consciousness of their situation and history as women" (Sayigh 1987, 10).

3. Even Jean Genet, not noted for his interest in women, praised Palestinian women's political effectiveness in his posthumously published *Prisoner of Love* (Genet 1992, 3–4).

4. Sayigh discusses the lack of systematic documentation of women's activities and particularly of lack of attention to any such records as might exist (Sayigh 1987, 10).

5. Terry Atwan puts the number of women jailed during the Intifada at 1,500 ("Life Is Struggle Inside and Outside the Green Line," in *Palestinian Women: Identity and Experience,* ed. Ebba Augustin [London: Zed Press, 1993], 57). Ahmad Dahbur wrote a poem entitled "You" in 1977 where he also refers to the Intifada: "For our people in the occupied territories . . . and for their great intifada / I remember the stone which my mother threw during the latest demonstration."

6. Among the names of women mentioned to me during a visit to the West Bank in the summer of 1991 are Hanan Awwad (poetry), Halima Jauhar (short stories), Basima Hallawa (short story), Nahida Nazzal (memoirs from prison), Samia al-Khalili (poetry), Khaula 'Uwayda al-Labadi (short story), Dima Samman (novel), Samira al-Sharabati (poetry; Hadi Daniel criticized for her not being political enough and for copying Nizar Qabbani). In Israel, Siham Dawud and Muna Abu 'Id (poetry).

7. Discussing a conference on the Intifada and women's issues in Jerusalem in December 1990, Basem Tawfeeq anticipates Rita Giacaman's fears. He writes that though the Intifada's first six months "witnessed a breaking of class, gender, religion and age barriers . . . the second phase returned women to their previous traditional roles. . . . Females became 'marginalized, then the Intifada set the stage' for a regression in women's rights . . . the nationalist leadership (a woman in the audience volunteered) use us as a media front" (Tawfeeq 1990, 8).

8. "Interview of the Month" between Farah and the poet Mahmud Darwish in *Al-Jadid,* April–May 1962.

9. Women writers like Samira 'Azzam, who left in 1948, wrote politically throughout. In "On the Road to Solomon's Pools," 'Azzam writes of the emasculation of Palestinian society. During an attack, he takes his family away from the village. He alone holds the baby until it is killed in his arms. He deliberately loses his wife in the crowd of refugees so as to be able to bury the son himself and alone, giving the mother no part in the family tragedy even when her child dies (story included in Cooke and Rustomji-Kerns 1994, 18–22).

10. Other Palestinian women writers' works also were introduced by men: e.g., Samih al-Qasim introduced Fadwa Tuqan's *A Mountainous Journey;* Samih Semah introduced Siham Dawud's anthology *And So, I Sing* (1979). A committee of three men—Muhammad Sulaiman, Mundhir Amir, and Samih Sammara—chose Dawud's poems from 1973 volumes of *Al-Ghad* and *Al-Ittihad* and she learned of the anthology *after* it was published.

11. See negative examples in "The Jailhouse" and "The Eldest Son" (Farah 1954, 71–81; 110–21). In "The Café Wise Man," another story from the collection, the waiter Hasan is fired after a rich client he accuses of not paying his bill accuses him of theft. The café wise man gives Hasan the half guinea the rich man claims to have paid with instructions to tell the owner that he had just found it under the table. The owner warns Hasan that "in future he should keep his eyes open to see the coins that were paid him." Hasan bites his tongue: "Can people only believe us if we are rich and wear elegant suits?" When Hasan tries to repay the wise man, the latter refuses despite his own need. Even when the rich man is exposed for gambling with his workers' wages, Hasan can do nothing. The story concludes wistfully: whenever an elegant suit enters the café, Hasan avoids serving its owner (50–58).

12. In "Regret," yet another story from the 1954 collection, Farah mocks the affectation of the use of French names and the interjection of foreign words like *manicure* and *tennis* into Arabic speech (40, 41). This kind of criticism was not new. Men like Iskandir Khuri al-Baytjalli had been saying the same things since the 1920s (see Peled 1988, 184).

13. We can read of the very same debauchery in the pre-1948 "Be Kind to the Children" (Farah 1954, 50–51).

14. For example, Hana Ibrahim's "The Tenth Anniversary Celebration" (1958) and "Infiltrators" (late 1950s); and Ghassan Kanafani's "Return to Haifa (1969).

15. Somekh divides the Palestinian depiction of Jews into three types: "The first (and the least frequent) kind is a description of Jews, in isolation, with no connection to the fate of the Arab population. . . . The second theme . . . is that in which contemporary Jewish society appears as opposed to Arab society, in confrontation or by comparison. Arab society is described as still backward, lagging behind the modern world, whereas Jewish society is shown as dynamic. . . . The third kind, and the most important: stories describing the bitter fate of the Arab population in Israel, while at the same time reflecting the partial or complete identification of Jewish individuals, simple people or intellectuals, with the sufferings of the Arabs. It should be noted that such stories . . . were generally written by Communist authors" (Somekh 1989, 116–17).

A striking example of a Palestinian writing about an Israeli is the poet Mahmud Darwish, who composed verses to Rita, his childhood friend and later lover whom the 1967 war tore from him for military service. 'Abdallah al-Shahham wonders why Darwish should write such poetry and surmises that Darwish may have wanted to prove that "he was more of a humanitarian than all of them because he enjoyed broader horizons, he was prepared for a dialogue with his enemy." He quotes the poet as having said: "I do not hate the Jews [but rather Zionism, which] is based on violence and militarism. . . . The more Rita is in love, the more she relinquishes Zionism" (al-Shahham 1988, 28–35).

16. Ibn Khaldun writes that some readers interpreted this story to advocate passivity and a dangerous acceptance of injustice and pain (editorial in *Al-Jadid,* April 1957, 22).

17. For *sumud,* says Jean Makdisi, "there is no single English sound-and-sense equivalent that I know of; rather it would have to be rendered by tapping the *thesaurus'* rich repository—tenacity, steadfastness, resolution, endurance, indomitability—all these words together, with their overlapping shades of meaning, give a sense of that noble word, *assoumoud*" (Makdisi 1990, 175).

18. The 1955 January issue of *Al-Jadid* published an editorial that demanded rights for women "so that they may fight side by side with men to destroy the chains of oppression" (6).

In a report presented at the symposium on the status of Israeli Arab women in Haifa on 7 March 1982, Miriam Mari distinguishes three stages in women's growing feminist consciousness (though she does not so identify it): (1) 1948–56, "when compulsory education laws brought many Arab girls into the schools"; (2) 1956–67, "when more Arab women began to work outside the villages, and, in some cases, came under the progressive influence of Mapam and the kibbutzim"; (3) post-1967 economic and academic opportunities (quoted in Tessler 1982, 6).

19. Hana Ibrahim's story "Rebel" (*Al-Jadid,* February 1956) tells the story of a blind girl who uses her miraculously regained sight to escape from everyone she knew, who persecuted her because of her sex and handicap.

20. While I was in the West Bank during the summer of 1991, I was given copies of stories by women that the Israeli censors had banned. They include Hanin 'Adnan Hindiya's "Al-janna al-da'i'a" and Khaula 'Uwayda al-Labadi's "Al-nabadat al-khalida."

21. In 1991 Najwa Qa'war Farah, who is now based in Amman, published a collection of short stories entitled *Intifadat al-'asafir* that openly indicts the Israeli occupation. Most of her protagonists are men who are trying to get back to the homeland to see family or to fight in the resistance. Farah is uncompromising about the evil of collaborators, as in "Memoir of an Ex-convict."

22. Khalifa tells of the difficulties she encountered trying to publish *Al-subar* (translated into English as *Wild Thorns*). First she tried two publishers in Beirut, one Lebanese and the other Palestinian. Both ultimately felt it was too dangerous to publish. Then she took the manuscript to Cairo but found the publisher who was interested in it too insistent on

changing the language, particularly the Palestinian colloquialisms. Upon her return to the West Bank, she was offered a contract by a joint Israeli-French publishing house. In 1976 the book came out simultaneously in Arabic, Hebrew, and French (Khalifa 1989).

23. Abu Hiyad in Muhammad Ayyub's *Al-kaff tunatihu al-makhraz* (Amman, 1987) says, "Where does the *sumud* money go? Who is the beneficiary? Do the poor get anything? The rich are steadfastly holding on to their wealth. They are the ones whose pockets are big enough to contain the *sumud* money."

24. Khalifa wrote *Sunflower* after having conducted one- to five-hour-long interviews with over fifty educated men (Khalifa 1989).

25. Khalifa repeats this plea almost verbatim in her next novel, *Memoirs*, 96.

26. For single women, according to Suha Sabbagh, "Since 1967, female employment has increased from 8.4% to 24.8% in 1980 . . . women who suddenly found themselves single heads of households were chastised by other women for departing from traditional modes of behavior by virtue of their new-found responsibility" (Sabbagh 1989, 75). A couple of Palestinian women whom Shaaban interviewed on women's independence said, "Arab societies under Israeli occupation preserve both the bad and the good for fear of losing their identity . . . sexually liberated women could in an instant turn into prostitutes in men's eyes; their sexuality remains a potential source of shame and social disgrace and it is still the most accessible means men have of subjugating them" (Shaaban 1988, 140, 162).

27. "Collaborators with the occupation were encircled and gradually rendered ineffective, as the entire mass of people under occupation came together in a block that opposed occupation" (Said 1989, 37).

28. Khalifa wrote *Memoirs* within six months, immediately upon completing *Sunflower* in 1979 but published the novel only six years later, on the eve of the Intifada (interview, Nablus, 29 May 1991).

29. Snitow writes: "The urgent contradiction women constantly experience between the pressure to be a woman and the pressure not to be one will change only through a historical process; it cannot be dissolved through thought alone. . . . The category woman is a fiction; then, post-structuralism suggests ways in which human beings live by fictions; then, in its turn, activism requires of feminists that we elaborate the fiction woman as if she were not a provisional invention at all but a person we know well, one in need of obvious rights and powers. Activism and theory weave together here, working on what remains the same basic cloth, the stuff of feminism" (Snitow 1989, 46–47).

30. When 'Afaf is accused of being from the oppressors' class, she retorts: "The oppressors' class has oppressed me" (Khalifa 1986, 51).

31. For a discussion of the constructive role of abortion in war, see the editors' introductory essay in Helen Cooper, Adrienne Munich, and Susan Squier 1989, 9–24.

32. "My silence under such circumstances would drive him crazy and make him wish to destroy" (Khalifa 1986, 78–79). After Fadwa Tuqan tells her mother about her imagined adventures, she is warned that she may be going crazy. Thereafter, Fadwa keeps her world to herself and continues to escape there for the rest of her life (Tuqan 1990 [1984], 58–59, 116). In Hanan al-Shaykh's *The Story of Zahra*, the protagonist's behavior and others' reactions to her are identical. Zahra also seeks refuge in the bathroom when others press in too closely.

33. In his review of the book in the Lebanese newspaper *Al-Safir*, 26 February 1991, Nadim Tawfiq Jarjura claimed that *Bab al-Saha* is a search for the answer to the question, who is allowed to kill? He sees the novel as Khalifa's attempt to "pierce the barrier between literature and reality. . . . As though literature has become necessary self-criticism." It was also a challenge to the author to see if "fiction could render the truth of what was happening in Palestinian society?" He quotes Khalifa as having said that the Intifada, unlike most experiences that need time for their articulation, had to be recorded at once. She had decided to focus on one aspect: the collaborators and their executions.

34. When 'Afaf's father discovers her in a cave with some young men preparing explosives, he is torn between shock at the flounting of social imperatives and pride in his daughter's nationalism: "But the family's honor! So he went from area to area and from café to café, saying, 'My daughter is honorable. My daughter is clean. My daughter is doing what men do.' The story got around until the governor heard about it and they arrested the revolutionaries and they beat one of them who could not stand it and he confessed from the first blow, another from the second blow" (Khalifa 1986, 137; cf. 6, 56).

35. Khalifa told me that Husam represents the Palestinian leadership and that she had "wounded him, crippled him so that all the lessons would pass in front of him consciously and unconsciously. Although he had at first advised Nuzha to go to the United States, by the time he has been with her for an extended period he advises her to stay. His previous rejection has turned into acceptance as he synthesized all these lessons and became wiser" (interview, Nablus, 29 May 1991).

36. Khalifa called Ahmad "a victim of the nationalist movement that cannot reeducate its cadre" (interview, Nablus, 29 May 1991).

37. Parallels from Djebar's revisionist Algerian text: "Abdelkader [narrator's and martyr's elder brother] and the partisans began to upbraid me: 'Your brother Ahmed died a martyr! We shall be happy to enjoy a similar end" (Djebar 1993, 130).

Abu Samra writes self-evidently of these ululations that women emit at a martyr's funeral. One woman refused to cry at her son's funeral, saying "Instead of weeping today everyone should ululate because today is Taysir's wedding" (Abu Samra 1989, 29). This transformation of a martyr's funeral into a wedding is repeated by other mothers. One said that she felt that "This wedding-funeral is better than the wedding of his marriage" (30). One martyr before dying had said to his mother: "We must sacrifice ourselves because Palestine is a bride with a very expensive dowry. How can we get her without paying the price?" (33).

38. In *Al-mutarada* (the pursued), Raja' Abu Ghazzala creates women who are frustrated by the men in their lives. Particularly striking is the short story "The Mad Woman's Tree." Two women meet after fifteen years' separation and review what they have accomplished during the intervening years. One of them remembers that she had wanted to "become a psychiatrist so as to be able to treat the boys of the alley for their superiority complex, their machismo and their aggression against the girls." Her companion reproaches her for not executing her plan, because all the men she knew needed help; they were "sick with love of power and tyranny. . . . We don't need one woman psychiatrist, we need an army" (Abu Ghazzala 1988, 33, 41). She denounces Anisa for allowing herself to become a pawn between her father and her husband. Anisa knows that this is true, but all she can do is paint violent paintings that no one understands. What is the use of art if it is directed at a society that is not ready to understand its message?

39. In her August 1991 letter, Khalifa writes, "the act of burning the flag of occupation is not an act of killing or violence, is it? It is a symbol of opposing oppression, an act of resistance, no? At least, this is how I think about it as a Palestinian citizen, even though I am a woman and a feminist."

40. According to Giacaman, "Women's traditional roles as homemakers are now imbued with new significance, as Palestinian society moves towards self-reliance through small-scale food production in order to cut dependency on imports" (Giacaman 1988b, 1).

41. "It is only *in* writing and *by* writing that the writer can be said to exist at all. The 'writer' is what exists in the interior of the activity of 'writing' . . . actions and their effects are conceived to be simultaneous; past and present are integrated rather than disrupted, and the subject and object of the action are in some way conflated" (White 1992, 179–87).

5. Flames of Fire in Qadisiya

1. The General Federation of Iraqi Women (GFIW) was founded in 1968 "to promote the status of women and to cooperate with international women's organizations" under the aegis of the Baath Party. Doreen Ingrams describes it as a "pressure group which can influence the Government to bring in reforms for the welfare of women." Among its achievements are the policing and prosecution of violations of women's rights, the widespread establishment of childcare facilities and women-run farms, and the assurance of decision-making positions for women throughout the bureaucracy (Ingrams 1983, 104–15). See also Abdel-Ghani 1980.

2. It has been easier—although not easy—to write critically of the war from outside. Before Kanaan Makiya revealed his name, he used the pseudonym Samir al-Khalil in order to say what he wanted about the Iraqi government and its war. Samira al-Mana has lived in London since the 1970s. Although most of her stories deal with the problems of exiles, her 1990 novel entitled *Habl al-surra* (The umbilical cord) takes on the Iran-Iraq War. The protagonist, 'Afaf, calls it "that terrible war" with its "rockets, poisonous gases, chemical weapons, destruction" and corpses floating on the waters of the Shatt al-'Arab and the Gulf. She writes of threats to the lives of Iraqis suspected of having Iranian blood. She describes the oppressiveness of life in Iraq, a place that the war has drained and turned into a desert: "travel is forbidden, letters get lost . . . everything is forbidden" (al-Mana 1990, 27–28). But the horror of the war is not restricted to Iraq; its terror can be felt in London. 'Afaf's uncle is visiting her from Iraq. The reunion is not joyful but plagued with suspicions. One day an agent calls. He had been waiting in anguish of this telephone call that would make him do the unthinkable: he has been ordered to kill his son who had escaped from the front. 'Afaf flashes back to the "photograph of a hanging that Arabic and British newspapers in London had published. It was of a father being awarded the Tigris and Euphrates medal, the most important medal in Iraq, because he had killed one of his sons who had escaped from the army. The medal honored the father as a symbol and a role model for all Iraqis. Her uncle raved on about this horrifying story and then asked: "What's the importance of the country without children? What's Iraq's importance without my children?" (133).

3. In several other stories in this collection, the war is called "the certain death" and it is described as "taking away our children" (cf. 66).

4. This is the case for other stories by Sa'id: the end of *Al-ihtiraq* (The burning) also is inconsistently patriotic. After the narrator's reluctance to fight, he is suddenly charging to the forefront.

5. In July 1994 during a visit to Urbana, Illinois, I talked with an Iraqi grocer about some of these writers. I wanted to know if any of them were known, real even. He was surprised to hear me mention Faysal ʿAbd al-Hasan Hajim because they were from the same town just west of Baghdad. The Hajims are a well-known literary family.

6. The critic ʿAbdallah Ibrahim explains that this generic naming of characters is common in Iraqi war novels. He claims that its function is to subordinate the character to the action (Ibrahim 1988, 88).

7. See discussion about Tim O'Brien's Vietnam novel, *The Things They Carried* (1990), in chapter one.

8. The state invoked medieval Iraqi writers as popular figures to "play upon the theme that the greatness of the Abbasid empire in its early days stemmed from its purely Arab quality and that its decline began once it was adulterated by the influx of minorities, such as the Persians and the Turks" (Davis and Gavrielides 1991, 132, 137, 139).

9. Basim ʿAbd al-Hamid Hammudi accuses Moosa of plagiarizing ʿUmar Muhammad al-Talib's *Al-qissa al-ʿiraqiya ʿala al-jabha al-ʿiraqiya* (Iraqi fiction at the Iraqi front [Baghdad, 1983]) and quotes passages to prove his point (Hammudi 1986, 45–48). Not having had access to al-Talib, I do not know whether Hammudi is overstating the case—Moosa does after all mention al-Talib's work in several places in his lecture ("Love, Death, Honor: Major Themes in Recent Iraqi Short Fiction," Marbid Festival 1985).

10. During the Lebanese civil war, women developed a new genre of journalistic prose poem they called the *billet* (Cooke 1988, 60–66).

11. For an English translation of the story, see Cooke and Rustomji-Kerns 1994.

12. ʿAdil ʿAbd al-Jabbar writes that the soldier refusing to give up the fight has become a major topos of the Iraqi war story (Hammudi 1986, 162).

13. Ibrahim writes that the War Story is typically divided between the front and somewhere else far away, and he goes on to quantify relationships that military men had with people away from the front: marriage 15 percent; love 42 percent; sex 7 percent; father 9 percent; child 12 percent; friend or colleague 12 percent. In other words, relationships with women amount to 64 percent (Ibrahim 1988, 59, 151).

14. Stanley Rosenberg writes that pilots' narratives from World War II evince neurosis that they combated with "such mechanisms as splitting, denial, projection, compartmentalization, and reversal of affect. These processes of distortion and self-alienation permitted the participants to live with death (their own potential death, their comrades' deaths, the

deaths of the victims of their bombs, cannon, and napalm) as if death were not real" (Rosenberg 1993, 60).

15. The problem of distance from target is increasing, as we saw during the Gulf War. Pilots saw a burst of fireworks on a screen and because their missions were so closely monitored, their bombs so smart, and their opponent so weak, they were in general spared the "anxiety" and fright, but also the consequent thrill, eroticism, and effectiveness. On 5 February 1991 J. Ledbetter reported in *The Village Voice* what has now become common knowledge: "pilots aboard the USS John F. Kennedy told AP that they'd been watching porn movies before bombing missions" (80).

16. The actual title *Ababil* means flocks of birds (*tayr ababil*) and comes from the Qur'an (Elephant sura, 105:3); the birds were supposed to have launched the equivalent of an aerial attack on the enemies of the Muslims. Saddam Hussein called "his new missile *hijarat ababil,* or flying stones," which he used against Israel during the Gulf War (Makiya 1993, 267).

17. After I met Edgerton and gave him a copy of an earlier version of this chapter, he sent me two pages that he told me were "the old ending of the story." In it, the male narrator who is a pilot imagines himself to be a pregnant woman.

18. Abouali Farmanfarmaian discusses an attempt at exploiting fantasies during the Gulf War. The eroticization of wives served as a kind of familial presentation of fantasy to American military men. "Operation Desert Cheer" took photographs of "soldier's wives half-nude, lace-clad, and sent the pictures to the husbands in the Gulf. For a military more than ever made up of family people, this can uphold fantasies without leaving the parameters of the family." He does not say what happened when these men returned home (Farmanfarmaian 1992, 133).

19. This remembering of a man's possessiveness once he has gone can be found in other women's writings on war, for example, Nuha Samara's "Two Faces One Woman" and Sa'adiya in *Sunflower* (see chapter 4).

20. "Son of my soul and foster son of the sorrows of the war. . . . Had God and the war not granted this beautiful boy to me, I would have dried up like a tree whom poisoned winds had scorched."—that is, war's victim helped her.

21. The internal opposition joined in a coalition of the Iraqi National Congress (INC) in late 1992. Their offices were in Salaheddin, where they employed Kurds, Arabs, Turkomans, and Assyrians. The local paper was published in Salaheddin and "20,000 to 30,000 copies are smuggled into government-controlled territory and distributed weekly in Baghdad and other cities. . . . The INC has infiltrated and circulated other opposition literature, such as statements, pamphlets, and posters, to the great anger

of the government and the Baghdad media" (*INC Newsletter,* spring 1994).

22. 'Abdallah refers to the Iraq-Iran War, but without naming it: it gave her some war experience to prepare her for what she was now having to go through; it was the reason they moved from Basra to Baghdad; she remembers watching TV during that war and seeing "mutilated corpses distributed throughout the mountains and valleys; swollen corpses with broken limbs floating on the waters, with crushed skulls and without heads." She remembers "the black posters we found in every street and alley throughout the years of the Eight-Year War announcing martyrs" ('Abdallah 1994, 114, 49, 88, 108). I thank Ghada al-Samman for sending me a copy of this book.

23. My thanks go to Nathalie Mansour, who sent me a copy of this book.

6. Reimagining Lebanon

1. Henri Zghaib's comments occurred during the Lebanese literature panel at the annual convention of the Middle East Studies Association in Durham, N.C., 13 November 1993. Mai Ghossoub writes: "Je crois que c'est cela être libanaise: une appartenance multiple, cette possibilité de vivre notre individualité, tout en sachant l'agencer avec les exigences de nos grandes familles, et cela quel que soit notre lieu de résidence" (Ghossoub 1993).

2. Anderson defines official nationalism as an "anticipatory strategy adopted by dominant groups which are threatened with marginalization or exclusion from an emerging nationally imagined community. . . . [Its policy levers are] compulsory state-controlled primary education, state-organized propaganda, official rewriting of history, militarism . . . and endless affirmations of the identity of dynasty and nation. . . . Such official nationalisms were conservative, not to say reactionary, policies, adapted from the model of the largely spontaneous popular nationalisms that preceded them" (Anderson 1991, 101, 110).

3. Evelyne Accad points out, however, that even at this earliest, "positive" stage, nationalism was not all good. During colonial rule to segregate, seclude, or veil one's women was proof that one was honorable and of superior culture. Nor did the exploitation of women in nationalist ideology stop beyond the first, "good" stage. Women were asked to fight for their country that they had been made to represent and that they were then asked to reproduce (Accad 1993).

4. For a discussion of the differences between imagining and inventing nations, see John A. Hall, "Nationalisms: Classified and Explained," *Daedalus* 122, no. 3 [1993]: 4.

5. Gellner writes that nationalism focused on individual agency is "held together above all by a shared culture, in place of a previous complex structure of local groups, sustained by folk cultures reproduced locally and idiosyncratically by the micro-groups themselves" (Gellner 1988, 57).

6. Aijaz Ahmad rejects the automatic reduction of third world literature to "the unitary insignia of nationalism and then to designate this nationalism as the determinate and epochal ideology for cultural production in non-Western societies" (Ahmad 1992, 243). See also Cooke 1987, 277–96.

7. The Freikorps writers "desire a father—a man less weak than their own fathers were in reality. . . . While real fathers are silenced by the soldier males, their texts express unmistakable desires for better ones" (Theweleit 1987–89, 2:369).

8. Absence as the ingredient essential to productive longing is in marked contrast to Rashid al-Daif, who claimed in an interview that when he said, "'From your absence comes the evening' I express the anguish of losing my beloved. This anguish is similar to that caused by war." It is a fear of losing the nation that he articulates in a poem: "WATANI (my nation / You've lost your W / You've lost your A / You've lost your T / You've lost your N." All that is left is the I that in Arabic denotes the first person singular possessive pronoun. All that is left is the possessing, not the belonging, individual (quoted in Takieddine-Amyouni 1993, 2).

Cited Works

'Abdallah, Ibtisam
    1994   *Matar aswad . . . matar ahmar* (Black rain . . . red rain).
            London: Bazzaz.

Abdel-Ghani, Hammam
    1980   *The General Federation of Iraq Women: A Practical Trans-*
            lation to the Objectives of the Revolution in Work and
            Creativity. Baghdad: GFIW Secretariat of Studies and Re-
            searches.

Abdul Razzaq, Abdullah
    1983   "Voices from Near and Far." In *Modern Arab Short Stories,*
            edited by Denys Johnson-Davies. London: Quartet.

Abu Ghazzala, Raja'
    1988   *Al-mutarada* (The pursued). Amman: Dar al-Shuruq.

Abu Samra, Akram
    1989   *Al-mar'a al-filastiniya: Dars fi al-intifada* (The Palestinian
            woman: a lesson on the Intifada). Carthage: PLO Unified
            Information.

Accad, Evelyne
    1993   "Transnational Aspects of War and Violence: Peace as an
            Alternative." Paper presented at the War and Gender Con-
            ference, Bellagio, August.

Adnan, Etel
    1978   *Sitt Marie Rose.* Paris: Editions des Femmes.

Ahmad, Aijaz
    1992   *In Theory: Classes, Nations, Literatures.* New York: Verso.

Al Sa'id, Shakir Hasan
  1988   *'Inda masharif khandaq al-istishhad* (Overlooking the mar-
             tyring trench). Baghdad: Dar-al Shu'un al-Thaqafiya al-
             'Amma.
al-'Alam, Ibrahim
  1991   "Al-riwaya al-filastiniya fi al-watan al-muhtall khilala
             khams wa 'ishrin sanna" (The Palestinian novel in the oc-
             cupied nation for twenty-five years). Manuscript.
al-Amir, Daisy
  1979   *Fi duwwamat al-hubb wa al-karahiya* (In the vortex of love
             and hate). Beirut: Dar al-'Awda.
———.
  1981   *Wu'ud li al-bay'* (Promises for sale). Beirut: al-Mu'assasa
             al-'Arabiya li al-Dirasat wa li al-Nashr.
———.
  1986   "Al-asatidha wa al-talamidh" (Teachers and pupils). *Al-
             Jumhuriya*, 5 April.
———.
  1988   *'Ala la'ihat al-intizar* (On the waiting list). Beirut: Dar al-
             Adab.
'Amran, Layla Karim
  1988   "Sama' al-Faw min jadid" (The sky of Fao again). In *Fi
             al-ghasaq 'adat 'arus al-bahr,* edited by Nu'man Majid.
             Baghdad: Dar al-Shu'un al-Thaqafiya al-'Amma.
Amrouche, Fadhma
  1989   *My Life Story: The Autobiography of a Berber Woman.*
  [1968]   Translated by Dorothy S. Blair. New Brunswick, N.J.: Rut-
             gers University Press.
Amrouche, Marguerite Taos
  1960   *La rue des tambourins.* Algiers.
Anderson, Benedict
  1991   *Imagined Communities.* New York: Verso.
———.
  1992   "Long-Distance Nationalism: World Capitalism and the
             Rise of Identity Politics." Paper delivered at University of
             Michigan, September.
al-'Ansari, Salah
  1988   *Abjadiyat al-harb wa al-hubb* (Alphabet of war and love).
             Baghdad: Dar al-Shu'un al-Thaqafiya al-'Amma.
Antonius, Soraya
  1983   "Fighting on Two Fronts: Conversations with Palestinian
             Women." In *Third World—Second Sex, Women's Struggles*

and National Liberation: Third World Women Speak Out,
edited by Miranda Davies. London: Zed Press.

Anzaldúa, Gloria
1987   *Borderlands/La Frontera: The New Mestiza.* San Francisco:
Aunt Lute.

Anzaldúa, Gloria, and Cherríe Moraga, eds.
1983   *This Bridge Called My Back.* New York: Kitchen Table—
Women of Color Press

Appiah, Kwame Anthony
1991   "Is the Post- in Postmodernism the Post- in Postcolonial?"
Critical Inquiry 17.

Arendt, Hannah
1970   *On Violence.* New York: Harcourt, Brace.

Aresu, Bernard
1983   "Female Characterization and Mythmaking in the Dramas
of Kateb Yacine." *Neophilologus* 67: 368–76.

Ashrawi, Hanan Mikhail
1982   "The Contemporary Literature of Palestine: Poetry and Fiction." Ph.D. dissertation, University of Virginia.

Atwan, Terry
1993   "Life Is Struggle Inside and Outside the Green Line." In
Palestinian Women: Identity and Experience, edited by
Ebba Augustin. London: Zed Press.

Aurbakken, Kristine
1986   *L'étoile d'araignée: une lecture de* Nedjma *de Kateb Yacine.*
Paris: Publisud.

Badran, Margot, and Miriam Cooke, eds.
1990   *Opening the Gates: A Century of Arab Feminist Writing.*
London: Virago; and Bloomington: Indiana University
Press.

Bamya, 'Ayda Adib
1982   *Tatawwur al-adab al-qassasi al-jaza'iri 1925–1967* (The
development of Algerian fiction, 1925–67). Algiers: Diwan
al-Matbu'at al-Jami'iyya.

Barakat, Huda
1990   *Hajar al-dahak* (The laughing stone). London: Riad El-
Rayyes Books.

———.

1993   *Ahl al-hawa* (People of passion). Beirut: Dar al-Nahar.

Barghuthi, Widad
1990   "Kayfa zaharat al-mar'a fi al-shi'r al-filastini al-mahalli"
(Women's images in local Palestinian poetry). Paper pre-

sented at Conference on the Intifada and Social Issues Concerning Women, Jerusalem.

Barthes, Roland

1978   *Writing Degree Zero.* Translated by Annette Lavers and
[1953]   Colin Smith. New York: Hill and Wang.

Benjamin, Walter

1969   *Illuminations: Essays and Reflections.* Translated by Harry
[1936]   Zohn and edited by Hannah Arendt. New York: Schocken.

Ben Slama, Raja

1991   "Les pleureuses." *Cahiers Intersignes,* no. 2.

Benson, Frederick R.

1967   *Writers in Arms.* New York: New York University Press.

Berg, Rick

1985   "Losing Vietnam: Covering the War in an Age of Technology." *Cultural Critique.*

Berkman, Joyce

1990   "Feminism, War, and Peace Politics: The Case of World War
        I." In *Women, Militarism, and War: Essays in History,
        Politics, and Social Theory,* edited by Jean Bethke Elshtain
        and Sheila Tobias. Savage, Md.: Rowman and Littlefield.

Bittari, Zoubeida

1964   *O mes soeurs musulmanes, pleurez!* Paris.

Boothby, Richard

1991   *Death and Desire: Psychoanalytic Theory in Lacan's Return to Freud.* New York: Routledge.

Boudjedra, Rachid

1969   *La répudiation.* Paris.

Brenkman, John

1993   "Multiculturalism and Criticism." In *English Inside and
        Out: The Places of Literary Criticism,* edited by Susan Gubar and Jonathan Kanholtz. New York: Routledge.

Brown, Kristin

1990   "From Abu Zayd to Abu Amar and Beyond: Palestinian
        Poetry, Song, and the Intifada." Paper presented to Middle
        East Studies Association, San Antonio, Texas.

Broyles, William, Jr.

1984   "Why Men Love War." *Esquire,* November.

Brownmiller, Susan

1975   *Against Our Will: Men, Women, and Rape.* New York:
        Simon and Schuster.

Bunster-Burotto, Ximena

1986   "Surviving Beyond Fear: Women and Torture in Latin

America." In *Women and Change in Latin America,* edited by June Nash and Helen Safa. Westport, Conn.: Bergin and Garvey.

Bunzi, John, and Nadia El-Masri, eds.

1989   *Der Aufstand.* Vienna: Passagen und Zeitgeschehen.

Cadi-Mostefai, Meriem

1978   "L'image de la femme algérienne pendant la guerre (1954–1962), à partir de textes paralittéraires et littéraires." Thesis, diplôme d'études approfondies, University of Algiers.

Campbell, D'Ann

1985   "Women at War with America." In *Women in War,* edited by Shelley Saywell. New York: Viking.

———.

1990   "The Regimented Women of World War II." In *Women, Militarism, and War: Essays in History, Politics, and Social Theory,* edited by Jean Bethke Elshtain and Sheila Tobias. Savage, Md.: Rowman and Littlefield.

Capa, Robert

1964   *Images of War.* New York: Grossman.

Cerovic, Stanko

1993   "La lumière de Sarajevo." *Peuples méditerranéens* 5.

Chapkis, Wendy

1988   "Sexuality and Militarism." *In Women and the Military System,* edited by Eva Isaksson. New York: St. Martin's.

Chomsky, Noam

1985   "Visions of Righteousness." *Cultural Critique.*

Clark, Michael

1985a   "Remembering Vietnam." *Cultural Critique.*

———.

1985b   "Vietnam: Representations of The Self and War." *Wide Angle* 7, no 4.

Clausewitz, Carl von

1976   *On War.* Translated by Michael Howard and Peter Paret. Princeton: Princeton University Press.

Cohen, Marshall, Thomas Nagel, and Thomas Scanlon, eds.

1974   *War and Moral Responsibility: A Philosophy and Public Affairs Reader.* Princeton: Princeton University Press.

Cohen, Roger

1954   "In Sarajevo, Victims of a 'Postmodern' War." *New York Times,* 21 May.

Cohn, Carol

1989   "Emasculating America's Linguistic Deterrent." In *Rocking the Ship of State: Toward a Feminist Peace Politics,* edited by Adrienne Harris and Ynestra King. Boulder: Westview Press.

———.

1990   "'Clean Bombs' and Clean Language." In *Women, Militarism, and War: Essays in History, Politics, and Social Theory,* edited by Jean Bethke Elshtain and Sheila Tobias. Savage, Md.: Rowman and Littlefield.

———.

1993   "Wars, Wimps, and Women: Talking Gender and Thinking War." In *Gendering War Talk,* edited by Miriam Cooke and Angela Woollacott. Princeton: Princeton University Press.

Cooke, Miriam

1987   "Literary Criticism: The State of the Art in Arabic." *Al-Arabiyya* 20.

———.

1988   *War's Other Voices: Women Writers on the Lebanese Civil War.* New York: Cambridge University Press.

———.

1989   "Deconstructing War Discourse: Women's Participation in the Algerian Revolution." Working paper on Women in Development, Michigan State University.

———.

1991   "Postmodern Wars: Phallomilitary Spectacles in the DTO." *Journal of Urban and Cultural Studies* 2, no. 1.

Cooke, Miriam, and Roshni Rustomji-Kerns, eds.

1994   *Blood into Ink: South Asian and Middle Eastern Women Write War.* Boulder: Westview Press.

Cooke, Miriam, and Angela Woollacott, eds.

1993   *Gendering War Talk.* Princeton: Princeton University Press.

Cooper, Helen, Adrienne Munich, and Susan Squier, eds.

1989   *Arms and the Woman: War, Gender and Literary Representation.* Chapel Hill: University of North Carolina Press.

Corradi, Juan

1982   "The Mode of Destruction: Terror in Argentina." *Telos* 54.

———.

1988   "Our Violence: Terrorism as a Mode of Post-Political Self-Reference." Paper presented at conference, Talking Terrorism, Stanford University, 4–6 February.

Darwish, Mahmud

1962   "Muqabalat al-shahr" (Interview of the month [with Najwa Qaʻwar Farah]). *Al-Jadid,* April–May.

Davies, Miranda, ed.

1983   *Third World—Second Sex, Women's Struggles and National Liberation: Third World Women Speak Out.* London: Zed Press.

Davis, Eric, and Nicolas Gavrielides, eds.

1991   *Statecraft in the Middle East: Oil, Historical Memory, and Popular Culture.* Miami: Florida International University Press.

de Beauvoir, Simone, and Giselle Halimi

1962   *Djamila Boupacha: The Story of the Torture of a Young Algerian Girl Which Shocked Liberal French Opinion.* New York: Macmillan.

Débèche, Djamila

1946   *Contactes en terre d'Afrique.* Paris.

———.

1955   *Aziza.* Algiers: Imbert.

Dejeux, Jean

1973   *Littérature maghrébine de langue française.* Naaman: Sherbroke.

Deleuze, Gilles, and Félix Guattari

1986   *Kafka: Toward a Minor Literature.* Translated by Dana
[1975].   Polan. Minneapolis: University of Minnesota Press.

Dib, Mohamed

1952   *La grande maison.* Paris: Editions du Seuil.

———.

1954   *L'incendie.* Paris: Editions du Seuil.

———.

1957   *Le métier à tisser.* Paris: Editions du Seuil.

———.

1985   *Who Remembers the Sea.* Translated by Louis Tremaine.
[1962]   Washington, D.C.: Three Continents Press. Originally published as *Qui se souvient de la mer* (Paris: Editions du Seuil).

Djebar, Assia

1957   *La soif.* Paris: Editions Julliard.

———.

1958   *Les impatients.* Paris: Editions Julliard.

———.

1962   *Les enfants du nouveau monde.* Paris: Editions Julliard.

———.

1967   *Les alouettes naïves.* Paris: Editions Julliard.

———.

1970   *Rouge l'aube.* Radio adaptation by Algerian radio.
[1960].

———.
1980   *Femmes d'Alger dans leur appartement.* Paris: Editions des
            Femmes.

———.
1987   *Ombre sultane.* Paris: J. C. Lattès.

———.
1993   *Fantasia: An Algerian Cavalcade.* Translated by Dorothy S.
[1985]   Blair. Portsmouth: Heinemann.

———.
1995   *Vaste est la prison.* Paris: Albin Michel.
Donadey, Anne
1993   "Assia Djebar's Poetics of Subversion." *L'Esprit créateur*
            33.
Drif, Zohra
1961   "La mort de mes frères." Bibliothèque nationale, Paris.
al-Dulaymi, Lutfiya
1988   *Budhur al-nar* (Seeds of fire). Baghdad: Dar al-Shu'un al-
            Thaqafiya al-'Amma.

———.
1988   "Fi al-ghasaq 'adat 'arus al-bahr" (At dusk the mermaid
            returned). In *Fi al-ghasaq 'adat 'arus al-bahr,* edited by
            Nu'man Majid. Baghdad: Dar al-Shu'un al-Thaqafiya
            al-'Amma.
During, Simon
1987   "Postmodernism or Postcolonialism Today." *Textual Prac-
            tice* 1, no. 1.
Dyson, Freeman
1985   *Weapons and Hope.* New York: Harper and Row.
Eagleton, Terry
1990   "Nationalism; Irony, and Commitment." In *Nationalism,
            Colonialism, and Literature,* edited by Terry Eagleton, Fre-
            dric Jameson, and Edward Said. Minneapolis: University of
            Minnesota Press.
Elshtain, Jean Bethke
1987   *Women and War.* New York: Basic Books.
Elshtain, Jean Bethke, and Sheila Tobias, eds.
1990   *Women, Militarism, and War: Essays in History, Politics,
            and Social Theory.* Savage, Md.: Rowman and Littlefield.
Enloe, Cynthia
1983   *Does Khaki Become You? The Militarization of Women's
            Lives.* Boston: South End Press.
Fanon, Frantz
1952   *Peau noire masques blancs.* Paris: Editions du Seuil.

———.

1956   *Résistance algérienne*. Paris.

———.

1975   *Sociologie d'une révolution*. Paris: Maspero.
[1959]

Farah, Najwa Qa'war

1954   *'Abiru al-sabil* (Passersby). Beirut: Dar Rihani.

———.

1956   *Durub wa masabih* (Paths and lanterns). Nazareth: Mat-
            ba'a al-Hakim.

———.

1963   *Li man al-rabi'?* (For whom is the spring?). Nazareth: Mat-
            ba'a al-Hakim.

———.

1981   *Rihlat al-huzn wa al-i'ta'* (Journey of sadness and giving).
            Beirut: Dar al-Kalima.

———.

1991   *Intifadat al-'asafir* (The intifada of the birds). Amman: Dar
            al-Jalil.

Farmanfarmaian, Abouali

1992   "Did You Measure Up? The Role of Race and Sexuality in
            the Gulf War." In *Collateral Damage: The 'New World
            Order' at Home and Abroad*, edited by Cynthia Peters. Bos-
            ton: South End Press.

Fernea, Elizabeth, and Fatima Bezirgan, eds.

1977   *Middle Eastern Muslim Women Speak*. Austin: Texas Uni-
            versity Press.

Foucault, Michel

1980   *Power/Knowledge: Selected Interviews and Other Writings
            1972–1977*, edited by C. Gordon. Brighton: Harvester.

Foulkes, A. Peter

1983   *Literature and Propaganda*. New York: Methuen.

Fralin, Frances Lindley

1985   *The Indelible Image: Photographs of War, 1846 to the
            Present*. New York: Harry N. Abrams.

Franco, Jean

1986   "Gender, Death, and Resistance: Facing the Ethical Vac-
            uum." *Chicago Review* 35, no. 4.

Freud, Sigmund

1961   *Beyond the Pleasure Principle*. Translated by James Stra-
[1919]   chey. New York: Liveright.

Friedrich, Otto

1990   "Master of the Universe." *Time,* 13 August.

Fuss, Diana
    1989   *Essentially Speaking: Feminism, Nature, and Difference.*
                New York: Routledge.
Gadant, Monique, ed.
    1986   *Women of the Mediterranean.* London: Zed Press.
Gellhorn, Martha
    1988   *The Face of War.* New York: Atlantic Monthly Press.
Gellner, Ernest
    1988   *Nations and Nationalism.* Oxford: Blackwell.
Genet, Jean
    1992   *Prisoner of Love.* Translated by Barbara Bray. Middletown,
    [1986]   Conn.: Wesleyan University Press.
Gerbner, George
    1992   "Persian Gulf War, the Movie." In *Triumph of the Image:
                The Media's War in the Persian Gulf—A Global Perspec-
                tive,* edited by Hamid Mawlana, George Gerbner, and Her-
                bert I. Schiller. Boulder: Westview Press.
Ghossoub, Mai
    1993   "Etre femme libanaise après la guerre." Paper presented at
                Institut du Monde Arabe, Paris, summer.
Giacaman, Rita
    1988a   "Palestinian Women in the Uprising: From Followers to
                Leaders?" Paper presented at Birzeit University.
———.
    1988b   "Changing Roles of Women." *Tanmiya,* September.
Giacaman, Rita, and Penny Johnson
    1989   "Palestinian Women: Building Barricades and Breaking
                Barriers." In *Intifada: The Palestinian Uprising against Is-
                raeli Occupation,* edited by Zachary Lockman and Joel
                Beinin. Boston: South End Press.
Giddens, Anthony
    1987   *The Nation-State and Violence.* Berkeley: University of Cal-
                ifornia Press.
Gilbert, Sandra, and Susan Gubar
    1988   *No Man's Land: The Place of the Woman Writer in the
                Twentieth Century.* Vol. 1. New Haven: Yale University
                Press.
Glenny, Misha
    1994   "Hope for Bosnia?" *New York Review of Books,* 7 April.
Gray, J. Glenn
    1970   *The Warriors: Reflections on Men in Battle.* 1959. Reprint,
                New York: Harper.

Green, Mary Jean
   1993   "Dismantling the Colonizing Text: Anne Hebert's 'Ka-mouraska' and Assia Djebar's 'L'Amour La Fantasia.'" *French Review* 66, no. 6.

Guendouz, Nadia
   1968   *Amal.* Algiers.

Habibi, Emile
   1955   Editorial. *Al-Jadid,* January.

——.
   1982   *The Secret Life of Saeed, the Ill-fated Pessoptomist.* Trans-
   [1974] lated by Salma Khadra Jayyusi and Trevor LeGassick. New York: Vantage.

Haddad, Malek
   1960   *L'élève et la leçon.* Paris: Editions Julliard.

——.
   1961   *Le quai aux fleurs ne répond plus.* Paris: Editions Julliard.

——.
   1978   *Je t'offrirai une gazelle.* Paris: Union générale d'éditions.
   [1959]

Haj, Samira
   1992   "Palestinian Women and Patriarchal Relations." *Signs* (summer).

Hajim, Faysal 'Abd al-Hasan
   1985   *Al-layl wa al-nahar* (Night and day). Baghdad: Dar al-Shu'un al-Thaqafiya al-'Amma.

——.
   1988   *Al-junud* (Soldiers). Baghdad: Dar al-Shu'un al-Thaqafiya al-'Amma.

Hall, John A.
   1993   "Nationalisms: Classified and Explained." *Daedalus* 122, no. 3.

Hammudi, Basim 'Abd al-Hamid
   1986   *Al-naqid wa qissat al-harb: Dirasa tahliliya* (The critic and the war story: an analytical study). Baghdad: Dar al-Shu'un al-Thaqafiya al-'Amma.

Harris, Adrienne, and Ynestra King, eds
   1989   *Rocking the Ship of State: Toward a Feminist Peace Politics.* Boulder: Westview Press.

Hart, Alan
   1984   *Arafat.* London: Sidwick and Jackson.

Harvey, David
   1989   *The Condition of Postmodernity.* Oxford: Basil Blackwell.

Havel, Vaclav
  1993   "How Europe Could Fail." *New York Review of Books*, 18
            November.
Hayslip, Le Ly, with Jay Wurts
  1989   *When Heaven and Earth Changed Places: A Vietnamese
            Woman's Journey from War to Peace*. New York: Dou-
            bleday.
Hélie-Lucas, Marie-Aimée
  1990   "Women, Nationalism, and Religion in the Algerian Strug-
            gle." In *Opening the Gates: A Century of Arab Feminist
            Writing*, edited by Margot Badran and Miriam Cooke.
            Bloomington: Indiana University Press.
———.
  1993   "Women Living under Muslim Laws." In *Ours by Right:
            Women's Rights as Human Rights*, edited by Joanna Kerr.
            London: Zed Press.
Herr, Michael
  1978   *Dispatches*. New York: Avon Books.
Higonnet, Margaret
  1993   "Not So Quiet in No Woman's Land." In *Gendering War
            Talk*, edited by Miriam Cooke and Angela Woollacott.
            Princeton: Princeton University Press.
Hijab, Nadia
  1994   "Palestinian Women: The Key to a Secular, Democratic
            State." In *Palestinian Self-Government: An Early Assess-
            ment*. Washington, D.C.: Center for Policy Analysis on
            Palestine.
Hobsbawm, Eric
  1993   "The New Threat to History." *New York Review of Books*,
            16 December.
Horne, Alistair
  1979   *A Savage War of Peace: Algeria 1954–1962*. New York:
            Penguin Books.
Hussein, Saddam
  1979   *Hawla kitabat al-ta'rikh* (On the writing of history). Bagh-
            dad: Ministry of Culture and Information.
Ibn Khaldun
  1956   "Opinions about Recent Books." *Al-Jadid*, July.
———.
  1957   Editorial. *Al-Jadid*, April.
Ibrahim, 'Abdallah
  1988   *Al-bina' al-fanni li-riwayat al-harb fi al-'Iraq* (The artistic

structure of the war novel in Iraq). Baghdad: Dar al-Shu'un al-Thaqafiya al-'Amma.

Ingrams, Doreen
1983   *The Awakened: Women in Iraq.* London: Third World Centre.

Isaksson, Eva, ed.
1988   *Women and the Military System.* New York: St. Martin's.

'Izz al-Din, Ahmad Jalal
1996   "Al-Jaza'ir: tuqa' harb ahliya idha lam yahsum al-jaysh al-ma'raka ma'a al-mutatarrifin mubkiran" (Algeria: there will be civil war if the army does not take on the extremists soon). *Al-Musawwar*, no. 3693, 21 July.

James, David
1985   "Presence of Discourse/Discourse of Presence: Representing Vietnam." *Wide Angle* 7, no. 4.

Jameson, Fredric
1991   *Postmodernism: or, the Cultural Logic of Late Capitalism.* Durham: Duke University Press.

Jarjura, Nadim Tawfiq
1991   "Bab al-Saha: Analyzing Details of the Intifada from Within." *Al-Safir*, 26 February.

Jeffords, Susan
1989   *The Remasculinization of America: Gender and the Vietnam War.* Bloomington: Indiana University Press.

Johnson-Davies, Denys, ed.
1983   *Modern Arab Short Stories.* London: Quartet.

Jones, Kathleen
1990   "Dividing the Ranks. Women and the Draft." In *Women, Militarism, and War: Essays in History, Politics, and Social Theory,* edited by Jean Bethke Elshtain and Sheila Tobias. Savage, Md.: Rowman and Littlefield.

Joseph, Suad
1991   "Elite Strategies for State Building: Women, Family, Religion, and the State in Iraq and Lebanon." In *Women, Islam, and the State,* edited by Deniz Kandiyoti. Philadelphia: Temple University Press.

Jovicic, Zoran
1992   *War Crimes Committed by the Yugoslav Army 1991–1992.* Zagreb: Croation Information Centre.

Kanaana, Sharif
1993   "The Role of Women in Intifada Legends." *Contemporary Legend* 3: 37–61.

Kanafani, Ghassan
    1993   *Al-rijal fi al-shams* (Men in the sun). Beirut.
Kandiyoti, Deniz, ed.
    1991   *Women, Islam, and the State*. Philadelphia: Temple University Press.
Keegan, John
    1978   *The Face of Battle: A Study of Agincourt, Waterloo, and the Somme*. New York: Penguin Books.
Kerr, Joanna, ed
    1993   *Ours by Right: Women's Rights as Human Rights*. London: Zed Press.
Kervin, Denise
    1985   "Reality according to Television News: Pictures from El Salvador." *Wide Angle* 7, no. 4.
Khalifa, Sahar
    1985a   *Wild Thorns*. Translated by Trevor LeGassick and Eliza-
    [1976]   beth Fernea. Austin: University of Texas Press. Originally published as *Al-subar* (Jerusalem: Galileo).
    ———.

    1985b   *'Abbad al-shams* (Sunflower). Amman: Department of In-
    [1979]   formation and Culture of the PLO.
    ———.

    1986   *Mudhakkirat imra'a ghayr waqi 'iya* (Memoirs of an un-realistic woman). Beirut: Dar al-Adab.
    ———.

    1989   "Lil-taghyir . . . 'alayya an akhtariqa al-judran" (To change . . . I have to pierce walls). *Al-Qabs,* 9 February.
    ———.

    1990a   *Bab al-Saha*. Beirut.
    ———.

    1990b   "Our Fate, Our House." *Middle East Report* (May–August): 30–31.
al-Khalil, Samir [Kanaan Makiya]
    1989   *Republic of Fear*. London: Hutchinson Radius.
    ———.

    1991   *The Monument: Art, Vulgarity, and Responsibility in Iraq*. Berkeley: University of California Press.
Khatibi, Abdelkabir
    1983   *Maghreb pluriel*. Paris: Editions Deno ël.
Khulusi, Natiq
    1988   "Al-diya' al-awwal li al-fajr" (The first light of dawn). In *Fi*

al-ghasaq 'adat 'arus al-bahr, edited by Nu'man Majid. Baghdad: Dar al-Shu'un al-Thaqafiya al-'Amma.

Knauss, Peter R.
1987 *The Persistence of Patriarchy: Class, Gender, and Ideology in Twentieth-Century Algeria.* New York: Praeger.

Kinney, Judy Lee
1985 "The Mythical Method: Fictionalizing the Vietnam War." *Wide Angle* 7, no. 4.

Kuberski, Philip Francis
1985 "Genres of Vietnam." *Cultural Critique.*

Lazreg, Marnia
1988 "Feminism and Difference: The Perils of Writing as a Woman on Women in Algeria." *Feminist Studies* 14, no. 1.

————.

1994 *The Eloquence of Silence: Algerian Women in Question.* New York: Routledge.

LeBlanc, Adrian Nicole
1994 "While Manny's Locked Up." *New York Times Magazine,* 14 August.

Lemsine, Aicha
1976 *La chrysalide: chroniques algériennes.* Paris: Editions des Femmes.

Lockman, Zachary, and Joel Beinin
1989 *Intifada: The Palestinian Uprising against Israeli Occupation.* Boston: South End Press.

Lorenz, Andrea W.
1991 "Ishtar Was a Woman." *Ms. Magazine,* May–June.

Loseff, Lev
1984 *On the Beneficence of Censorship: Aesopian Language in Modern Russian Literature.* Munich: Otto Sagner.

Lyotard, Jean François
1987 *The Postmodern Condition: A Report on Knowledge.* Minneapolis: University of Minnesota Press.

Majid, Nu'man, ed.
1988 *Fi al-ghasaq 'adat 'arus al-bahr* (At dusk the mermaid returned). Baghdad: Dar al-Shu'un al-Thaqafiya al-'Amma.

Makdisi, Jean Said
1990 *Beirut Fragments: A War Memoir.* New York: Persea Books.

Makiya, Kanaan
1993 *Cruelty and Silence: War, Tyranny, Uprising, and the Arab World.* London: Jonathan Cape.

Mammeri, Mouloud
 1965   *L'opium et le bâton.* Paris: Plon.
al-Mana, Samira
 1990   *Habl al-surra* (The umbilical cord). London: Manshurat al-lghtirab al-Adabi.
Manasra, Najah
 1993   "Palestinian Women: Between Tradition and Revolutions." In *Palestinian Women: Identity and Experience,* edited by Ebba Augustin. London: Zed Press.
Mandelstam, Nadezhda
 1971   *Hope against Hope: A Memoir.* Translated by Max Hayward. London: Collins.
Mani, Suha Hindiyeh, and Afaf Ghazawneh
 1993   "The Socio-Economic Conditions of Female Wage Labour in the West Bank." In *Palestinian Women: Identity and Experience,* edited by Ebba Augustin. London: Zed Press.
Marcus, Jane
 1989   "The Asylums of Antaeus: Women, War, and Madness—Is There a Feminist Fetishism?" In *The New Historicism,* edited by H. Aram Veeser. New York: Routledge.
Marin, Peter
 1981   "Living in Moral Pain." *Psychology Today,* November.
McKinnon, Catherine
 1994   "Rape, Genocide, and Women's Human Rights." In *Mass Rape: The War against Women in Bosnia-Herzegovina,* edited by Alexandra Stiglmayer. Omaha: University of Nebraska Press.
McLuhan, Marshall, and Quentin Fiore
 1968   *War and Peace in the Global Village.* New York: Bantam Books.
McMahon, Janet
 1991   "Suha Sabbagh." *Washington Report on Middle East Affairs,* March.
Mechakra, Yasmina
 1986   *La grotte éclatée.* Algiers: ENAL.
 [1979]
Mikha'il, Dunya
 1995   *Yawmiyat mawja kharij al-bahr* (The journal of a wave outside the sea). Baghdad: Dar al-Shu'un al-Thaqafiya al-'Amma.
Miller, Laura L., and Charles C. Moskos
 1994   "Humanitarians or Warriors? Race, Gender, and Combat Status in Operation Restore Hope." Manuscript.

Mogannam, Matiel
    1937   *The Arab Woman and the Political Problem.* London: Herbert Joseph.
Mohanty, Chandra Talpade
    1991   "Under Western Eyes: Feminist Scholarship and Colonial Discourses." In *Third World Women and the Politics of Feminism,* edited by Chandra Talpade Mohanty, Ann Russo, and Lourdes Torres. Bloomington: Indiana University Press.
Monego, Joan Phyllis
    1984   *Maghrebian Literature in French.* Boston: Twaine.
Moore, Barrington
    1967   *Social Origins of Dictatorship and Democracy: Lord and Peasant in the Making of the Modern World.* Boston: Beacon.
Moosa, Matti
    1985   "Love, Death, Honor: Major Themes in Recent Iraqi Short Fiction." Lecture delivered at Marbid Festival, Iraq.
Moraga, Cherríe
    1993   *The Last Generation.* Boston: South End Press.
Mosteghanemi, Ahlem
    1985   *Algérie, femmes, et écritures.* Paris: L'Harmattan.
———.
    1993   *Dhakirat al-jasad* (Body memory). Beirut: Dar al-Adab.
M'Rabet, Fadela
    1964   *Révolution africaine.* Paris.
———.
    1983   *La femme algérienne—Les algériennes.* Paris: Maspero.
al-Musawi, Muhsin Jassim
    1991   "The Socio-Political Context of the Iraqi Short Story: 1908–1968." In *Statecraft in the Middle East: Oil, Historical Memory, and Popular Culture,* edited by Eric Davis and Nicolas Gavrielides. Miami: Florida International University Press.
Nagan, Winston
    1994   "Human Rights as a Negotiating Tool in Peacemaking." Manuscript.
Najjar, Orayb Aref, ed.
    1992   *Portraits of Palestinian Women.* Salt Lake City: University of Utah Press.
Nash, June, and Helen Safa, eds.
    1986   *Women and Change in Latin America.* Westport, Conn.: Bergin and Garvey.

Nasrallah, Emily

1980   *Al-iqla' 'aks al-zaman* (Flight against time). Beirut: Nawfal.

———.

1984   *Al-mar'a fi 17 qissa* (Woman in seventeen stories). Beirut: Nawfal.

———.

1985   *Al-tahuna al-da'i'a* (The lost mill). Beirut: Nawfal.

———.

1992   *A House of Her Own.* Charlottetown, Canada: Ragweed.

O'Brien, Tim

1990   *The Things They Carried.* New York: Penguin Books.

Parin, Paul

1994   "Open Wounds: Ethnopsychoanalytic Reflections on the Wars in the Former Yugoslavia." In *Mass Rape: The War against Women in Bosnia-Herzegovina,* edited by Alexandra Stiglmayer. Omaha: University of Nebraska Press.

Parker, Andrew, Mary Russo, Doris Sommer, and Patricia Yaeger, eds.

1992   *Nationalisms and Sexualities.* New York: Routledge.

Pejic, Nenad

1992   "Media and Responsibility in the War." *Peuples méditerranéens* (Special edition, Yugoslavie: logiques de l'exclusion), no. 61 (October–December).

Peled, Mattityahu

1988   *Aspects of Modern Arabic Literature.* Louvain and Paris: Peeters.

Peters, Cynthia, ed.

1992   *Collateral Damage: The 'New World Order' at Home and Abroad.* Boston: South End Press.

Poole, Ross

1985   "Structures of Identity: Gender and Nationalism." In *War/Masculinity,* edited by Paul Patton and Ross Poole. Sydney: Intervention Publications.

Priebe, Richard O., and Thomas A. Hale, eds.

1979   *Artist and Audience: African Literature as a Shared Experience.* Washington, D.C.: Three Continents Press.

Qaraman, Su'ad

1990   "Shakhsiyat al-'adad" (Personality of the issue). *'Alam al-mar'a* (Woman's world), 1 December.

Radhakrishnan, R.

1992   "Nationalism, Gender, and Narrative." In *Nationalisms and Sexualities,* edited by Andrew Parker, Mary Russo, and Patricia Yaeger. New York: Routledge.

Reeves, Minou

  1989   *Female Warriors of Allah: Women and the Islamic Revolution*. New York: Dutton.

Remarque, Erich Maria

  1929   *All Quiet on the Western Front*. New York: Little, Brown.

Rose, Gillian

  1993   *Feminism and Geography: The Limits of Geographical Knowledge*. Minneapolis: University of Minnesoto Press.

Rosenberg, Stanley

  1993   "The Threshold of Thrill." In *Gendering War Talk*, edited by Miriam Cooke and Angela Woollacott. Princeton: Princeton University Press.

Rowe, John Carlos

  1988   "Bringing It All Back Home: American Recyclings of the Vietnam War." University of Wisconsin-Milwaukee Center for Twentieth-Century Studies, working paper no. 3, fall.

Ruddick, Sara

  1989   *Maternal Thinking: Towards a Politics of Peace*. Boston: Beacon.

Sabbagh, Suha

  1989   "Palestinian Women Writers and the Intifada." *Social Text* 22 (spring).

Sabbah, Fatna A.

  1984   *Woman in the Muslim Unconscious*. New York: Pergamon.

Sa'id, 'Ali Lufta

  1988   *Imra'a min al-nisa'* (A woman among women). Baghdad: Dar al-Shu'un al-Thaqafiya al-'Amma.

Said, Edward

  1989   "Intifada and Independence." In *Intifada: The Palestinian Uprising against Israeli Occupation,* edited by Zachary Lockman and Joel Beinin. Boston: South End Press.

———.

  1990   *Nationalism, Colonialism, and Literature*. Minneapolis: University of Minnesota Press.

———.

  1993   "Intellectual Exile: Expatriates and Marginals." Reith Lecture, *The Independent* (London), 8 July.

Salman, Nur

  1986   *Ila rajul lam ya'ti* (To a man who did not come). Beirut.

Salman, Suhayla

  1988   *Al-liqa'* (The meeting). Baghdad: Dar al-Shu'un al-Thaqafiya al-'Amma.

Samara, Nuha
    1990   "Two Faces One Woman." In *Opening the Gates: A Century of Arab Feminist Writing*, edited by Margot Badran and Miriam Cooke. London: Virago; and Bloomington: Indiana University Press.

al-Samman, Ghada
    1980   *Kawabis Bayrut* (Beirut nightmares). Beirut: Manshurat Ghada al-Samman.

Sasser, Charles W.
    1992   "Women in Combat? One Grunt's Opinion." *Soldier of Fortune,* March.

Sayeh, Mai
    1986   "Choosing the Revolution." In *Women of the Mediterranean,* edited by Monique Gadant. London: Zed Press.

Sayigh, Rosemary
    1987   "Palestinian Women: A History in Search of Historians." *Revue d'études palestiniennes.*

———.
    1988   "Palestinian Women: Triple Burden, Single Struggle." *Peuples méditerranéens.*

———.
    1992   "Palestinian Women: A Case of Neglect." In *Portraits of Palestinian Women,* edited by Orayb Aref Najjar. Salt Lake City: University of Utah Press.

Saywell, Shelley, ed.
    1985   *Women in War.* New York: Viking.

al-Sayyid, 'Abd al-Razzaq
    1980   *Harb Lubnan: Suwar watha'iq ahdath* (Lebanon's war: photographs, documents, events). 1977; reprint, Beirut: Dar al-Masira.

Sbouai, Taieb
    1985   *"La femme sauvage" de Kateb Yacine.* Paris: Arcantère.

Scarry, Elaine
    1985   *The Body in Pain: The Making and Unmaking of the World.* New York: Oxford University Press.

Schwartz, William, and Charles Derber
    1990   *The Nuclear Seduction: Why the Arms Race Doesn't Matter—and What Does.* Berkeley: University of California Press.

Schweik, Susan
    1991   *A Gulf So Deeply Cut: American Women Poets and the Second World War.* Madison: University of Wisconsin Press.

Sedgwick, Eve

1990   *Epistemology of the Closet.* Berkeley: University of California Press.

——.

1992   "Nationalisms and Sexualities in the Age of Wilde." In *Nationalisms and Sexualities,* edited by Andrew Parker, Mary Russo, and Patricia Yaeger. New York: Routledge.

Segal, Mady W., and David R. Segal

1983   "Social Change and the Participation of Women in the American Military." In *Research in Social Movements, Conflicts, and Change.* Vol. 5. Greenwich, Conn.: JAI Press.

Shaaban, Bouthaina

1988   *Both Right and Left Handed.* London: Women's Press.

al-Shahham, 'Abdallah

1988   "A Portrait of the Israeli Woman as the Beloved: The Woman-Soldier in the Poetry of Mahmud Darwish after the 1967 War." *British Society for Middle Eastern Studies Bulletin* 15, no. 1–2: 28–35.

al-Shaykh, Hanan

1986   *The Story of Zahra.* London: Quartet.

Shehadeh, Lamia Rustum

1993   "Sexual Conflict in Lebanon." Paper presented at conference, Conflict Resolution in the Middle East, Larnaka, Cyprus, July.

Showalter, Elaine

1985a   *The Female Malady: Women, Madness, and English Culture, 1830–1980.* New York: Penguin Books.

——.

1985b   *The New Feminist Criticism: Women, Literature, and Theory.* New York: Pantheon.

al-Shuwayli, Dawud Salman

1986   *Ababil* (Flocks). Baghdad: Dar-al Shu'un al-Thaqafiya al-'Amma.

Smith, Helen Zenna

1989   *Not So Quiet . . .* Edited by Jane Marcus. London: Virago.
[1930].

Smith, R. R. R.

1991   *Hellenistic Sculpture: A Handbook.* London: Thames and Hudson.

Snitow, Anne

1989   "A Gender Diary." In *Rocking the Ship of State: Toward a Feminist Peace Politics,* edited by Adrienne Harris and Ynestra King. Boulder: Westview Press.

Somekh, Sasson
    1989   "Cold, Tall Buildings: The Jewish Neighbor in the Works of Arab Authors." *Jerusalem Quarterly* 52 (fall).

Sontag, Susan
    1977   *On Photography.* New York: Farrar, Straus and Giroux.
    ———.
    1993   "Godot Comes to Sarajevo." *New York Review of Books,* 21 October.

Spivak, Gayatri Chakravorty
    1985   "Subaltern Studies: Deconstructing Historiography." In *Selected Subaltern Studies,* edited by Ranajit Guha. New York: Oxford University Press.

Springer, Claudia
    1985   "Military Propaganda: Defense Department Films from World War II and Vietnam." *Cultural Critique.*

Stam, Robert
    1992   "Mobilizing Fictions: The Gulf War, the Media, and the Recruitment of the Spectator." *Public Culture* 4, no. 2: 101–26.

Stanley, Sandra C., and Mady W. Segal
    1988   "Military Women in NATO: An Update." *Armed Forces and Society* 14, no. 4.

Stetkevych, Suzanne
    1992   *The Mute Immortals Speak: Pre-Islamic Poetry and the Poetics of Ritual.* Ithaca: Cornell University Press.

Stiehm, Judith
    1983   *Men's and Women's Wars.* Oxford: Pergamon.
    ———.
    1988   "The Effect of Myths about Military Women on the Waging of War." In *Women and the Military System,* edited by Eva Isaksson. New York: St. Martin's.
    ———.
    1989   *Arms and the Enlisted Woman.* Philadelphia: Temple University Press.

Stiglmayer, Alexandra, ed.
    1994   *Mass Rape: The War against Women in Bosnia-Herzegovina.* Omaha: University of Nebraska Press.

Stiles, Kristine
    1994   "Remembering Invisibility: Photography and the Formation of Community in the Nuclear Age." Manuscript.

Stork, Joe
    1989   "The Significance of Stones: Notes from the 7th Month." In *Intifada: The Palestinian Uprising against Israeli Occupa-*

tion, edited by Zachary Lockman and Joel Beinin. Boston: South End Press.

Swerdlow, Amy

1990   "Motherhood and the Subversion of the Military State: Women's Strike for Peace Confronts the House Committee on Un-American Activities." In *Women, Militarism, and War: Essays in History, Politics, and Social Theory*, edited by Jean Bethke Elshtain and Sheila Tobias. Savage, Md.: Rowman and Littlefield.

Tagg, John

1988   *The Burden of Representation: Essays on Photography and Histories*. Amherst: University of Massachussetts Press.

Takieddine-Amyouni, Mona

1993   "Style as Politics in the Poems and Novels of Rashid al-Daif." Paper presented to Middle East Studies Association, Durham, N.C.

Talib, 'Aliya

1988   *Al-mumirrat* (Corridors). Baghdad: Dar al-Shu'un al-Thaqafiya al-'Amma.

al-Talibani, Makram Rashid

1987   *Al-mawdi' 'al-turabi* (The dusty place). Baghdad: Dar al-Shu'un al-Thaqafiya al-'Amma.

Tamari, Salim

1989   "What the Uprising Means." In *Intifada: The Palestinian Uprising against Israeli Occupation*, edited by Zachary Lockman and Joel Beinin. Boston: South End Press.

Tawfeeq, Basem

1990   "Openness and Frankness Dominate Discussion on Women's Role." *Al-Fajr*, 24 December.

Tawil, Raymonda

1983   *My Home My Prison*. Translated by Peretz Kidron. Lon-
[1980]   don: Zed Press.

Taylor, Diana

1991   *Theatre of Crisis: Drama and Politics in Latin America*. Lexington: University Press of Kentucky.

Tessler, Mark

1982   "Arab Women's Emancipation in Israel." In *University Field Staff International Reports*, no. 21.

Theweleit, Klaus

1987–89   *Male Fantasies*. Vol. 1, translated by Stephen Conway; vol. 2, translated by Erica Caster and Chris Turner. Minneapolis: University of Minnesota Press.

———.
1993   "The Bomb's Womb." In *Gendering War Talk*, edited by
            Miriam Cooke and Angela Woollacott. Princeton: Prince-
            ton University Press.
Thomas, Dorothy Q., and Regan E. Ralph
1994   "Rape in War: Challenging the Tradition of Impunity."
            SAIS Review (winter–spring): 81–99.
Thompson, Mark
1994   *Forging War: the Media in Serbia, Croatia, and Bosnia-
            Herzegovina.* Article 19, International Centre against Cen-
            sorship.
Tremaine, Louis
1979   "The Implied Reader in Kateb Yacine's *Nedjma.*" In *Artist
            and Audience: African Literature as a Shared Experience,*
            edited by Richard O. Priebe and Thomas A. Hale. Wash-
            ington, D.C.
Tuqan, Fadwa
1990   *A Mountainous Journey: An Autobiography.* Translated by
[1985]   Olive Kenny. London: Women's Press. Originally published
            as *Rihla jabaliya rihla sa'ba: sira dhatiya* (Mountainous
            journey, difficult journey; 3d ed., Amman: Dar al-Shuruq li
            al-Nashr wa al-Tawzi', 1988).
Usher, Graham
1992   "Palestinian Women, the Intifada and the State of Inde-
            pendence: An Interview with Rita Giacaman." *Race and
            Class* 34, no. 3.
al-'Uthman, Layla
1994   *Al-hawajiz al-sawda'* (Black barricades). Kuwait: Matabi'
            al-Qabs al-Tijariya.
Valeriani, Richard
1991   "Covering the Gulf War: Talking Back to the Tube." *Co-
            lumbia Journalism Review,* March-April.
Veeser, H. Aram, ed.
1989   *The New Historicism.* New York: Routledge.
Virilio, Paul
1983   *Pure War.* New York: Semiotext.

———.

1989   *War and Cinema: The Logistics of Perception.* Translated
            by Patrick Camiller. New York: Verso.
Walzer, Michael
1974   "World War II: Why Was This War Different?" In *War and
            Moral Responsibility: A Philosophy and Public Affairs*

Reader, edited by Marshall Cohen, Thomas Nagel, and Thomas Scanlon. Princeton: Princeton University Press.

Wells, Donald A.

1967   *The War Myth.* New York: Pegasus.

White, Hayden

1992   "Writing in the Middle Voice." *Stanford Literature Review* 9, no. 2.

Wolf, Christa

1988   *Cassandra.* New York: Farrar, Strauss and Giroux.

Woodhull, Winifred

1993   *Transfigurations of the Maghreb: Feminism, Decolonization, and Literatures.* Minneapolis: University of Minnesota Press.

Woollacott, Angela

1994   *On Her Their Lives Depend: Munitions Workers in the Great War.* Berkeley: University of California Press.

Wyschogrod, Edith

1985   *Spirit in Ashes: Hegel, Heidegger, and Man-Made Mass Death.* New Haven: Yale University Press.

Yacine, Kateb

1959   *Le cercle de représailles.* Paris: Editions du Seuil.

———.

1966   *Le polygone étoilé.* Paris: Editions du Seuil.

———.

1991   *Nedjma.* Translated by Richard Howard. Charlottesville:
[1956]   University Press of Virginia. Originally published as *Nedjma* (Paris: Editions du Seuil).

Yared, Nazik

1986   *Al-sada al-makhnuq* (The stifled echo). Beirut: Nawfal.

Index

'Abd al-'Amir, Khudayyir, 237
'Abd al-Jabbar, 'Adil, 318n12
'Abd al-Majid, Muhammad, 239
'Abdallah, Ibtisam, 264, 320n22; *Matar aswad . . . matar ahmar* (Black rain . . . red rain), 265–66
Abdul Razzaq, Abdullah, 234–35; "Voices from Near and Far," 233, 234
abortion: Abortion Wars, 296; clinic shootings, 86; in Khalifa work, 209
absence, 287–88, 321n8
Abu Ghazaleh, Ilham, 178
Abu Ghazzala, Raja', *Al-mutarada* (the pursued), 316n38
Abu Khalid, Khalid, 177
Abu Samra, Akram, 173–74, 316n37
Accad, Evelyne, 320n3
L'Action, 123
Adhana, Amair, 34
Al-Adib, 182, 183
Adnan, Etel, 281
Aesopian language, 230, 242, 247, 262, 263
Afghanistan: children combatants, 108; rocket launchers, 97
African Americans, U.S., 96
aggression: and gender, 15, 35, 303n13. *See also* violence
Ahmad, Aijaz, 285, 321n6
Ahrar, Lebanese, 269
al-Akhyaliyya, Layla, 168

Algeria, 118–66, 307–10; Armée de Libération Nationale, 128; education, 120–21, 123–24, 150; Etoile Nord-Africaine (1930s), 130; FLN, 105–6, 121, 124; French burning rebels (1845), 90–91; French takeover (1830), 71, 90; Islamicists, 8, 83; Kahina (702 C.E.), 131, 308n9; War Story, 140, 142
Algerian Lesson (silence is the real crime), 8, 166, 174
Algerian men: and Algerian women, 7, 8, 111–23 passim, 127–40 passim, 155–64; feminization by colonizers, 110–12; *goumiers,* 159; women tougher than, 159; writing, 7–8, 122, 127, 129–40, 146, 157, 162–64, 308–9
Algerian Radio, 143, 146
Algerian war of independence (1954–62), 4, 119, 121–22, 129–66, 307–10; Arabs idealizing, 115; battle of Algiers (1957), 122; beginning/ending, 83; and feminization by colonizers, 110–12; and French schools, 120; just war, 10; men's writings, 7–8, 127, 129–40, 162–64, 308–9; Palestinians idealizing, 115; silence on women's roles in, 7–8, 119, 125, 126, 127, 146–66; violence sanctioned, 10, 42, 99, 119; women denounced, 146; women's participation, 105–6, 111–12, 121–22, 129, 146–47, 158–62, 308–9; women's writings, 7–8, 123–29, 140–66, 307–10

Algerian women, 118–66, 307–10; Algerian men and, 7, 8, 111–23 passim, 127–40 passim, 155–64; Algerian Radio and, 143, 146; combatants, 7, 105–6, 111–12, 121–22, 129, 146, 158–62, 308–9; denounced, 146; dress, 105–6, 111, 116, 119, 123, 137, 144, 146, 150, 307n3; and feminism, 7–8, 122–28 passim, 140–43, 148–49, 160–62; femmes sauvages, 132, 134, 309n10; *fitna,* 129; foreign, 126–27; French co-opting, 119–20, 307n3; French intellectuals and, 119–20, 122; French men understanding, 160; in lived reality, 307n1; mother role, 135; Mothers of Algiers, 36; as national symbols, 120, 121, 123, 130, 132, 307n3; and Palestinian women, 115–16, 165–66, 174, 177, 218–19; Personal Code, 142; political liberation, 119, 141–42, 161; postbellum, 7, 8, 115–16, 119, 122, 123, 131, 141, 146, 164–65, 218–19; reassessment by, 146–66; resistance history, 131, 151–61, 307n2; revolutionary heroines, 122, 128–29, 144; silence about war roles, 7–8, 106, 119, 125, 126, 127, 143, 146–66; tortured, 106, 116, 122, 129, 159; tougher than men fighters, 159; writing, 7–8, 10–11, 41, 122–29, 140–66, 307–10
Algiers: Algiers Pact (1964), 142; battle of (1957), 122; University of, 124
Aliens, 35, 36
allegories, national, 273–80
Al Sa'id, Shakir Hasan, *'Inda masharif khandaq al-istishhad* (Overlooking the martyring trench), 232
Amal, Lebanese, 269
Amazons, 5, 36
ambiguities: in Iraqi art, 232. *See also* binarism; dichotomies
ambulance drivers, women, 104
Americans. *See* United States
Amin, Qasim, 169
al-Amir, Daisy, 9, 221–23; *'Ala la'ihat al-intizar* (On the waiting list), 223; "Al-asatidha wa al-talamidh" (Teacher and pupils), 238–39; *Fi duwwamat al-hubb wa al-karahiya* (In the vortex of love and hate), 223; "Thaman bakhs" (A bargain), 223; *Wu'ud li al-bay'* (Promises for sale), 223
Amir, Mundhir, 311n10
Amran, Daniele, 161

'Amran, Layla Karim, "Sama' al-Faw min jadid" (The sky of Fao again), 241
Amrouche, Fadhma, 123; *My Life Story,* 120–21
Amrouche, Marguerite Taos, 161; *La rue des tambourins,* 123–24
Anderson, Benedict, 5, 284, 285, 320n2
androgyny, 280
al-'Ansari, Salah, 235, 249; "Two Walls," 254
'Antar (classic hero), 178
Anzaldúa, Gloria, 118, 206–7, 292
Appiah, Kwame Anthony, 70
Arabic language: Algerian, 122–23, 140, 152, 155, 309n12; dictionaries, 251; foreign words in, 312n12; teaching, 123; and women's silence, 152, 155
Arabic literature, 3; Algerian, 122–23, 140; early, 168–69, 183; Iraqi, 236, 237; Palestinian, 188, 193
Arab men: early writing, 169, 183; Tawil's condemnation, 193; writing about defeat of 1967, 192. *See also* Algerian men; Lebanese men; Palestinian men
Arab Revolt (1936), 172, 177
Arab wars, 4, 115–16; and resistance literature, 236; in Suez (1956), 1, 129. *See also* Algeria; Iraq; Lebanon; nationalism; Palestinians
Arab women, 14, 16; center stage, 169; early writings, 168–69, 183; feminist, 7–8; Iranian, 8, 35, 115, 178; Iraqi women's reputation among, 220; organizations, 171, 182, 191, 194; pan-Arab conference, 171; politico-literary history, 168; rape as weapon against, 37; Tuqan's writings on, 194; writing about war, 3–5, 192–95, 298–300. *See also* Algerian women; Iraqi women; Lebanese women writing about war; Palestinian women
Arab Women's Congress of Palestine (1929), 171
Arab Women's Union, 171, 182, 191
Arafat, Yasser, 21, 79
architecture: Iraqi war monument, 9, 70, 73, 232–33; postmodern, 114–15
Arendt, Hannah, 85, 95, 96–98
Argentina, mother warriors, 36, 107, 306n18
Armée de Libération Nationale, 128
art: military leaders enlisting, 9, 71, 73, 115, 223–25, 232–48, 262–64; as political tool, 208. *See also* films; literature; photography; writing

al-Ashqar, Habshi, 150
Ashrawi, Hanan Mikhail, 178
Atwan, Terry, 311n5
Augustin, Ebba, 179
Aurbakken, Kristine, 133–34
authority: men over women, 146; television, 73–74; war literature, 3, 5, 41. *See also* legitimacy; power
autobiography: Djebar, 151–59; early Arab women's, 168–69; Tuqan, 195
'Awad, Walid, 129
Ayyub, Muhammad, 314n23
al-'Aziz, Balqis Ni'mat, "Swing of Fire," 234
'Azzam, Samira, 169, 311n9

Baathists, Iraqi, 9, 220–21, 231, 240, 317n1
Bab al-Saha (Khalifa), 197–98, 211–16
Badaw, Yahia, 177
Barakat, Huda, 9–10, 273–80, 281–82, 289–90; *Ahl al-hawa* (People of passion), 279–80; *Hajar al-dahak* (The laughing stone), 273–79, 283, 287
Barghuthi, Widad, 177
Barthes, Roland, 236; *Writing Degree Zero*, 219
al-Baytjalli, Iskandir Khuri, 312n12
BDM International, 73
beginnings, vs. endings, 6, 82–84
Beirut: bus shootings of Palestinians, 20; hotels battle, 266; Mathaf traffic circle, 21
Beirut Decentrists, 161, 217–18, 280–81
Ben Bella, Ahmed, 141–42
Ben Bouali, Hassiba, 122, 307n3
Bengalis: Pakistani rapes against, 37; self-rule struggle, 89
Benjamin, Walter, 26–27, 291, 304n3
Ben Slama, Raja, 168
Benson, Frederick R., 29
Berbers: Kahina, 131; language, 152, 155; Pelissier massacre, 157
Berg, Rick, 92
Berkman, Joyce, 30
binarism, 7, 9, 15, 254–64, 294, 296; blurring of, 15, 42–43, 68, 296; and gender, 14–15, 22–23; and Intifada reinscription, 212; War Story, 6–7, 14–23 passim, 31–32, 39–42 passim, 68, 69, 80–81. *See also* dichotomies
Bird, Thomas, "Man and Boy Confront the Images of War," 72
birthing, nationalist, 274–76, 289

Bittari, Zoubeida, *O mes soeurs musulmanes, pleurez!*, 140–41
Black Panther Militia, Milwaukee, 96
Bloch, Alexandre, 39
Block, Robert, 76
Boban, Mate, 76
bodies: injuries as signs, 90–91; in Khalifa work, 206, 209, 217–18; in Lebanese women's writings, 289; in Salman work, 243–44; sexed, 14; unveiled, 105; and voice, 152, 153, 154–55. *See also* torture
Bogside Marches (1969), 305n11
Bonaventure Hotel, Los Angeles, 114–15
Bosnia, 297; genocide, 91–92; media, 74–77; rape as weapon, 37; reporters targeted, 72; violent women, 35; women tortured, 106; women writing about war, 41. *See also* Croatia; Serbs
Boudjedra, Rachid, *La répudiation*, 163
Boumedienne, Houari, 115, 142
Boupacha, Jamila, 122, 144
boys: fathers killing, 317n2; in French schools in Algeria, 120; gang, 305n13; guerrilla group, 306n21; with submachine guns, 97. *See also* children
Brando, Marlon, 29
Brenkman, John, 310n1
British: Arab Revolt against (1936), 172, 177; and Ireland, 89, 96, 305n11; and Palestine (1940s), 8, 161; and South Asia, 89; Suez Canal attack, 129; writers after World War I, 164
Brokaw, Tom, 304n5
Brown, Kristin, 178
Broyles, William, Jr., 101
al-Buhaysh, Raja', "Tales of Iraqi Suns," 235
Buhrayd, Jamila, 122, 129, 144, 174, 307n3
Bunster-Burotto, Ximena, 106–7
Burma, rapes by military, 37
Bush, George, 79, 83, 84, 86

Cable News Network (CNN), Gulf War, 69, 74, 305n12
Cadi-Mostefai, Meriem, 308n5
Campbell, D'Ann, 34, 161, 302–3
Camus, Albert, 130
Capa, Robert, 27
Cassandra, Arab, 205
categorization: and instability, 69; of wars, 6, 82, 88. *See also* dichotomies
cedar tree, in Lebanese war album, 19–20

censorship: Aesopian language and, 230, 262; Israeli, 196, 313n20; and propaganda, 229–30, 262–63; Tuqan's work, 196. *See also* silence

Central America: jungle guerrilla warfare, 87; torture of women, 106; warships off coast, 86. *See also* El Salvador

Cerovic, Stanko, 76

chaos: creative, 110; in women's war stories, 16

Chapkis, Wendy, 249, 252

Chechnya, mothers, 36

chemical weapons, Iraqi, 247

children: combatants, 36, 78, 82, 97, 108–10, 112–13, 306; Iraqi, 110, 317nn2,3; victims, 38, 306n20; in war-torn countries/inner city, 88. *See also* boys; girls

"Child Warriors" (*Time*), 88, 108, 306n20

Chile, mother warriors, 107

Chinese women, Japanese rapes against, 37

Chinkin, Christine, 303n11

Chomsky, Noam, "Visions of Righteousness," 92

citizenship: in democracies, 30, 310n1; Lebanese, 275, 281, 289; masculinization for, 275; and nationalism, 268, 275, 281, 289, 290; and ruler/ruled binary, 80; and war readiness, 31; and women in military, 30, 31, 34–35

civilians: combatant, 38, 41, 70, 81, 85, 87, 100–110, 116, 252–54, 306; vs. combatants, 6, 19, 32, 42, 70, 80, 81, 88, 100, 116, 296; international military law regarding, 32; military counterparts, 33–34; raped, 38; targeted, 38, 72, 100–102, 106–7, 305n15

Clark, Michael, 73, 92–93

Clausewitz, Carl von, 31, 84, 102

Cohen, Roger, 76–77

Cohn, Carol, 14–15, 292

Cold War, 30, 38, 88

collaborators: with Israeli occupation, 205, 313n21, 314n27, 315n33; with silencers, 263

colonialism: anticolonial vs. postcolonial nationalism, 10–12; in Asia and Africa (general), 80, 94, 99, 119; double critique, 134, 170, 192; French in Algeria, 119–21, 123, 132–33, 134, 151–61; in Lebanon, 269; masculinity of, 110–11; Palestinian renewed, 8, 169; postmodern break with, 70–71; sex segregation,

320n3. *See also* imperialism; postcolonialism

combatants: children, 36, 78, 82, 97, 108–10, 112–13, 306; civilian, 38, 41, 70, 81, 85, 87, 100–110, 116, 252–54, 306; vs. civilians, 6, 19, 32, 42, 70, 80, 81, 88, 100, 116, 296; peacekeeping operations and, 103; raped women as, 38. *See also* front; military

committees: Palestinian, 172, 174–75. *See also* organizations, women's

Communists, Arab, 181, 312n15

community: imagined, 5, 217–18, 268, 271; individuals creating, 95; of oppositional writers, 5; of women, 149; women's responsibilities to, 218. *See also* nation

computer simulations: of war, 73, 113–15. *See also* game models

conflict resolution: without organized and lethal violence, 4, 11–12, 35, 41, 217, 299. *See also* war

Conrad, Joseph, 29

control: of Algerian women, 129, 134, 135, 136, 137, 146, 150; anonymous/"rule by Nobody," 96; denial of loss of, 248–49; of media images, 78; and men's fear of dissolution in the feminine, 131–32, 137; and peace/war ambiguity, 39; by photographer, 24–25, 27; wars fought for, 91–92. *See also* power

Coppola, Francis, *Apocalypse Now*, 29, 78, 81–82

Corradi, Juan, 97, 110

Crane, Stephen, *Red Badge of Courage*, 3

creativity, of chaos, 110

crimes: binarism sanctioning, 42; against humanity, 38, 75; media, 75; of silence, 8, 118–66, 298–99; terminology for, 42–43; war, 38, 42–43, 75, 303n11. *See also* killing; violence

criticism: of Iraq, 226–27, 248, 317n2, 319–20; in Israeli Occupied Territories, 197; literary, 3, 235–40, 263; and nationalism, 170; of representation of war and writer, 248; of war, 226–27, 248, 317n2. *See also* double critique

Croatia: violent women, 35; war albums, 17, 25

Cultural Critique, 92

Dahbur, Ahmad, "You," 311n5

al-Daif, Rashid, 268–69, 321n8

Dar al-Mu'allimat, 182

Darwish, Mahmud, 177, 191, 312–13

Dawud, Siham, 311n10
death: anxiety/fear/fright reactions, 248–
49; celebration of death in battle, 243;
denial of, 87, 248–49, 318–19; and desire, 248–61; experience of, 305n14;
flashbacks, 249–50; "man-made mass
death," 88; nationalism and, 275–77;
nucleocide, 88. *See also* killing
de Beauvoir, Simone, 119; *Djamila
Boupacha,* 122
Débèche, Djamila, 7, 161; *Aziza,* 123
Deer Hunter, 93
defeat, vs. victory, 7, 80, 89–94
de Klerk, Frederik Willem, 110
Delacroix, Eugène, 160
Delbrueck, Hans, 31
Deleuze, Gilles, 154, 175–77
democracy, 299; citizenship, 30, 310n1;
defined, 167; and equal access to national service, 30; language and, 167–
68, 310n1; in military, 31; Palestinian,
174, 179; talking, 167–219; writing
central to, 219
denial, of death, 87, 248–49, 318–19
Derber, Charles, 88
Der Derian, James, 73, 293
Derrida, Jacques, 71
desire: and death, 248–61. *See also* sexuality
Desparmet, J., "L'Oeuvre de la France
en Algérie jugée par les indigènes,"
111
Details magazine, 88
deterritorialization, 154, 176
Dib, Mohamed, 8, 112, 129, 132, 250; *La
grande maison,* 134; *L'incendie,* 134;
Le métier à tisser, 134; *Qui se souvient
de la mer* (Who remembers the sea),
112, 134–37
dichotomies, 6–7, 14–23 passim, 69, 80,
296; beginnings/endings, 6, 82–84;
breaking up, 6–7, 15, 42–43, 68, 82–
117, 296; civilian/combatant, 6, 19, 32,
42, 70, 80, 81, 88, 100–110, 116, 296;
home/front, 7, 14, 23, 80, 88, 113–14,
246, 296; homosexual/heterosexual, 69;
private/public, 69, 304n18; ruler/ruled,
80; victory/defeat, 7, 80, 89–94; those
who could and could not write, 169;
war/peace, 19, 21, 39, 80, 82–89,
304n18; women's space and men's
space, 7, 19, 22–23, 80, 113, 116. *See
also* binarism
Al-Diyar, 97
Djabali, Leila, 161

Djebar, Assia, 7, 124–28, 151–61,
308n8, 310; *Les alouettes naïves,* 126,
143–45, 146, 151, 161, 163–64; on
artists brought by French forces, 71;
Les enfants du nouveau monde, 126–
28, 144, 159; *Fantasia,* 119, 151–59,
310n15; "Femmes d'Alger dans leur
appartement," 145; *Femmes d'Alger
dans leur appartement,* 151; "Il n'y
a pas d'exil," 125; *Les impatients,*
124–25; "Les morts parlent," 151;
El-Moudjahid articles, 146, 308n5;
Ombre sultane, 150–51; *Rouge l'aube,*
146; on silence, 150–59; *La soif,* 124;
Vaste est la prison, 310n15; on victory,
90, 94
Donadey, Anne, 310n16
Doolittle Report (1954), 101
Dos Passos, John, 236
double critique, 134, 170, 192
dress: Algerian women, 105–6, 111, 116,
119, 123, 137, 144, 146, 150, 307n3.
See also veils
Drif, Zohra, 106, 122; "La mort de mes
frères," 128–29
al-Dulaymi, Lutfiya, 9, 235, 245–48, 253–
61; *Budhur al-nar* (Seeds of fire), 245–
48, 253–61; "Dinner for Two," 235;
"Fi al-ghasaq 'adat 'arus al-bahr" (At
dawn the mermaid returned), 245; "Returning from Abroad," 245
During, Simon, 81–82
Dyson, Freeman, 2, 39

Eagleton, Terry, 272
Eastern Europe, postcolonial, 70–71, 94
Edgerton, Clyde, 252, 319n17
education, women's, 150, 191; Algerian,
120–21, 123–24, 150, 307n4; Iraqi,
221; Palestinian, 182, 191, 313n18
Ehrhart, W. D., "Guerrilla War," 101–2
elegies: early Arab women's, 168; Salman,
285–86; Tuqan, 195–96
Eliot, T. S., 164
El Salvador: civil war, 74; FMLN's children combatants, 108; mother warriors,
107
Elshtain, Jean Bethke, 35, 161, 271,
304n18
endings, vs. beginnings, 6, 82–84
Enloe, Cynthia, 113
equal opportunity, sexual, 174–75; military, 30, 31, 35, 108, 303n10, 313n18.
See also democracy; feminism
Eritrean People's Liberation Front, 34

Eritrean women: military and civilian roles, 34; writing about war, 41

Eros: and Thanatos, 248–61. See also sexuality

ethnicity, 75, 88, 95, 270. See also genocide; race

experience: and death event, 305n14; war, 3–4, 5, 30, 41, 90, 105–6, 161–62. See also civilians; combatants; reality

families: Iraqi state support for, 220–21; military as, 33; nationalist groups displacing, 274–78; as protectees, 33, 38. See also children; fathers; men; mothers; women

Fanon, Frantz, 119, 167; on Algerian women, 105, 111–12, 122, 161; on violence, 42, 99

Fao Island liberation, literature, 237, 240–41, 245, 261

Farah, Najwa Qa'war, 169, 181–91, 192, 200–201, 216–17, 313n21; 'Abiru al-sabil (Passersby), 181–83; "Baha," 187; "Bitterer Choice," 189–90; "Café Wise Man," 190, 312n11; "Call of Damascus and the Pomegranates' Censure," 190; "Call of the Ruins," 188–89; Durub wa masabih (Paths and lanterns), 182–83, 184; "Granny's Things," 190; "Hired Hand on His Own Land," 189; "Inspiration from the Holy War," 183; Intifadat al-'asafir (The intifada of the birds), 182, 313n21; "Layla and the Fragrance of Oranges," 186–87; Li man al-rabi'? (For whom is the spring?), 182; "Mandelbaum Gate," 190–91; "Memoir of an Ex-convict," 313n21; "Newspaper Vendor," 184; "Regret," 312n12; Rihlat al-huzn wa al-i'ta' (The journey of sadness and giving), 182; "Story of a Generation," 184–85; "Stumbling Block," 187–88; "Two Beggars," 184; "When Nairuz Returns," 185–86; "Which of the Two Paths?," 183–84

Farmanfarmaian, Abouali, 319n18

fathers: Algerian, 122, 151, 155, 310n15; Exaggerated Oedipus, 175–76; Freikorps, 321n7; Intifada Legends and, 173; killing sons, 317n2; and new face of military, 33; Tuqan's, 195. See also patriarchy

Fatima, Prophet's daughter, 115

Fawwaz, Zaynab, 169

femininity/feminization: of colonized Algerians, 110–12; in War Story, 24–25, 80; and women civilian-combatants, 103–4; and women in military, 111, 295; of women writing about war, 11. See also masculinity/masculinization

feminism, 3, 7–8, 43, 292; Algerian women and, 7–8, 122–28 passim, 140–43, 148–49, 160–62; early Arab women's writings and, 169; and fiction woman, 314n29; Montreal massacre, 86–87; vs. nationalism, 272; pacifist, 30, 35, 36; Palestinian women and, 8–9, 170–75 passim, 183, 191–97 passim, 202–4, 218–19, 313; war of sexes, 86; war viewed by, 38; and women in military, 30–31, 34–35, 36, 161, 313n18; Zionist settlements, 271

Ferenczi, Sandor, 135

Ferocious Few, 35–36, 271

feudalism, Lebanese identities and, 269

fiction: and autobiography in enemy's language, 252–53; injuries and, 90; and propaganda, 247–48; and reality, 90, 241, 315n33; war story, 92; woman as, 314n29. See also literature

films, 6, 73, 82, 304–5; Aliens, 35, 36; Apocalypse Now, 29, 78, 81–82; "cine-commando units," 72; Eros-Thanatos in war, 249; Full Metal Jacket, 103–4; Hollywood, 72, 304n4; impression of being there, 27–28; military propaganda, 72, 304n4; models for war, 76; mother warriors in, 36; new narrative frame, 29–30; organization of, 26–27; Serb rapes, 91; Star Wars, 36; Terminator 2, 36; Top Gun, 76, 249; after Vietnam War, 29, 78, 81–82, 93, 103–4; before Vietnam War (war movies), 68, 72; violent women in, 35. See also photography; television

Fiore, Quentin, 81, 106

Foucault, Michel, 85, 236

Foulkes, A. Peter, 229–30, 246

Fralin, Frances Lindley, 305n10

France: Algerian takeover (1830), 71, 90; Algerian views postbellum, 141; Arab League women's conference, 306n19; Berber massacre (1830s), 157; burning Algerian rebels (1845), 90–91; colonialism in Algeria, 119–21, 123, 132–33, 134, 151–61; co-opting Algerian women, 119–20, 128, 307n3; French men writing about Algeria, 129–30, 156–58, 160; Moroccan and Tunisian independence (1956), 129; schools in Algeria, 120–21; Suez Canal attack,

129. *See also* Algerian war of independence; French language

Franco, Jean, 107

French language, 120–21, 122–23, 152–56

Freud, Sigmund, 248, 251; *Interpretation of Dreams*, 134–35; *Medusa's Head*, 136

Friedrich, Otto, 230

front, 14, 110, 112, 115; vs. home, 7, 14, 23, 80, 88, 113–14, 246, 296; Iraqi, 246, 318n13. *See also* men's space

Front de Libération Nationale (FLN), 105–6, 121, 124

Front Islamique de Salut, Algeria, 8

game models: for war, 69, 73. *See also* computer simulations

gangs, inner-city, 86, 87, 305n13

Gaza. *See* Israeli Occupied Territories

Gellhorn, Martha, 304–5

Gellner, Ernest, 270, 271, 273, 321n5

gender, 14–15; and aggression, 15, 35, 303n13; death and desire, 254–61; as dominant paradigm, 13–16; and War Story, 6, 7, 15–23 passim, 30–40, 80. *See also* boys; femininity/feminization; girls; masculinity/masculinization; men; sex segregation; sexuality; women

Gendering War Talk (Cooke & Woollacott), 251–52

General Federation of Iraqi Women (GFIW), 220–21, 317n1

General Union of Arab Women, 194

General Union of Palestinian Women, 172, 197

Genet, Jean, 79, 310n3

Geneva Convention, 32, 297, 303n11

genocide: Bosnia, 91–92, 106; control by, 91–92; Hague International Tribunal and, 75; intervention and, 297; Nazi, 38

Germany: Freikorps, 224, 250, 275, 321n7; Nazis, 37, 38; women raped by Soviets, 37

Ghossoub, Mai, 320n1

Giacaman, Rita, 174–75, 178–79; on women's committees, 167, 174–75; and women's traditional roles, 218, 311n7, 316n40

Giddens, Anthony, 271

Gilbert, Sandra, 164

Gilbert, W. S., 164

girls: in French schools in Algeria, 120–21; gang, 305n13; guerrilla group,

306n21; in Vietnam War, 103–4, 306n21. *See also* children

Glenny, Misha, 75

Glucksmann, André, 74

Goldstone, Richard, 75

governments: media used by, 9, 75; Palestinian committees in absence of, 175; positive terms for war, 89; rape sanctioned as weapon, 37; War Story, 28–29; without peace/war ambiguity, 39; and women and families in military, 34–35. *See also* Iraq; military; propaganda; state

Gray, J. Glenn: on Eros and Thanatos, 248, 250; on *homo furens*, 15; on killing, 42; on lust of the eye, 301–2; on men nurturing and loving each other, 39; on peace, 302n9; on sex segregation, 14

Green, Mary Jean, 157

Greki, Anna, 161

groups: Algerian warriors, 128–29; family displaced by, 274–78; Lebanese, 95–96, 99, 269, 274–78, 281; powerful, 94–100, 274. *See also* identities

Guattari, Félix, 154, 175–77

Gubar, Susan, 164

Guendouz, Nadia, 161, 164–65

guerrilla warfare: Algerian women's adaptation to, 122; Central America, 87, 108; children in, 108, 306n21; and civilian/combatant distinction, 101–2

Gulf War, 30, 37, 82, 264–66, 293–94; beginning/ending, 83–84; distance from target, 319n15; Gulf War Syndrome, 85; international military lawyers, 32; Iraq invasion of Kuwait, 73, 83, 264–65, 297; Iraqi rapes against Kuwaitis and Palestinians, 37; line-in-the-sand front, 69; media, 69, 74, 79, 83, 93–94, 305n12; and new face of military, 33; Operation Desert Cheer, 319n18; outcome, 93–94; veterans in Somalia, 103; War Story, 80–81, 84; weapons, 69, 79, 85, 319n16; women in combat duty, 33, 103; women writing about, 264–66

Habibi, Emile, 172–73, 181, 309n11; "Mandelbaum Gate," 190–91; *Secret Life of Saeed*, 175–77

Habibi, Sami, 183

Haddad, Malek, 8, 127, 129, 137–40, 162, 309n12; *L'élève et la leçon*, 137, 138–39; *Je t'offrirai une gazelle*,

Haddad, Malek (*continued*)
137, 138; *Le quai aux fleurs ne répond plus*, 137, 139–40
Hague International Tribunal, 38, 75, 305n15
Haj, Samira, 213
Hajim, Faysal 'Abd al-Hasan, 226–29, 240, 255, 318n5; "'Asha' akhar" (A last supper), 227–28; "Dhubul" (Withering), 228; *Junud* (Soldiers), 227–29; *Al-layl wa al-nahar* (Night and day), 226–27; "Ma'an wa ila al-abad" (Together forever), 229; "Risala mu'ada" (A returned letter), 229
Halimi, Giselle, 119; *Djamila Boupacha*, 122
Hall, John, 270
Hammudi, Basim 'Abd al-Hamid, 224–25, 235, 236, 237–38, 318n9; *Al-naqid wa qissat al-harb* (The critic and the war story), 239
Harb Lubnan (Lebanon's war) photo album, 17–28
Harford, Gustav, *The Short Timers*, 104
Harvey, David, 14
Havel, Vaclav, 271
Hayslip, Le Ly, 103
Hebrew language, 193
Hélie-Lucas, Marie-Aimée, 118, 160–61
Hemingway, Ernest, 164, 236
heroines: Algerian, 122, 128–29, 144; Arab historical, 115, 178
heroism: heroic killing, 42; in Iraqi war literature, 234, 237–38, 241; Palestinian, 178; repudiated, 128, 241
Herr, Michael, 68; *Dispatches*, 115, 240–41
Hijab, Nadia, 172
Hiroshima, 38, 88, 266
historians, military, 15, 28–29, 31, 81, 115
history: Iraqi, 231; multiple stories, 4; Saddam Hussein, 230–31. *See also* postcolonialism; War Story
Hitler, Adolf, 247
Hizbollah, Lebanese, 269
Hobsbawm, Eric, 267
Hollywood, 72, 304n4
home, 14, 203–4; vs. front, 7, 14, 23, 80, 88, 113–14, 246, 296; Iraqi, 246, 318n13. *See also* women's space
homoerotics: in *Harb Lubnan*, 19; and men in military, 19, 32, 39–40; Stonewall rebellion, 69, 304n1
honor: Palestinian men's, 212, 213; *sharaf/'ird*, 212

Hrawi, Muna, 306n19
humanist nationalism, 10, 272–80, 290
humanitarianism: and equal opportunity in military, 31; in Iraqi war literature, 234, 241; in Palestinian writing about Israelis, 312–13
Human Rights Watch, 37
al-Hurani, Fathiya 'Awad, 173–74
Husayn, Rashid, 177
Hussein, King of Jordan, 109–10
Hussein, Saddam, 263–64; artists enlisted by, 9, 71, 73, 223–25, 232; claims to lineage, 230–31; compassion extolled, 234; Gulf War, 73, 83–84, 94, 265; *Hawla kitabat al-tarikh* (On the writing of history), 231; *hijarat ababil* missile, 319n16; Iraq-Iran War, 73, 115, 222, 223–24; Iraqi women and, 221

Ibn Khaldun, 183, 313n16
Ibrahim, 'Abdallah, 227, 235–37, 318nn6,13
Ibrahim, Hana, 181, 313n19
Ibrahim, Khalida Khadar, "Tears of Joy," 233–34
identities: certainties of space and, 7; national, 268–90; politics based on, 23, 99–100; postcolonial, 270; religious, 23; of women writers, 299. *See also* civilians; combatants; gender; groups; nationalism; race
imagined community, 5, 217–18, 268, 271
imperialism: cultural, 3; European, 70; neo-, 82. *See also* colonialism
incest, 132, 133
independence: Arab countries, 169; Asian and African wars of, 80; Moroccan and Tunisian (1956), 129. *See also* Algerian war of independence; nationalism; postcolonialism; resistance
individuals: Algerian warriors, 128–29; and nationalism, 272–73; violent, 94–100. *See also* civilians; combatants; gender
Ingrams, Doreen, 317n1
injuries: as signs, 90–91. *See also* torture
insecticide in war, 246–47
intellectuals: and Algerian women, 119–20, 122; Iraqi, 240; Mechakra vs., 147; Palestinian women, 191. *See also* writing
International Tribunal, Hague, 38, 75, 305n15

Intifada (1987–93), 4, 78–79, 195–216, 311; children combatants, 36, 78, 82, 108–10, 112–13; civilian combatants (general), 112–13; committees, 175; Irish, 305n11; men's roles, 173, 175, 197–99, 211–12, 218; men writing about, 177; poetry and songs during, 178; women beginning (1967–87 phase), 82–83, 165–66, 173, 212; women jailed and martyred, 173–74, 175, 311n5; women's organizations, 172; women's resistance tactics, 9, 12, 36, 78, 82, 107–9, 113, 173–74, 197–201, 211–12, 218–19; women writers anticipating, 196, 202; women writing about, 8–9, 109, 113, 161, 179, 195–216, 218, 315n33

Iran: children combatants, 97; silent women, 8; violent women, 35; women in military, 115, 178. *See also* Iraq-Iran War

Iraq, 10, 220–66; Baathists, 9, 220–21, 231, 240, 317n1; children combatants, 110, 979; criticism of, 226–27, 248, 317n2, 319–20; history rewritten, 231; identity politics, 99; Israeli attack, 83–84; Ministry of Culture and Information, 223, 231, 232, 266; mother warriors, 107; postcolonial, 70–71; *taba'iyya iraniyya* (out), 99; *taba'iyya 'uthmaniyya* (in), 99; war monuments, 9, 70, 73, 232–33; War Story, 73, 236, 239, 241, 243, 318n13. *See also* Gulf War; Hussein, Saddam; Iraq-Iran War; Iraqi women

Iraqi National Congress (INC), 319–20

Iraq-Iran War (1980–88), 4, 9, 73, 220–66, 317–20; artists/writers enlisted for, 9, 71, 73, 223–25, 232–48, 262–64; casualties, 222; compassion of Iraqis for Iranis, 233–34; criticism of, 225–26, 227, 248, 317n2; game model, 73; Iraqi men writing about, 9, 99, 222–43 passim, 248–51, 317n2; Iraqi women writing about, 9, 222, 224, 233–48 passim, 254–55, 317–20; propaganda, 9, 223–25, 229–30, 246–48, 262–64; Qadisiya name, 115, 223–24; violence in, 99; warrior character, 236–37, 318

Iraqi women: freedoms curtailed, 221; General Federation of, 220–21, 317n1; importance recognized, 220–21; in military, 252; patriotic symbols, 234–35; writing about war, 9, 10, 11, 41, 221–

23, 233–48 passim, 254–55, 264–66, 317–20

Ireland, Northern, 89, 96, 305n11

Islam, Algerian, 8, 83, 142

Israel, 89; censorship, 196, 313n20; colonialist role, 8, 169; establishment of (1948), 1, 169, 172, 180–81; Farah leaving, 190–91; Ferocious Few, 271; green line, 169, 173; Gulf War, 74; Iraq attacked by, 83–84; Lebanon invasion (1969), 1; Lebanon invasion (1982), 1, 9–10, 73–74, 267, 281; Palestinian depiction of Jews in, 185–86, 188, 190–91, 197, 312–13; peace process, 11–12, 89; Six-Day War (1967), 1, 10, 170, 177, 191–95. *See also* Intifada; Israeli Occupied Territories

Israeli Occupied Territories, 173, 313–14; age of population, 110; collaborators, 205, 313n21, 314n27, 315n33; combatant-civilian, 112–13; media, 70, 78–79, 174; torture, 91, 106; violent women, 35; women speaking out, 165. *See also* Intifada; Palestinians

'Izz al-Din, Ahmad Jalal, 83

Jabra, Jabra Ibrahim, 236, 249

James, David, 77

Jameson, Fredric, 81, 114–15, 273

Japanese: rapes against Chinese and Koreans, 37; war crimes, 38

Jarjura, Nadim Tawfiq, 315n33

Jauhar, Halima, 8–9

Jeffords, Susan, 85–86, 103–4

Jencks, Christopher, 70

Jews: Nazi rapes of, 37; Palestinian depiction of Israeli, 185–86, 188, 190–91, 312–13; women fighting British, 161. *See also* Israel

Johnson, Penny, 218

Jones, Kathleen, 30

Joseph, Suad, 220–21

Jovicic, Zoran, *War Crimes Committed by the Yugoslav Army 1991–1992*, 17

Jumblat, Kamal, 20–21

"Just War—Gulf War" conference, Vanderbilt, 33

just wars, 10, 21, 30

Kafka, Franz, 154

Kahina (702 C.E.), 131, 308n9

Kamil, 'Adil, "Symbol," 234

Kanaana, Sharif, 173

Kanafani, Ghassan, *Al-rijal fi al-shams* (Men in the sun), 201

Kataib, Lebanese, 269
Keegan, John, 15, 28, 31, 32
Kervin, Denise, 74
Khalifa, Sahar, 8–9, 170, 179–80, 191–
   219 passim, 314–15; '*Abbad al-shams*
   (Sunflower), 109, 180, 196, 202–5, 212,
   214, 306n22, 314nn24,28, 319n19;
   Bab al-Saha, 197–98, 211–16, 315n33;
   on flag burning, 316n39; *Mudhakkirat
   imra'a ghayr waqi'iya* (Memoirs of an
   unrealistic woman), 205–11, 212, 217,
   259, 314n28; "Our Fate, Our House,"
   216; publishing problems, 313–14; *Wild
   Thorns*, 78–79, 91, 197, 198–201, 202,
   211, 313–14; women's organizations,
   175
al-Khalil, Samir, 99, 230–31, 240; pseudonym, 317n2; *Republic of Fear*, 222
al-Khansa' bint Tumadir, 168, 175
Khatibi, Abdelkabir, 134, 170
Khayyun, 'Ali, 224–25; "Mourning Is Inappropriate for Martyrs," 239; "Time
   Has Three States," 234
Khomeini, Ayatollah, 35, 222
Khulusi, Natiq, "Al-diya' al-awwal li al-
   fajr" (The first light of dawn), 240–41
Khusbak, Shakir, "Years of Terrorism,"
   225
killing: fathers killing sons, 317n2; genocide, 38, 75, 91–92, 106, 297; heroic,
   42; Montreal feminists massacred, 86–
   87; nucleocide, 88; suicide, 143; terminology, 42–43. *See also* death; war
Kinney, Judy Lee, 93
Korean women, Japanese rapes against,
   37
Kuberski, Philip Francis, 81
Kubrick, Stanley, *Full Metal Jacket*, 103–4
Kurds: Iraqi purge, 233, 247; Iraqi rapes,
   37; nationalism, 270
Kuwait: Iraqi invasion, 73, 83, 264–65,
   297; Iraqi rapes, 37; women writing
   about Gulf War, 264

land: deterritorialization, 154, 176; Lebanese loyalty to, 281–84
languages: Aesopian, 230, 242, 247, 262,
   263; of body, 152; in democracies,
   167–68, 310n1; four Algerian women's,
   152; French, 120–21, 122–23, 152–56;
   Hebrew, 193; Lybico-Berber, 152, 155;
   nationalist claims associated with, 270.
   See also Arabic language; writing
Latin America: identity politics, 99–100;
   mother warriors, 36, 107, 306n18; terrorism, 110; women tortured, 106–7.
   See also Central America; Peru
lawyers, international military, 32
Lazreg, Marnia, 105–6, 111, 119–20,
   307nn1,3, 308n7
Lebanese civil war (1975–92), 16; all
   fighters corrupt, 278–79; al-Amir, 221–
   22, 223; Arab League women's conference (1987), 306n19; children combatants, 110; civilians as combatants,
   108, 110, 112, 252–53; groups, 95–96,
   99, 269, 274–78, 281; after Israeli invasion (1982), 9–10, 281–90; and nationalism, 268–90; postmodern war, 70;
   reporters taken hostage, 72; "the situation" / *les événements* / *al-hawadith*, 83,
   89; sniper, 24; television, 73–74, 79;
   "two-year war," 83; and uncertainties
   about war, 10; and U.S. inner-city violence, 87, 88, 108; war albums, 17–28,
   77; War Story, 16–28; women writing
   about, 3, 16, 161, 208, 217, 266, 273–
   90, 318n10
Lebanese men: emigrating, 269, 285; writing about war, 16
Lebanese women writing about war, 3, 4,
   9–10, 11, 189–90, 273–90; and Algerian women postbellum, 116; art as political tool, 208; Beirut Decentrists, 161,
   217–18, 280–81; *billet* prose poem,
   318n10; discursive activism only, 218–
   19; hotels battles, 266; and nationalism,
   10, 269–70, 272–90; vs. War Story, 10,
   16, 27, 41, 217
Lebanon, 1, 82, 267–90, 320–21; emigration from, 269, 284, 285; *ghuraba'* (foreigners), 99; Institute for Women's
   Studies in the Arab World, 220; Israeli
   invasion (1982), 1, 9–10, 73–74, 267,
   281; nationalism, 10, 268–90; Phalangists, 20, 98; postcolonial, 70–71.
Lemsine, Aicha, 161; *La chrysalide*,
   148–50
Lévi-Strauss, C., 84
literary criticism: double role, 263; feminist, 3; of Iraqi war literature, 235–40
literature: autobiography, 151–59, 168–
   69; biographies of women, 169; control
   in, 27; English and American after
   World War I, 164; meaning found in, 2;
   national allegories, 273–80; as propaganda and anti-propaganda, 229–30;
   and reality, 315n33; reason for focusing
   on, 3–4; resistance, 236. *See also* Arabic
   literature; poetry; war literature; writing

Los Angeles: gang wars, 86, 87; Westin Bonaventure Hotel, 114–15

Loseff, Lev, 230, 247, 262, 263

Lyotard, Jean François, 70, 81, 231

machismo, men in military and, 32

madness: of victims, 147–48, 279–80; women's, 209–11, 215, 253, 258. *See also* psychiatric hospital

madres of the Plaza de Mayo, 36, 107, 306n18

Mahfuz, Najib, 236

Mailer, Norman, 164

Majid, Jihad, "Al-dhikra al-mi'wiya" (Centennial jubilee), 261

Majid, Nu'man, 237, 238, 240; *Fi al-ghasaq 'adat 'arus al-bahr* (At dusk the mermaid returned), 237, 240

Makdisi, Jean Said, 95, 97, 108, 313n17

male bonding, 32

Malraux, André, 29, 128

Mammeri, Mouloud, *L'opium et le bâton*, 162–63

al-Mana, Samira, 263, 317n2

Manasra, Najah, 175, 179

Mandelstam, Nadezhda, 118

Marcus, Jane, 104, 210

Mari, Miriam, 313n18

Marin, Peter, 101

martyrs: Iraqi ethos, 241; Iraqi monuments, 9, 232–33; Palestinian women, 173–74, 175, 311n5; wedding-funeral, 215, 316n37

Marxists: Lebanese, 269; and Vietnam, 81. *See also* Communists

masculinity/masculinization: birthing, 275–76; and civilian combatants, 110–13; desire and death, 250, 260–61; of French colonizers, 110–11; in military, 24, 32–33, 80, 110–15, 275–76, 280, 295; and nationalism, 275–76, 280; and shell shock, 104; of space, 110–11; and women civilian-combatants, 103–4. *See also* femininity/feminization

al-Mashat, Mohamed, 83

al-Masri, Ghassan, 78, 173–74

Mater Dolorosa, 5, 15, 107, 158

McKinnon, Catherine, 75

McLuhan, Marshall, 74, 81, 106

Mechakra, Yasmina, *La grotte éclatée*, 147, 308n9, 309n11

media, 6, 73–80, 262, 304n5; Bosnia, 74–77; "cine-commando units," 72; governments using, 9, 75; Gulf War, 69, 74, 79, 83, 93–94, 305n12; Irish Bog-side Marches, 305n11; Israeli Occupied Territories, 70, 78–79, 174, 305n11; Palestinian women as media image, 78, 311n7; positive role, 75; radio, 77, 143, 146, 251–52; reporters in war zones, 37, 71–72, 74; on urban violence, 87–88; and victory/defeat, 92, 93–94; Vietnam War, 77–78, 81, 92. *See also* films; literature; propaganda

men: control over women, 129, 135, 136, 137, 146, 150; male bonding, 32; sexual arousal in war, 249–52, 254; and statist nationalism, 271; War Story roles, 15–16; women writing against war and management by, 10, 11–12. *See also* Arab men; fathers; masculinity/masculinization; patriarchy

men in military, 110–14; German Freikorps, 224, 250, 275, 321n7; *goumiers*, 159; Iraqi characterizations, 236–37, 318; masculinization, 24, 32–33, 80, 110–15, 275–76, 280, 295; and women in military, 31, 32–33, 36, 39–40, 111–12, 295; women tougher than, 159

men's space, 14, 110–11, 116, 254; death and desire, 254–61; dichotomy with women's space, 7, 19, 22–23, 80, 113, 116; women writing and, 41, 156, 254–61. *See also* front

men writing about war, 117, 193; Algerian, 7–8, 127, 129–40, 162–64, 308–9; French men about Algeria, 129–30, 156–58, 160; Iraqi, 9, 99, 222–43 passim, 248–51, 317n2; Lebanese, 16; new narrative frame, 40–41; Palestinian, 9, 175–78; War Story mode, 16; after World War I, 164

Mikha'il, Dunya, 264; *Yawmiyat mawja kharij al-bahr* (The journal of a wave outside the sea), 266

Milhis, Thuraya, 181

military, 110; artists enlisted by, 9, 71, 73, 115, 223–25, 232–48, 262–64; boycotting, 31; "cine-commando units," 72; civilian counterparts, 33–34; clarity essential for, 39; historians, 15, 28–29, 31, 81, 115; international military lawyers, 32; "neo-mercenary," 33; new face of, 33; as privileged space, 14; protectees, 15, 16, 33, 38; rape as weapon, 37; socially progressive, 34; U.S., 30–37 passim, 72, 102–3, 113, 294–95, 302–3. *See also* combatants; front; men in military; war; weapons; women in military

Miller, Laura, 103, 108
Milwaukee, Black Panther Militia, 96
Mirsky, Jonathan, 77
Mohanty, Chandra Talpade, 3, 5, 292
Monego, Joan Phyllis, 124
monuments, Iraqi war, 9, 70, 73, 232–33
Moore, Barrington, 167
Moosa, Matti, 222, 234–35, 318n9;
"Love, Death, Honor," 234, 318n9
Moraga, Cherríe, 293
morality: in postcolonial wars, 298; war
album and, 18–19, 25
Moskos, Charles, 103, 108
Mosteghanemi, Ahlem, 148, 149, 160;
Dhakirat al-jasad (Body memory), 122–
23, 309n12
mothers: Iraqi, 233; and Lebanese nation-
alism, 283–84, 288–89; literary sym-
bols, 135; *madres* of the Plaza de
Mayo, 36, 107, 306n18; Mater Dolorosa, 5, 15, 107, 158; Patriotic, 5, 15;
Spartan, 5, 15, 177; warriors, 6, 33,
36–37, 69, 107, 109, 115, 174, 294;
Women Strike for Peace and, 303
M'Rabet, Fadela, 133; *Les algériennes*,
141–43; *La femme algérienne*, 141–42
Al-Muntada, 182
murder: terminology, 42–43. See also killing
al-Musawi, Muhsin Jassim, 225
myths: of origin, 270; primitive, 84; War
Story, 33

Nablus, women's writing in, 192–94,
196–97
Nabulsi, Lina, 173–74
Nagan, Winston, 303n11
Nagasaki, 38, 88
Nasir, 'Abd al-Sattar, 224–25, 238;
"Fighter's Wife," 234–35
Nasrallah, Emily, 9–10, 281–84, 288,
289–90; *al-tahuna al-da'i'a* (The lost
mill), 282; *Al-iqla' 'aks al-zaman* (Flight
against time), 189–90; "Kulluhunna
ummuhu" (All of them are his mother),
282–84
nation: definitions of, 267–73, 299; Iraqi,
226; Lebanese, 10, 268–90. See also
nationalism; state
nationalism, 95–96, 169, 267–90, 320–21;
Algerian, 7–8, 121–22, 123, 126–27,
128, 161, 307n3; anticolonial vs. postcolonial, 10–12; classifications of, 270;
definitions of, 267–73, 299, 320n2; ethnic, 95; humanist, 10, 272–80, 290;

Kurdish, 270; Lebanese, 10, 268–90;
long-distance, 284; metaphysics of,
272–73; naive, 170, 191; Palestinian,
8–9, 170–82 passim, 193, 196–97, 218–
19, 270, 310n2, 315n36; post–Cold
War, 88; postcolonial, 10–12, 70, 268–
69, 273, 289–90; real, 170–71, 276; sex
segregation, 320n3; statist, 270–72,
273, 274, 285; and War Story reality,
29; women's organizations and, 172–
73, 310n2; women writers and, 10–11,
170–71, 179, 182, 193, 196–97, 218–
19, 269–70, 272–90, 315n36. See also
independence; women as national symbols
National Public Radio, 77, 251–52
al-Na'uri, 'Isa, 183
Nebuchadnezzar, 230–31
Nietzsche, F., 302n9
nuclear age, 293–94, 297; changing nature
and representation of wars in, 6–7, 29–
30, 38, 68–117; nationalisms, 96; nuclear escalation, 97; nuclear tests, 86;
nuclear war, 31, 38, 88–90; and women
in military, 31. See also postcolonialism;
postmodern wars
nucleocide, 88

O'Brien, Tim, 15, 40–41, 92; *Things They
Carried,* 35
Oedipus, Exaggerated, 175–76
Oklahoma City bombing, 296–97
Operation Desert Cheer, 319n18
Operation Lina, 98
Operation Restore Hope, 102, 103
oppositions: War Story, 6–7. See also binarism; dichotomies
order: artists creating, 115; War Story,
15–16
organizations, women's: Arab, 171, 182,
191, 194; Iraqi, 220–21, 317n1; Palestinian, 171–72, 175, 197, 310n2
Orwell, George, *Homage to Catalonia*, 29
outcomes: as discursive constructions, 89–
94. See also defeat; victory
Owen, Wilfred, 1–2, 241

pacifism: Arab women and, 299; feminist,
30, 35, 36; and gender, 15; Mechakra
vs., 147; and sanctioned killing, 42
Paklina, L. J., *Iskussto inoskazatel'noj
reci,* 262
Palestine Liberation Organization (PLO),
21, 109–10, 165, 172, 178
Palestinian Arab Women's Congress, 171

Palestinian men: honor, 212, 213; staying/ leaving, 201, 212; Tawil's condemnation, 193; views of women, 172–74, 175–78, 179–80, 183; ways of fighting, 173, 197–99, 211–12, 218; women writers introduced by, 183, 311n10; writing, 9, 175–83 passim, 190–91, 192

Palestinians, 89, 110, 169–219, 310–16; Algerian war of independence idealized by, 115–16; and British (1940s), 8, 161; colonized anew, 8, 169; committees, 172, 174–75; green line, 169, 173; Jews depicted by, 185–86, 188, 190–91, 197, 312–13; just war by, 10; media attention, 78–79, 174; nationalism, 8–9, 170–82 passim, 193, 196–97, 218–19, 270, 310n2, 315n36; Palestinian-Israeli war (1948), 1, 4, 173, 177, 180–91; peace process, 11–12, 89; Six-Day War (1967), 1, 10, 170, 177, 191–95; Society for Women's Welfare, 194; women's importance, 8, 166, 172–77. *See also* Intifada; Israeli Occupied Territories

Palestinian women, 169–219, 310–16; and Algerian women's postbellum oppression, 115–16, 165–66, 218–19; economic roles, 314n26, 316n40; education, 182, 191, 313n18; erasure faced by, 174–80, 212, 216, 311n7; and feminism, 8–9, 170–75 passim, 183, 191–97 passim, 202–4, 218–19, 313; General Union of Palestinian Women, 172, 197; Intifada started by, 82–83, 165–66, 173, 212; martyrs and prisoners, 173–74, 175, 311n5; as media image, 78, 311n7; mothers, 36, 107, 174; as national symbols, 177, 178, 180; organizations, 171–72, 175, 197, 310n2; politics, 171–72, 174–80, 182–83, 195–97, 202, 310–11; raped, 37, 213; resistance during 1948 war, 173; sexually liberated, 314n26; and silence, 170, 178–80, 209, 315n32; violent, 35; ways of fighting, 9, 12, 36, 78, 82, 107–9, 113, 173–74, 197–201, 211–12, 218–19; writing about war, 8–9, 10–11, 41, 109, 113, 161, 169–71, 177–219, 311–16; writing about women's issues, 169–71, 178–81, 185–88, 191–95, 197, 216–19

paradigms: derailing, 30–38; dominant, 13–43; two, 13–16; War Story as, 39

Parin, Paul, 75

patriarchy: Algerian, 124, 142; Arab, 193; gender-specific spaces in, 14, 261; Is-

raeli, 197; Palestinian, 8, 173, 181, 192, 193, 195; U.S. (South), 3; women's experiences articulated by, 5

Patriotic Mother, 5, 15

patriotism: in Iraqi war literature, 225–26, 234–35, 317n4. *See also* nationalism

peace, 39; dichotomy with war, 19, 20, 39, 80, 82–89, 304n18; Gray on, 302n9; just, 31; Palestinian-Israeli process, 11–12, 89; Perpetual, 39, 304n18; and sex segregation, 13–14, 15–16; war/peace continuum, 6, 39, 82–89; and war-sanctioned crime, 43; women waging, 11

peacekeeping operations, and combat definition, 103

Pejic, Nenad, 75

Peled, Mattityahu, 183

Pelissier, 157

Persian Gulf war. *See* Gulf War

Peru: rapes by military, 37; Shining Path (Sendero luminoso), 35, 271

photography: "cine-commando units," 72; control in, 24–25, 27; *Harb Lubnan*, 17–28; impression of being there, 25–28; Operation Desert Cheer, 319n18; organization of, 26–27; and reality, 26, 302nn7,8; role of photographer, 25–26; Sontag on, 25, 26, 27, 28, 301n4, 302n7; war albums, 17–28, 77; War Story, 17–29. *See also* films; television

pilots: desire and death, 249–52, 318–19; hyperspace, 113–14

poetry: Algerian women's, 161, 164–65; al-Amir, 238–39; Dahbur, 311n5; al-Daif, 321n8; Darwish, 177, 312–13; Dawud, 311n10; early Arab, 168; Ehrhart, 101–2; Lebanese *billet* prose poem, 318n10; by Palestinian men, 177–78; Salman, 284–89; Tuqan, 193–94, 195–96; women models, 177

politics: Algerian women's liberation, 119, 141–42, 161; art as tool for, 208; Communists, 181, 312n15; early Arab women's writings and, 168, 169; and gender, 15; identity, 23, 99–100; Lebanese group, 95–96, 99, 269, 274–78, 281; Marxists, 81, 269; maternal activism, 37, 107; Palestinian women's, 171–72, 174–80, 182–83, 195–97, 202, 310–11; of representation, 78; of sexual equality, 35; silence allowing exclusion from, 167, 179–80; and social change, 11; torture of women and, 106–7; war experience a stepping stone for, 30;

politics (*continued*)
women's traditional roles transformed,
218. *See also* democracy; feminism; nationalism; power; propaganda; state
politikon, vs. *oikon*, 15
polygamy, Algerian, 141, 143
Poole, Ross, 104, 271
postcolonialism, 80, 94–95, 99, 270; Algeria as emblematic, 119; Beirut Decentrists and, 218; described, 70; double critique, 134, 170, 192; easy access to violent means, 100; "infantile diseases" of, 133; Lebanese, 268–69; nationalism, 10–12, 70, 268–69, 273, 289–90; wars, 70–71, 94, 115–16, 293–99. *See also* independence; nationalism; nuclear age; postmodern wars
postmodernism, 69–71, 81, 231; architecture, 114–15
postmodern wars, 68–117, 266, 297; denial of death, 249; dichotomies breaking up, 68, 82–117; Intifada epitomizing, 212. *See also* nuclear age; postcolonialism
poststructuralism, 94, 314n29
power: and gender, 14; group, 94–100, 274; space allocation and, 14; violence transformed into, 96–100; as war, 85; and women in military, 30; and women writing, 164. *See also* authority; control; politics
prison: Algerian women in, 128, 307n4; Palestinian women in, 173–74, 175, 311n5
private-public dichotomy, 69, 304n18
propaganda, 229–30; American military, 72, 304n4; in Bosnia, 75; integration, 246; Iraqi, 9, 223–25, 229–30, 246–48, 262–64, 318n8
prostitution: in Algeria, 119–20; and Palestinian sexually liberated women, 314n26
psychiatric hospital, 145, 163, 176, 279–80. *See also* madness

Qadisiya, 115, 223–30; Iran-Iraq War, 115, 220–66, 317–20
Qadisiyat Saddam competitions, 226, 227, 229, 232, 237
Qaraman, Su'ad, 194
al-Qasim, Samih, 177, 311n10
Qa'war, Taufiq, 183
qissat al-harb, term for Iraqi war literature, 236
queer theory, 69. *See also* homoerotics

race, 95, 96, 292. *See also* ethnicity; genocide
Radhakrishnan, R., 272, 289–90
rapes: French of Algerians, 157; Palestinian women, 37, 213; Serbs of Muslims, 37, 38, 91, 106; as weapon, 37–38, 213
Reagan, Ronald, 79, 86, 92
reality: Algerian women's lived, 307n1; injuries as, 90; literature and, 241, 315n33; and photography, 26, 302nn7,8; and representation, 90, 241; War Story shaping, 28–29. *See also* experience
real nationalism, 170–71, 276
religion: Algerian, 8, 83, 123, 142; of competing groups, 95, 269; identity in, 23; Palestinian Muslim-Christian women's unions, 171–72
Remarque, Erich Maria, 39, 226, 236; *All Quiet on the Western Front*, 104
reporters, in war zones, 37, 71–72, 74
representations. *See* art; media; war representations
resistance: in Algerian history, 131, 151–61, 307n2; burning flag, 316n39; children's ways of fighting, 36, 78, 82, 108–9, 113; contrasting, 216–19; grassroots movements, 102; literature of, 236; men's ways of fighting, 173, 197–99, 211–12, 218; mimicry and, 310n16; vs. victimization, 107; women's ways of fighting, 9, 12, 36, 78, 82, 107–9, 113, 173–74, 197–201, 211–12, 218–19. *See also* Algeria; independence; Palestinians; postcolonialism
responsibility: collective, 281, 290, 299; for ending war, 16, 18–19; to group, 128; women's, 218; by women writers, 299
revolution: women's, 202. *See also* feminism; independence; resistance
revolutionary women: Algerian heroines, 122, 128–29, 144; models, 205
Rosenberg, Stanley, 249–50, 318–19
Rowe, John Carlos, 81
Ruddick, Sara, 35, 107, 281; *Maternal Thinking*, 88
al-Rukkabi, 'Abd al-Khaliq, 224–25
ruler/ruled binary, 80. *See also* governments; state
Russians: Aesopian writers, 230; Afghanis vs., 97; Chechnya mothers and, 36; Nazi rapes, 37. *See also* Soviets
Rwanda, 297

Sabbagh, Suha, 172, 314n26
Sabbah, Fatna A., 121
Saddam Hussein. *See* Hussein, Saddam
Sa'id, 'Ali Lufta, 240; "Imra'a min al-nisa'" (A woman among women), 225–26, 243; *Imra'a min al-nisa'* (A woman among women), 225–26
Said, Edward, 78–79
St. Vincent Millay, Edna, 37
Sakakini, Milia, 171
Sakakini, Widad, 169
Salim, Nayif, 177
Salman, Nur, 9–10, 289–90; *Ila rajul lam ya'ti* (To a man who did not come), 284–89
Salman, Suhayla, 9, 107, 243–45; "Khalti Umm Malik 'addaha hisan" (A horse bit my aunt Umm Malik), 107, 245; "Lara," 243–44; *Al-liqa'* (The meeting), 244–45; "Mashhad," 244–45
Samara, Nuha, "Two Faces One Woman," 252–53, 319n19
al-Samira'i, Salim 'Abd al-Qadir, 237
al-Samman, Ghada, *Kawabis Bayrut* (Beirut nightmares), 266, 281
Sammara, Samih, 311n10
Sarafina, 91
Sasser, Charles W., 294–95
Saut al-Mar'a, 182
Sayeh, Mai, 167, 170, 177–78
Sayigh, Rosemary, 192, 310n2, 311n4
al-Sayyid, 'Abd al-Razzaq, 24–26, 27, 77
Scarry, Elaine, 86, 90
Schwartz, William, 88
Schwarzkopf, General, 73
Schweik, Susan, 37
Sedgwick, Eve, 14, 268
Segal, David, 33–34
Segal, Mady, 33–34
Semah, Samih, 311n10
separatist movements: in the sixties, 95. *See also* groups; nationalism
Serbs: films depicting rapes, 91; and media, 75, 76; rapists, 37, 38, 91, 106; violent women, 35, 271
sexes: war of, 86. *See also* gender
sex segregation: Algerian war and, 159; in colonialism and nationalism, 320n3; Lebanese war album, 22; war/peace and, 13–14, 15–16. *See also* men's space; women's space
sexual equality. *See* equal opportunity; feminism
sexuality: and Algerian prostitution, 119–20; androgyny, 280; and death, 248–61;

homoerotics, 19, 32, 39–40, 69, 304n1; homosexul/heterosexual, 69; incest, 132, 133; of liberated Palestinian women, 314n26
sexual violence. *See* rapes
Shaaban, Bouthaina, 170–71
al-Shahham, 'Abdallah, 312–13
Shatt al-'Arab, 97
Shaw, George Bernard, *Arms and the Man,* 68
al-Shaykh, Hanan, *Story of Zahra,* 253, 315n32
shell shock, and masculinity, 104
Shihabi, Zulaikha, 171
Shining Path (Sendero luminoso), Peru, 35, 271
Showalter, Elaine, 29, 104
al-Shuwayli, Dawud Salman, 249; *Ababil* (Flocks), 250–51
silence, 7–8, 118–66, 167, 263, 293; and Algerian women's war roles, 7–8, 106, 119, 125, 126, 127, 143, 146–66; crime of, 8, 118–66, 298–99; Palestinian women and, 170, 178–80, 209, 315n32; war imposing, 91–92. *See also* censorship
simulacra, martial, 230–33
Six-Day War (1967), 1, 10, 170, 177, 191–95
Smith, Helen Zenna, 40; *Not So Quiet,* 3, 104
Smith, R. R. R., 302n6
sniper, Lebanese, 24
Snitow, Ann, 306n18, 314n29
society: military-civilian links, 33–35; military pioneering in social reform, 34. *See also* civilians; politics; religion; state
Society for Women's Welfare, 194
soldiers. *See* combatants; military
Somalia: children combatants, 108; Operation Restore Hope, 102, 103
Somekh, Sasson, 181, 186, 312n15
Sontag, Susan: on media in Bosnia, 74; on photography, 25, 26, 27, 28, 301n4, 302n7
South Africa, 82, 110; mother warriors, 36, 107; torture, 91
Soviets: Aesopian writers, 230; Cold War, 38; demonized by U.S., 101; Iraqi war underwritten by, 243–44; postcolonial, 94; rapes of German women, 37. *See also* Russians
Soweto, mother warriors, 36
space allocation, 7, 110–15; Algerian women and, 121; hyperspace, 110–16;

space allocation (*continued*)
  inner-city gang, 87; power and privilege constructed by, 14. *See also* men's space; women's space
Spanish civil war, 29, 278
Spartan Mother, 5, 15, 177
spectator's eye: one with weapons, 79–80. *See also* photography
speech. *See* languages; silence; voice
Stam, Robert, 79, 93–94
Star Wars, 36
state: comparison of Iraqi and Lebanese building of, 220; nationalism independent of, 10, 95, 269–90; at war, 88–89; without peace/war ambiguity, 39. *See also* citizenship; governments
statist nationalism, 270–72, 273, 274, 285
Stetkevych, Suzanne, 168
Stiehm, Judith, 30–31, 32–33, 34, 36, 291–92
Stonewall rebellion, 69, 304n1
Stork, Joe, 109–10
suicide, Algerian women, 143
Sulaiman, Muhammad, 311n10
sumud/sumood (steadfastness), 189, 204, 310n2, 313n17, 314n23
survivors, vs. victims, 5, 108
Swerdlow, Amy, 303n15

Tagg, John, 302n8
tagging, 87, 305n13
Talib, 'Aliya, 9, 241–43, 244, 254; "Al-ikhdirar" (Greening), 242, 243; "Al-'inaq al-madi'" (The luminous embrace), 243; "Intizar jadid" (A new wait), 243; *Al-mummirat* (Corridors), 241–43; "Al-nawaris" (The gulls), 242–43; "'Uyun ukhra" (Other eyes), 241–42
al-Talib, 'Umar Muhammad, 318n9
al-Talibani, Makram Rashid, 233–34; *Al-maudi' al-turabi* (The dusty place), 233–34
Tamari, Salim, 110
Tawfeeq, Basem, 311n7
Tawil, Raymonda, 192–93, 197; *My Home My Prison,* 193
Taylor, Diana, 99–100, 110
al-Taymuriya, 'A'isha, 169
technology. *See* media; war technology
television, 72–81 passim; Gulf War, 69, 74, 83, 93–94, 305n12
Terminator 2, 36
terrorism: Corradi on, 97, 110, 306n23; Drif on, 128–29; Malraux's definition, 128

Thanatos: Eros and, 248–61. *See also* death
Theweleit, Klaus, 35, 94, 134–37 passim, 295; on German Freikorps men, 224, 250, 275, 321n7; *Male Fantasies,* 224, 275
Thirty Years War (1618–48), 116
Thurmond, Max, 102–3
Time magazine, 88, 92, 108, 306n20
Tobias, Sheila, 30
Todorov, Tzvetan, 236
Top Gun, 76, 249
torture: Mechakra's father, 147; men giving in to, 159; and victory/defeat, 91; of women, 106–7, 116, 122, 129, 159
Toumi, Moustapha, "Femme, femme, femme," 146
tourism, sex, in Algeria, 119–20
Tremaine, Louis, 130
tribal groups, and Lebanese citizenship, 281
Tripoli Program (1962), 142
Tubi, Asma, 181
Tuqan, Fadwa, 8–9, 170, 192–97, 200, 216; *Mountainous Journey,* 193–95, 311n10; salon, 196; silence, 315n32; "Song of Becoming," 196
Tuqan, Ibrahim, 177
turath, Iraqi invention of, 231–32

unions, women's, 171–72, 182, 191, 194, 197
United Nations: Bosnia forces, 76–77, 106; Charter, 303n11; children combatants, 108; Commission of Human Rights, 2
United States: anti-militarists, 30; Civil War, 104–5; Cold War, 38; Doolittle Report (1954), 101; film propaganda, 72, 304n4; Gulf War, 83, 84, 93–94, 265–66, 293–94; intervention in wars, 297; and media coverage, 69, 73–74, 79; military, 30–37 passim, 72, 102–3, 113, 294–95, 302–3; Oklahoma City bombing, 296–97; patriarchy in South, 3; Presidential Commission for the Assignment of Women to the Military, 103; State Department terminology for killing, 42–43; third world populations, 293; urban violence, 82, 86, 87–88, 96, 305n13; War on Drugs, 86; war as positive term, 89; writers after World War I, 164. *See also* Vietnam War
urban violence, 82, 86, 87–88, 96, 305n13

al-'Uthman, Layla, *Al-hawajiz al-sawda'* (Black barricades), 264–65

veils, 14; Algerian, 105–6, 111, 116, 123, 137, 144, 146, 150, 307n3; Iranian, 115
victims: child, 38, 306n20; gangs depersonalizing, 305n13; madness, 147–48, 279–80; photographing, 24–26; vs. resisters, 107; vs. survivors, 5, 108; targeted civilians, 38, 72, 100–102, 106–7, 305n15. *See also* injuries; killing; martyrs; rapes; torture
victory: vs. defeat, 7, 80, 89–94; as goal of war, 13–14; Iraqi artists and, 9, 73, 237
Vietnam magazine, 93
Vietnam War, 70–71, 73, 80–82; American rapes of Vietnamese women, 37; boredom, 40; combatant-civilian distinction, 101–2; desire and death, 249–50; Edgerton story, 252; films after, 29, 78, 81–82, 93, 103–4; films before (war movies), 68, 72; Herr on, 68, 115; media coverage, 77–78, 81, 92; outcome reversed, 93; representation of, 6, 29, 40, 77, 81–82; ten-year anniversary literature, 92–93; women and girls fighting, 103–4, 306n21
violence, 10, 87, 94–100, 297; conflict resolution without organized, lethal, 4, 11–12, 35, 41, 217, 299; easy access to, 97, 100; of Ferocious Few, 35–36, 271; transformed into power, 96–100; urban, 82, 86, 87–88, 96, 305n13; war sanctioning, 10, 42–43, 99, 119. *See also* killing; rapes; terrorism; torture; war
Virilio, Paul, 71, 80, 81; *Pure War*, 85, 86
voice: and female body, 152, 153, 154–55. *See also* languages; silence; writing
voyeurism, war album, 25, 27

Walker, Alice, *Color Purple*, 149
war, 100, 297; alive-ness in, 161–62; brevity motivations, 33; categories of, 6, 82, 88; constant presence of, 13; defined, 13–14, 84, 85–86, 303n11; desire and death in, 248–54; dichotomy with peace, 19, 21, 39, 80, 82–89, 304n18; as dominant paradigm, 13–14; experience, 3–4, 5, 30, 41, 90, 105–6, 161–62; global, 88–89; good, 21, 28; guerrilla, 87, 101–2, 108, 122, 306n21; idealization of, 29; just, 10, 21, 30; nationalism tied to, 271; nuclear, 31, 38,

88–90; as positive term, 89; pure, 85–86; readiness for, 31; of sexes, 86; sex segregation in, 13–14, 15–16; taxonomy, 32; terms for, 89; threat of, 38–39; total, 116; unjustifiably destructive, 10; urban, 82, 86, 87–88, 96, 305n13; war/peace continuum, 6, 39, 82–89. *See also* dichotomies; postmodern wars
war albums: Croatian, 17, 25; Lebanese, 17–28, 77
war correspondents, 37, 71–72, 74
war crimes, 38, 42–43, 75, 303n11
war literature, 236; authority, 3, 5, 41; fictive, 92; Iraqi management of, 9, 73, 223–25, 232–48, 262–64; military historians, 15, 28–29, 31, 81, 115; new narrative frame, 40–42; *qissat al-harb*, 236; and resistance literature, 236. *See also* men writing about war; War Story; women writing about war
war monuments, Iraqi, 9, 70, 73, 232–33
War on Drugs, U.S., 86
war representations, 69–80, 304–7; Iraqi criticism of, 248; with Iraqi war monuments, 9, 70; military enlisting artists for, 9, 71, 73, 115, 223–25, 232–48, 262–64; during nuclear age, 6–7, 29, 68, 80, 84; and reality, 90, 241; Vietnam War, 6, 29, 40, 77, 81–82. *See also* art; films; media; war literature
warriors. *See* combatants; military
wars, 6, 82; Abortion, 296; American Civil, 104–5; Cold, 30, 38, 88; El Salvador civil war, 74; Great Northern (1700–1721), 116; naming, 297; Spanish civil, 29, 278; Thirty Years (1618–48), 116. *See also* Arab wars; Israel; Vietnam War; World War I; World War II
War's Other Voices (Cooke), 1, 4, 16–17, 223
War Story, 5–7, 15–31, 68–69, 96, 263, 295–97; Algerian, 140, 142; binarism, 6–7, 14–23 passim, 31–32, 39–42 passim, 68, 69, 80–81; and gender, 6, 7, 15–23 passim, 30–40, 80; Gulf War, 80–81, 84; Iraqi, 73, 236, 239, 241, 243, 318n13; Khalifa vs., 217; Lebanese, 16–28; Lebanese women writers vs., 10, 16, 27, 41; little war stories, 38–43; new narrative frame vs., 29–30, 40–42; photography, 17–29; *qissat al-harb*, 236; shaping reality, 28–29; and women writing about war (general), 29–30, 39, 41, 43, 293, 295–96. *See also* war literature

war technology, 71, 72, 96–97, 116, 304n3; chemical, 247; and civilian-combatant distinction, 102; computer simulations, 73, 113–15; cost, 97; Hiroshima/Nagasaki, 38, 88, 266; and pure war, 85; seeing screen of warhead, 69, 79. *See also* nuclear age; weapons

weapons: chemical, 247; Gulf War, 69, 79, 85, 319n16; Hiroshima/Nagasaki, 38, 88, 266; rape, 37–38, 213; spectator's eye one with, 79–80; violence as, 96–97. *See also* war technology

Wells, Donald A., 68

West Bank. *See* Israeli Occupied Territories

Westmoreland, William C., 77

Wollstonecroft, Mary, 35

womb: masculine, 295; in Salman work, 288–89

women, 38, 116–17, 293; ambulance drivers, 104; civilian combatants, 103–9, 112–13, 252–54, 306; erased, 180; Ferocious Few, 35–36, 271; fictitious category, 314n29; Jewish, 37, 161, 185–86, 188; and madness, 209–11, 215, 253, 258; men's fear of dissolution in the feminine, 131–32, 137; military targets, 38, 106–7; organizations, 171–72, 175, 182, 191, 194, 197; protectees, 15, 16, 33, 38; reporters in war zones, 37; sexual arousal in war, 252–54; silence, 8, 106, 118–66; and statist nationalism, 271; tortured, 106–7, 116, 122, 129, 159; traditional roles transformed, 218; War Story roles, 15–16, 21, 22; and war/urban violence, 87–88; writing (general), 167–69. *See also* Arab women; bodies; dress; education; feminism; femininity/feminization; mothers; rapes

Women and War film, 87–88

women as national symbols: in Algeria, 120, 121, 123, 130, 132, 307n3; in Iraq, 234–35; Palestinian, 177, 178, 180

women in military, 6, 30–41, 106–7, 115, 291–92, 295; Algerian, 7, 105–6, 111–12, 121–22, 129, 146, 158–62, 308–9; combat positions, 30, 33, 103, 113; decision-making positions, 303n10; feminism and, 30–31, 34–35, 36, 161, 313n18; Iranian, 115, 178; Iraqi, 252; military roles/civilian roles, 33–34; mother warriors, 6, 33, 36–37, 69, 107,

109, 115, 174, 294; and nationalism, 280; *stratégie-femme*, 111–12; tougher than men, 159; U.S., 30, 31, 34, 102–3, 103, 113, 294–95, 302–3

women's space, 14, 116, 254; death and desire, 254–61; dichotomy with men's space, 7, 19, 22–23, 80, 113, 116. *See also* home

Women Strike for Peace (1960s), 303

women writing about war, 41–42, 43, 116–17, 293; Algerian, 7–8, 10–11, 41, 122–29, 140–66, 307–10; Arab women (general), 3–5, 192–95, 298–99; authority of, 3, 5, 41; and conflict resolution without violence, 4, 11–12; Gulf War, 264–66; Iraqi, 9, 10, 11, 41, 221–23, 233–48 passim; and morality, 298; and nationalism, 10–11, 170–71, 179, 182, 193, 196–97, 218–19, 269–70, 272–90; new narrative frame, 41–42; Palestinian, 8–9, 10–11, 41, 109, 113, 161, 169–71, 177–219, 311–16; self-consciously feminine, 11; and war-sanctioned crime, 43; and War Story, 29–30, 39, 41, 43, 293, 295–96; and women in military, 6, 41; after World War I, 164. *See also* Lebanese women writing about war

Woodhull, Winifred, 112, 119, 121, 130

Woolf, Virginia, 201

Woollacott, Angela, 252, 306n17

World War I: civilian-combatants, 116, 306n17; English and American writings after, 164; and gender, 104; and Hollywood, 72; and left-wing mentality, 29

World War II: alive-ness in, 161–62; civilian-combatants, 116; concentration camps, 247; crimes, 303n11; genocide, 91–92; and Hollywood, 72; and Palestinian women's organizations, 172; Picasso's *Guernica* on, 134; pilots, 318–19; rapes, 37; representations, 21, 27; women after, 161; women in military, 302–3

writing, 167–69, 219, 292, 316n41; Aesopian, 230, 242, 247, 262, 263; dichotomy between those who could and could not write, 169; Djebar on, 154–58; Farah on, 182, 183; Haddad on, 137, 139, 140; Khalifa on, 196–97; mimicry, 310n16; and nationalism, 281–82; oppositional, 4, 5; Tuqan on,

194–95. *See also* literature; men writing about war; women writing about war
Wyschogrod, Edith, 88

Yacine, Kateb, 129–34, 147, 308–9; *Le cadavre encerclé*, 131, 308n8; *Nedjma*, 129–34, 308–9
Yared, Nazik, 289–90; *Al-sada al-makhnuq* (The stifled echo), 284

al-Yaziji, Warda, 169
Yugoslavia, 82; media role, 75–77. *See also* Bosnia

Zaynab, Prophet's granddaughter, 115, 178
Zghaib, Henri, 269
Zionism: feminist settlements, 271; Palestinians writing about Jews and, 312–13
Ziyada, Mayy, 169

Compositor: Braun-Brumfield, Inc.
Text: 11/13.5 Sabon
Display: Sabon
Printer and Binder: Braun-Brumfield, Inc.